UNIVERSITY COLLEGE
WINCHESTER

Ma **Martial Rose Library**
Te **Tel: 01962 827306**

To be returned on or before the day marked above, subject to recall.

Aphra Behn's Afterlife

Angellica confronts Willmore in an eighteenth-century illustration from
Behn's most frequently-performed play, *The Rover* (1735 edn.). Bodleian
Library, University of Oxford. Shelfmark Vet A4f. 706 (4)

Aphra Behn's Afterlife

JANE SPENCER

OXFORD
UNIVERSITY PRESS

OXFORD
UNIVERSITY PRESS

Great Clarendon Street, Oxford OX2 6DP

Oxford University Press is a department of the University of Oxford.
It furthers the University's objective of excellence in research, scholarship,
and education by publishing worldwide in

Oxford New York

Athens Auckland Bangkok Bogotá Buenos Aires Calcutta
Cape Town Chennai Dar es Salaam Delhi Florence Hong Kong Istanbul
Karachi Kuala Lumpur Madrid Melbourne Mexico City Mumbai
Nairobi Paris São Paulo Shanghai Singapore Taipei Tokyo Toronto Warsaw
and associated companies in Berlin Ibadan

Oxford is a registered trade mark of Oxford University Press
in the UK and certain other countries

Published in the United States
by Oxford University Press Inc., New York

British Library Cataloguing in Publication Data
Data available

Library of Congress Cataloging in Publication Data
Data available

ISBN 0-19-818494-8

1 3 5 7 9 10 8 6 4 2

Typeset in Baskerville
by J&L Composition Ltd, Filey, North Yorkshire
Printed in Great Britain
on acid-free paper by
Biddles Ltd
Guildford and King's Lynn

In memory of

GARETH ROBERTS
1949–1999

most wonderful colleague and friend

Acknowledgements

SOME material in Chapter 4 appeared in an earlier form in my article 'Adapting Aphra Behn: Hannah Cowley's *A School for Greybeards* and *The Lucky Chance*', in *Women's Writing*, vol. 2 no. 3 (1995), 221–34. I am grateful to Triangle Journals for permission to use this. Part of Chapter 5 is a revised version of my '*The Rover* and the Eighteenth Century', in Janet Todd (ed.), *Aphra Behn Studies* (Cambridge University Press, 1996), 84–106. I am grateful to Cambridge University Press for permission to incorporate this. Lines from W. H. Auden, *Collected Shorter Poems, 1927–1957*, are quoted by permission of Faber and Faber Ltd. and Random House, Inc.

My work on this book has been generously supported by several institutions. Some of the research was done while I held a William A. Ringler, Jr. Fellowship at the Huntington Library in 1994. The British Academy provided travel grants and, crucially, a Research Leave Award. As well as granting me research terms in 1994 and 1997, Exeter University School of English gave the matching funding that allowed me to take up the British Academy award and have two terms' leave in 1998–9, during which time most of the book was written.

That I was able to think of writing it in the first place is due to James Booth, who introduced me to Aphra Behn back in the 1970s, before anyone else was lecturing on her; and to Marion Shaw, who taught me how to read as a feminist.

My colleagues at Exeter have supported me in many ways. Many of them have read and commented helpfully on some part of the work in progress. In addition, I'd especially like to thank Regenia Gagnier for giving me courage; Helen Taylor for providing a listening ear; Peter New for minimizing my duties in the summer term of 1999; Chris Brooks for taking on an enormous workload during that term which, among other things, lightened mine; Diane Purkiss for not allowing me to slow down towards the end; and Ashley Tauchert for challenging and nourishing me over the course of many conversations. My debt to the late Gareth Roberts is inadequately acknowledged in the dedication.

I have received enormous help from the community of scholars working in seventeenth- and eighteenth-century studies. Jeslyn Medoff very generously allowed me to make use of her unpublished research on the early biographies of Behn, and provided me with a number of leads, as well as sustaining me with her conversation. Mary Ann O'Donnell has passed on information and shared the results of bibliographical work in progress with her usual great generosity. She and Bernard Dhuicq organized the hugely enjoyable Aphra Behn conference in July 1999, where I learned a great deal that was new at an uncomfortably late stage in the book's composition. Warren Chernaik very generously made his unpublished work on *Oroonoko* available to me. Carol Barash was extremely kind in answering my questions and providing me with access to the Folger MS of Anne Finch's poetry. Conversations and communications with Cathrin Brockhaus, Alan Downie, Germaine Greer, Ludmilla Jordanova, Paulina Kewes, Joyce Green MacDonald, Anita Pacheco, Sarah Prescott, Marjorie Stone, and Janet Todd, have been especially helpful. I would also like to thank all those who have listened to me give papers on Behn over the last few years for their comments and suggestions, which have opened up new directions for me. Warren Chernaik and Susan Wiseman read the entire book in draft. They criticized, offered suggestions, and saved me from errors, and the book is a much stronger work for their help. The errors that remain, of course, are all my own.

My parents, Margaret and Philip Spencer, have given me every help and encouragement, and have spent many half-term holidays looking after their granddaughters. Jacquie Rawes, Richard Simmons, and Peninah Thomson have been never-failing sources of handy accommodation and sustenance of all kinds, practical, intellectual, and emotional. Kate Spencer listened to me patiently while I talked about the book, and solved a major structural problem for me on the way home from school one day. I am proud to say that I am Eleanor Spencer's favourite author, even though (or perhaps because) she has not yet read my work. Hugh Glover has been my constant support, and the help he is to me is beyond my power to describe.

J.S.

Exeter
December 1999

Contents

Contents

Introduction

I value Fame as much as if I had been born a *Hero*.[1]

The words of a dead man
Are modified in the guts of the living.[2]

IT is well known, and has now been the subject of much discussion, that women's writing has a very much smaller space in literary history than men's. The two reasons for this are sometimes falsely placed in mutual opposition. They are first, the history of women's relatively low access to all the advantages that writers need, beginning at a basic level with literacy itself; and second, the masculinist biases, conscious and unconscious, of our records of literary activity. The first of these must surely have caused the greatest loss: loss that by its nature we cannot ascertain, measure, or redress, though it has been eloquently mourned.[3] It is the second that commands our attention as subject to change. Over the last twenty-five years, feminist research has given us knowledge of women writers who had been (almost) erased from the record, and has made it necessary to revise the records we already had. The processes by which women writers are placed in—or excluded from—literary histories, and the ways in which considerations of gender enter into the formation of literary canons, are crucial to feminist literary study.

In Restoration and eighteenth-century England, the relations between women and the literary canon carried a special significance. Because of the expansion of print culture, women as writers were much more visible in this period than in the preceding one, and those whose privilege it was to define literary traditions began to recognize

---

[1] Aphra Behn, Preface to *The Lucky Chance* (1686); *The Works of Aphra Behn*, ed. Janet Todd, 7 vols. (London: Pickering and Chatto; Columbus, Oh.: Ohio State University Press, 1992–6), vii. 217. Hereafter abbreviated as *Works*.

[2] W. H. Auden, 'In Memory of W.B. Yeats', *Collected Shorter Poems 1927–1957* (London and Boston: Faber and Faber Ltd., 1981), 141.

[3] See Tillie Olsen, 'Silences' and 'Women Who are Writers in Our Century', both reprinted in *Silences* (London: Virago, 1980) for a moving account of the social and cultural forces working against women's development as writers.

that the writing of women needed in some way to be taken into account. The development of the literary market led to an increase in the number of writers of both sexes; but the increase was probably proportionally greater, and certainly more noticeable, in the case of women.[4] At the same time, the growth of literature as a trade encouraged the reflections on writers and writing that became a flourishing branch of that trade. Lives of poets and dramatists, essays on criticism, reviews of recent publications, scholarly editions of Shakespeare, and histories of the novel all contributed to the growing sense of a national literature. While this literature was seen by many people as the natural preserve of the man of letters, there was a growing tendency to incorporate a certain kind of proper woman writer into the critical picture.

In this book, I approach the construction of literary authority and the literary canon during the eighteenth century through a study of the reception of the work of Aphra Behn. As one of the first professional writers of either sex in England, she participated in the redefinition of the author that attended the new literary market;[5] and as the most prominent woman writer of the Restoration, she had an immense and complex significance for women writers in following generations. Her large *œuvre*, the variety of her work, and the extent of her success in her lifetime, meant that she had the potential to be very influential after her death. The eighteenth-century construction of Restoration writing in general, and Behn's in particular, as decadent and salacious, had profound effects on the tenor of that influ-

---

[4] Numbers of female writers publishing cannot be computed exactly because of the widespread practice of anonymous publication. Cheryl Turner's *Living by the Pen* (London: Routledge, 1992) charts the development of female professional writing. See also Judith Stanton, 'Statistical Profile of Women Writing in English from 1660 to 1800', in Frederick M. Keener and Susan E. Lorsch (eds.), *Eighteenth-Century Women and the Arts* (Westport, Conn.: Greenwood Press Inc., 1988), 247–54. The idea that women wrote the majority of novels in this period, derived from 18th-c. comments on the startling growth of female writing, is mistaken. James Raven's *British Fiction 1750–1770: A Chronological Check-List of Prose Fiction Printed in Britain and Ireland* (Newark, Del.: University of Delaware Press; London: Associated University Presses, 1987) shows that male novelists predominated in the mid-century period. However, Judith Stanton's work suggests that in 1770–1800, women's writing was expanding at a greater rate than men's. See 'The Production of Fiction by Women in England, 1660–1800: A Statistical Overview', paper given at the Eighth International Congress on the Enlightenment, Bristol, 1991. James Raven's forthcoming *The English Novel 1770–1829: A Bibliographical Survey of Prose Fiction Published in the British Isles* (Oxford: Oxford University Press, 2000) will provide a comprehensive basis for answering this question.

[5] See Catherine Gallagher, *Nobody's Story: The Vanishing Acts of Women Writers in the Marketplace 1670–1820* (Oxford: Clarendon Press, 1994), esp. chs. 1 and 2.

ence, and made her legacy to later female writers an uneasy one. Over the hundred years following her death, her image played an important, and very mixed, part in the process of the legitimation of the woman writer.[6]

When I first worked on Aphra Behn it was in the context of other early women novelists, most of them writing in the eighteenth century. The comments on Behn I came across were hostile ones, and the century's most famous writers—Richardson, Swift, Pope, Fielding, Steele, Johnson—were among her detractors. Indeed, going on the record with a good insult to Aphra Behn could almost be taken as an entrance qualification to the eighteenth-century literary world. Yet her novels clearly remained popular for much of the century, with her collected fiction being republished until the 1750s, and *Love-Letters between a Nobleman and his Sister* till the 1760s, while *Oroonoko* was still being reprinted in 1800. When I began to look at Behn's stage history, I found more indications of her continued popularity. In an age when the theatre depended heavily on revivals of seventeenth-century plays, *The Rover* was one of the Restoration comedies that were regularly performed, and Behn's status as major Restoration playwright was confirmed by successive editions of her complete plays. The story of Behn's reception in the eighteenth century is one of high, though gradually declining, popularity, coupled with critical mockery and detraction.

I am concerned with Behn's afterlife up till 1800, by which time her period of greatest influence on the literary tradition was over. However, she has never been completely dropped from the literary records. Even during the nineteenth-century nadir of her reputation, a six-volume edition of her works was published, shortly followed by a pamphlet from the publisher, offering 'Two Centuries of Testimony in Favour of Mrs. Aphra Behn'.[7] In the last twenty-five years, though, she has undergone a remarkable revival, helped by the growth of feminist cultural analysis but influenced by several other factors. The twentieth-century renewal of interest in Restoration drama spread

---

[6] Behn's relation to later female writers is discussed in Ros Ballaster, *Seductive Forms: Women's Amatory Fiction from 1684 to 1740* (Oxford: Clarendon Press, 1992); Jeslyn Medoff, 'The Daughters of Behn and the Problem of Reputation', in I. Grundy and S. Wiseman (eds.), *Women, Writing, History 1640–1740* (London: Batsford, 1992), 33–54; Jacqueline Pearson, 'The History of *The History of the Nun*', in Heidi Hutner (ed.), *Rereading Aphra Behn: History, Theory and Criticism* (Charlottesville, Va., and London: University Press of Virginia, 1993), 234–52.

[7] *Two Centuries of Testimony in Favour of Mrs. Aphra Behn* (London: John Pearson, 1872).

rather late to the most successful female dramatist of the period, but a number of her plays, especially *The Rover*, have been produced since the 1970s.[8] In the 1970s, too, the interest that has always been aroused by her eventful and elusive life resulted in two biographies, and new investigations into her life have continued since.[9] Colonial studies have provided a context for renewed interest in *Oroonoko*, with its setting in Surinam in the early years of the slave-trade. Her other fiction, especially *Love-Letters between a Nobleman and his Sister*, has attracted attention from historians of the novel. Her complete works have been edited in seven volumes.[10] She has become a part of the canon studied on university courses.[11]

One aspect of Behn that attracts a good deal of attention is the sheer scale of her professional success. Her eighteen certain plays (there are others of doubtful attribution) performed throughout the 1670s and 1680s, with two produced posthumously in the 1690s, make her one of the most prolific Restoration dramatists. Her longest novel, the three-part *Love-Letters*, inaugurated the scandal-novel in England. Her shorter stories became extremely popular after her death. She published a variety of poems and translations, and attempted the role of court poet, producing Stuart panegyrics. Her third-night payments, booksellers' fees, and the patchy patronage obtained through dedications did not bring her a good living, but they seem to have been her main support for a number of years. This is all the more remarkable in an age when a woman's making her writing public was strongly associated by many with public access to her body.[12] If the prostitute is, according to Pierre Bourdieu, 'a figure who is symbolic of the artist's relationship to the market',[13] this figure acquires peculiar force in the late seventeenth-century reaction to women writers, who were sometimes satirically depicted as literal rather than metaphorical whores. Catherine Gallagher has argued

[8] For a discussion of recent performances see *The Rover and Other Plays*, ed. Jane Spencer (Oxford: Oxford University Press, 1995), pp. xx–xxii.

[9] Maureen Duffy, *The Passionate Shepherdess: Aphra Behn 1640–89* (London: Jonathan Cape, 1977); Angeline Goreau, *Reconstructing Aphra: A Social Biography of Aphra Behn* (Oxford: Oxford University Press, 1980). The most recent biography is Janet Todd, *The Secret Life of Aphra Behn* (London: André Deutsch, 1996).   [10] *Works.*

[11] For a discussion of Behn's reputation, including its recent revival, see Janet Todd, *The Critical Fortunes of Aphra Behn* (Columbia, Oh.: Camden House, 1998).

[12] See Goreau, *Reconstructing Aphra*, 150.

[13] Pierre Bourdieu, *The Field of Cultural Production: Essays on Art and Literature*, ed. Randall Jackson (Cambridge: Polity Press, 1993), 167.

that this should not be seen as a necessarily disabling comparison for the woman writer. She describes Behn as capitalizing on the poetess–whore analogy to create her own version of the professional writing role, a role in which self-alienation ensures survival in the marketplace. The 'rhetoric of female authorship' in Behn and later women writers only differs 'from that of authorship in general by exaggerating and sexualizing the common theme' of the dispossession of the writer who becomes an author by virtue of being sold. Women writers, for Gallagher, are 'representatives of the condition of the author in the eighteenth century . . . special in their extreme typicality', and Behn's authorial persona, 'the professional playwright as newfangled whore', enables both commercial success and the production of 'dark comedy' that exposes the commodification of women.[14]

Behn's very professional success, however, became one of the factors demoting her in subsequent literary histories. She herself was well aware of the difference between the commercial success she pursued and the literary status she increasingly came to desire. Her discussions of her profession mingle defence of commercial writing with claims of a status beyond it. In 1678, defending her comedy *Sir Patient Fancy* from charges that it offended the ladies by its bawdy, she declared that she was 'forced to write for Bread and not ashamed to owne it'; in 1686, facing similar accusations about *The Lucky Chance*, she alluded to its box-office success as a better indication of true audience opinion: 'I found by my receipts it was not thought so criminal'. Yet in *Sir Patient Fancy* she described writing for money as a thing 'even I despise as much below me', and in *The Lucky Chance* she declared herself 'not content to write for a Third day only', and equated literary reputation with the 'Fame' that was seen in the seventeenth century as the proper motive for heroic action.[15]

If the commercial writer's position was the feminized one of whore, Behn here clearly sees the more elevated concept of literary fame as masculine. In *The Lucky Chance*, she refers to 'my Masculine Part the Poet in me'.[16] In another late bid for literary reputation, however, she made an audacious claim for the inclusion of femininity in the notion of literary honour. In the 1680s Nahum Tate asked Behn

[14] Gallagher, *Nobody's Story*, pp. xxi, xv, 14.
[15] 'To the reader', *Sir Patient Fancy*, in *Works*, vi. 5; and Preface to *The Lucky Chance*, *Works*, vii. 217. [16] *Works*, vii. 217.

to contribute to an English translation of Cowley's Latin poem, *Of Plants*. Her portion was Book 6, one of two books on trees. The introduction of the laurel tree is Cowley's occasion for elevating the poet's role while claiming for himself a properly modest share of the honour of the laurel wreath. Laurels are the greatest honour of a king, and poets are second only to kings in their claim to them. In Behn's version:

> And all the Glories of immortal Fame
> Which conquering Monarchs so much strive to gain,
> Is but at best from thy triumphing Boughs
> To reach a Garland to adorn their Brows,
> And after Monarchs, Poets claim a share
> As the next worthy thy priz'd wreaths to wear.
> Among that number, do not me disdain,
> Me, the most humble of that glorious Train.

Behn then added five lines, glossed in the margin as 'The Translatress in her own Person speaks':

> I by a double right thy Bounties claim,
> Both from my Sex, and in *Apollo*'s Name:
> Let me with *Sappho* and *Orinda* be
> Oh ever sacred Nymph, adorn'd by thee;
> And give my verses Immortality.[17]

From a post-Romantic perspective, it may seem odd for Behn to place her claim to immortality in the middle of a translation rather than a work of original genius; but for a seventeenth-century writer, for whom imitation and translation, especially from the Latin, are high arts, this is the appropriate place. In Behn's time, and for some time after, knowledge of Latin, the central grammar school subject for all gentlemen, generally marked a scholar's social status and gender.[18] Not very much is known of Behn's education, but she seems to have been ill qualified for the honour of translating Cowley. In a poem to her friend Thomas Creech, 'To the Unknown Daphnis on his Excellent Translation of Lucretius', she had lamented her ignorance of the classical languages,[19] and she had been satirized as 'our

---

[17] 'Of Plants', *Works*, i. 325.
[18] See Elizabeth Spearing, 'Aphra Behn: The Politics of Translation', in Janet Todd (ed.), *Aphra Behn Studies* (Cambridge: Cambridge University Press, 1996), 154–77.
[19] *Works*, i. 25–8.

blind Translatress Behn' for an earlier contribution to Dryden's edition of Ovid's *Heroides*, published with his explanation that she had
no Latin.[20] Despite this, Behn not only accepted Tate's commission,
but used her translation to appropriate the classical myth of Apollo
and Daphne, traditionally used to elevate the poet's role. The god of
poetry's attempt to rape Daphne, who escaped him by turning into a
laurel tree, was a myth of the origins of poetic authority peculiarly
suited to feminine revision, and panegyrics to women writers
included the claim that while male writers aggressively and un-
successfully tried to seize poetic power, women received it as
Daphne's gift. Katherine Philips, the 'Orinda' of Behn's lines, had
received a poetic tribute from a woman calling herself 'Philo-
Philippa'. The poem, published in the 1667 edition of Philips's work,
proclaimed:

> Let the male poets their male *Phoebus* choose,
> Thee I invoke, *Orinda*, for my Muse;
> He could but force a Branch, *Daphne* her Tree
> Most freely offers to her Sex and thee,
> And says to Verse, so unconstrain'd as yours,
> Her Laurel freely comes, your fame secures:
> And men no longer shall with ravish'd Bays
> Crown their forc'd Poems by as forc'd a praise.[21]

'Philo-Philippa', turning from Phoebus Apollo to Daphne, rereads
the myth so as to posit a distinct and superior feminine poetic tradition. Behn, even as she recalls this revision in her own attempt to
place herself in Orinda's line, adds a new twist. Claiming the laurels
in the roles of both aggressor (in Apollo's name) and that of
Daphne's female beloved (from my sex), she refuses to confine herself
to either a masculine or a feminine tradition. Having it both ways,
she also revises the mocking reference to herself in a poem of
the 1670s, 'A Session of the Poets', which took the conventional
seventeenth-century theme of a group of poets vying with each other
to be awarded the laurels by Apollo. In this poem she was also
depicted making a dual claim:

---

[20] Matthew Prior, 'A Satire on the Modern Translators', *Dialogues of the Dead and Other Works in Prose and Verse*, ed. A.R. Waller (Cambridge: Cambridge University Press, 1907), 50.
[21] 'To the Excellent Orinda', in Germaine Greer *et al.* (eds.), *Kissing the Rod: An Anthology of Seventeenth-Century Women's Verse* (London: Virago Press, 1988), 204.

> Next poetess Afra then showed her sweet face,
> And swore by her poetry and her black Ace
> The laurels by a double right were her own,
> For the poems she had writ, and the conquests she'd won.[22]

Writing and sex are her double claim in both poems, but while 'A Session' defines her sex as her genitals and her sexual conquests, in 'Of Plants' 'my sex' becomes the reason for Daphne's love, and also her fellowship with other women poets. The place she claims with Sappho, most famous of ancient women poets, and Orinda, the epitome of the good modern woman writer, was granted her for some years after her death.

In these lines, we see Behn making her bid for inclusion in what Pierre Bourdieu terms the 'literary field', in which artistic value is understood to be in opposition to wide audience appeal and financial success. There are two hierarchical principles at work, one of '*success*, as measured by indices such as book sales, number of theatrical performances, etc. or honours, appointments, etc.', and the other, more powerful as the literary field gains greater autonomy, of '*degree specific consecration* (literary or artistic prestige)'.[23] Bourdieu's analysis, developed in the study of nineteenth-century French culture, can be more widely applied. We can see the period 1660–1800, in which a consumer culture was developing in England, as a time when the literary field was in the process of development, with the growth of the literary market accompanied by a growing tendency to define literary prestige in opposition to mere commercial success. The power of the literary field explains the stigma often attached in literary history to writers who were popular with their contemporaries, and explains, too, the anxiety of a writer like Behn to detach herself to a degree from her commercial success.

Bourdieu does not discuss the effects of gender, but they can be seen to play a significant part in the construction of the literary field. If we consider seventeenth- and eighteenth-century women aiming for success in the literary field, the immediately striking point is that

---

[22] 'A Session of the Poets', in *The Poems of John Wilmot Earl of Rochester*, ed. Keith Walker (London, 1984), 135. The poem has sometimes been attributed to Rochester, sometimes to Buckingham. David M. Vieth, in the most thorough discussion of its attribution, concludes that it was written *c.* Nov. 1676, either by Settle or by some other writer, but not Rochester or Buckingham. See his *Attribution in Restoration Poetry: A Study of Rochester's Poems of 1680* (New Haven and London: Yale University Press, 1963), 298–9 and 303.

[23] Bourdieu, *The Field of Cultural Production*, 38, 39.

honours and appointments were institutionally closed to them, while the market was not. Both the writers and critics who defined prestige, and the groups who controlled honours and appointments, were overwhelmingly, though not exclusively, male, while the market was more mixed. Relative to men, therefore, women writers were more restricted to the market end of Bourdieu's 'success'. The 'honours' end included the royal offices of Poet Laureate and Historiographer Royal, both held by Dryden and later by Shadwell, and potentially lucrative appointments in theatrical management, such as Steele's appointment to the governorship of Drury Lane in 1714. These honours were generally given in recognition of (and inducement for) political services, and some writers hoped for even higher rewards (Steele was disappointed that his services to the Whigs did not bring him a high ministerial post).[24] Women writers might certainly receive some reward for political writing—Behn repeatedly sought Tory patronage for her work, with some success, and in the following generation, George I and the Prince of Wales commanded performances of Susanna Centlivre's Whig plays—but royal appointments and government posts were not offered to them.[25] This not only cut them off from a potential source of financial success, making them more dependent on audiences and book sales; it deprived them of a degree of power, influence, and prestige, as well. The appointments that were closed to women are that part of Bourdieu's literary 'success' which had most in common with literary prestige; in some ways a part of prestige, rather than part of its opposition. In other words, the gendering of the literary field produced new kinds of hierarchy within it, including the devaluation of success in the market, perceived as feminized in terms both of producers and consumers, and the higher valuation of the kind of official recognition that was generally granted on mingled political and literary grounds.

In *Toward an Aesthetic of Reception,* Hans Robert Jauss claims that a literary work should be judged on the basis of its reception and influence. Central to his theory is the concept of the 'horizon of

---

[24] John Loftis, *Steele at Drury Lane* (Berkeley and Los Angeles: University of California Press, 1952), 51.

[25] For a discussion of Behn's search for political patronage, see Virginia Crompton, '"Forced to write for bread and not ashamed to owne it": Aphra Behn, Court Poetry and Professional Writing in the 1680s', Ph.D. thesis, University of East Anglia, 1994. Hanoverian patronage of Centlivre is discussed in J. B. Bowyer, *The Celebrated Mrs. Centlivre* (Durham, NC: Duke University Press, 1952), 105.

expectations'. A literary work enters and evokes a certain 'horizon of expectations' familiar from earlier texts, and then varies, corrects, alters or even just reproduces these. Aesthetic value is determined by the extent to which a work challenges the expectations of its first audience, and can only later be understood and absorbed—a theory which depends on an assumption of the progressive nature of audience response.[26] It can easily be seen how this distinction echoes the poles of mere commercial success and more prestigious artistic recognition which, for Bourdieu, operate in the literary field. This is a theory of aesthetic value which is unlikely to challenge the dominant gender relations within literary reception. A typical reception pattern for known women writers is not initial shock followed by gradual understanding, but initial acceptance followed by downgrading and forgetting. This certainly is the general trajectory of Aphra Behn's reception in the period covered by this book. Jauss's aesthetic would thus place her in the lowest of all positions: mere entertainment, because of her initial ability to fulfil audience expectations; and not of lasting value, because of the adverse reactions of (presumably more discerning) later generations. If, in a search for women's work of literary value, we turn instead to the work of women who failed to achieve lifetime popularity, and have been neglected in literary history, Jauss's aesthetic does not help here either. Such writers are equally devalued, because aesthetic value is made dependent on the ability to change the horizon of expectations, not just on refusal or inability to conform to it. In effect, deferred audience acceptance is the criterion of value.

Of course, the saving grace of this apparently closed system of aesthetic value is that reception never ends; it is always open to a later generation to discover the aesthetic value that has not been found before. In all such re-evaluations, though, the question arises: who judges the aptness of the new reading? We are returned to the struggle for authority, central to Bourdieu's account. In considering the reception of Behn as a manifestation of the contest for authority I am indebted to the work of Ina Ferris, whose feminist reception study of Scott's Waverley novels has important implications for the writing of literary history. As Ferris argues, 'a key project for feminist literary history of any period is to understand the *relations* of gender

---

[26] See Hans Robert Jauss, *Toward an Aesthetic of Reception*, trans. Timothy Bahti (Brighton: Harvester, 1982), 20–5.

that structure the literary field'. Central to my study will be the relations of gender structuring the literary field in the eighteenth century, and the way the reception of Behn's work affects that process.
My concern, like Ferris's, is with the function of gender, 'specifically
with the ways in which gender-constructs inform and maintain the
distribution of genres (their status, territory, value, and so forth) at a
given historical moment'.[27]

My approach to literary value is the relativist one argued by
Barbara Herrnstein Smith: not a refusal to attach literary value to
writing, but a constant awareness of the way such values are created
in particular historical contexts. As Smith writes: 'All value is radically contingent, being neither a fixed attribute, an inherent quality,
or an objective property of things but, rather, an effect of multiple,
continuously changing, and continuously interacting variables, or, to
put this another way, the product of the dynamics of a system.'
Smith's analysis informs my work in several respects. Her view that
'what are commonly taken to be the *signs* of literary value are, in
effect, its *springs*', is important for the study of aesthetic reception.
The canonization of a work becomes understood as the process by
which its literary value is created and maintained:

the repeated inclusion of a particular work in literary anthologies not only
promotes the value of that work but goes some distance towards creating this
value, as also does its frequent appearance on reading lists or its frequent
citation or quotation by professors, scholars, and academic critics. . . . all
these institutional acts have the effect . . . of drawing the work into the orbit
of attention of a population of potential readers . . . they make it more
likely both that the work will be experienced at all and also that it will be
experienced as valuable.[28]

Tracing the ways in which Aphra Behn is anthologized and cited in
the eighteenth century is thus to trace the creation of the value(s) of
her work and authorial status. As I do this I pay attention to the
changing function of her work, following Smith's description of lasting literary value as the ability to perform desired or desirable
functions under changing conditions and for changing readers.
My discussion of the lasting fame and influence of *The Rover*

[27] Ina Ferris, *The Achievement of Literary Authority* (Ithaca, NY, and London: Cornell University Press, 1991), 4.
[28] Barbara Herrnstein Smith, *Contingencies of Value* (Cambridge, Mass.: Harvard University Press, 1988), 30, 50, 46.

and *Oroonoko* turns on their adaptability to particular desires of eighteenth-century audiences and readers.

Feminist literary historians have always paid attention to literary reception, especially to the construction and use of reputation, a term which when applied to women writers mingles personal and sexual considerations with consideration of the writing. This has been as true of Aphra Behn as of other women writers, and it is not surprising that a woman who, in the relatively free atmosphere of the Restoration, wrote about sexual freedom, should have been attacked for her life as well as her writing during the moral clampdown of the eighteenth century. In recent years feminist critics have examined the eighteenth-century decline in Behn's reputation and argued that it had a constricting effect on later women writers' authorial identities. Jeslyn Medoff argues that: 'The women who wrote in the generation after Aphra Behn were strongly affected by society's reception (or rejection) of her, well aware that they were writing in a new era that required different methods for coping with the problem of combining femaleness and fame.'[29] Jacqueline Pearson has also demonstrated the anxiety caused by the reputation of this prominent female precursor, who came to be understood as a kind of 'bad mother' to eighteenth-century women writers, in contrast to the personally respectable Katherine Philips, 'Orinda', the 'good mother'.[30] Women writers proved their respectability by showing how greatly they differed from Aphra Behn.

Though these critics are undoubtedly correct in finding an eighteenth-century tendency to reject Behn, the full picture of her reception in the period includes the continuation in a number of places (editions, anthologies, histories of the theatre and of women's poetry) of her high reputation as 'the ingenious Mrs Behn'. The men of letters who seem in retrospect to be the arbiters of eighteenth-century taste were not the only powerful voices speaking of Behn. Moreover, reputation is only a part of reception. More significant is the continuing effect of the work, which is operational, as Jauss writes, 'if those who come after it still or once again respond to it— if there are readers who again appropriate the past work or authors who want to imitate, outdo, or refute it'.[31] Many of Behn's writings

[29] Medoff, 'The Daughters of Behn', 35.
[30] Pearson, 'The History of *The History of the Nun*', 243.
[31] Jauss, *Toward an Aesthetic of Reception*, 22.

remained current in this sense throughout the eighteenth century. Her low reputation among eighteenth-century men of letters is a sign of her continued membership of the literary field, according to Bourdieu's criterion of 'the objective fact of producing effects within it'; attacks on her, like all polemics, 'imply a form of recognition'.[32] Attacks on Behn were perfectly compatible with the continued commercial success her work was achieving during this period: indeed, that success was one argument against her artistic value.

Behn's effects on eighteenth-century culture, then, are not to be gauged by reputation alone. The influence of her work on eighteenth-century writing is a crucial consideration; and a writer's power to influence, while obviously affected by her current reputation, cannot be simply deduced from it. Behn inspired more conscious imitations in the 1690s, when her reputation was still relatively high, than in later decades; but the continued currency of her work, in print and on the stage, in the eighteenth century, generated a continuing influential power. Jacqueline Pearson is one of the first to do full justice to this power. Eighteenth-century women writers, as she notes, may have felt uneasy about being identified with Behn, but they imitated her, whether they were willing to admit it or not.[33] Following Pearson's example, I shall be concerned in this book to trace the workings of unacknowledged influence in Behn's literary afterlife.

In my study of Behn's reception I aim both to do justice to the degree of 'fame' and influence she achieved and to chart the processes of demotion and exclusion that, by 1800, pushed her work to the margins of literary and theatrical tradition. It is a complex narrative, not to be simply characterized as the story either of success or failure, and it stands necessarily, and somewhat uneasily, beside the success stories of the canonization of writers such as Shakespeare and Milton during the same period. Recent work on the progress of literary reputations has stressed the importance of the *making* of the canon: studies of Shakespeare, especially, showing that his pre-eminence is not to be taken for granted but was the outcome of a historical process. Michael Dobson argues that the emergence of Shakespeare as 'an Enlightenment culture hero' and a British 'national habit' was part of the cultural expression of the success of

---

[32] Bourdieu, *The Field of Cultural Production*, 42.
[33] Pearson, 'The History of *The History of the Nun*', 243.

the Hanoverian commercial empire: 'Shakespeare was declared to rule world literature at the same time that Britannia was declared to rule the waves'.[34] In comparison to such work, a study of Aphra Behn's relation to the canon is bound to seem secondary: why give so much attention to the making of a reputation that was patchy and compromised, to the creation of a marginal figure?

There are, I think, two reasons. One is that cultural tradition is made up of failures as well as successes, the secondary as well as the primary, the marginal as well as the central: writers of the 'first rank', as eighteenth-century critics liked to call them, can only be so by virtue of the existence of a second rank. To understand canon-formation as a process, then, we need not only to consider, for example, how Dryden came to be seen as pre-eminent among Restoration writers, but also how Cowley did not.

When the object of study is a woman writer, a second reason comes into play. Part of what makes Behn particularly significant is her position at the beginning of the history of professional women's writing; in the minds of eighteenth-century women, she was a notable first example whom they followed in second position. Behn can be a first, then, but only in a tradition understood as secondary, for women writers have long been understood as secondary not in particular cases or by accident, but by definition. Patricia Parker's analysis of 'Coming Second: Woman's Place' offers a way of understanding the deep roots of this attitude in biblical and other creation stories. The Genesis story of the creation of Eve after Adam 'has for centuries authorized women's place as second place, a coming after, in which priority in the temporal sequence has hierarchical superiority as its consequence or result'.[35] Parker also argues for the importance of a different creation myth, equally persistent, in which a mother–goddess is imagined, conversely, as coming first: as the source of an original, disorderly female rule which needed to be replaced in a male takeover. The Babylonian creation story in which the male god Marduk triumphs over the original mother Tiamat, and Hesiod's *Theogony*, in which Zeus replaces the rule of the earth goddess, are examples. Both these contradictory accounts of the female position have served the purpose of justifying female subordination.[36]

---

[34] Michael Dobson, *The Making of the National Poet* (Oxford: Clarendon Press, 1992), 5, 7–8.

[35] Patricia Parker, *Literary Fat Ladies: Rhetoric, Gender, Property* (London and New York: Methuen, 1987), 179.   [36] Ibid. 187–91.

They have also, as the story of Behn's reception will show, affected the process of responding to women writers and placing them in literary tradition. The belief in female secondariness, encouraging the view of women writers as essentially imitators of an earlier male, has coloured critical reaction to Behn's drama. Conversely, the myth of the female as original but unruly, in need of replacement by male order, can illuminate our understanding of the way Behn has been treated within histories of the novel. In other words, Behn's 'secondary' position is not just an incidental fact and certainly not a bar to the significance of her afterlife: it is a crucial part of the wider problem which this study investigates, the problem of the complex effects of gendered beliefs on the creation of literary and cultural histories.

My study is divided into three parts. In the first part, 'Reputations', I show that Behn had very different kinds of afterlife in different genres. She had a very different image within dramatic history from the one that prevailed in discussions of the novel. Overall, however, the image of her as an erotic woman and writer became the prevalent one: built up, especially, in the early biographies and in discussion of her poetry, the erotic Behn coloured eighteenth-century attitudes to all women's writing. In Part II, 'Influences', I look at Behn's effects on eighteenth-century writing, showing how important she was as a role-model for later women writers, and arguing that women's literary influence, especially influence on men, has been undervalued within a literary history built on father–son genealogies. In the final part, 'Receptions', I give a detailed analysis of the eighteenth-century afterlife of her two most famous works, *The Rover* and *Oroonoko*.

Aphra Behn was an influential force in eighteenth-century literature. Her work was significant in the development of stage comedy, the novel, the sentimental tradition, and the discourse against slavery. In all of these very different areas, her meanings were reshaped towards others' ends. Yet her words, modified as they were in the guts of the living, continued to have their effects.

PART I

Reputations

PART I

Reparations

Pleasure and Poetry: The Behn Myth

WHEN, in the preface to *The Lucky Chance,* Aphra Behn demanded recognition for 'the Poet in me' (*Works,* vii. 217), she was no doubt using 'poetry' in its accepted seventeenth-century sense, to mean 'fine writing' or 'literature' in general; her main concern, though, was to be immortalized for her verse and her plays. Her fiction, an experiment started relatively late in her career, was always something of a sideline; and for her and her contemporaries, it was probably not included in that older, more comprehensive sense of poetry. References to her during her lifetime, from slanders to encomia to the more measured assessments of early dramatic encyclopaedias, treat her as a poet, whether the emphasis is on dramatic poetry or her volumes of verse. *The Ladies Dictionary,* published a few years after her death, is typical of contemporary emphases, listing her as '*Astera Behen,* [*sic*] a Dramatick Poetess, whose well known Plays have been very taking; she was a retained Poetess to one of the Theatresses [*sic*], and writ, besides, many curious Poems'.[1] Novels were not the route to literary eminence in the seventeenth century.

By the last two decades of the eighteenth century the picture was completely altered: Behn's verse was out of fashion, her plays were rarely performed, and for many readers her main claim to remembrance was the authorship of *Oroonoko.* Indeed, this short novel was singled out quite early as one of her most important works, so that Behn can be said to have contributed to the new trend for novelists to gain fame. By the late eighteenth century, of course, fiction stood much higher in the literary hierarchy; yet Behn was not hailed as an important early novelist. The novel's rise in status entailed a rejection of many of its early practitioners as immoral, and Behn's reputation suffered as a result. As the next chapter will show, she was condemned by the eighteenth-century novelists who were intent on

---

[1] *The Ladies Dictionary* (London: John Dunton, 1694), 419.

raising the status of fiction in the same years as she was being honourably remembered by the writers of dramatic history. The reason *Oroonoko* received special treatment was the immense popularity of Thomas Southerne's stage-adaptation of it, first performed late in 1695 and one of the most frequently performed plays of the eighteenth century. By 1785 Clara Reeve could treat his play as the main reason for remembering her: 'Mrs. *Behn* will not be forgotten, so long as the Tragedy of *Oroonoko* is acted.'[2]

Behn's reputation, then, does not have a single chronology, but follows different trajectories in the annals of poetry, of the stage, and of the novel. One key to understanding reactions to her is the position a particular critic or historian occupies in relation to the formation of one or other of the eighteenth-century literary canons: her picture varies according to whether it is being drawn by someone who is most concerned with establishing a tradition in the novel, in poetry, or in drama. At the same time, all discussions of her were affected by the biographical tradition that grew up around her, centring on the influential 'Memoirs' included in her collected novels.

In this chapter I consider three aspects of the making of Behn's reputation: discussions of her within her lifetime; the growth of Behn biography in the years following her death; and the reception of Behn's verse. What unites these different parts of her story is the growth of a myth about Behn, which both drew on received notions of the relationship between a female writer and her work, and set the tone for the reception of later women writers. The myth is that Behn's writing reflects a life pre-eminently concerned with sexual love. The 'Memoirs', first published in the 1696 collection of Behn's novels and expanded in later editions, concentrated on its subject's early life and supposed adventures, offering a very succinct account of her literary career: '[t]he Rest of her Life was entirely dedicated to Pleasure and Poetry'.[3] The image of Aphra Behn which was to become dominant in the eighteenth century was that of a woman for whom (sexual) pleasure and poetry were intermingled. This view began to emerge in her lifetime, representing the narrowing-down of an originally much wider conception of her as a writer. It was

---

[2] Clara Reeve, *The Progress of Romance* (Colchester: W. Keymer, 1785) i. 118.

[3] 'Memoirs on the Life of Mrs. Behn', in *The Histories and Novels Of the Late Ingenious Mrs. Behn* (London: S. Briscoe, 1696), sig. C2ᵛ. I have reversed the italics in this quotation, and do so silently throughout the book when quoting works entirely or in large proportion printed in italics.

developed and emphasized in the biographical tradition. Finally, in the story of Behn's poetic reputation during the eighteenth century we can see how the view of her as primarily a poet of love affected her place in the poetic canon and contemporary assumptions about femininity and writing.

THE ESTABLISHMENT OF BEHN'S REPUTATION, 1670–1688

To discuss an author's life in this way—as the story of her writing career—always risks leaving the impression that this is the way she herself thought about it. Behn started writing verse early in her life and was probably trying her hand at heroic drama during her visit to Surinam in her early twenties,[4] so she was not simply driven to write from financial necessity, but nor did she plan her life, as in a later generation Alexander Pope seems to have done, as the pursuit of literature. She may have progressed from anonymous hackwork for the stage, and even work as a copyist, to writing plays under her own name. The hardship involved in attempts to live by the pen in the late seventeenth century should not be underestimated. Behn's contemporaries remarked, with varying degrees of sympathy, on the great poverty of her later years, during which she had to beg her publisher for an extra £5 for *Poems Upon Several Occasions*, writing: 'I shou'd really have thought 'em worth thirty pound . . . I have been without getting so long that I am just on the poynt of breaking, especially since a body has no creditt at the Playhouse as we used to have.'[5] Nevertheless, as the years went by she became, not less dependent on her writing, but more openly concerned about its prestige as well as its profitability. Behn's involvement in the new commercialization, not only of literature but of authorship, has been emphasized in recent accounts: she is seen as a canny self-promoter, marketing her own image as 'author–whore',[6] but this is only part of the story. As Dustin Griffin has argued, the period 1650–1750 was a transitional one between a court-based literary culture and a market-based print culture. Aphra Behn, like Milton and Dryden, belonged 'to both cultures—the old world of patronage and the new world of

---

[4] Todd, *Secret Life*, 63–5. [5] Ibid. 324–5.
[6] Catherine Gallagher, 'Who was that Masked Woman? The Prostitute and the Playwright in the Comedies of Aphra Behn', in Hutner (ed.), *Rereading Aphra Behn*, 65–85.

booksellers'.[7] Her plays aimed to please political patrons as well as the wider audience. Many of her verses, like those in 'Our Cabal', originated as coterie verse, circulating in manuscript among friends after the old, amateur fashion; but then she collected and published them for money. Griffin suggests two possible models for literary careers at this time: 'the Virgilian career', an older model in which the poet aims for perfection and works towards a culminating great poem; and the newer model of the 'professional man of letters', who tailors each work to its particular audience, takes different writing opportunities as they come his way, and does not worry about revising or sequencing his works.[8] Behn's career most closely fits that of the professional: her extraordinary versatility came from seizing opportunities as they arose, and writing for different audiences (though she was not indifferent to revision). Like her contemporary Dryden, she combined writing for money with a frank desire for literary fame. The complex, by no means wholly commercially driven role of 'professional man of letters' was not only very new in Behn's time: it was also, of course, of doubtful applicability to her. Her literary career can be seen in effect—and in her later years, I think, in conscious intention—as an experiment in whether there could be a professional *woman* of letters.

It was as a playwright that Behn the author first came to public notice. Her early work was accepted by Thomas Betterton, thus beginning Behn's long association with the Duke's Company. Her tragicomedy *The Forc'd Marriage: or the Jealous Bridegroom* had a moderately successful six days' run in the 1670–1 season.[9] A second play, *The Amorous Prince,* followed a few months after, in February 1671. Behn made enough of a mark with these early efforts to be noticed, even if some of the notice was mockery: in Buckingham's burlesque play, *The Rehearsal,* Behn's tragicomic heroics were laughed at along with the more eminent target, Dryden.[10] She turned next to publishing verse, editing the *Covent-Garden Drolery* (1672), in which she included some of her own poems.[11] A third play, *The Dutch Lover,* in 1673,

[7] Dustin Griffin, 'The Beginnings of Modern Authorship: Milton and Dryden', *Milton Quarterly*, 24/1 (1990), 2.   [8] Ibid. 5–6.

[9] [John Downes], *Roscius Anglicanus* (London: H. Playford, 1708), 34.

[10] Todd, *The Critical Fortunes*, 3–4.

[11] The poems are four songs and 'Prologue to The Double Marriage', which is probably hers, and was later used as an epilogue to her posthumously produced play, *The Widdow Ranter.* See Mary Ann O'Donnell, *Aphra Behn: An Annotated Bibliography of Primary and Secondary Sources* (New York and London: Garland, 1986), 213–15.

marked a new departure: Behn turned to intrigue comedy, set in Spain but mocking, in the eponymous comic butt, England's rival nation. It was not a success on the stage: Behn blamed the actors, and published the play with a defensive and witty preface, addressing the 'Good, Sweet, Honey, Sugar-candied READER' with complaints about prejudice against women writers, and mockery of the pedants who thought plays should keep to the rules or convey a moral (*Works*, v. 160). At this point, refusing the apologetic stance and the reverence for literary tradition that might have gained her a more respectable position, she established herself as a bold woman, a professional, a modern ready to try out new staging techniques, and with not much respect for the ancients and the rules. By 1675, with three plays to her name and a few poems published, she was well known enough to be included in Edward Phillips's compendium, *Theatrum Poetarum*, where she appeared as: '*Astrea Behn*, a Dramatic writer, so much the more considerable as being a Woman, to the present English Stage'.[12] In the following year she staged two more plays: her one tragedy, *Abdelazer*, adapted from *Lust's Dominion*, a play that had been attributed to Marlowe;[13] and the comedy *The Town-Fopp*, from George Wilkins's *The Miseries of Inforst Marriage*. Around this time, too, she was included in 'A Session of the Poets', which contributed to Behn's public image as a bold, lascivious woman whose poetry was bound up with her sexuality.[14] Still, the remarkable thing is that she was considered a contender at all.

In March 1677 came the play that more than any other would carry her name into the next century: *The Rover; or, the Banish't Cavaliers*. Like most of Behn's plays it drew on earlier sources: this time, very heavily, on Thomas Killigrew's ten-act closet-drama *Thomaso, or, the Wanderer*, published in the 1650s. Perhaps to avoid attacks on her as a plagiarist, she had the play staged, and at first published, anonymously: unusual practice for her, and not kept up for long. The first edition went through three issues in 1677, and by the third her name was on the title-page. Despite the criticisms of her use of Killigrew, the play was a great success on the stage, and gained

---

[12] Edward Phillips, *Theatrum Poetarum, or a Compleat Collection of the Poets, Especially the most Eminent, of all Ages* (London: Charles Smith, 1675), 255.

[13] *Lust's Dominion* was attributed to Marlowe on its publication in 1657 but is more likely to be by a later anonymous writer imitating his style: see Todd's introduction to *Abdelazer* in *Works*, v. 242.

[14] 'A Session of the Poets', in *The Poems of John Wilmot Earl of Rochester*, ed. Walker, 135.

Behn the praise of—and hopes of patronage from—James, Duke of York himself. It was revived several times in the following years, in public and Court performances; and when her next comedy, *Sir Patient Fancy*, was published in 1678, it was 'by Mrs. A. Behn, the Authour of the *Rover*'.

Behn was now an established playwright, and in the next few years a succession of comedies were performed at the Duke's: *The Feigned Courtesans* (1679), *The second part of the Rover* (1681), *The False Count* (1681), *The Roundheads: or the Good Old Cause* (1681), and *The City-Heiress: or, Sir Timothy Treat-all* (1682). An early composition, the tragicomedy *The Young King*, may have been performed in 1679, but presumably with little success, as it was not published till several years later. In the increasingly politicized climate following the Popish Plot of 1678, her plays became conspicuously Tory, pro-James and anti-Monmouth. To the image of Behn the poetess–whore could now be added Behn the Tory hack: the two identities were combined in Shadwell's *The Tory Poets: A Satyr* (1682), where *The City-Heiress* and *The Roundheads* are attacked, and Otway is called Behn's pimp. In Alexander Radcliffe's satire on contemporary poets, further insults are added, including the basic one that she did not write her works at all: it is said, recorded Radcliffe, that:

> The Plays she vends she never made.
> But that a *Greys Inn* Lawyer does 'em,
> Who unto her was Friend in Bosom.[15]

Having had a lover (John Hoyle) was taken as evidence that he had written her work.

Not all notices of Behn's work were so sceptical or so damning. She had friends—and political allies—among her contemporaries writing for the stage (all men), and she soon proved an inspiration to the very few women writing for publication. 'Ephelia' praised her in *Female Poems on Several Occasions* in 1679, and included three of Behn's own poems (without attribution) in the second edition in 1682.[16] John Dryden invited her to contribute to his collection of *Ovid's Epistles, translated by Several Hands*. Published by Jacob Tonson in 1680, this was a prestigious volume, and Behn's inclusion is an indication that she had gained some recognition among those she liked to think of as her

[15] Alexander Radcliffe, *The Ramble* (London, 1682), 6.
[16] O'Donnell, *Bibliography*, 255.

brother poets. She chose, or was assigned, a female voice, writing a paraphrase of Oenone's epistle to Paris. Though she was promptly satirized by Matthew Prior for her lack of Latin, this publication represented a foothold in the classical tradition that still defined who could and who could not be considered true poets.

A place in that tradition mattered to Behn, and mattered more as she grew older. Early in her career, she tended to treat men's learning with defensive scorn, as she had in the preface to *The Dutch Lover*; later, as her confidence grew, she had more desire for the classical knowledge that seemed necessary if writing was to be heroic authorship rather than hackwork. In 1683 she expressed a sense of frustration at being shut out from 'The Godlike *Virgil* and Great *Homers* Muse', praising Thomas Creech for the translation of Lucretius that allowed unlearned women into a male world of knowledge:

> Thou by this *Translation* dost advance
> Our Knowledge from the State of Ignorance;
> And Equallst Us to Man!

Behn wanted to follow in men's footsteps, both classical and modern: she used the metaphor more than once. In the poem to Creech she records that she has cursed:

> the scanted Customs of the Nation,
> Permitting not the Female Sex to tread
> The Mighty Paths of Learned *Heroes* Dead.
>
> (*Works*, i. 25–6)

In the preface to *The Lucky Chance* (1686), she demanded the right to 'tread in those successful Paths my Predecessors have so long thriv'd in, to take those Measures that both the Ancient and Modern writers have set me'. Her context, here, was her need for the same freedom that men had to introduce sexual references and jokes. Audaciously, but accurately, identifying the freedom to write bawdily with the freedom to pursue literary fame, she threatened not to write at all if she could not write as men did: 'If I must not, because of my Sex, have this Freedom, but that you will usurp all to your selves; I lay down my Quill, and you shall hear no more of me' (*Works*, vii. 217).

However, Aphra Behn could not afford to lay down her quill at any time before her death, and her final decade was one of remarkable productivity. When its one rival, the King's Company, collapsed in 1682, the Duke's Company took it over to become the United

Company. This was bad news for playwrights: in the following years there was much less demand for new plays, and Behn was among those forced to look for other ways of writing for bread. During the next few years, despite the beginnings of illness, this modern 'Sapho, famous for her Gout and Guilt' kept up a rapid and diverse stream of literary invention.[17] Political developments provided her with one opportunity. Ford, Lord Grey of Werke, a prominent ally of Monmouth, was involved in a scandal and court-case over his elopement with his sister-in-law, Lady Henrietta Berkeley, in 1682, and shortly afterwards was implicated in the Rye House plot against the King. Behn drew on these events for the first part of *Love-Letters between a Nobleman and his Sister*, published in 1684.[18] Appearing at first anonymously, this innovative piece of epistolary fiction was to become one of Behn's most popular works, read for its eroticism long after its topical resonance had faded. A second part of *Love-Letters* came out in 1685, and a third in 1687. Meanwhile Behn continued to write and publish poetry. Translating and considerably augmenting the Abbé Paul Tallemant's *Voyages de l'Isle d'Amour* as *A Voyage to the Island of Love*, she put it together with some of her original poems, and published *Poems Upon Several Occasions* with Jacob Tonson in 1684.

This volume of poetry helped build up Behn's now prominent reputation as an erotic writer. The following year she published her translation of La Rochefoucauld's maxims, *Seneca Unmasqued*. At this time she also extended her repertoire as a Tory poet, hoping for patronage in connection with her Pindarics on Charles's death and James's coronation. Other translations, including a version of Balthazar de Bonnecourse's *La Montre*, followed. In 1688 she returned to the formula she had adopted in *Poems Upon Several Occasions*, adapting Tallemant's *Le second voyage de l'isle d'Amour* as *Lycidus: or the Lover in Fashion*. She also continued the experiment with fiction that she had begun with *Love-Letters*, writing a number of short novels, some of them set in the countries she had visited in her early years, Holland (*The Fair Jilt*, 1688) and, more exotically, Surinam (*Oroonoko*, 1688). She carried on translating, both fiction (*Agnes de Castro*, 1688) and philosophical prose (Fontenelle's *A Discovery of New Worlds* and *History of Oracles, and the Cheats of the Pagan Priests*, both 1688). In addition to

---

[17] [Robert Gould], *A Satyrical Epistle to the Female Author of a Poem, call'd Silvia's Revenge* (London: R. Bentley, 1691), 5.

[18] According to Todd, Behn was asked by 'someone in the government' to write *Love-Letters* as a piece of Tory propaganda: see *Secret Life*, 302.

all this, she was back on the stage. *The Lucky Chance*, a newly reflective London comedy with a bitter undertone, was performed in 1686, and *The Emperor of the Moon*, a lively farce with spectacular stage-effects, had begun its long and successful stage history in 1687.

By now she was a writer of considerable fame. Though she presented herself to her readers in a great variety of ways, according to occasion—proud writer, needy scribbler, knowledgeable poet of love, member of the London writing fraternity, theorist of translation, loyal Tory, and many more—the public identities most encouraged by the performances and publication of her works so far can be summed up as follows. There was the professional dramatist, who combined anti-Whig political points with entertaining comedy, and claimed a place in a man's tradition; and there was the poet of love, who drew on French writing in particular to create lyrical, pastoral, and erotic verse. In her lifetime both these aspects of her writing identity received recognition, but most emphasis was given to the poet of love.

Early histories of English writers began to notice her. William Winstanley left her out of *The Lives of the Most Famous English Poets* in 1687, but she did figure in Gerard Langbaine's *Momus Triumphans: or, The Plagiaries of the English Stage* (1688) where her borrowings were noted but, on the whole, condoned. Her fellow-writers had, throughout the 1680s, continued to include her in their circulating manuscripts of sessions and satires; and whether the tone was vicious, as in Robert Gould's various satirical attacks, or more jocular, as in Wycherley's '*To the* Sappho *of the* Age, *suppos'd to Ly-In of a* Love-Distemper*',[19] these poems all strengthened the idea that, in Aphra Behn, sexuality and writing were inseparable. In a different vein, the commendatory poems by her friends, used to introduce her various volumes of verse, praised her for her beauty, wit, and knowledge of love. Repeatedly compared to Sappho as well as to the great Orinda, she was celebrated for the breadth of her talents, but most of all for eroticism. Whether she was mocked as a harlot suffering 'Poverty, Poetry, Pox',[20] or hailed as the 'wonder of thy Sex!' whose poetry revealed 'th'unfathom'd thing a Woman's Heart',[21] the image of her

---

[19] William Wycherley, *Miscellany Poems* (London: C. Brome, J. Taylor, and B. Took, 1704), 191–2.

[20] MS Epistle to Julian. BL Harleian 7317, fol. 58; quoted in *The Works of Aphra Behn*, ed. Montague Summers (London: William Heinemann, 1915), i, p. lvii.

[21] '*To the Lovely Witty* Astraea, *on her Excellent Poems*', in *Poems Upon Several Occasions* (London: R. and J. Tonson, 1684), sig. A8ᵛ–B1ʳ.

established during her lifetime as an example of womankind was
going to be hard for the next generation of female poets to ignore.

Another aspect of Behn's image, her libertinism, deserves consideration. Behn as love-poet was always more than a singer of soft
verses. Her erotic writing was linked to the libertine philosophy
which also strongly marked her public image. Like Rochester, whose
work she admired and lavishly praised, Behn combined ideas of sexual liberty with a sceptical attitude towards religion. She chose to
head *Poems Upon Several Occasions* with 'The Golden Age', a celebration of a mythical past of free love and free-thinking before kings,
priests, or laws existed; the fact that it was an adaptation from a
French original did not stop it being controversial. In another poem,
she praised Thomas Creech's translation of Lucretius, who wrote
that the world was made up of atoms and denied an afterlife. Behn
was outspoken in her enthusiasm for the pagan philosopher, who
offered a liberating Reason which conquered the reader:

> Beyond poor Feeble Faith's dull Oracles.
> Faith the despairing Souls content,
> Faith the Last Shift of Routed Argument.[22]

Creech, who was nervous of being too closely identified with the
atheism he had translated, was none too pleased with this, and the
lines were altered for their place in his work;[23] but Behn cared enough
to restore the original version for inclusion in *Poems Upon Several
Occasions*. Connections with free-thinking libertinism characterized
her personal life, too. She was well known for her affair with another
'admirer of *Lucretius*', as she called him (*Works*, i. 167): John Hoyle, 'an
Atheist, a Sodomite professed, a corrupter of youth, & a Blasphemer
of Christ', as he was described after his death.[24] This aspect of Behn
disturbed many of her contemporaries. Bishop Burnet warned Anne
Wharton in 1682 that Behn 'is so abominably vile a woman, and
rallies not only all Religion but all Virtue in so odious and obscene a
manner, that I am heartily sorry she has writ any thing in your com-
mendation'.[25] Attacks on Behn are sometimes represented—as she

---

[22] *Poems Upon Several Occasions* 53.
[23] In Creech's volume these lines run: 'As strong as Faiths resistless Oracles, | Faith the
Religious Souls content, | Faith the secure retreat of Routed Argument' (*Works*, i. 26).
[24] Bulstrode Whitelocke's entry in his Commonplace Book, made on 27 May 1692 just
after Hoyle was killed during a quarrel: cited in Summers, *The Works of Aphra Behn*, i,
p. xxxvi.   [25] Cited in Greer *et al.* (eds.), *Kissing the Rod*, 290.

liked to represent them herself—as just silly prudery, so it is worth emphasizing that she aligned herself with the most extreme sentiments of Restoration libertinism, quite unacceptable to all but a small group of her contemporaries.

Behn's pursuit of fame, then, was not, or at least not consistently, a clever marketing of her image: she made too few compromises for that. She linked herself politically with the Stuarts and philosophically with the libertines, and hoped for fame on those terms. In her later years she wrote several times about her hopes for a position in literary history. She thought that her reputation as a comic dramatist should have been higher, writing in the preface to *The Lucky Chance* that 'had the Plays I have writ come forth under any Mans Name, and never known to have been mine; I appeal to all unbyast Judges of Sense, if they had not said that Person had made as many good Comedies, as any one Man that has writ in our Age' (*Works*, vii. 217). Writing the story of the heroic slave Oroonoko, she expressed the belief that 'the Reputation of my Pen' would make his name live on in the future (*Works*, iii. 119). When the 1688 revolution put an end to her hopes as a court poet, and as her illness grew more severe, she began to fix her thoughts even more on her posthumous reputation. Being asked to contribute to the translation of Cowley's Latin poem on plants gave her another chance to bid for literary immortality, which she did in her now-famous prayer to Daphne.

BEHN AT HER DEATH

When she died, in April 1689, Behn's literary reputation was indeed a considerable one. Despite the fact that she was politically out of favour, she was buried 'most scandalously but rather appropriately', as Virginia Woolf was to remark,[26] in Westminster Abbey, which had recently become recognized as the resting-place of honour for poets. (In fact, Behn is buried in the east cloisters rather than in the spot now known as Poets' Corner, but eighteenth-century references make it clear that she was considered to have received a poet's honour with her burial.) The lines, possibly by John Hoyle, that were carved on her gravestone were dismissed as 'wretched Verses' by her early biographer, but they make a poignant tribute:

[26] *A Room of One's Own* (London: Vintage, 1996), 61.

> Here lies a Proof that Wit can never be
> Defence enough against Mortality.[27]

There were no folios of verse laments, as there would be eleven years later for Dryden; but a couple of broadside elegies indicate that her death was felt as significant. The first of these was licensed only a few days after her death, suggesting a personal connection between the anonymous writer and her subject; but its tone is generalized, saying little about Behn herself.[28] It is fascinating for the insight it gives into what Behn had come to represent. The loose Pindarics refer to Behn by the soubriquet 'Astrea', which had become so firmly identified with her that it was entered in the burial register,[29] and used in some early critical accounts. The name was connected to Behn as early as her Surinam days, and linked her with the heroine of Honoré d'Urfé's *L'Astrée*.[30] It was common enough for women to write verse under a name from romance, and Behn's association with Astrea seems to have carried no other significance during her lifetime, but the fact of her death brought other resonances into play. As her elegist laments 'Summon the Earth (the fair *Astrea's* gone)', the reader is reminded of Astrea the goddess of justice and innocence, who left the earth when it became sinful at the end of the Golden Age.[31] For a poet who had celebrated the Golden Age as innocent because the concept of sin had not been invented, the goddess's name might strike the reader as either very apt or horribly ironic, depending on one's point of view. The elegist goes on to treat Behn as a female champion, forming with Orinda a short line of female poetic succession, now broken:

> Who now of all the inspired Race,
> Shall take *Orinda's* Place?

[27] 'The History of the Life and Memoirs of Mrs. Behn', in *All the Histories and Novels Written by the Late Ingenious Mrs Behn, Entire in One Volume. The Third Edition, with Large Additions* (London: Samuel Briscoe, 1698), 50. The writer suggests that the couplet was written by 'the very Person, whom the Envious of our Sex, and the Malicious of the other, wou'd needs have the Author of most of hers' (50). This may be Hoyle. Todd suggests Ravenscroft as another possibility: see *Secret Life*, 510, n. 19.

[28] Behn died on 16 Apr. 1689 and was buried on 20 Apr; the elegy was licensed on 22 Apr. G. Thorn-Drury (ed.), *A Little Ark* (London: P. J. and A. Dobell, 1921), 57.

[29] Todd, *Secret Life*, 435.

[30] Harrison Platt, 'Astrea and Celadon: An Untouched Portrait of Aphra Behn', *PMLA*, 49 (1934), 544–99.

[31] *An Elegy Upon the Death of Mrs. A. Behn; The Incomparable Astrea*. By a Young Lady of Quality, in Thorn-Drury (ed.), *A Little Ark*, 53–5.

> Or who the Hero's Fame shall raise?
> Who now shall fill the Vacant Throne?

The idea that a great poet's death left a vacant throne for which his successors must vie was a favourite conceit of the male elegiac tradition. This use of the figure for a female poet is pessimistic in tone; no successor is envisaged:

> Of her own Sex, not one is found
> Who dares her Laurel wear,
> Withheld by Impotence or Fear . . .

Moreover, making a link between female writing and female status which was common in the period, the poem presents the loss of Astrea as a triumph for men, who can now reassert their rule over women:

> Let all our Hopes despair and dye,
> Our Sex for ever shall neglected lye;
> Aspiring Man has now regain'd the Sway,
> To them we've lost the Dismal Day . . .

The idea of Behn as a female champion for other women to emulate proved a potent one in the following decade, and is discussed in Chapter 4. This 'Young Lady', however, also anticipated the worries of many later women writers when she lamented Astrea's 'failure' in virtue, deciding: '"Twas pity that she practis'd what she taught' (the arts of love).[32]

A more personal tribute came from Behn's friend, the dramatist Nathaniel Lee, who wrote a broadside elegy on her death:

> I lov'd thee inward, and my Thoughts were true;
> And after Death thy Vertue I pursue.
> Thou hadst my Soul in secret, and I swear
> I found it not, till thou resolv'dst to Air.

He thought that Behn should have the literary immortality she had craved:

> *Melpomene* the stateliest of the Nine;
> And more Majestick where thy Numbers shine;
> Commands my Thoughts a mightier Urn to raise,
> And crown thy verse with an Immortal praise.[33]

---

[32] Ibid. 55–6.
[33] Roswell Gray Ham, *Otway and Lee: Biography from a Baroque Age* (New Haven: Yale University Press, 1931), 219.

However, the rather tongue-in-cheek praise Behn received from Dryden was more prophetic of the kind of reputation she was to have in the years to come. In his epilogue written for *The Widdow Ranter*, he wrote teasingly of Behn as mistress of erotic writing and purveyor of sexual pleasure:

> She who so well cou'd Love's kind Passion paint,
> We piously believe, must be a Saint.
>
> .   .   .   .
>
> Yet tho her Pen did to the Mark arrive,
> 'Twas common Praise, to please you, when alive;
> But of no other Woman, you have read,
> Except this one, to please you, now she's dead.
>
> (*Works*, vii. 354)

THE BIOGRAPHICAL TRADITION

Nothing much seems to have been known about Behn's background during her lifetime, and when 'G.J.' (probably her friend George Jenkins) published posthumously her play *The Widdow Ranter* he said very little about its author, other than that she was a true '*Judge of Wit*' and that she would have been horrified to see her play so badly produced and acted (*Works*, vii. 292). In 1691 Langbaine published his *Account of the English Dramatick Poets*, which included an assessment of Behn, who was described as 'a Person lately deceased, but whose Memory will be long fresh amongst the Lovers of Dramatick Poetry, as having been sufficiently Eminent not only for her Theatrical Performances, but several other Pieces both in Verse and Prose; which gain'd her an Esteem among the Wits, almost equal to that of the incomparable *Orinda*'.[34] Langbaine was concerned with listing plays and evaluating authors, rather than with biography, and beyond noting that Behn wrote for money, he said nothing about her life. A more personal recollection seems to have been recorded in *The History of the Athenian Society* the same year, possibly written by Charles Gildon: this work calls her an 'excellent Poetess' who 'discoursed very refinedly on any Subject that came in her way'.[35] 'Astera Behn' was

---

[34] Gerard Langbaine, *An Account of the English Dramatick Poets* (Oxford: L.L. for George West, and Henry Clements, 1691), 17.
[35] *The History of the Athenian Society* (London,[1693]), 27.

noted in John Dunton's *The Ladies Dictionary*, 1694, in an entry deriving from Philips's 1675 account; but there was no Behn biography
until 1696, when Charles Gildon published posthumously a second
play, *The Younger Brother*, with a brief biographical notice, 'An Account
of the Life of the Incomparable Mrs. Behn', which gave her maiden
name as Johnson, described her father as 'a Gentleman of a good
Family in *Canterbury* in Kent', and claimed that she travelled to
Surinam with her family in her youth. Her husband, 'Mr *Behn*, an
Eminent Merchant', and her espionage in Flanders were mentioned.
Behn's later poverty and illness were described: 'the latter part of her
Life found her Circumstances much below her Desert; and after a
tedious Sickness, and several years foregoing Indisposition, she dy'd
soon after the Revolution.'[36]

Charles Gildon, then, can be called Behn's first biographer, and he
also had, at the very least, connections with the other early biographical accounts. Also in 1696, Samuel Briscoe published the
Histories and Novels in one volume. Here was a much longer biographical piece, 'Memoirs on the Life of Mrs. Behn. By a Gentlewoman of
her Acquaintance', which repeated and elaborated on the information given by Gildon. Gildon signed the dedication of the *Histories and
Novels*, and of the subsequent revised and expanded versions of the
collection, and may have been the author of the 'Memoirs'. He certainly was the author of *The Lives and Characters of the English Dramatic
Poets* (1699), a revised version of Langbaine's *Account*. Whereas
Langbaine had only said that Behn almost equalled Katherine
Philips, Gildon compared Behn's fire and easiness favourably to
Philips's coldness,[37] and concluded that Behn 'excell'd not only all
that went before her of her own Sex, but great part of her
Contemporary Poets of the other; she had a great Facility in Writing,
and much of Nature in all she writ' (*Lives and Characters*, 9). Charles
Gildon is the source of or is connected to most of the early biographical work on which Behn's reputation was built, and some of
the highest praise that was given to her came from him. Yet his
influence on her posthumous fame was in many ways pernicious. A
friend of Behn's in her later years, Gildon spent his family inheritance in early adulthood and then made his living as a prolific

---

[36] *The Younger Brother* (London: J. Harris, 1696), sig. A4[r-v].
[37] *The Lives and Characters of the English Dramatic Poets* (London: William Turner, 1699),
110–11.

writer, and, at times, literary forger. He was well known as a Grub Street author and later became one of Pope's targets in *The Dunciad*. To be edited and promoted by Charles Gildon was to enter the eighteenth-century literary field as the protégée of a hack writer.[38] His praise of her did her no good in the eyes of the eighteenth-century biographer who remarked that 'Mr Gildon's judgment will hardly pass for current with persons of a good taste', and hinted that sexual attraction had made Gildon overrate her: 'great deductions ought often to be made from the Applauses of a Writer of our sex, when bestowed on a beautiful woman of genius, with whom he is intimate.'[39] In his treatment of Behn, Gildon had certainly helped to spread the myth which this later detractor was using: the myth that linked female writing almost exclusively to sex.

The 1696 'Memoirs' of Behn, whether composed, compiled, or merely commissioned by Gildon, were responsible for a decisive shift in the way she was received: from Behn the witty author to Behn the amorous adventuress. The 'Gentlewoman' begins by claiming an 'intimate Acquaintance with the admirable *Astrea*' as her authority for celebrating this 'Honour and Glory to our Sex' (sig.[a5^{r-v}]). Behn is presented in the biographical tradition of the remarkable child who shows early indications of future greatness: her father takes with him to Surinam '*Afra*, his Promising Darling, our Future *Heroine*, and Admir'd *Astrea*; Who, ev'n in the first Bud of Infancy, discover'd such early Hopes of her riper Years, that she was equally her Parent's Joy and Fears; for they too often mistrust the Loss of a Child, whose Wit and Understanding outstrip its Years, as too great a Blessing to be long enjoy'd' (sig.[a5^v-a6^r]). The child's remarkable abilities are soon identified as having as much to do with love as with writing. Her literary talents are construed in amatory terms: 'at the first use almost of Reason in Discourse, she wou'd Write the prettiest, soft-engaging Verses in the World', and she is credited with breaking hearts in her extreme youth: 'as she was Mistress of uncommon Charms of Body, as well as Mind, she gave infinite and raging Desires, before she cou'd know the least her self' (sig.[a6^{r-v}]).The conflation of Behn's mental

---

[38] See Ruthe T. Sheffey, who argues in 'The Literary Reputation of Aphra Behn' (Diss., Univ. Pennsylvania, 1959) that Gildon's support lowered Behn's status (73). She suggests that Pope's dislike of Behn may have been increased by her association with Gildon (99–100).

[39] *A General Dictionary, Historical and Critical*, vol. iii (London: James Bettenham for G. Strahan, *et al.*, 1735), 143.

and bodily attractions, which in the commendatory verses advertising her poetry could be understood as conventional hyperbole, has a dual function: it still serves as a puff for the publication it prefaces, but it is also hardening into a part of the emerging biographical tradition. The life offered here concentrates on the early travel to Surinam and Antwerp, because these are the settings of *Oroonoko* and *The Fair Jilt*, both of which were reprinted in this volume for the first time since 1688. Because of the fame of Southerne's adaptation, *Oroonoko* is particularly emphasized, and the biography is partly conceived as an introduction to the author of *Oroonoko*. Taking Behn's narrator at her word when she insists on the truth of her story, the 'Memoirs' treat *Oroonoko* as a source for the life—a life in which amatory rather than literary matters are considered significant. The 'Gentlewoman' takes it upon herself to refute 'some unjust Aspersions' on Behn's relationship with the royal slave (sig. b1ʳ). 'She' assures the reader that she knew Behn too well not to have been told of any such affair between the writer and her hero; that Oroonoko was too much in love with Imoinda to fall in love with another woman, especially a white one; and that Astrea, who in this account is still a very young girl in Surinam, was too well guarded by her family to be able to enter into any amorous involvement. This elaborate denial serves, of course, to draw attention to the titillating idea of a sexual relationship between Oroonoko and Astrea. As the 'Memoirs' form the earliest source we have for the rumour, the 'Gentlewoman' either made it up or was at least the main reason it was given currency. The repetition of this rumour and denial in subsequent editions of the *Histories and Novels* ensured that eighteenth-century readers approached *Oroonoko* alerted to the idea of intimacy between the writer and a hero who was understood to be authentic.

Behn is at any rate in no danger, here or later, of being placed in her husband's shadow. Her marriage takes place in a subordinate clause within a long sentence more concerned with her spying mission: 'After she was Marry'd to Mr. *Behn*, a Merchant of this City, tho' of *Dutch* Extraction, [King Charles] committed to her Secrecy, and Conduct[,] Affairs of the highest Importance in the *Dutch* War' (sig. b1ᵛ). The stay at Antwerp seems at first to serve, like the voyage to Surinam, as a way of introducing the novel set in that place: her mission 'Obliging her to stay at *Antwerp*, presented her with *The Adventures of Prince* Tarquin, *and his false wicked Fair One* Miranda: the full Account of which, you will find admirably writ in the following

Volume' (sig. b1^{v-b}2^r). At this point, the biographer takes a strange turn, veering off to describe 'some other Adventures' supposed to have happened during Behn's stay in Antwerp. These adventures, and the return voyage, take up the next nine pages of the eighteen-page text. They read like one of the short, jokey tales of intrigue then in vogue. Behn was sent to Holland to negotiate with the republican William Scot, with whom she had had contact in Surinam; here, these exchanges are transformed into a comic trick played by the heroine Astrea, a woman who unusually combines beauty, wit, and judgement, and turns all these advantages to the service of her king. Her contact is a comic, vain, amorous Dutchman, Vander Albert, from whom she gets valuable information while preserving her own honour by the old comedy ploy of the bed-trick, sending his abandoned love Catalina into his arms instead of herself. When this is discovered and Albert plots revenge by substituting himself in Astrea's bed for the old woman, Astrea's companion, Astrea inadvertently foils him by going with a group of her friends to surprise the old woman. The old woman, having aided and abetted Albert's attempt on Astrea, is dismissed, while Albert himself goes to Amsterdam and suddenly dies of a fever; and Astrea returns home, seeing a strange vision of a marble '*Pageant*' of pillars and waving streamers on the voyage. The 'Memoirs' end with their brief indication of Astrea's subsequent literary career.

This odd mixture of circumstantial, if twisted, biographical detail with fictional convention is such a strange choice for conveying the author's life that it has been suggested that the biographer was patching together an inadequate knowledge of Behn's life with pieces of unfinished fiction found in her papers.[40] Whatever the source of the 'Memoirs', their effect was to present Behn as more of a heroine of intrigue than an author. The novels were presented to the world as stories of amorous adventure written by the heroine who starred in them.

The *Histories and Novels* proved popular, going through a second issue in the same year, and a new, expanded 'third' edition was published in 1698, containing several new stories and a much bigger biographical preface, 'The History of the Life and Memoirs of Mrs. *Behn*. Written by one of the Fair Sex'. Much of the new material comes in the form of letters, purportedly by Behn herself, but

---

[40] R. A. Day, 'Aphra Behn's First Biography', *Studies in Bibliography*, 24 (1969), 227–40.

probably not genuinely hers. The Antwerp account here takes up twenty-eight pages. It makes more of Behn's importance as a spy, claiming that she gave the English warning of the Dutch plan to sail up the Thames, but was ignored. It also makes more of Behn the writer, but not by describing her professional career, which at this date was still mainly understood as her dramatic career. As a dramatist, she had of course already been detailed by Langbaine. For the author of the 1698 'Memoirs', who is marketing her as a writer of prose fiction, most of her professional career is irrelevant. Astrea is portrayed as an entrancing story-teller and letter-writer, whose literary efforts serve as a kind of compensation to her for the failures of her political mission.

A 'particular Friend of hers', finding out that her warning letters were mocked by the minister she was writing to, suggests that she should give up her spying 'and divert her Friends with some pleasant Adventures of *Antwerp*, either as to her Lovers, or those of any other Lady of her Acquaintance; [assuring her] that in this she wou'd be more successful than in her Pretences of State, since here she wou'd not fail of pleasing those she writ to'.[41] This serves to introduce Astrea's letter of reply, in which she tells the story of her friend Lucilla's adventures: a comic tale in the style of many a short novel of the period, involving Don Miguel and Don Lopez, whose tricks on their miserly father bring him to repentance and provide the sons with the means to marry Lucilla and her cousin. In her next letter, Astrea writes of her own adventures, both with the Vander Albert who appeared in the earlier memoirs, and his older kinsman Van Bruin. Both men are in love with Astrea, and Van Bruin's absurd love-letters, with Astrea's mocking replies, are inserted into the narrative. These letters seem to have been written in the 1690s with an eye to capitalizing on Behn's current reputation: Astrea's jokes about Van Bruin's attempted voyage for 'the *Island of Love*' would remind the readers of 1698 of the poetic *Voyage to the Island of Love* which had recently been reprinted in the second edition of Behn's *Poems Upon Several Occasions*.

The story of Astrea's trickery of Vander Albert, and her subsequent return to London, is given as in the 1696 'Memoirs'. Astrea's London life is then conveyed through tales of comic and serious

---

[41] 'The History of the Life and Memoirs of Mrs. *Behn*', *All the Histories and Novels Written by the Late Ingenious Mrs. Behn* (London: Samuel Briscoe, 1698), 8.

involvements with men. In the first of these, she is represented talking to the biographer, her friend, about the life of a foolish admirer of hers who has been repeatedly tricked by the aunt he married for money. The biographer joins in the fun by pretending an affection for the would-be lover, who ends up being tossed in a blanket. The second amorous intrigue, obliquely introduced when Astrea mentions that Lysander is growing jealous of 'this ridiculous Amour' (43), is presented as a much more serious affair. This is her passion for a 'Gentleman', to whom she has written a short series of letters inserted in the text. The claim of the memoir is that these are authentic letters: they are headed: 'Love-Letters to a Gentleman, By Mrs. *A. Behn*' (44). These letters had already appeared in the 1696 edition, and are more likely than the Van Bruin and Vander Albert letters to be genuine. In 1696 they were placed after the stories; but in 1698 they were treated as an important part of the author's biography, woven into the introductory 'Memoirs'. Referred to as Lysander in the text, and Lycidas in the letters, the 'Gentleman' has multiple connections with Behn's poetry. 'Lisander' or 'Lysander', and 'Lycidas' or 'Lycidus' appear in the *Voyage to the Island of Love* and its sequel, *Lycidus: or the Lover in Fashion*; and both names are used elsewhere in Behn's writing. In 'Our Cabal', 'Lysidas' is '*Mr.* J. H.', probably John Hoyle; and some of Behn's love-poetry, as well as her dedication to *Seneca Unmasqued*, is addressed to 'Lysander'. It is not surprising, then, that love-letters apparently addressed by Behn to 'Lycidas' should have been interpreted biographically, and it is possible that the 'Love-Letters to a Gentleman' were originally written by Behn to John Hoyle; but they may have been addressed to someone else, or alternatively, they may have been written as part of an unfinished fiction. We cannot be entirely certain that they were written by Behn at all.[42] Whatever the truth of the matter, the letters serve in the memoir to introduce Astrea in a new vein: instead of the assured, witty heroine laughing at her lovers' follies, she becomes the passionate lover, owing something to the desperate, abandoned woman found in Ovid and in recent epistolary novels, but rendering this convention in a direct, individuated, intimate voice, simultaneously pleading and proud: 'I must have a better Account of your Heart to Morrow, when you come. I grow desperate fond of you, and

---

[42] See Todd, *Secret Life*, 177–83, for an account of the letters in which they are understood as addressed to Hoyle; and Todd's note in *Works*, iii. 260, for other possibilities.

wou'd fain be us'd well; if not, I will march off: But I will believe you mean to keep your Word, as I will for ever do mine' (52–3). These letters, eight in all, take up most of the rest of the memoir. Astrea the writer, then, is presented as the writer of love-letters. The professional writer appears only indirectly, in occasional references: 'I stay'd after thee to Night, till I had read a whole Act of my new Play' (52). As a writer's biography, the 1698 'Memoirs' is concerned not with the literary works in themselves but with creating a sense of intimacy with their creator. Above all, the reader is encouraged to feel intimate with the writer as passionate woman.

The 1698 'Memoirs', reproduced in the many editions of the *Histories and Novels* that were published during the following forty years, formed the most influential single basis for the eighteenth-century understanding of Behn's life. When entries on Behn began to appear in dictionaries of biography they used this memoir, along with the novels themselves, especially *Oroonoko*, as a main source. One of the effects of this was to elevate Behn's social status, ensuring that she continued to be represented as a gentlewoman of birth, and that the narrator's account in *Oroonoko* about her travelling to Surinam as daughter of the doomed Lieutenant Governor was taken as autobiographical. Discussions of Behn throughout the eighteenth and nineteenth centuries, until twentieth-century interest prompted new biographical scrutiny, placed her as a gentlewoman of Kent.[43] The 1698 'Memoirs' had other, more far-reaching effects on Behn's reception. It both fictionalized her life and emphasized fiction as her own most important mode. While her role as a dramatist was also recorded, most prominently in Charles Gildon's continuation of Langbaine's *Lives and Characters*, itself expanded by Giles Jacob as *The Poetical Register*, it was Behn the novelist who was most thoroughly and, it appeared, intimately revealed to her readers. Moreover, this identity as a writer of fiction was closely bound up with that of the heroine of her own adventures: the witty and 'innocent' player in light-hearted games of intrigue, and the passionate lover baring her soul in letters. This distorted and personalized account worked well as a way of marketing Behn's fiction. In the longer term, it provided ammunition for an eighteenth-century reaction against her as a

---

[43] See Duffy, *The Passionate Shepherdess*, 17–20, and Todd, *Secret Life*, 13–14, for the testimony of two contemporaries of Behn, Thomas Colepepper and Anne Finch, Countess of Winchilsea, who also place her in Kent but in a lower social rank. It is from Colepepper and Finch that the account of Behn as the daughter of a barber and a wet-nurse derives.

writer at best frivolous, at worst immoral. The romps with Vander Albert and Van Bruin, which in 1698 served to suggest both Astrea's cleverness and her essential modesty, would seem less innocent in a more sober age. The love-letters, so prominently placed at the beginning of the works, would continually remind eighteenth-century readers of her legendary susceptibility to passion.

By the early eighteenth century, Behn's authority as a writer on love was firmly connected to the received view of her personal experience of it. In Richard Steele's periodical *The Lover*, she appears in a letter addressed to the editor by 'Charles Lasie', as one of the writers he has consulted to help him overcome his tendency to fall for every woman he sees. After Ovid and Abraham Cowley, 'The third I went to was Mrs. *Behn*. She indeed, I thought, understood the Practick Part of Love better than the Speculative; but she was a dangerous Quack, for a sight of her always made my Distemper return upon me.'[44] The phrase about her practical knowledge of love passed into later biographies. The amorous image was further developed a few years later in one of Samuel Briscoe's publications, *Familiar Letters of Love, Gallantry, and Several Occasions* (1718). Eight letters were included under the heading 'Love-Letters, By Mrs. A. Behn, never before Printed'. Some of these letters, or some parts of them, may be genuine, but the way Briscoe mingled letters addressed to 'Mr. [John] Hoyle' and to 'Mrs. [Emily] Price', known members of her circle, with passionate letters upbraiding an unfaithful 'Philander', the name of the hero of *Love-Letters between a Nobleman and his Sister*, conflated Behn the author with Behn the heroine of an unhappy love-story. The effect was compounded when three of the letters to Philander were signed 'A.B.' or 'A. Behn', and a fourth 'Silvia', the name of Philander's lover in the novel. The letters to 'Philander', like those of the famous Portuguese nun, suggested a panicking, abandoned woman:

How, have you then forgot those blessed Moments! If for any Neglect of mine, or one unhappy, undesigned Glance cast on another, tell me, but inform me of my Fault, and I will give you the most severest Proof of an unfeigned, unalterable passion. But what do I say? Your Coldness proceeds from an Indifference only, and I am, too sure, the most unhappy Wretch on Earth.[45]

---

[44] *The Lover. By Marmaduke Myrtle, Gent*, no. 23, Sat. 17 Apr. 1714. I am indebted to Jeslyn Medoff for drawing this reference to Behn to my attention.

[45] *Familiar Letters of Love, Gallantry and Several Occasions* (London: Sam Briscoe, 1718), i. 35.

Whoever actually wrote these lines, *Familiar Letters* added to the myth of Behn the epistolary heroine.

By the 1730s, biographical dictionaries were becoming an important way of spreading a writer's reputation. In 1735 appeared *A General Dictionary*, a translation from the French of Bayle's *Dictionary* with new lives added. Among the additions was a long entry, covering ten folio pages, on 'Aphara' Behn, possibly written by John Lockman, one of the three named authors of the work, whose signature 'I' it bears, or perhaps by the antiquary William Oldys, who claims it as his in his marginalia to Langbaine's *Account*.[46] This is a scholarly compilation, including personal anecdotes derived from the actor John Bowman, drawing widely on printed sources, and using extensive footnotes. It uses Langbaine's and Gildon's discussions of her drama, the 1698 'Memoirs', and, extensively, *Oroonoko* itself. The tone is a good deal less admiring than that of the 'Memoirs', but the image created of Behn is rather similar: she is an amorous woman and writer. When *Oroonoko* is judged the best of her works, it is because she 'has therein drawn the passion of love with great delicacy and softness'.[47] The wit and tenderness of the African hero is partly accounted for by similarities between races: '[a] difference of colour does not make any difference in the soul', and partly by the author's amorousness: 'as the Author of Oroonoko's Life was herself so susceptible of the fond passion of love, there is no doubt but she heightened the expressions of her Hero, on this and other occasions" (iii. 141). The rumour spread by the 'Memoirs' about Behn's sexual involvement with her hero is revived here. The writer in *A General Dictionary* is not convinced by the earlier denials. Perhaps influenced by Southerne's dramatic version of *Oroonoko*, in which the central relationship is a mixed-race one, he sees Behn's whiteness as an attraction for Oroonoko rather than a bar to their relationship: 'possibly the sight of so beautiful a white woman, might efface the idea of the charms he till then had found in his Imoinda, and substituted that of our Poetess'.[48] Some, he concedes, may not believe this possible, because of the contrast in their

---

[46] Several copies exist of Langbaine's 1691 *Account of the English Dramatic Poets* with Oldys's comments. The one I have consulted is in the Bodleian Library, shelf-mark Malone 129, in which Oldys's notes have been transcribed by Edmond Malone.

[47] *A General Dictionary*, iii. 41.

[48] This point is made by Jeslyn Medoff in '"Very Like a Fiction:" Two Early Biographies of Aphra Behn', in Ursula Appelt and Barbara Smith (eds.), *Write or be Written: Early Modern Women Poets and Cultural Constraints* (Scholar Press, forthcoming). I am greatly indebted to Jeslyn Medoff's research on *A General Dictionary* and to discussions with her on the early biographies.

complexions, but 'might not this contrast excite a certain curiosity, and are not miracles daily wrought by love?' (iii. 141). If *Oroonoko* is reduced to the story of its author's desires, 'Love-Letters to a Gentleman' are taken as further proof of her amorous disposition. They are seen as biographical evidence that she loved 'Lycidas' while he was cold and indifferent, and the biographer seems uncertain whether to blame Lycidas for failing to respond to her, for 'what man could have resisted those raving expressions [?]', or to sympathize with a man pursued by an amorous poetess, for women like that never stop writing letters, and 'Love is ever predominant in their minds' (iii. 146, 145). When he compares Behn to Dido and Lycidas to Aeneas, it is not just as an individual but as a type of the female poet that she is characterized as 'a doating, distracted, forsaken woman' (iii. 146).

A few years later Behn was given five folio pages in the *Biographia Britannica*, another account deriving from the same printed sources. Again, *Oroonoko* is taken as biographical evidence, and the Antwerp stories from the 'Memoirs' are recounted in detail. Once again the rumour of Behn's affair with Oroonoko is repeated, though this time the writer does not argue for its truth. If the *Biographia Britannica* is less obsessed with Behn's love-life than *A General Dictionary*, it marks a drop in her literary reputation. Quoting Charles Gildon's defence of Behn, the writer admits that he may be right about her moral character, but:

how far she may deserve the high encomiums bestowed on her as a writer, and what abatements it may be necessary to make in settling her true merit, the reader of her works will easily judge. Her *Novels, Oroonoko* excepted, are chiefly translations: Her *Poetry* is none of the best; and her *Comedies*, though not without wit and humour, are full of the most indecent scenes and expressions.[49]

A further drop in Behn's reputation as a writer is evident in the revised edition of the *Biographia Britannica* in 1780. Andrew Kippis admitted to having read very little of her work, but he took it on authority that it was indecent.[50] He did, however, quote extensively from William Oldys' manuscripts, which described her as a significant author. Behn, according to Oldys:

[49] *Biographia Britannica* (London: W. Innys, *et al.*, 1747), i. 669.
[50] *Biographia Britannica* (2nd edn.; London: W. and A. Strahan, 1780), ii. 146. The main part of this entry, signed B, repeats the 1747 entry, but is followed by additional material on 145–6 signed K for Kippis.

was of a capacity above most of her sex who have obliged the public. She had a ready command of pertinent expressions, and was of a fancy pregnant and fluent: whence it is that she wrote with a facility, spirit, and warmth, especially in amorous subjects, superior to every other Poetess of the Age, and many of the Poets too: so that none among us may, perhaps, more justly be called the ENGLISH SAPPHO; equalling her either for description, or perhaps experience, in the flames of love; and excelling in her personal temptation to it . . . (ii. 146)

The later eighteenth-century biographies of Behn, then, continued to spread the notion that she was significant as an example of the amorous woman who writes.

THE POET

While Behn was known during her lifetime for Stuart panegyric, satire on Whigs, libertine verse, and Latin and French translation, she was most prominent as a love-poet. In the twenty years after her death, this reputation was consolidated. The evidence of editions, anthologies, and comments on her suggests that other aspects of her work were gradually obscured, and she was generally accorded a place as a significant poet, but mainly a love-poet.

Not long before her death, Behn was prominent enough as a court poet for Gilbert, Bishop Burnet, to try to enlist her as an encomiast of the new regime of William and Mary; her refusal fixed her as a Stuart poet, and in the years after her death her political verse would have the smallest share in building her reputation. The occasional new piece of political verse emerged soon after her death: eight lines 'On a Conventicle' were included among three 'VERSES by Madam *Behn*, never before printed' in 1692.[51] Early in the 1690s her Tory loyalties made her vulnerable to gibes: in 1692 the *Athenian Mercury*, in answer to a question '*Whether* Sappho *or Mrs.* Behn *were the better* Poetess?' replied by applying to Behn the story that '*In the City of Ardebil in Persia are a Corporation of Whores, all Poetesses, whose chief Subject is the praise of the Emperor.* This unlucky Story was brought to mind by some woful Loyal Plays, which for 2 Reigns together pester'd the Theaters and Stationers, which is all we will say of 'em, considering whose they were'.[52] During the next few years, however, Behn's

---

[51] [Gildon] (ed.), *Miscellany Poems upon Several Occasions* (London: Peter Buck, 1692), 84.
[52] *Athenian Mercury*, vol. 5, no. 13, Tues. 12 Jan., 1691/2.

politics became less important: rather than a dangerous Tory, she simply seemed outmoded. While her verse-collections came out in new editions, there was no call to reprint her political Pindarics; and while anti-Monmouth songs like 'Young Jemmy was a Lad' were reprinted along with the rest of her *Poems Upon Several Occasions* in 1697, their political point was probably not much noticed any more. By 1707, when the *Muses Mercury* printed a group of Behn poems probably taken from manuscripts (though most had been published in some form earlier), the poet's politics had become little more than a historical curiosity. Introducing 'The Complaint of the Poor Cavaliers', a previously unpublished Behn poem, in June 1707, the *Muses Mercury* editors commented: 'All the World knows Mrs. *Behn* was no *Whig*, no *Republican*, nor *Fanatick*; her Zeal lay quite on the other Side: And tho her Manners was no Honour to any, yet her Wit made her acceptable to that which she espous'd.' By this time it was thought necessary to point out to the reader that Behn was 'a *Politician* [a political writer], as well as a *Poet*', and to gloss her poem on the cavaliers: ''Tis well known, that the Gentlemen she speaks of . . . had too much reason to complain; and that the very Men, who had been so much instrumental in keeping King *Charles* the II. out of his Dominions, were most caress'd after his *Restoration*.'[53]

Behn's foothold in the tradition of classical translation was more enduring, though this aspect of her writing received little comment. Her paraphrase on Oenone's epistle to Paris continued to be pub-lished, along with Dryden's praise, in editions of *Ovid's Epistles*, even after a more exact translation of the epistle had been provided by John Cooper. There were ten editions by 1720; in 1725 a revised and expanded *Ovid's Epistles. With his Amours* was published, still contain-ing Behn's work, and went through six editions up till 1776. Her trans-lation of Cowley's 'Of Trees' also continued to be published throughout the eighteenth century in successive editions of his works.

However, the 'blind *Translatress*' never really managed to establish herself among the poetic élite, entry to which still required a classical education. During this period two strands of canon-making can be discerned in the burgeoning volumes of anthologies and histories of poetry: one inclusive, with a wide variety of modern writers, who are ranked alongside the ancients; the other much more exclusive, giving more weight to the ancients and to a select company of moderns.

---

[53] *Muses Mercury: or the Monthly Miscellany* (London: J.H. for Andrew Bell, 1707), 139.

The latter canon was much less likely to include women, although Anne Wharton and Katherine Philips had a better chance of representation than Behn. Her place was in more generous canons constructed by the lowlier editors and critics. She was not a contributor to the Dryden–Tonson *Miscellanies*, published in a series of volumes from 1685 until the early eighteenth century. These collections, the earlier ones edited by Dryden and the later ones by Nicholas Rowe, were 'by the most Eminent Hands'. The first edition was arranged by classical author translated, and though there were some original poems the main selling-point was the publication of new translations of Virgil, Ovid, Lucretius, and Horace.[54] Given this emphasis it is not surprising that Behn was not asked to contribute. The Dryden–Tonson *Miscellanies* played a significant part in eighteenth-century cultural development, helping to define 'cultural literacy as the knowledge of both [classical and contemporary] traditions', and establishing 'the printed anthology as a haven for high literature'.[55] The contributors, including Dryden himself, Roscommon, Otway, Denham, Lee, Sedley, Prior, Caryll, Tate, Creech, and Anne Wharton, were therefore presented as élite cultural guides.[56] Behn's omission indicates her relatively low status, and begins to set the tone for the eighteenth-century reception of her as a poet. Instead, she made it into the less prestigious and influential imitation of the Dryden–Tonson *Miscellany*, Gildon's *Miscellany Poems upon Several Occasions* (1692). This, too, contained Latin translations and original English poetry, and included three new poems by Behn alongside the work of Milton, Cowley, and Prior. Behn tended to be ignored by those historians of poetry who sided with the ancients: she was omitted from Blount's *De Re Poetica* (1694) with its strong emphasis on ancient poets. He included Sappho and Orinda, but implicitly denied Behn's request to be placed with them: Katherine Philips, he wrote, echoing her English publisher, might well be called 'The *English Sapho*', but after her death she did not leave 'any of her Sex, her Equal in *Poetry*'.[57] When Behn was praised it was generally by the

[54] *Miscellany Poems ... By the most Eminent Hands* (London: Jacob Tonson, 1684).

[55] Barbara M. Benedict, *Making the Modern Reader* (Princeton: Princeton University Press, 1996), 98, 99.

[56] *Miscellany Poems: The First Part. ... By the Most Eminent hands. Publish'd by Mr Dryden. The Third Edition* (London: Jacob Tonson, 1702).

[57] Sir Thomas Pope Blount, 'Characters and Censures of the Most Considerable Poets, whether Ancient or Modern', 168; in *De Re Poetica* (London: R. Everingham for R. Bently, 1694).

Grub Street moderns, the popularizers: John Dunton's Athenian Society accorded her a high rank as 'among the chief of Latin and English Poets'.[58] Daniel Defoe placed her with Cowley, Milton, Ratcliff, Waller, Roscommon and Howard as one of the 'Giants . . . of Wit and Sense'.[59]

Where Behn was accorded most recognition was as an amatory poet. Love-poetry was, of course, also an important part of the classical and native traditions; it was one of those paths her predecessors had used, and Behn could tread those worn paths well, producing tuneful pastoral lyrics about the encounters of Strephons and Amintas, and sometimes splendidly, as in the lovely baroque of 'Love in Fantastique Triumph satt'; while occasionally she could lead off in new directions. Her 'The Disappointment' reworks Ovid's theme of the failed erotic encounter by imagining the effect of male impotence on his female partner: 'The *Nymph*'s Resentments none but I | Can well Imagine or Condole'. Her poem adapts a recent French version of the theme, de Cantanac's 'Sur une Impuissance'; instead of ending the poem, as her source does, on the restoration of potency, she leaves the nymph disappointed and the man cursing the female attractions that had 'Damn'd him to the *Hell* of Impotence' (*Works*, i. 69). However, Behn's treatment of love was not received as a contribution to tradition, but as the unproblematic expression of a feminine self. Behn was either giving voice to her own passionate feelings, or displaying her own attractions to seduce the male reader. The customary poems of praise with which her 1680s' volumes of verse were packaged commended her for all sorts of virtues: for her political loyalties, for uniting manly strength and feminine sweetness, for comic skill, and for proving that women had souls; but the most constant note they sounded was her erotic pre-eminence. Her *Voyage to the Island of Love*, it was said, both seduced men and rendered women more susceptible to men's seductions:

> thy Pen disarms us so,
> We yield our selves to the first beauteous Foe;
> The easie softness of thy thoughts surprise,
> And this new way Love steals into our Eyes;

---

[58] 'An Essay Upon all sorts of Learning, Written by the Athenian Society', in *The Young Students Library* (London: John Dunton, 1692), p. xiii.

[59] *The Pacificator*, 1700, cited in Paula Backscheider, *Daniel Defoe: His Life* (Baltimore and London: Johns Hopkins University Press, 1989), 73.

. . . .

> You Nymphs, who deaf to Love's soft lays have been,
> Reade here, and suck the sweet destruction in . . .[60]

Charles Cotton's '*To the Admir'd* Astrea' summed up the line taken by most of Behn's encomiasts: she was good at everything, but best of all at love.

> Some Hands write some things well; are elsewhere lame:
> But on all Theams, your Power is the same.
> Of Buskin, and of Sock, you know the Pace;
> And tread in both, with equal Skill and Grace.
> But when you write of Love, *Astrea*, then
> *Love* dips his arrows, where you wet your Pen.
> Such charming Lines did never Paper grace;
> Soft, as your Sex; and smooth, as Beauty's Face.
> And 'tis your Province, that belongs to you:
> Men are so rude, they fright when they wou'd sue.
> You teach us gentler Methods; such as are
> The fit and due Proceedings with the Fair.[61]

Conflating Behn's physical attractions, themselves not individual but simply emblematic of femininity, and her writing, Cotton helped establish what would become critical commonplaces about female writing: that it was a natural extension of the female body and equally to be valued for sexual purposes.

The reception of Behn's poetry played a significant part in establishing this commonplace in England. The second edition of *Poems Upon Several Occasions* and the reissue of *Lycidus* in 1697 continued to introduce Behn to readers not only as primarily an erotic poet, but as representative of the essential sexiness of women's verse. *La Montre* was frequently reprinted from 1696 onwards: 'The Lover's Watch' and 'The Lady's Looking-Glass' (both part of the 1686 *La Montre*) were included in *Histories and Novels*. During the 1690s and early 1700s Behn's poetry also appeared in various collections besides Gildon's *Miscellany*. George Granville included ten poems by Behn (two of them previously unpublished) in his *The History of Adolphus*, a prose romance with a miscellany of poems, in 1691. Not all of Behn's

---

[60] 'T.C.', '*To the Authour, on her Voyage to the Island of Love*', *Poems Upon Several Occasions*, sig. A7ᵛ–A8ʳ.
[61] Charles Cotton, '*To the Admir'd* Astrea', *La Montre: or the Lover's Watch* (London: R.H. for William Canning, 1686), sig. A7ʳ.

poems are attributed to her in the volume, but Granville contributed to her image as poet-seducer by including his own poem in her praise, '*To. Mrs.* B——. *By Mr.* GRANVILLE':

> Where'er you look, with every glance you kill,
> Whene'er you write, you triumph with your Quill.
> *Diana* did the Bow and Quiver bear,
> *Cybell* had Lyons, *Pallas* had the Spear;
> Such were the Emblems of those Powers Divine;
> Hearts bleeding by the Dart, and Pen, be thine.[62]

The continuing power of Behn's name was demonstrated in a false attribution in *Chorus Poetarum* (1694). Probably another of Gildon's collections (the dedication is signed by him) this advertises itself as the work of Buckingham, Rochester, Etherege, Marvell, Denham, Spenser, 'Madam *Behn*', and other 'Eminent Poets of this Age'. The only poem ascribed to Behn here, 'The Gods are not more blest than he', is a translation of Sappho's Ode in Longinus, and is not by Behn, but probably by William Bowles;[63] the ascription to Behn suggests the readiness with which the best-known woman poet of the age could be associated with Sappho, with a love-poem, and perhaps simply with a poem whose speaker is female.

By the beginning of the eighteenth century, Behn was established as the poet of love for women writers to imitate and be measured against. When John Froud wanted to praise Sarah Fyge under the name 'Clarinda', he said that she was an even better love-poet than her predecessor: 'Not Behn herself with all her softest Art | So well could talk of love, or touch the heart'.[64] In *The Art of Love: In Imitation of Ovid De Arte Amandi* William King, construing all women's writing as amatory, advised women who would write to imitate Behn: '*Astrea*'s Lines flow on with so much ease, | That she who writes like them must surely please'.[65] Behn was also considered one of the standard English poets to be quoted in collections and anthologies—part of the amorous

[62] *The History of Adolphus, Prince of Russia; and the Princess of Happiness. By a person of Quality. With a Collection of Songs and Love-verses. By several hands* . . . (London: R.T., 1691), 54. A revised version of this poem appeared as '*To Mrs.* AFRA BEHN' in *The Genuine Works in Verse and Prose, of the Right Honourable George Granville, Lord Lansdowne* (London: J. Tonson and L. Gilliver, 1732), 59.   [63] O'Donnell, *Bibliography*, 316–18.

[64] *The Grove: or, the Rival Muses. A Poem* (London: John Deeve, 1701), 12. For the identification of 'Clarinda' as Sarah Fyge see Jeslyn Medoff, 'New Light on Sarah Fyge (Field, Egerton)', *Tulsa Studies in Women's Literature*, 1/2 (1982), 170–1.

[65] William King, *The Art of Love* (London: Bernard Lintot, 1709), 170.

branch of the English tradition. When Edward Bysshe published *The Art of English Poetry* (1702), a kind of how-to book for aspiring writers, with poetic extracts arranged alphabetically by subject, he included two pieces from Behn. One extract from the poem 'On a Juniper-Tree', describing a lovers' encounter ('I saw 'em kindle to desire'), was placed under the heading 'Enjoyment'; the second passage, a mixture of lines from 'The Golden Age' and *Voyage to the Island of Love*, was filed under 'Honour'.[66] The selections underlined Behn's identity as an erotic poet, in favour of enjoyment and opposed to honour. When the *Muses Mercury* of 1707 printed twelve Behn poems in successive issues, the editors' prefatory remarks show how thoroughly by this time Behn was identified as an amorous women whose poetry was a kind of natural extension of her sexuality. Introducing 'Cupid in Chains' they remarked: 'The Poem we now print under her Name has something in it so soft, so amorous, so pretty, and so perfect, that it shews the Author to have been both a Poet and a Lover; both of which Mrs. *Behn* was in a high Degree; few of her Sex having distinguish'd themselves more by their Wit and Amours than she has done.'[67] The verses 'On a Pin that hurt Aminta's eye' were 'so tender, that one may see that the Author writ 'em with no affected passion. And indeed she had no need to affect what was so natural to her'.[68]

This emphasis on the naturalness of Behn's verse was in line with the increasing value attached to the natural and sincere in poetry, especially in poetry by women. Journals like the *Muses Mercury* were, in effect, beginning to rewrite Behn as the kind of woman poet who would appeal to eighteenth-century readers and receive the approval of eighteenth-century critics. This process, however, could only be taken so far. Behn's libertine eroticism was not chaste enough for eighteenth-century tastes. Even in the 1680s it had subjected her to criticism, not only from enemies but from her anxious admirer, Anne Wharton; and after Behn's death it became increasingly common to lament that her life and her poetry were both too loose. Her anony-mous 'Young Lady' elegist thought it a pity she practised what she taught, and Richard Ames wrote that 'Afra' would miss out on the poetic immortality accorded to Orinda because she was a 'fond *Sappho*' who '*too many Phaons* Lov'd'.[69] The 'indecency' of her verse became famous, and there were some claims to fit Behn's poetry for

[66] Edward Bysshe, *The Art of English Poetry* (London: H. Knap, E. Castle and B. Tooke, 1702).   [67] *Muses Mercury*, May 1707, 112.   [68] *Muses Mercury*, June 1707, 140.
[69] Richard Ames, *The Pleasures of Love and Marriage* (London: R. Baldwin, 1691), 8.

the new age by revision, though it is not entirely clear whether the *Muses Mercury* was really toning down her work, or just emphasizing its erotic appeal, when it claimed to have 'reduc'd' her verses 'to bring them within the Rules of Decency'.[70]

It was not just Behn's morality that jarred on eighteenth-century readers. They wanted a modesty and purity of style, too. Behn wrote in an age dominated by the poetry of Abraham Cowley, who made an English version of Pindar's verse fashionable. Cowley's Pindarics were long, irregular, odes, with lines of varying length and a complex rhyme-scheme. They treated lofty subject-matter in an elevated tone, and the verses were ornamented with extended metaphors. Behn adopted the Pindaric for many of her most ambitious poems: her poems to James and Charles, and 'The Golden Age', which opened her *Poems Upon Several Occasions*. Her verse also shows the influence of seventeenth-century fashion in its baroque love of lavish detail. This style of writing fell from favour early in the eighteenth century, which developed the plainer, tighter, more elegant style later called 'Augustan', with stricter use of the heroic couplet and pointed use of balance and antithesis. Behn's fondness for love-scenes in groves also marked her out as old-fashioned in the age of the mock-heroic, when pastoral conventions were being modified and questioned. Some of her more familiar verses, especially her addresses to friends and the poems of 'Our Cabal', were rather more suited to the urban concerns and urbane tones of the Augustans, but they lacked the feminine propriety the Augustans expected from a woman writer: Behn's conversational 'Letter to a Brother of the Pen in Tribulation', for instance, was a jokey commiseration with her friend's bout of venereal disease, the sort of topic eighteenth-century readers thought quite unsuitable for a woman. Besides, such light coterie verse tended to lose its appeal once the social circle in which it had flourished was gone. The eighteenth century had a different social scene to explore.

For all these reasons, Behn's poetry soon began to seem old-fashioned after 1700. Her name could still be a draw: two poems in Buckingham's *Dramatick Works* (1715) were (probably wrongly) ascribed to her,[71] and Samuel Briscoe placed her, with Dryden, as one of the

---

[70] See Todd, *The Critical Fortunes*, who thinks this comment aims to make Behn's verse seem more scandalous (28).

[71] One was a version of the Sappho translation wrongly attributed to Behn in *Chorus Poetarum*; the other, an elegy on Buckingham first published in 1687, is of doubtful attribution. See O'Donnell, *Bibliography*, 322–4.

wits of the last age which that age had failed properly to acknowledge: in these more cultivated times, he flattered his readers, these poets would be better appreciated.[72] However, when Behn's poetry was mentioned by the new Augustan writers, it was as an example of what to avoid. Jonathan Swift dismissed the seventeenth-century use of the Pindaric by imagining Pindar himself overcoming his modern imitators in *The Battle of the Books* (written 1697, published 1710). Among his vanquished enemies are '*Afra* the *Amazon*', whose poetic shortcomings he deftly indicated in the teasing phrase, 'light of foot'.[73] Even the generally favourable *Muses Mercury* considered that 'Mrs Behn had no Notion of a Pindaric Poem, any farther than it consisted of irregular Numbers, and sav'd the Writer the Trouble of even Measure; which indeed is all our common Pindarick Poets know of the Matter'.[74]

In Alexander Pope's criticism of Behn, the mockery of an outmoded style of poetry is sharpened with a particular sexual animus: the standard-bearer of neo-classical correctness dismisses an earlier style of poetry by comparing it, in effect, to a loose woman. Pope's own poetry was not free of Behn's influence. Several echoes of her verse can be found in his, especially where he is adopting the voice of a female lover, and the phrases 'lovely Youth' and 'sad Statue' in his *Sapho to Phaon* have been traced to her *Oenone to Paris*.[75] His discussion of her poetry, however, is entirely disparaging. He quotes and comments on some lines from 'The Golden Age' in *Peri Bathous, or the Art of Sinking in Poetry* (1728). Behn's first stanza describes the setting for the free love-making of the Golden Age:

> The Groves appear'd all drest with Wreaths of Flowers,
> And from their Leaves dropt Aromatick Showers,
> Whose fragrant Heads in Mystick Twines above,
> Exchang'd their Sweets, and mix'd with thousand Kisses,
>   As if the willing Branches strove
>   To beautify and shade the Grove
>   Where the young wanton Gods of Love
> Offer their Noblest Sacrifice of Blisses.

> (*Works*, i. 30)

[72] *Familiar Letters of Love, Gallantry and Several Occasions*, sig. A2ʳ.

[73] *A Tale of a Tub With Other Early Works 1696–1707*, ed. Herbert Davies (Oxford: Basil Blackwell, 1939), 158.   [74] *Muses Mercury*, Oct. 1707, 237.

[75] Alexander Pope, *Pastoral Poetry and An Essay on Criticism*, ed. E. Audra and Aubrey Williams [The Twickenham Pope, vol. i] (London: Methuen and Co.; New Haven: Yale University Press, 1961), 393, 399. For this reference I am grateful to Bernard Dhuicq, whose forthcoming article 'Aphra Behn, écrivain professionnel: du plagiat aux droits d'auteur' fully explores Pope's debts to Behn.

Pope quotes all but the last two of these lines as an example of 'the FLORID Style'. The lines are very carefully chosen and deployed. As Janet Todd points out, 'by cutting Behn off in mid-sentence he makes her thought appear more pointlessly fanciful than it really is' (*Works*, i. 385); he has also taken care to choose a passage which mingles flowers and sex. Flowers, decorative in themselves and metaphorical for poetic decoration, make a good target for a neo-classical attack on poetic excess; and it is a gendered attack. Not only are flowers associated with the feminine, but the fault of the florid style is its overelaboration of merely fanciful detail; and detail, as Naomi Schor argues, has long been understood as feminine, in contrast to the masculinity of sublime generality. Schor argues that 'one of the enabling gestures of neo-classicism' was its rejection of a 'particularity' which was implicitly understood as feminine. The 'identification of crowded ornament with feminine taste' enabled the Augustans to mock the overelaboration of the baroque in the name of a sparer, more masculine style given to abstractions.[76] Pope's attack on flowers encompasses their association with female beauty and sexual invitation, an association strengthened in 'The Golden Age' by the sexual activities of the flowery branches, and the known femininity and amorous reputation of the poem's author. The florid style is an excellent example of bathos, Pope argues, because 'flowers which are the *Lowest* of vegetables, are most *Gaudy*, and do many times grow in great plenty at the bottom of *Ponds* and *Ditches*'.[77] His friend Swift represented women as 'gaudy Tulips rais'd from Dung';[78] Pope, more implicitly, makes a similar point here, forging a chain of association between flowers, dirt, women, sex, and the female poet.

There was an attempt to update Behn's verse to fit it for the new age. *The Land of Love* (1717) was a version of Behn's *Voyage to the Island of Love*, anonymously revised. The point was not to rehabilitate Behn, whose name did not appear in the edition at all, but to make use of an originally very popular poem to create a more modern, and moral, volume for a politer generation of readers. For the most part the adaptation closely follows its original, with the hero (Lisander in

[76] N. Schor, *Reading in Detail: Aesthetics and the Feminine* (New York and London: Methuen, 1987), 3–4, 19.

[77] *The Prose Works of Alexander Pope*, ed. Rosemary Cowler (Oxford: Basil Blackwell, 1986), ii. 219.

[78] 'The Lady's Dressing Room' (1730), in *The Poems of Jonathan Swift*, ed. Harold Williams (2nd edn.; Oxford: Clarendon Press, 1958), ii. 530.

Voyage, Lysander in the revision) telling of his visit to the land of love and his relationship with Aminta, tragically ended by her death. The progress of their affair is charted in separate poems with headings like 'Love's Power', 'Love's Resentment', 'The Den of Cruelty', and 'The River of Despair': personifications such as the God of Love, the princess Hope, Honour, and Respect converse with the lovers. The reviser cuts the length, and makes small verbal changes to create a smoother verse. Some revisions improve the rhyme: Behn's 'The Sails were hoisted, and the Streamers spread, | And chearfully we cut the yielding Floud' becomes 'The Streamers spread, the Sails all hoisted stood, | And chearfully we cut the yielding Flood'.[79] Others regularize the couplets by getting rid of the occasional hexameters. The description of the isle of love is generalized: where Behn located her isle in '*the Calm* Atlantick *Sea*', in sight of '*the Coast of* Africa', the 'LAND of LOVE' is placed vaguely in 'that pleasing Country' where 'the Seat of CUPID' is found.[80]

The most extensive adaptations, though, were made for moral more than stylistic effect. Behn's *Voyage* describes Lisander's eventually successful seduction of Aminta: the claims of Honour are dismissed by Love, and Respect, having insisted on being present to temper Lisander's first advances, leaves the lovers with his blessing: '*Go happy Lovers, perfect the desires,* | *That fill two Hearts that burn with equal Fires*' (*Voyage*, 113). The section called 'Love's Temple' explains that Hymen's priests rarely officiate here:

> For Priest cou'd ne'r the Marriage-cheat improve,
> Were there no other Laws, but those of Love!
> A Slavery generous Heav'n did ne'r design,
> Nor did its first lov'd Race of men confine.
>
> (101)

There is some erotic description of the lovers' embraces in the Bower of Bliss. Lisander, like other lovers in Behn, suffers a temporary fit of impotence when Aminta first yields to him, but he soon recovers; their love is consummated, and they live for some time together, 'the wonder of the groves' for their mutual devotion, until on one occasion, while they are together in the grove, Aminta suddenly dies:

---

[79] *A Voyage to the Isle of Love*, 5 (separately paginated within *Poems Upon Several Occasions*); *The Land of Love* (London: H. Meere and A Bettesworth, 1717), 5.
[80] *Voyage*, 9; *The Land of Love*, 6.

> never did the Charmer ere impart,
> More Joy, more Rapture to my ravisht Heart:
> 'Twas all the first; 'twas all beginning Fire!
> 'Twas all new Love! new Pleasure! new Desire!
> ——Here stop my Soul——
> Stop thy carreer of Vanity and Pride,
> And only say,——'*Twas here* Aminta *dy'd*.
>
> (125)

This startling mid-intercourse collapse might, of course, be morally construed—death as a punishment for illicit sex—but despite the reference to vanity and pride, the general impression the poem gives is that the lovers are unlucky rather than faulty, and there is no retraction of the scorn poured on priests and marriage. The poem ends on Lisander's grief and his appeal for pity from Lycidas.

In *The Land of Love*, the final third of the poem is considerably altered, making the lovers far less open to charges against their sexual morality, yet punishing them anyway. Some of Behn's lines, including a twenty-six-line attack on priests and marriage, are omitted, and several new passages in favour of Hymen and chastity are added. Once again, Honour attempts to draw Aminta away from the hero, but he does so with more authority. Lysander has to admit he was wrong to try to seduce Aminta:

> Why, why did I not HYMEN's Priests obey,
> And for the Marriage-Ceremonies stay?
> Tho' 'twas the farthest, 'twas the safest Way.
>
> (*The Land of Love*, 65)

When Aminta eventually yields to the God of Love, it is on condition that her chastity is respected:

> LOVE's Speech is pow'rful; indeed, 'tis true;
> But still what HONOUR dictates, I'll pursue.
>
> (67–8)

Lysander agrees to the new condition of no sex before marriage; but Aminta dies on the morning of their wedding.

The Land of Love represents the most thorough attempt to adapt Behn's love-poetry for polite readers. Before long, though, her poems were too old-fashioned to be worth extensive alteration. While for Swift and Pope she represented the faults of the previous age, useful for helping them define their contrasting Augustan virtues, in the middle and later years of the century her style was thoroughly out-moded, as the more introspective and emotional poetic sensibility represented by Thomson, Gray, Collins, Goldsmith, and Cowper dominated the literary scene. A new canon of English poets was being created, with the emphasis on modern writers. Influential here were the twelve editions of James Dodsley's *Collection of Poems* (1748–82), especially popular with the gentry and professional classes and 'generally regarded as the epitome of polite taste in poetry during the second half of the eighteenth century'.[81] Behn, of course, was not included; more significantly, she was not accorded the historical importance of a place in Johnson's famous *Lives of the Poets* (1779–81).

However, while Behn fairly rapidly lost her place as one of the 'standard' English poets, she was almost simultaneously awarded a place of special significance as a female poet. In the first half of the eighteenth century, women's poetry flourished as never before, prompting critics to consider and publishers to market it in a category of its own. Much eighteenth-century discussion of Behn is motivated by the wish to place her in relation to a newly constructed feminine tradition, or to consider her as an example of the female poet.

Some eighteenth-century canon-making was designed to exclude women, and in this endeavour Behn's image could be made useful, as the negative example proving women's unfitness to join the select company of male poets. One of many celebrations of English poetic achievement was published in a multi-part article in the *Gentleman's Magazine* in 1738. The occasion was an event of symbolic importance in the making of the English canon: Milton, whose political allegiances had previously deprived him of official honours, was given, in 1737, the belated homage of a monument in Westminster Abbey.[82] 'The Apotheosis of Milton' describes a vision in which the narrator is shown Milton's entry into the great assembly of English poets gathered in the Abbey. A ghostly guide, the Genius of the Abbey, carries

---

[81] M. F. Suarez, SJ, 'Trafficking in the Muse: Dodsley's *Collection of Poems* and the Question of Canon', in A. Ribeiro (ed.), *Tradition in Transition* (Oxford: Clarendon Press, 1996), 297.

[82] As recently as 1710 the Dean of Westminster had refused to let Milton be named on a monument to John Philips, so the erection of Milton's monument in 1737 shows a marked change in attitude to him. See Dustin Griffin, *Regaining Paradise* (Cambridge: Cambridge University Press, 1986), 15.

him to a large room '*sacred to the Spirits of the Bards, whose Remains are buried, or whose Monuments are erected within this Pile*', each of whom has a seat. The poets are pointed out and described in turn, beginning with Chaucer, '*the Father of* English Poesy'.[83] Milton does not take his seat without opposition: Chaucer, the president of the assembly, speaks strongly in his favour, but Abraham Cowley tries to exclude him for his rebellion against Charles I. The article details not only Milton's qualifications, but those of the rest of the assembly: each seat has to be justified. Spenser, Jonson, Dryden, and a few more are described in glowing terms, but the Genius of the Abbey has his doubts about some of the other members: Thomas Shadwell only '*has a Seat here by the Indulgence of a Tasteless Court, who bestowed on him the Laurel in prejudice of the Great* Dryden' (*Gent. Mag.* 8: 235). Still, he is allowed to stay. Thomas Otway barely deserves his place, for although 'his Genius entitled him to a Place in the first Rank of Men . . . the Habits he contracted, threw him into the lowest'; nevertheless, the other poets all look on him with 'paternal Affection and Pity', and he remains (*Gent. Mag.* 8: 469, 235). Nathaniel Lee is allowed to stay, though some of his fellow-poets are uneasy about having a madman among them; and even Mr Stepney, who isn't a poet at all but had his monument in the Abbey as a statesman, is not actually asked to leave, though Matthew Prior sneers at him (*Gent. Mag.* 9: 74). Only one member is ejected:

But observe that Lady dressed in the loose *Robe de Chambre* with her Neck and Breasts bare; how much Fire in her Eye! What a passionate Expression in her Motions! And how much Assurance in her Features! Observe what an Indignant Look she bestows on the President, who is telling her, *that none of her Sex has any Right to a Seat there.* How she throws her Eyes about, to see if she can find out any one of the Assembly who inclines to take her Part. No! not one stirs; they who are enclined in her favour are overawed, and the rest shake their Heads; and now she flings out of the Assembly. That extraordinary Woman is *Afra Behn*   (*Gent. Mag.* 8: 469).

Milton's entry into Westminster Abbey is made the occasion for Behn's expulsion: figuratively exhuming her, the writer of 'The Apotheosis of Milton' tries to undo the mistake that led to a woman being honoured as a poet. The representation of Behn here—sexy, haughty, and histrionic—classes her with the tragedy-queens of the Restoration stage, and implies that her type is outmoded. No

---

[83] *Gentleman's Magazine*, 8 (1738), 233.

such 'extraordinary' women, it implies, are to be found any more: eighteenth-century women are too modest and feminine to attempt to claim a place among the poets.

In this respect, if not in others, the writer of 'The Apotheosis of Milton' was swimming against the stream, and his views should not be taken as typical of the *Gentleman's Magazine* line: the periodical printed and praised poetry by several women, notably Elizabeth Carter. The consensus in polite society was that ladies could become eminent writers, and in the middle of the century there was a spate of publications commemorating the literary achievements of Englishwomen of the past, and celebrating those of the present. They dealt with Aphra Behn in remarkably different ways. The antiquarian George Ballard ignored her altogether, along with other commercial playwrights, in his scholarly *Memoirs of Several Ladies of Great Britain* (1752): his female canon was a distinctly genteel one.[84] In his poem *The Feminiad* (1754) John Duncombe adopted a common eighteenth-century strategy of praising virtuous women writers by comparing them with immoral ones. Behn figures, alongside Delarivier Manley and Susanna Centlivre, as one of 'Vices friends and Virtues female foes', with 'bold unblushing mien'. Even if their poetry had merit in itself, such writers could not be praised, for: 'Nor genuine wit nor harmony excuse | The dang'rous sallies of a wanton Muse'.[85]

In the following year, a substantial selection of Behn's poetry was published in George Colman and Bonnell Thornton's *Poems by Eminent Ladies*. In contrast to Duncombe and Ballard, who in their different ways were each interested in establishing a female canon along moral lines, Colman and Thornton extended their approval to a wide range of recent women writers, including Aphra Behn. The anthology contained poetry by eighteen women, from Katherine Philips and Margaret Cavendish, Duchess of Newcastle, in the mid-seventeenth century, to living contemporaries such as Mary Barber, Elizabeth Carter, Mary Jones, and Lady Mary Wortley Montagu. Each selection was introduced by an account of the writer. The six-page introduction to Behn contains the usual stories of her adventures, derived from the 'Memoirs', and the editors acknowledge their use of the most favourable recent biography of her, the account in

---

[84] Margaret Ezell, *Writing Women's Literary History* (Baltimore: Johns Hopkins University Press, 1993), 85, 84.   [85] John Duncombe, *The Feminiad* (London, 1754), 15.

Cibber's *Lives of the Poets*. Behn is presented, almost as warmly as she had been at the beginning of the century, as the poet of love.[86] *Voyage to the Island of Love* is reprinted, followed by seventeen other poems from *Poems Upon Several Occasions* and *Lycidus*. Some of the more explicit and irreverent poems about sex, such as 'The Disappointment', and those which hint at lesbian and bisexual themes, such as 'To Clarinda' and 'Hadst thou, Alexis' are not included. Apart from these concessions to eighteenth-century decency, however, there is very little attempt to sanitize Behn. 'The Golden Age', with its celebration of free love, is included, though in deference to religious sensibilities the couplet 'Not kept in fear of Gods, no fond Religious cause, | Nor in Obedience to the duller Laws' is omitted. The poet's most unladylike admission of 'loving two equally' is printed. The section of the 'Ode to Desire' which is included is not chosen for being any safer than the part which is cut. *Voyage to the Island of Love* is not revised, as it had been for *The Land of Love* nearly forty years earlier. Here, the poem is presented not as a modern piece which must conform to current standards, but as the work of another age, to which some historical licence can be granted. The anti-clerical, anti-marriage, anti-Honour verses are left untouched, and so is the lovemaking with its strange climax.

Perhaps Colman and Thornton were more generous to Behn because they were less serious about defending women writers, an activity that always tied gallant male critics of this period into moral knots. The extensive advertising feature they provided for their own venture in their periodical the *Connoisseur* shows them taking an irreverent line towards many of the contributors to the anthology. The article, written in the persona of Mr Town, does, of course, make high claims for the poems: 'my female readers in particular' are assured that the eminent ladies have written many pieces 'which cannot be surpassed by the most celebrated of our male-writers'.[87] The question—can women poets take a place among the men?—which 'The Apotheosis of Milton' had answered so firmly in the negative, is raised again in yet another vision, in which Mr Town is transported to the court of Apollo to hear Juvenal and Sappho take sides on 'whether the ladies, who had distinguished themselves in poetry,

---

[86] *Poems by Eminent Ladies*, vol. i (London: R. Baldwin, 1755).
[87] [George Colman and Bonnell Thornton], *The Connoisseur* [no. 69, Thur. 22 May 1755], vol. i (London: R. Baldwin, 1755), 409.

should be allowed to hold the same rank, and have the same honours paid to them, with the men' (*Connoisseur*, i. 410). Apollo orders that ladies who think they can ride Pegasus should demonstrate their skill; and there follows a description of each woman's attempt, in which her style of riding corresponds to the received view of her writing and character. The Duchess of Newcastle keeps a good seat, though the horse runs away with her (i. 411); Katherine Philips rides smoothly, but 'never ventured beyond a canter or a hand-gallop' (i. 412); while Letitia Pilkington, 'despising the weak efforts of her husband to prevent her', jumps into the saddle and takes 'particular delight in driving the poor horse, who kicked and winced all the while, into the most filthy places; where she made him fling about the dirt and mire' (i. 414).

The 'free-spirited Mrs. BEHN' appears in this company as a Restoration libertine. Now that femininity had become synonymous with delicacy, female sexual display was construed, paradoxically, as manlike, and Behn is represented as a 'BOLD masculine figure . . . in a thin, airy, gay, habit, which hung so loose about her, that she appeared to be half undrest', who leaps across the side-saddle provided for the ladies and insists on riding astride. She shows her legs as Pegasus leaps about, and makes the muses blush at her performance, but Thalia (the comic muse) and Erato (the amorous muse) are pleased with her. She is last seen being helped to dismount by the famous rake and poet Rochester, who recites her own 'Ode to Desire' (a footnote here helpfully directs the reader to the right page in the anthology), but carries her off to lines from Milton's description of Adam seducing Eve: '*To a myrtle bower | He led her nothing loth*' (i. 413). Behn is a fallen Eve, loose, bold, and erotic. Her poetry is still expected to appeal, but it is clearly the poetry of a very different age, an age which many condemn but which 'Mr Town' regards with amused toleration.

Poems by Eminent Ladies became the most available text of Behn's poetry in the later years of the century. There was a Dublin edition in 1757, with the same selection, and a revised and enlarged version in 1773, in which Behn is again represented by the same poems.[88]

---

[88] *Poems by Eminent Ladies* (Dublin: D. Chamberlaine for Sarah Potter, 1757); *Poems by the most Eminent Ladies of Great-Britain and Ireland*, ed. G. Colman and B. Thornton, vol. i (London: T. Becket and T. Evans, 1773). A jumbled selection of the poems was also included in *A Select Collection Of the Original Love Letters of Several Eminent Persons, of Distinguish'd Rank and Station . . . To which are subjoin'd, Poems by Eminent Ladies* (London, 1755).

Some years later, a new and very much altered edition appeared, which Ezell has described as showing a shift from the variety and inclusiveness of the earlier version towards a much more uniform definition of female writing.[89] More women are included (thirty-three as against eighteen), but most poets are represented by very few poems, and the focus is far more on contemporaries and on 'delicate' poetry. In this edition, Behn's contribution, like those of other earlier poets, is drastically cut. She is represented only by four poems, which show her simply as a pastoral lyricist.

By the later eighteenth century, then, Behn's poetry was read—when it was read at all—as something of a historical curiosity. She dropped out of most general discussions and anthologies of poetry,[90] her place taken by more recent women writers who better fitted the developing idea of delicate feminine expression. A typical late-century collection, the *Lady's Poetical Magazine* (1781), concentrated heavily on recent and contemporary writers: few poets, and no women, were included from before the eighteenth century.[91] Behn's poetry was not entirely forgotten, however, and its reputation for being natural and spirited was carried forward into the nineteenth century. Selections were published in Alexander Dyce's *Specimens of British Poetesses* (1827) and Frederic Rowton's *The Female Poets of Great Britain* (1848). Her poetry did not appeal to Wordsworth,[92] but it did to Leigh Hunt, whose praise of Behn's lyrics pointed the way to a revival of interest later in the century. In an essay discussing Dyce's anthology, he printed some of her poems, including 'Love Arm'd', with comments on her fine, musical lines. 'APHRA herself', he admitted, 'affects and makes us admire her, beyond what we looked

---

[89] Ezell, *Writing Women's Literary History*, 112–16; *Poems by the Most Eminent Ladies . . . Republished from the Collection of G. Colman and B. Thornton, Esqrs. With considerable alterations, additions, and improvements* (London: W. Stafford, 1785?). One of the British Library copies (Harding c. 267–8) has been dated in pencil, '178——'. Ezell suggests 1780. The Eighteenth-Century Short Title Catalogue gives a likely date of 1785 because W. Stafford was trading in 1784–5.

[90] She does make a brief late appearance in a four-volume *Poetical Dictionary* published by Newbery in 1761, which like the *Art of Poetry* arranges extracts alphabetically by subject. Three lines from 'Behn's Abdelazar' are included under 'Kisses'.

[91] *The Lady's Poetical Magazine, or Beauties of British Poetry*, 4 vols. (London: Harrison and Co., 1781–2).

[92] He wrote that *Poems By Eminent Ladies* was 'miserably copious' in its selection from Behn's work. Wordsworth to Alexander Dyce, 30 Apr. 1830, in *The Letters of William and Dorothy Wordsworth: The Later Years*, ed. Ernest de Selincourt (Oxford: Clarendon Press, 1939), i. 473.

for.' Here, once again, Behn's poetic reputation was mingled with ideas derived from the biographical tradition to create a picture of the woman writer as lover: 'Aphra Behn is said to have been in love with Creech. It should be borne in mind by those who give an estimate of her character, that she passed her childhood among the planters of Surinam; no very good school for restraining or refining a lively temperament.'[93] The myth of Aphra Behn continued to spread.

[93] Leigh Hunt, *Men, Women, and Books* (London: Smith, Elder and Co., 1847), ii. 125.

2

The Dramatist and the Novelist

IN a letter to Sarah Chapone in 1750, Samuel Richardson attacked three contemporary women writers of scandalous memoirs by saying that they were even worse than three women writers of previous generations, who—it went without saying—were dreadful: 'Mrs. Pilkington, Constantia Phillips, Lady V——, . . . what a Set of Wretches, wishing to perpetuate their Infamy, have we—to make the Behn's, the Manley's, and the Heywood's, [*sic*] look white. From the same injured, disgraced, profaned Sex, let us be favoured with the Antidote to these Womens Poison!'[1] Putting Behn together with Manley and Haywood, Richardson is thinking of her as a novelist, specifically as a writer of scandal fiction. His vituperation contrasts with the altogether more measured tones of David Erskine Baker, fourteen years later. In his *Companion to the Play-house*, Baker assesses Behn's plays:

In all, even the most indifferent of her Pieces, there are strong Marks of Genius and Understanding.—Her Plots are full of Business and Ingenuity, and her Dialogue sparkles with the dazzling Lustre of genuine Wit, which every where glitters among it.—But then she has been accused, and that not without great Justice, of interlarding her Comedies with the most indecent Scenes, and giving an Indulgence in her Wit to the most indelicate Expressions. . . .The best . . . Excuse that can be made for it is, that altho' she might herself have had as great an Aversion as any One to loose Scenes or too warm Descriptions, yet, as she wrote for a Livelihood, she was obliged to comply with the corrupt Taste of the Times.[2]

Baker's view of Behn was not an original one: his entry on her is highly derivative, taking a good deal from the 'Memoirs', and in this

---

[1] *Selected Letters of Samuel Richardson*, ed. J. Carroll (Oxford: Clarendon Press, 1964), 173. In fact Haywood was still writing in the 1750s, but her scandalous reputation had been established much earlier, in the 1720s.

[2] D. E. Baker, *The Companion to the Play-House* (London: T. Becket and P. A. De Hondt, 1764), ii. B3^r.

particular passage from Theophilus Cibber's 1753 *Lives of the Poets*. My point is that this is the view of Behn that is being disseminated in the 1760s (and indeed later, in subsequent editions of Baker's work) within dramatic history. According to this view Behn's plays belong to an earlier age and would be problematic to stage in the more refined theatrical milieu of the late eighteenth century; but her dramatic achievements can be appreciated and allowances made for changes in taste. Of course, there are many distinctions to be made between Baker and Richardson, besides the fact that one is thinking about drama and the other of fiction. Richardson is expressing his feelings in a private letter, Baker drawing on the most readily available sources to produce an inclusive dictionary of dramatists for a wide audience. Richardson is writing as a rival practitioner, Baker as a historian: it is in Richardson's interests to magnify the difference between older fiction and the new, moral variety he writes himself, while it is in Baker's to show that England has a rich dramatic heritage. Nevertheless the two comments reflect, among other things, the difference between Behn's status as a dramatist and as a novelist. This chapter traces the different trajectories of Behn's eighteenth-century life as a dramatist and as a writer of fiction.

Behn's fiction remained current in the later eighteenth century, with editions of *Love-Letters between a Nobleman and his Sister* being published up to the 1760s and of *Oroonoko* until 1800. In 1780 one of her biographers considered that it was only her fiction that was much read any more: 'Mrs. Behn's works are now little regarded, her Novels excepted, which, we suppose, have still many readers among that unhappily too numerous a class of people who devour the trash of the circulating libraries.'[3] As this comment indicated, by this date the popularity of her fiction was thought to reflect more discredit to her readers than credit to the author. The decisive shift in Behn's reputation as a novelist came with the novel's rise in status in the middle years of the century. In particular, the moralization of popular fiction, already under way with Penelope Aubin's work in the 1720s and consolidated by Richardson in the 1740s, led to new and unfavourable assessments of her novels. Richardson's comment lumps together the writing of Behn, Manley, and Haywood as the immoral work of a previous age, which the good women of the present mid-eighteenth-century world (to say nothing of Richardson

---

[3] *Biographia Britannica* (2nd edn.; London: W. and A. Strahan, 1780), ii. 146.

himself) must counteract by their virtue. Women writers will do it by being virtuous; Richardson himself by creating 'a new species of writing'[4] in which female virtue is central. Wanting to elevate the status of fiction, Richardson casts out the woman who might be conceived as an originary point for the English novel, and claims primacy for himself.

The moralization of drama preceded that of fiction. As early as the 1690s popular dramatists were advertising the fact that they were cleaning up their work. As a result we might expect Behn's reputation to plummet earlier in dramatic circles than novelistic ones, but this is not what happened. Certainly there were early and influential attacks on the indecency of her plays, but against that we have to set the very great continuing popularity of *The Rover*. This chapter argues that the era of stage-reform, far from ruining her dramatic reputation, actually helped Behn to achieve the status of the first woman dramatist to become a long-running success on the London stage. Popularity on the stage, as we will see, often went together with critical disdain; but, comparing the treatment Behn received in discussions of the novel and of the stage, on the whole I have found a more generous, inclusive treatment of her among those whose main concern is drama. These writers did not have Richardson's reasons for writing Behn out of the picture. Eighteenth-century historians of the drama had their own anxieties, often being concerned to prove that the stage could be a force for morality or to argue that working in the theatre should be accorded a higher social status; but they did not have the same anxieties that eighteenth-century novelists had about their genre. They knew that drama had an ancient lineage, and one that was (mainly) male. It could, much more comfortably than the novel, incorporate a woman writer of the Restoration. The inclusion of Behn did not threaten a general picture in which women's work came second.

THE PLAYWRIGHT: PERFORMANCE HISTORY AND CRITICAL REACTIONS

Behn was one of the most popular of the stock Restoration dramatists who appeared regularly in the early eighteenth-century repertoire, and though performance of her work fell off markedly after 1750, she was still being occasionally revived in the late eighteenth

---

[4] Richardson, letter to Aaron Hill, 1741; in *Selected Letters,* ed. Carroll, 41.

century. Successive editions of her complete *Plays* in the first three decades of the century indicate a respectable place in the dramatic canon. The anonymous editor of the first of these, in 1702, wrote that her 'Theatrical Performances have entitled her to such a distinguishing Character in that way, as exceeds That of any of the Poets of this Age, Sir *William Davenant* and Mr. *Dryden* excepted.'[5] Charles Gildon's favourable comments in the *Lives and Characters of the English Dramatick Poets* were repeated during the eighteenth century in editions of Giles Jacob's *Poetical Register* (1719 and 1723).

In the early eighteenth century, then, Behn's drama achieved both popularity and critical esteem. It is worth emphasizing this, because twentieth-century views of her early reception have been unduly coloured by famous disparagements uttered by two prestigious men of letters, Richard Steele and Alexander Pope. Steele put her and Mary Pix together in 1711 as examples of the 'Writers of least Learning', who were 'best skill'd in the luscious Way'. He criticized *The Rover* for the activities of its rake–hero, who is seen leaving the stage to have sex 'above once every Act' (Steele exaggerates: the incident happens once in the play), and for making another character, Ned Blunt, 'strip to his Holland Drawers' on-stage.[6] Even better known is a couplet by Pope, published a quarter of a century after Steele's attack. In 'The First Epistle of the Second Book of Horace. To Augustus' (1737) Pope glances at Behn the playwright:

> The boards how loosely does Astraea tread,
> Who fairly puts all Characters to bed.[7]

Repeated in a number of works on Behn, this couplet certainly contributed to the eighteenth-century downfall of Behn's reputation. However, Steele's and Pope's attacks both need to be seen in context. Each wrote from a particular position in a changing cultural scene, and neither can be taken as simply representative of the opinion of their time.

Steele wrote as a practising dramatist himself, an exponent of stage-reform whose plays to date, *The Funeral* (1701), *The Lying Lover*

---

[5] *Plays Written by the late Ingenious Mrs. Behn* (London: Jacob Tonson, 1702), Preface, sig. A2ʳ.
[6] Richard Steele, *Spectator* (no. 51, Sat. 28 Apr. 1711), ed. D. F. Bond (Oxford: Clarendon Press, 1965), i. 217–18.
[7] Alexander Pope, *The First Epistle of the Second Book of Horace Imitated* (1737), ll. 290–1, in *The Poems of Alexander Pope*, ed. John Butt (London: Methuen and Co., 1963), 645.

(1703), and *The Tender Husband* (1705), attempted to infuse a new moral tone into contemporary comedy. However, it was in his collaboration with Addison on the *Tatler* and the *Spectator*, perhaps the most influential organs for the dissemination of the new polite culture, that he produced a more effective attack on the immorality of Restoration drama, criticizing Etherege's *Man of Mode* in particular for its depiction of corrupted and degenerate human nature.[8] His attack on Behn and Pix is part of this campaign, and while it certainly affected Behn's position in critical esteem there is no reason to believe that it stopped performances of *The Rover*, which was to reach the peak of its popularity some years later. Indeed, Steele himself, when on the face of things he had the power to do it, did nothing to purge the stage of her. When he took over as patent-holder of Drury Lane in 1714, its performances of *The Rover* during the next few years remained unchanged at between one and four per season. In 1720 he was anonymously criticized for doing so little towards the reform of the stage that he had been widely expected to carry out:

[Steele] has not at any time, during his administration, made one step towards those glorious ends proposed by his Majesty, for the service of religion and virtue, nor reformed the least abuse of either. The same lewd Plays being acted and revived without any material alteration, which gave occasion to that universal complaint against the English Stage, of lewdness and debauchery . . . thus, among other Plays, they have revived 'The Country Wife', 'Sir Fopling Flutter', 'The Rover', 'The Libertine destroyed;' and several others.[9]

Steele disappointed this critic because he did not supervise the day-to-day running of Drury Lane at all closely, leaving the trio of Colley Cibber, Robert Wilks, and Barton Booth to manage the theatre;[10] and they, however much they were credited in later years with improving the tone of the stage, chose plays primarily for economic reasons. Old plays were cheaper to put on because there were no author's payments, and they could be revived season after season at short notice. Early eighteenth-century theatre was often a theatre of revival and repetition: only in those times when competition was created by more than one playhouse was there much theatrical innovation, and

[8] Steele, *Spectator* (no. 65, Tue. 15 May 1711), ed. Bond, i. 278.
[9] *The State of the Case Restated* (1720), quoted in Loftis, *Steele at Drury Lane*, 77.
[10] Ibid. 76, 78.

even then there remained a significant dependence on stock plays from the previous century.[11] In these conditions it made sense to revive Restoration comedy in the face of moral criticism, since audiences evidently still came to watch it.

Pope's famous lines belong in a different context. Where Steele's interest in stage-reform was the interest of a man deeply committed to the theatre, Pope's side-swipe at a loose woman on the boards was the comment of a man who took the modern stage as an example of the decay of modern culture. The lines had a powerful effect later in the century on the opinions of people who had never seen Behn's plays performed, but took their indecency on trust from Pope. In 1780 Pope's words were quoted as 'well known' by Andrew Kippis, whose views on Behn's drama had been formed without any contaminating contact: 'The wit of her Comedies seems to be generally acknowledged, and it is equally acknowledged, that they are very indecent; on which account I have not thought myself under any obligation to peruse them.'[12] Nevertheless Pope did not, of course, represent the whole of current opinion, either when he wrote or later in the century. That he made Behn a target at all indicates that she still had some currency, enough to be taken as a conveniently immoral representative of the debased culture that he attacked most thoroughly in *The Dunciad*. This attack on Behn, coming from a man fiercely opposed to many of the cultural developments of the eighteenth century, should prompt us to consider how far Behn was, in fact, in tune with some of those developments. Remembering Pope's treatment of Colley Cibber helps to put his treatment of Behn in perspective. It has been easy for literary critics and historians, overwhelmed by the brilliant character-assassination performed on the hero of the revised *Dunciad,* to forget that not only was Cibber a successful playwright and powerful theatre-manager, but that not everybody at the time agreed that these were the activities of cultural degeneration. On the contrary, Drury Lane under the management of Cibber, Wilks, and Booth was hailed within the theatre world as a stage 'in full Perfection', a stage raised from infamy to 'the greatest Theatre in the Universe', a proof 'that the Stage, under a due Regulation, was capable of being . . . the most rational Scheme . . . to alleviate the Cares of Life; to allure the ill-disposed, from less innocent

---

[11] R. D. Hume, *Henry Fielding and the London Theatre 1728–1737* (Oxford: Clarendon Press, 1988), 15–17.　　　　　　　　　　[12] *Biographia Britannica,* ii. 146.

Amusements, and to give the Hours of Leisure from Business, an instructive and delightful Recreation'.[13] The point is not that these praises were any more impartial than Pope's attacks—the first comes from William Chetwood, for twenty years the Drury Lane prompter—but that there was more than one way of viewing the moral tendency of the early eighteenth-century theatre. For many commentators the years up to 1730 were a successful era of stage-reform. They were also the years in which Behn's best-known comedy was most frequently performed, and the conjunction of these two facts need not be seen as paradoxical. It was perfectly possible at this time to view Behn's work as tending, like other Restoration comedies, towards indecency, while recognizing the elements that made it worthy of continued performance and praise.

For a fuller understanding of the reception of Behn's drama in the eighteenth century we need to look beyond Steele and Pope, and take into account a wide range of different sorts of evidence, bearing in mind not only the difference between popularity in the theatre and a place in the literary canon,[14] but also the differences between some aspects of canon-formation and others. On the one hand, Behn's popularity in the repertory, especially in farce, encouraged some critics to use her as an example of depravity or frivolity, and thus exclude her from serious literary consideration. On the other hand, men of the theatre, more favourably disposed towards her than the poets and novelists who were outlining their views of what made good literature, were constructing canons of their own—more inclusive ones, which took theatrical success as a positive rather than a negative sign, but equally made historical allowances for work not deemed fit for contemporary representation. In their catalogues and collected biographies the full range of her plays received critical attention, whereas only a narrow selection of her work was regularly performed on the stage. The reception of Behn's drama needs to be studied through a variety of evidence, including performance history, publication history, catalogues of plays, volumes of dramatic biography, and stage histories.

---

[13] W. R. Chetwood, *A General History of the Stage* (London: W. Owen, 1749), 235; *The Female Tatler*, quoted in Chetwood, 238; Baker, *A Companion to the Play-House*, i, p. xxvi.

[14] See Paulina Kewes, *Authorship and Appropriation* (Oxford: Clarendon Press, 1998) for a discussion of dramatic canon-formation in the period 1660–1710, arguing that 'the literary canon was only tangentially influenced by popularity in the theatre' (223).

From early on in her career, Behn's plays had been subject to attacks for their indecency; yet the stage-reform of the early eighteenth century, far from banishing her from the stage, actually provided the context for her continued dramatic success. Collier's famous attack on the stage, published in 1698, did not start the process of reform but made it more urgent. In response to this and other anti-theatrical attacks, men and women with significant interests in the theatre as playwrights or managers undertook the reform of the stage as a way of defending it. One of the ways this was done, of course, was by writing new, moral plays, and pointing out how much better they were than the work of the previous age; but another way, much favoured by theatre-managers, was to perform old plays in new ways, more consonant with the fashion for decency and morality. The point made by Steele's critic, that old lewd plays should not be acted without revision, had already been understood by the theatre-managers, and many seventeenth-century plays were advertised in playbills of the first quarter of the century as 'revised' or 'corrected'. The reform of the stage was a mixed and gradual process in these early years, involving no wholesale rejection of the drama of a previous age; and stage histories reflected this in their inclusive and mainly generous assessment of seventeenth-century drama. Novelists and their critics in the eighteenth century were to describe the new moral fiction as a radical break with fiction of the past; but dramatic history told a similar story of moralization and sentimentalization within a discourse of continuity.

In this climate there was no need to reject Behn, whose work still drew audiences, but it was necessary to select from her and to adapt her work to suit changing tastes. The earlier part of her stage career coincided with the vogue for sex comedy, and her plays, like those of Etherege and Wycherley in the same years, presented successful rakes, adultery, and fornication, and made frequent use of bawdy and *double entendre*. Especially in the early 1680s, her plays were also strongly partisan in their politics. *The City-Heiress* (1682) combined both characteristics: it drew criticism for its portrait of the 'rich City-Widow' Lady Galliard, whose affair with Wilding was one of many indications that women of the City fell for young Tories, not Whig merchants. Robert Gould wrote that 'to please a vicious age', Behn had brought:

> A far more Vicious Widow on the stage,
> Just reaking from a Stallion's rank Embrace
> With rifled Garments, and disorder'd Face;
> T'acquaint the audience with her slimy case.[15]

In the 1690s, Behn's well-known Stuart loyalties went against the grain of the times, and after the Whig ascendancy of 1714 they were quite outmoded. Her treatment of sex was increasingly out of tune with the reforming stage of the 1690s and later. However, there were other elements in her work which anticipated later trends. Her serious treatment of the position of the cast-off mistress in *The Rover*, and of a woman trapped in an unhappy marriage in *The Lucky Chance*, anticipated the problem comedies of Vanbrugh, Southerne, and Farquhar in the 1690s and 1700s. Her comedies used the intrigue conventions, derived from the Spanish, which would continue to entertain audiences in new plays of the eighteenth century, such as Susanna Centlivre's. Her use of farce and *commedia dell'arte* techniques in *The Emperor of the Moon* fitted well with the new turn to stage spectacle in the early 1700s. There was plenty in Behn's plays to make some of them suitable for continued performance and others for revision, adaptation, or the inspiration for new work.

The Rover, an immediate success in 1677, emerged early as Behn's most popular play. Stage records before 1700 being radically incomplete, it is impossible to be exact about performances in these years, but there were four revivals of the play at Court between 1680 and 1690, and it was also revived in the public theatres in the 1680s and 1690s.[16] By the 1690s it was the play by which she was most generally known. The *Athenian Mercury*, in answer to a question about who was 'the best Dramatick Professor in this Age', chose Dryden, but first gave an honourable mention to some other contenders, including Behn, 'whose *Rovers* are pretty natural things'.[17] Other Behn plays were revived during the 1680s and 1690s: *The Forc'd Marriage*

---

[15] Robert Gould, *The Playhouse* (London, 1689), quoted in *Works*, vii. 5.

[16] Unless otherwise stated, all performance data in this study is taken from the calendars in *The London Stage 1660–1800*, 5 parts (Carbondale, Ill.: Southern Illinois University Press, 1960–8). For the years 1700–11, *The London Stage 1660–1800. Part 2: 1700–1729. A New Version . . . Draft of the Calendar for Volume I. 1700–1711*, ed. J. Milhous and R. D. Hume (Carbondale, Ill.: Southern Illinois University Press, 1996) has been used. There was probably a performance of *The Rover* in the 1696–7 season, though no record exists: a second edition of the play was published in 1697, 'As it was acted by His Majesty's Servants, at the Theatre in Little-Lincolns-Inn-Fields'.   [17] *Athenian Mercury*, 5/2 (Sat. 5 Dec. 1691).

probably in 1687–8,[18] *The Feigned Courtesans* in 1680 and possibly in 1696,[19] and *The Emperor of the Moon*, first performed in 1687, was probably revived the following year[20] and was performed in 1691. In April 1695, *Abdelazer* was used by the patent company to reopen the theatre, closed since Queen Mary's death in December 1694. At this point the London theatre world was undergoing a major upheaval. The United Company which had monopolized production since the early 1680s was split when the most senior actors, including Thomas Betterton, Elizabeth Barry, and Anne Bracegirdle, rebelled against John Rich's management and left to form their own company at Lincoln's Inn Fields. This brought back competition to the stage, creating pressure both to mount new plays and to revive a greater variety of old ones.[21] In the frenzied 1695–6 season Behn's previously unperformed play, *The Younger Brother*, became one of seven new comedies put on at Drury Lane.[22] It failed, but further Behn revivals followed in the next few years, with three of her plays, *The Roundheads*, *The City-Heiress*, and *The Young King* being reprinted in 1698, probably indicating performances in 1697–8.

At the beginning of the eighteenth century the two theatre companies continued to compete. Drury Lane, at first the loser by the split, was beginning to recover its position as the new generation of actors matured, and as it gained the services of Farquhar and Vanbrugh. The success of Farquhar's *The Constant Couple* in 1699 (while Congreve's *The Way of the World* failed at Lincoln's Inn Fields in 1700) established Drury Lane as the house for the best new comedy.[23] The companies united again in 1710, and a new management trio of Wilks, Cibber, and Doggett was set up. Wilks and Cibber, with Barton Booth, who replaced Doggett, managed Drury Lane for more than twenty years. It became established as the main house for drama, though theatrical competition began again in 1714 when John Rich reopened Lincoln's Inn Fields.

---

[18] This is inferred from the publication of a 2nd edn. in 1688 'As it is Acted by His Majesties Servants at the Queens Theatre'.

[19] The 1696 performance is conjectured from the advertisement of the play as 'not acted these 20 years' in 1716.

[20] This is inferred from the publication of a 2nd edn. in this year.

[21] See Judith Milhous, *Thomas Betterton and the Management of Lincoln's Inn Fields 1695–1708* (Carbondale, Ill.: Southern Illinois University Press, 1979), esp. 42–55 and 97–102, for a discussion of the theatrical situation in 1695. [22] Ibid. 102.

[23] S. S. Kenny, 'Theatrical Warfare, 1695–1710', *Theatre Notebook*, 27/4 (1973), 130–45.

During these years it is much easier to trace the fortunes of Behn's plays on the London stage, because of the regular playbills appearing in newspapers after 1700. *The City-Heiress,* despite its lewdness, had a revival at Drury Lane in 1701 and at the Queen's Theatre in 1707. There were revivals of *The False Count* (in 1715 and 1716), *The Feigned Courtesans* (in 1716 and 1717), and *The Lucky Chance* (in 1718), all at Lincoln's Inn Fields, and another revival of *The False Count* at the Little Theatre in the Haymarket in 1730. The main Behn plays, however, were *The Emperor of the Moon* and *The Rover.* The first indication that *The Emperor of the Moon* was playing at the beginning of the century comes from the provinces: it was in the repertory of a company of strolling players, led by Thomas Doggett, who toured in the east of England in 1701.[24] It was revived at Drury Lane in 1702 with William Penkethman playing Harlequin: he was to become well known in the part. *The Emperor* continued to be played in at least one of the London theatres in nearly every year until the 1730s. *The Rover* opened at Drury Lane in 1703 with Robert Wilks as Willmore, and was regularly performed up to the 1740s.

During the first thirty years of the century, *The Rover* and *The Emperor* were among the most popular Restoration revivals on the London stages. In a period when the type of audience—relatively small and including many regulars—encouraged a high turnover, many Restoration plays were revived, but only for a few performances each per season. Even great new successes, like Farquhar's *Beaux' Stratagem,* soon settled down to seasonal runs not much higher than those enjoyed by stock plays from the previous century. To give some sense of how Behn's plays fared, I have selected seven successful plays and compared them against *The Rover* and *The Emperor,* noting the number of performances recorded in each set of five seasons, from the season 1700–1 to the season 1729–30 (see Table 1). Three are Restoration comedies close in time to *The Rover,* and all of these, like Behn's play, were attacked for indecency: Wycherley's *The Country Wife,* Etherege's *The Man of Mode,* and Ravenscroft's *The London Cuckolds.* Three are from the 1690s. Two of them, Vanbrugh's problem-comedy *The Provok'd Wife* and Congreve's *Love for Love,* had

---

[24] This tour is documented because Doggett was prosecuted by the Cambridge University authorities for the attempt to perform at Sturbridge Fair in Sept. 1701. *The Emperor* was added to the company's repertoire some time between then and Dec. 1701, when the company broke up. See J. Milhous and R. D. Hume, 'Thomas Doggett at Cambridge in 1701', *Theatre Notebook* 51/3 (1997), 147–65.

been attacked by Jeremy Collier for indecency and profanity, but they became popular stock plays nevertheless. Another is Farquhar's extremely popular comedy *The Constant Couple*. One is an example of the new eighteenth-century comedy of stage-reform, Steele's *The Tender Husband*.

Performances of selected plays, 1700–1 to 1729–30

	1700–1 to 1704–5	1705–6 to 1709–10	1710–11 to 1714–15	1715–16 to 1719–20	1720–1 to 1724–5	1725–6 to 1729–30	Total perform-ances 1700–1 to 1729–30
Country Wife (1675)	—	2	2	16	11	39	70
Man of Mode (1676)	4	10	12	13	16	13	68
Rover (1677)	8	15	10	15	20	30	98
London Cuckolds (1682)	5	12	6	13	20	8	64
Emperor of the Moon (1687)	13	17	12	32	17	8	99
Love for Love (1695)	3	19	25	32	23	28	130
Provok'd Wife (1697)	—	5	2	24	8	38	77
Constant Couple (1699)	10	12	12	26	18	32	110
Tender Husband (1705)	7	16	8	15	12	14	72

During the period as a whole, *The Rover* is clearly the most popular of the 1670s comedies considered, with 98 performances as against 70, 68, and 64 respectively for the other three. This suggests that despite criticisms of its indecency, it was less objectionable than other works of its day. That Restoration comedy could succeed if revised for the new age is suggested by the figures for *The Country Wife*, which was rarely put on in the early years of the century, but was revived in the season 1714–15 as 'Not Acted these Six Years. Written by

Mr Wycherley. Carefully Revis'd'. After this date it was frequently performed and had overtaken *The Rover* by the last five years of the period. The importance of revision is also suggested by the records for *The Provok'd Wife*. No performances are recorded for the first five years of the period. It was revived in 1705–6 'with alterations' and had five performances, but after that it had very little success, with only two more performances recorded, until the season of 1715–16, when it was advertised as 'Not Acted these Eight Years. Carefully Revis'd'. James L. Smith conjectures that the revisions of 1705–6 and 1715–16 were probably minor, involving the removal of outdated references and of lines which had been attacked as 'profane'.[25] At any rate it seems that the revisions of 1715–16 were successful, since from then on the play was performed every season. Its big increase in popularity dated from the 1725–6 season, when it was put on at Drury Lane for the first time, 'Revised by the Author'. It was probably for this revival that Vanbrugh provided the revised scenes in which Sir John Brute disguises himself as a lady instead of a clergyman, thus getting rid of the attack on clerical dignity which had caused great offence to Collier and others.[26] This play, too, had overtaken *The Rover* in popularity by the last five years of the period.

Behn's 1670s comedy stands up surprisingly well against the competition of some of the most popular of the works of the new generation of playwrights who began writing in the 1690s and dominated the eighteenth-century repertoire.[27] That *The Rover*, overall, did better than *The Provok'd Wife* in this period can be explained by the particular notoriety of Vanbrugh's play before alteration, but it at least shows that Behn's comedy was not one of the worst offenders against decency in eighteenth-century eyes. *The Rover* was significantly less popular than *Love for Love*, with 130 performances in the period, and *The Constant Couple*, with 110, but the difference is not so great as might have been expected between a 1670s comedy and the work of two of the 'perennial favourites'. During the first ten years of the period it actually marginally outperformed *The Constant Couple*,

---

[25] See his discussion in *The Provok'd Wife*, ed. James L. Smith (New Mermaids ed., London: Ernest Benn, 1974), 113.   [26] Ibid. 112–14.

[27] See S. S. Kenny, 'Perennial Favourites: Congreve, Vanbrugh, Cibber, Farquhar and Steele', *MP* 73 (1976), S4–S11, for a discussion of the popularity of these writers, whose work taken together 'accounted for a large percentage of the comedies which played in London for three-quarters of a century' (S4). My comparison of the records of selected individual plays suggests that this dominance was not fully entrenched in the first thirty years of the century.

and drew level with it again during the last ten years; and during the last five seasons of the period *The Rover* was performed slightly more often than *Love for Love*. During the period as a whole, it was significantly more popular than Steele's moral comedy *The Tender Husband*, which only just managed to be performed more often than the other 1670s comedies. This may, of course, have affected the great reformer's attitude to his 'luscious' female rival.[28]

The Rover's success in this period suggests that it proved easy to assimilate to the new theatrical climate. Without the harsher, more cynical notes sounded by Etherege and Wycherley, and by Behn herself in some of her 1680s comedies, it could be made to resemble the genial comedy typical of the early eighteenth century.[29] The play's continuing popularity, and the alterations made to ensure it, are discussed in detail in Chapter 5, where I show how well it lent itself to revival in the spirit of eighteenth-century comedy.

The figures for *The Emperor of the Moon* in the same period show that the farce rapidly gained a prominent position in the repertory, being performed more often during the first ten years of the century than popular recent comedies like *The Constant Couple* and *Love for Love*. From 1715 to 1725 it was also very popular, having been taken up by Rich at Lincoln's Inn Fields. After this date its performances began to fall off. The success of the new pantomimes, *Necromancer* and *Harlequin Dr Faustus*, in 1723–4 started a new vogue, and in the following years the development of pantomime began to make the kind of proto-pantomime of *The Emperor* old-fashioned.[30] The phenomenal success of *The Beggar's Opera* at Lincoln's Inn Fields in 1728–9 also tended to push other productions to one side. For twenty-five years, however, Behn's farce was one of the most popular productions in London.

Its appeal was multiple. It had the slapstick antics of Harlequin and Scaramouch, with typical *commedia dell'arte* scenes such as Harlequin trying to tickle himself to death, jousting with Scaramouch for the hand of Mopsophil, and tricking a gatekeeper

---

[28] Steele's later work, of course, was much more popular than this, but *The Conscious Lovers* (1722) was omitted from the table because of its later date.

[29] R. D. Hume finds that the change from hard, satiric comedy to a more humane comedy had occurred by 1708 or 1710. See 'The Multifarious Forms of Eighteenth-Century Comedy', in G. W. Stone (ed.), *The Stage and the Page* (Berkeley, Los Angeles, and London: University of California Press, 1981), 4.

[30] Leo Hughes, *The Drama's Patrons* (Austin, Tex., and London: University of Texas Press, 1971), 98.

with a carriage that he can transform instantaneously into a cart. Its props included a 20-foot-long telescope and a 'speaking head', a kind of ventriloquist's dummy that was a recent craze when the play was first performed, but continued to entertain audiences for years after. As well as slapstick and farcical props, the play offered a visual spectacle comparable to those of the grandest operatic entertainments of the late seventeenth century. Using the whole of the long Dorset Garden stage, Behn planned a series of discoveries culminating in the final-act appearance of the temple at the back of the stage. Various characters flew across the stage in small chariots, and there was a spectacular scene in which a large flying-machine descended from the roof, bearing actors dressed as signs of the zodiac, and Cinthio and Charmante as the emperor of the moon and the prince.[31]

This kind of spectacle was new in Behn's time, and hers was one of the most elaborate developments of it. It was clearly a major part of the play's attraction. Revivals were often advertised with reference to the use of its 'Scenes and Machines'. These being a big expense for theatrical companies, the same ones were used for years, and swapped from one play to another. When new scenes and machines were prepared they formed an added attraction. A short piece of only three acts, the farce lent itself particularly well to the common practice of adding new songs and dances to dramatic performances as interludes. Sometimes it was listed as a mainpiece, with singing and dancing to follow, and at other times as the afterpiece to another play. *The Emperor* was used, in effect, as one of the elements in a kind of variety show; and the wide, cross-cultural appeal of its entertainment, so much more dependent on the visual and musical than the verbal, meant that the theatre was frequently requested to perform it for the entertainment of foreign dignitaries. When it opened on 18 September 1702 the *Daily Courant* advertised it as performed 'At the desire of some Persons of Quality . . . A Comedy wherein Mr Penkethman acts the part of Harlequin without a Masque, for the Entertainment of an African Prince lately arrived here, being Nephew to the King of Bauday in that Country. With several Entertainments of Singing and Dancing, and the last new Epilogue never spoken but once by Mr Penkethman.' Later in the season, in April 1703, it was performed again 'For the Entertainment of his Excellency Hogdha Bawhoon, envoy to Her Majesty from the great

---

[31] See the discussion of the play's staging in *The Rover and Other Plays*, ed. Spencer.

King of Persia', this time with a new piece of music 'in which Mr Paisible, Mr Banister and Mr Latour play some extraordinary Parts upon the Flute, Violin and Hautboy', and 'a new dance by the Devonshire Girl in Imitation of Mlle Subligne'. In the following season, new scenery was added to the play's attractions, 'additional Scenes, being the Changes in the Dome, which were originally us'd in the Opera of the *Virgin Prophetess*',[32] and 'an Additional Grotesque Scene, and the Grand Machine, both taken out of the opera of *Dioclesian*'.[33] These scenes continued in use for some years, while other attractions were added in the form of new songs and dances, an epilogue spoken by Penkethman while riding on an ass, and a new gadget to interpret the scene in which the main characters trick Doctor Baliardo by freezing into the illusion of a set of tapestry hangings: 'a New Invention first Contriv'd by Monsieur St Everimont, which Represents a Suit of Hangings, which in an Instant is Transform'd to Men and Women'. This last was advertised in 1710 for a performance of the farce at the new theatre at Greenwich, opened by Penkethman himself. On this occasion Harlequin was played by another comedian, Spiller, but by this time Penkethman was legendary in the part. One collection of essays included an anecdote about a lady who is drinking punch with her women friends when her lawyer calls, prompting a swift change to more ladylike beverages: 'the scene was immediately chang'd, and the drinking of Cold Tea with the *Indian* Punchbowl, by the Contrivances of their Madamships, their Chambermaids and Waiting-Women, was as soon turn'd into Chocolate and Coffee, as *Pinkethman* in the *Emperor of the Moon* makes a *Metamorphosis* of his Chariot and Baker's Cart, the better to carry on and humour what was Madam *Afra*'s Design'.[34]

Lincoln's Inn Fields began performing *The Emperor* in 1715, and from 1717 until 1731 it was the only theatre staging the play, which it put on at least once every season and often four or five times. The play fitted in well with the general repertoire of the Lincoln's Inn Fields company, which specialized in farce, singing, dancing, and acrobatics. As far as theatrical rivals and critics of the drama were concerned, *The Emperor*'s genre, and its popularity, were points to be used against it. It was used as a byword for low and ridiculous entertainment. In *A Comparison Between the Two Stages* the critic Sullen uses

---

[32] Advertised for 27 Dec. 1703.   [33] Advertised 31 Dec. 1703.
[34] *Serious and Comical Essays* (London: J. King, 1710), 39.

it to help disparage Dryden's *Amphitryon*, which should not lay claim
to the status of a comedy since it is 'as very and substantial a *Farce* as
Scapin, or the *Emperor of the Moon* . . . as vile *Farce* as ever he rail'd
against'.[35] Colley Cibber used an anecdote about the play as evidence
that farce is ridiculous and unnatural. The best excuse for
Harlequin's mask is that:

the low, senseless, and monstrous things he says, and does in it, no theatrical
Assurance could get through, with a bare Face: Let me give you an Instance
of even *Penkethman*'s being out of Countenance for want of it: When he first
play'd *Harlequin* in the *Emperor of the Moon*, several Gentlemen . . . insisted,
that the next time of his acting that Part, he should play without it: Their
Desire was accordingly comply'd with—but, alas! In vain—*Penkethman* could
not take to himself the Shame of the Character without being concealed—
he was no more *Harlequin*—his Humour was quite disconcerted! his
Conscience could not, with the same *Effronterie* declare against Nature,
without the Cover of that unchanging Face, which he was sure would never
blush for it! . . . Now if this Circumstance will justify the Modesty of
Penkethman, it cannot but throw a wholesome Contempt on the low Merit of
an *Harlequin*.[36]

According to Thomas Wilkes, writing in 1759, 'Dryden and his
brother bards' had been greatly 'mortified' by Behn's success with
The Emperor. Whether or not this was the case, Wilkes certainly found
its success mortifying himself, and explained it by disparaging the
audience: 'Entertainments of this nature are fit only for weak minds,
which cannot bear the impression of reflection; and the Managers
are only excusable in exhibiting them, inasmuch as it is inconsistent
with honesty to advise them *To be wise to empty boxes*.'[37] This critical disdain for art that appeals to the senses more than the intellect intensified among twentieth-century academics, and has coloured today's
views of eighteenth-century performances and audiences: even Leo
Hughes, one of the first critics to give serious consideration to
eighteenth-century farce, deplores 'a further flight from head to ears
and eyes' in the popular tastes of the 1720s.[38] *The Emperor* is a classic
case of the conflict between success and prestige: the ability of Behn's

[35] *A Comparison Between the Two Stages (1702)*, ed. S. B. Wells (Princeton: Princeton
University Press, 1942), 79.

[36] Colley Cibber, *An Apology for the Life of Mr. Colley Cibber, Comedian, and Late Patentee of the
Theatre-Royal* (London: John Watts, 1740), 90–1.

[37] Thomas Wilkes, *A General View of the Stage* (London: J. Coote, 1759), 80.

[38] Hughes, *The Drama's Patrons*, 97.

farce to entertain eighteenth-century audiences only lowered her reputation among the critics.

The rapid change in theatrical conditions at the end of the 1720s has been delineated by Robert Hume.[39] The unprecedented success of *The Beggar's Opera* in 1728, together with the not quite so remarkable run of Vanbrugh and Cibber's *The Provok'd Husband*, sparked off competition for the growing London audience, and pirate theatres at the Little Haymarket and Goodman's Fields began to challenge the monopoly of the patent companies. Innovation and experimentation blossomed in the early 1730s, and the older plays began to lose their importance in the repertoire. Both *The Rover* and *The Emperor* had fewer performances in the 1730s than the 1720s. *The Rover*, however, held its place well during the early years of the decade, being performed six times in 1729–30, seven times in 1730–1, and eight times in 1731–2. After the Licensing Act of 1737 suppressed the fringe theatres and restored the patent companies' monopoly, there was a return to the safe practices of earlier years, with a poor market for new plays.[40] Behn's plays did not return to their earlier prominent position, however. *The Emperor*, now outmoded, was performed three times in the 1740s and then dropped altogether in the 1750s and 1760s. *The Rover* carried on longer, with more efforts to revise it for the changing times; but after a revival at Covent Garden in 1748, and another one that played for three seasons in the years 1757–60, it too was dropped.

The period from the 1740s onwards was a time of increasing stage refinement. While earlier stage histories, like Downes's *Roscius Anglicanus* (1708), tended simply to chronicle the year-by-year activities of managers and actors, and the performances of plays, later ones aimed to raise the theatrical world in public esteem. The cultural status of working on the stage lagged behind that of writing for it, and in 1749 W. R. Chetwood attempted to elevate theatrical professions in his stage history. Dedicating his work to the theatre-managers Garrick, Lacy, Rich, and Thomas Sheridan, he began by referring to the theatre's origins in Greece, and continued with a declaration of its virtuous tendency: 'So reasonable an Entertainment, as the Drama in its Purity, must be, in some sort, a Promoter to Virtue; therefore every Manager of a Theatre should make it his Study to exhibit no other Pieces but what aim to that End; and, by

---

[39] Hume, *Henry Fielding and the London Theatre*, esp. 37–44.   [40] Ibid. 202, 253, 260.

Degrees, throw off the looser Drama, and constitute, in its place, those that the wisest, most virtuous, need not be asham'd to partake of the innocent Amusement.' Chetwood criticized audiences for throwing things at actors on stage, and contrasted this rudeness with the respect given to actors in France, where they were 'acceptable in the Company of Rank and Figure in that polite Nation'. Drury Lane under Robert Wilks was praised in terms of its social refinement: its 'Green-Rooms were free from Indecencies of every Kind, and might justly be compared to the most elegant Drawing-Rooms of the Prime Quality . . . even Persons of the First Rank and Taste, of both Sexes, would often mix with the Performers, without any Stain to their Honour or Understanding'.[41] Benjamin Victor went further, writing that Colley Cibber, Robert Wilks, and Anne Oldfield, performing *The Careless Husband,* turned the theatre into 'the *School of Politeness,* where persons of the first Rank might have learned such behaviour, as would have added to their Dignity'.[42] Through such retrospective judgements, the years up to 1730 were seen as the time the stage was reformed; but it was the period in which these judgements were recorded that shows the greatest concern for politeness and elegance on the stage. It was this refining phase in the theatre's rise to respectability, not the earlier period of stage-reform, that ended Behn's tenure of the stage. While Robert Wilks, the man given most of the credit for raising Drury Lane to morality and politeness in the years up to 1730,[43] not only staged *The Rover* but played its leading role for thirty years, David Garrick, who inaugurated a new era of greater delicacy when he took over the theatre's management in 1747, dropped Behn from the repertoire. During his management of Drury Lane *The Emperor of the Moon* was revived there only once, for two performances in December 1748, and *The Rover* was not performed there at all.

After 1760 the theatrical world livened up into what Hume calls the 'High Georgian' period, with Goldsmith and Sheridan's work being produced alongside other new plays by Macklin, Murphy, Foote, Colman, and Garrick.[44] Comedies of the 1690s and early 1700s by

---

[41] Chetwood, *A General History of the Stage,* 40, 44, 235–6.

[42] B. Victor, *The History of the Theatres of London and Dublin* (London: T. Davies *et al.*, 1761), ii. 55.

[43] Chetwood acknowledges all three managers but gives most of the glory to the 'sole Directions' of Wilks: *A General History of the Stage,* 235.

[44] Hume, 'The Multifarious Forms', 7.

Congreve, Farquhar, Centlivre, Cibber, and others were still popular, but the satiric and bawdy comedies of the 1670s were no longer suitable for the stage in their original form. Restoration comedy did not disappear altogether. Instead, there was a vogue for new, sanitized versions of older plays.[45] *The Country Wife* emerged transformed by Garrick into *The Country Girl* in 1776, shorn of its original point, the rake–hero Horner. From 1760 onwards Behn, too, was considered unfit for representation without transformation. *The Rover* was no longer put on under its original title, but was revived in John Philip Kemble's revised version, *Love in Many Masks*, in 1790.

Though the new pantomimes superseded *The Emperor of the Moon*, it returned in the 1770s in an altered form, billed as a 'Dialogue-Pantomime', and performed with marionettes at the Patagonian Theatre. This puppet-theatre, in a room above Exeter Change in the Strand, operated from 1776 to 1781, putting on ballad operas and literary burlesques. Its founder was a scene-painter, and the shows were elaborate displays of scenic art.[46] Advertisements for the production of *The Emperor* promised 'a great Variety of magnificent Scenes, the whole of which are entirely new . . . to conclude with a magnificent Piece of perspective Architecture'.[47] Judging by the new edition of the play printed to accompany the production,[48] Behn's original staging was followed very closely in this miniature version, with the final act including the gallery, the view of Parnassus, and the last scene with the temple and altar. There was a representation of the zodiac, with transparencies used for the signs; a moon globe which descended carrying the emperor and prince; and chariots to carry Harlequin and Scaramouch. An added attraction were the new songs, taken from a number of recent musical performances.[49] The final spectacular scene was accompanied by the singing of 'let this bright Seraphim in burning Row' from the Oratorio of Samson. This show proved to be a popular attraction. It was first performed

---

[45] Hughes, *The Drama's Patrons*, 124.

[46] For the Patagonian Theatre see George Speaight, *A History of the English Puppet Theatre* (London, 1955).   [47] *Gazetteer and New Daily Advertiser*, Sat. 22 Mar. 1777.

[48] *The Emperor of the Moon. A Dialogue-Pantomime . . . As performed at The Patagonian Theatre* (London: T. Sherlock, 1777). The newspaper announcement of the opening performance suggests that this new edition was prepared beforehand and was on sale at the theatre.

[49] These were Gay's *Polly*; Dryden's *Alexander's Feast,* being performed with Handel's music during the 1750s; Garrick's *Cymon: A Dramatic Romance* (1766); Moses Mendez' *The Chaplet: A Musical Entertainment* (1761); and Robert Lloyd's comic opera *The Capricious Lovers* (1764).

in March 1777, was put on eighteen times that season,[50] and revived in April 1778 'for the benefit of the Scene Painter', with the novelty of 'entire new Scenery and Decorations, Particularly a superb Colonado, and the Silver Palace of the Moon'.[51]

As well as their long life on the London stages, Behn's plays travelled. Both *The Rover* and *The Emperor* were being performed in Dublin by the 1720s. There was a command performance of *The Rover* for the Duke and Duchess of Dorset at Smock Alley on 16 October 1721, and other performances of the play are noted at Smock Alley in 1728–9, 1732–3, and 1751–2.[52] Editions of the comedy were published in Dublin in 1724 and 1741. Three performances of *The Emperor of the Moon* are recorded for the 1720s. It was performed at the Aungier Street theatre in 1739 and 1740,[53] and at Smock Alley in 1747–8, cut down to one act. The three-act version was performed eight times in 1756–7 and nine times in 1757–8.[54] A new edition was published in Dublin in 1757. The farce also travelled to Cork, where performances are recorded in 1760 and 1775.[55]

Behn's work does not seem to have been much performed in the English provinces, although, as we do not have complete calendars for all the provincial theatres, there may have been some performances which are not recorded. *The Rover* was performed by the Norwich players in 1711–12.[56] By the time English provincial theatres became fully established in the second half of the century, with new theatres being built in a number of provincial towns, and royal patents being granted to players in Bath, Norwich, York, Hull, Liverpool, and Chester,[57] Behn's plays were no longer popular. The calendar of Tate Wilkinson's Yorkshire circuit from 1766 to 1803, for example, does not include *The Rover*, and records *The Emperor of the*

[50] *Gazetteer and New Daily Advertiser,* 22 Mar.; 1, 3, 5, 8, 10, 12, 15, 17, 22, 26, 29 Apr.; 8, 13, 15, 24, 29 May; and 3 June 1777.

[51] *Morning Chronicle and London Advertiser,* Friday 10 Apr. 1778.

[52] J. Greene and G. L. H. Clark, *The Dublin Stage, 1720–1745* (London and Toronto: Associated University Presses, 1993), 59, 96, 120; Esther K. Sheldon, *Thomas Sheridan of Smock-Alley . . . including a Smock-Alley Calendar for the Years of his Management* (New Jersey: Princeton University Press, 1967), 459.   [53] Greene and Clark, *The Dublin Stage,* 430.

[54] Sheldon, *Thomas Sheridan of Smock-Alley,* 416–17.

[55] William Smith Clark, *The Irish Stage in the County Towns 1720 to 1800* (Oxford: Clarendon Press, 1965), 295.

[56] S. Rosenfeld, *Strolling Players and Drama in the Provinces, 1660–1765* (Cambridge: Cambridge University Press, 1939), 50. Rosenfeld discusses the repertoire of Norwich, York, Bath, and Canterbury up to 1765. *The Rover* is mentioned only in connection with Norwich.   [57] Ibid. 2.

Moon only once, as an afterpiece performed in Hull in November 1775.[58]

The stage popularity of *The Rover* was reflected in the number of new editions published during the eighteenth century: there were separate editions in 1709, 1724, 1729, 1735, 1741, and 1757 (altered), and an edition of *Love in Many Masks* in 1790. As a farce *The Emperor of the Moon* was not considered to have so much to offer the reader, but the later revivals prompted new editions in 1757 and 1777. However, it was not only the plays still in performance that were published. As Paulina Kewes has shown, a canon of English drama was being formed by the later years of the seventeenth century, and by the early eighteenth century, the increasing critical prestige being accorded to contemporary and recent plays was reflected in the publication of complete editions of the plays of writers such as Dryden, Otway, Wycherley, Southerne, Rowe, Farquhar, Lee, and Behn.[59] Behn's dramatic works were published four times in the first twenty-five years of the century.[60]

As we have already seen, Behn was included and assessed favourably in the main accounts of English drama in the late seventeenth and early eighteenth centuries, begun by Langbaine and continued by Gildon and Jacob. She was considered firmly a part of the new dramatic canon, and these accounts continued to influence later works. By the middle years of the century, however, there is a change of tone. Chetwood's *The British Theatre* (1750), intended as a 'more regular and exact Account of the *English* Dramatic Writers' to replace Langbaine and Jacob,[61] is very comprehensive, with fairly short entries on each writer. Behn is given a generally favourable treatment in a three-page entry deriving from earlier accounts, but Gildon's high praise of her is not repeated. In later accounts, supporters of Behn became defensive. Shiels, writing on her for Theophilus Cibber's *Lives of the Poets,* remarked that 'Mrs. Behn suffered enough at the hands of supercilious prudes, who had the

---

[58] Linda Fitzsimmons and Arthur W. McDonald (eds.), *The Yorkshire Stage 1766–1803* (Metuchen, NJ, and London: The Scarecrow Press Inc., 1989), 211.

[59] Kewes, *Authorship and Appropriation*, 180–224.

[60] *Plays Written by the late Ingenious Mrs. Behn* (London: Jacob Tonson, 1702); *Plays Written by the late Ingenious Mrs. Behn. The Second Edition* (London: W. Meadows, 1716); *Plays Written by the late Ingenious Mrs. Behn* (London: Mary Poulson, 1724). The 'second edition' is really a reissue of the 1702 edition. The plays also appeared in *The Works of Mrs. Behn. Entire in three volumes . . . The second volume. Plays* (London: R. Wellington, 1711).

[61] W. R. Chetwood, *The British Theatre* (Dublin: Peter Wilson, 1750), p. i.

barbarity to construe her sprightliness into lewdness; and because she had wit and beauty, she must likewise be charged with prostitution and irreligion' (iii. 27). On the vexed question of indecency in the comedies, he appealed to a historical understanding of changing times: 'let those who are ready to blame her, consider, that her's was the sad alternative to write or starve; the taste of the times was corrupt'.[62] The most substantial dramatic history of the late eighteenth century to deal favourably with Behn was Baker's *Companion to the Play-house*. His first volume, containing a dictionary of plays, shows how much Behn, despite the corrupt taste of her times, was still considered a current dramatist in the 1760s. Not only is *The Rover* praised, both parts of the play being described as 'very entertaining, and contain much Business, Bustle, and Intrigue, supported with an infinite deal of Sprightliness', and *The Emperor* noted as 'even yet sometimes played, and seldom without Applause'; but most of her plays are listed, often with a brief comment, and the entry on *Abdelazer* suggests that it could be a candidate for revival: 'The Plot is intricate, much interlarded with trivial Circumstances, and the Catastrophe on the whole too bloody, yet with a little Alteration might be render'd very fit for the present Stage'.[63] Towards the end of the century, disapproval took over from historical excuse in dramatic histories. Charles Dibdin included a five-page entry on Behn in his five-volume history, attacking her for her looseness and for plagiarism.[64] By now, Behn was being dropped from the dramatic canon as expressed in new collections of the best English plays: her plays were not included Elizabeth Inchbald's collection, *The British Theatre*, in 1808.[65] However, Baker's assessment of her continued to have currency in later editions of his work, and her comedies were still receiving praise in the nineteenth century.[66]

Though subject to criticism, Behn was not written out of dramatic history. Early in the eighteenth century she was popular on the stage, and she was considered part of the dramatic canon, valued for

[62] T. Cibber, *The Lives of the Poets of Great Britain and Ireland* (London: R. Griffiths, 1753), iii. 27, 26.

[63] D. E. Baker, *Companion to the Play-House*, i, entries on *Rover*, *Emperor*, and *Abdelazer*.

[64] Charles Dibdin, *A Complete History of the English Stage* (London, 1797–1800), iv. 198–203.

[65] *The British Theatre*, ed. E. Inchbald, 25 vols. (London: Longman, Hurst, Rees and Orme, 1808).

[66] See John Genest, *Some Account of the English Stage*, 10 vols. (Bath: H. E. Carrington, 1832), i. 120, 145, 210, 214–17, 270–1.

her genial comedy and entertaining farce. The indecency of *The Rover* and the genre of *The Emperor* denied her access to the highest literary ranking, but in theatrical circles she was remembered with respect. In the second half of the century her works were altered and eventually altogether dropped; but she was a witty and entertaining representative of an earlier age—no longer fit for the contemporary stage, but worth an honourable place in history.

BEHN AND THE NOVEL

The reception of Behn as a novelist during the eighteenth century is particularly interesting, complex, and significant, because it is so intimately bound up with the reception of the novel as a form. While the idea that the novel rose in eighteenth-century England as a new form adapted to specially English social conditions has now been strongly challenged by critics and historians pointing, among other things, to the pervasive influence of French and Spanish fiction on English writers,[67] the consensus remains that something new was happening, not so much within fiction itself as with the place of fiction in eighteenth-century culture. Not only has the numerical rise of the novel and novelists been amply demonstrated by statistical study,[68] but critics have recently been arguing that the novel was established as a central cultural form in this period, whether they call this a 'making', an 'elevation', a 'novelization', or an 'institutionalization'.[69] They date the process differently, William Warner and Brean Hammond[70] placing the decisive shift in the 1740s with Richardson's and Fielding's novels and critical discussions, Homer Brown and

---

[67] See, e.g. E. Showalter, *The Evolution of the French Novel 1641–1782* (Princeton: Princeton University Press, 1972); R. Ballaster, *Seductive Forms*; J. A. Downie, 'The Making of the English Novel', *Eighteenth-Century Fiction*, 9/3 (1997), 249–66. They are all in different ways answering Ian Watt's classic study *The Rise of the Novel* (1957).

[68] For the growth of fiction 1750–70 see J. Raven, *British Fiction 1750–1770: A Chronological Check-List of Prose Fiction Printed in Britain and Ireland* (Newark, Del.: University of Delaware Press, 1987). For the growth in fiction by women throughout the century see Turner, *Living By the Pen*, 31–59. James Raven and Antonia Forster's forthcoming *Bibliography of English Fiction*, i., *1770–1799* will demonstrate the steep rise in novel production in the final thirty years of the century.

[69] See Downie, 'The Making of the English Novel'; W. Warner, 'The Elevation of the Novel in England', *ELH* 59 (1992), 577–96; B. Hammond, *Professional Imaginative Writing in England 1670–1740* (Oxford: Clarendon Press, 1997), 303 ('novelization'); and H. O. Brown, *Institutions of the English Novel* (Philadelphia: University of Pennsylvania Press, 1997).

[70] B. Hammond, 'Mid-Century English Quixotism and the Defence of the Novel', *Eighteenth-Century Fiction*, 103 (1998), 247–68.

Alan Downie opting for the late eighteenth and early nineteenth
centuries with the steep growth in fiction publishing and the promotion of a canon in histories and edited collections of fiction. The different dates depend, as Downie argues, on whether you emphasize
the roles of authors and readers or of publishers and critics.[71] The
novel did not come either into being or into prominence at any
single 'moment', but moved gradually to take up a central cultural
position by the early nineteenth century. The reception of Behn's
fiction was a part of the process.

We have quite rightly been warned against finding Behn, or anyone
else, the winner in a competition to become 'first' English novelist, a
game where the players' scores shift as the critics move the goal-
posts.[72] What concerns me here is not some mythical 'first', but the
relation between the reception of Behn's fiction and the establishment of the novel as a distinct genre worthy of definition, critical
attention, and a history. When Behn was writing her fiction, 'novel'
was not a stable term, but was beginning to be used in England to
refer to short pieces of fiction. In this the English were following
recent French developments. The shorter *histoires* or *nouvelles* of the
later seventeenth century were replacing the multi-volume romances
of the earlier part of the century, and French criticism by the 1680s
was praising these new works as more realistic, closer to contemporary life, and more psychologically acute than the romances.[73] Behn
drew on the *nouvelles* of writers like Madame de Lafayette as well as
on other French fictional models such as the *chronique scandaleuse*, and
she also used anglicized versions of the French terms for fiction, publishing most of her fictions as 'histories' and one, *The Lucky Mistake,*
as a 'novel'.[74] Behn herself, as we have seen, based her claims to fame
on her verse and drama. Her dedications to the novels published in
her lifetime typically refer to the work in question as a *'little piece'* or a
'little Trifle', or, in the case of *Oroonoko,* as the result of a mere *'few*

[71] Downie, 'The Making of the English Novel', 263–6.

[72] See W. Warner, *Licensing Entertainment* (Berkeley: University of California Press, 1998),
1–44. For an argument for seeing Behn's *Love-Letters* as 'the first English novel' while recognizing 'that such a claim about origin and priority is necessarily fallacious', see J. K. Gardiner,
'The First English Novel', *Tulsa Studies in Women's Literature*, 8/2 (1989), 201–22 (201).

[73] The Sieur du Plaisir's *Sentimens sur les lettres et sur l'histoire* (1683) praised the new kind of
fiction. His work was paraphrased by the abbé de Bellegarde in 1702, and his ideas were
disseminated in England in the preface to *Queen Zarah* in 1705. See J. L. Sutton, Jr., 'The
Source of Mrs. Manley's Preface to *Queen Zarah*', *Modern Philology*, 82/2 (1984), 167–72.

[74] *The Lucky Mistake, A New Novel, By Mrs. A Behn* (London: Richard Bentley, 1689).

Hours' of writing (*Works*, iii. 166, 208, 56), and her main claim for
them was usually the common one that they were not really fictions
at all but true histories. However, her fiction was soon exploited in
some of the earliest attempts by publishers to market the novel in
England as a distinct and distinctly modern form, one that could be
the basis of an authorial *œuvre*. William Canning was the first to group
her novels together for publication, reissuing *Oroonoko* and *The Fair Jilt*,
together with the translated novel *Agnes de Castro*, as *Three Histories . . .
By Mrs. A. Behn* in 1688. Richard Bentley seems to have originally
intended *The Lucky Mistake*, which he published in the year of Behn's
death, as the first in a collection of novels;[75] in the event it was published alone, but he reissued it three years later as part of the first volume in a twelve-volume collection of *Modern Novels*.[76] In 1696, Behn's
Histories and Novels capitalized on and extended this movement.
Coming six years before the first collected edition of her plays, it
presented her to the public as a novelist. The publication of her collected novels at this date, together with those trappings of authorial
canonization, a preliminary biography and, in the second issue in the
same year, an engraved portrait, is remarkable. The trend for publishing the collected works of playwrights was already well under way,
but no other English author of the seventeenth century was represented by a collected edition of novels. In fact, quite what belonged in
such an edition was not at all clear at the time. Not only was the full
title of the collection, *All the Histories and Novels Written by the Late
Ingenious Mrs. Behn, Entire in One Volume,* deceptive because not all
Behn's stories were included, but some of the work which was included would not in later times strictly be considered prose fiction. As
well as *The Lucky Mistake* and the three novels from *Three Histories,*
Briscoe included the mixed poetry and prose of *La Montre*, which he
reprinted in two parts as *The Lover's Watch* and *The Lady's Looking-
Glass,* and he also printed for the first time 'Love-Letters' (in later
editions 'Love-Letters to a Gentleman'), a work of uncertain status,
placed after the novels in the 1696 edition, and presented more
clearly as Behn's own correspondence in 1698.

---

[75] The novel was published with a head-title 'The First Novel', suggesting that it had
been planned as part of a collection, perhaps of Behn's fiction. See O'Donnell, 153.

[76] *Modern Novels: In XII Volumes,* vol. 1 (London: R. Bentley, 1692). *The Lucky Mistake* is the
fifth and last in the volume, coming after *The Earl of Essex, and Queen Elizabeth, The Duke of
Alancon, The King of Tamaran,* and *Homais, Queen of Tunis.*

The success of *Histories and Novels* ensured sequels. The expanded edition of 1698 added three previously unpublished novels, *Memoirs of the Court of the King of Bantam*, *The Nun, or the Perjured Beauty*, and *The Adventure of the Black Lady*. Briscoe also published a new collection, *Histories, Novels, and Translations*, originally planned as a companion volume to the 1698 *Histories and Novels* but not published until 1700.[77] *Histories, Novels, and Translations* included Behn's two translations from Fontanelle and her *Essay on Translation and Translated Prose*, all first published in 1688; it also included five more novels that had not been published in Behn's lifetime, *The Unfortunate Bride: or, The Blind Lady a Beauty*, *The Unfortunate Happy Lady*, *The Wandring Beauty*, *The Unhappy Mistake: or the Impious Vow Punish'd*, and *The Dumb Virgin*. All except the last of these had been printed in 1698, but they were not issued until 1700.[78] The publication of these substantial collections of fiction indicates the considerable selling power of the name of '*the late Celebrated Mrs*. Behn' at this period (*Works*, iii. 338). Briscoe, who of course had a vested interest in magnifying her contribution, even credited her with single-handedly saving the reputation of the novel, writing in his dedication to *The Wandring Beauty* that '[t]he humour of Novels is so sunk for some Years, that it shews an extraordinary desert in Mrs *Behn*, that they are still in general esteem' (*Works*, iii. 391).

In recent years doubt has been cast on the provenance of the previously unpublished works in these collections of novels, and it has been suggested that they were actually written by Thomas Brown or Charles Gildon to fill out a profitable volume for Samuel Briscoe.[79] I discuss this unsettled question in more detail in the following chapter; here I only want to note that wherever they came from, the new stories made the collections of her fiction much larger, and so had a considerable effect on her eighteenth-century reception. The existence of two big collections meant that Behn the novelist could be seen as a figure equally substantial with Behn the dramatist. The collections went through a number of eighteenth-century editions. The first collection, *Histories and Novels*, proved the most successful, with further editions in 1699, 1700, 1705, 1718, 1722, 1735, and 1751. *Histories, Novels and Translations* was also republished, with probably a second edition

[77] O'Donnell, *Bibliography*, 201.   [78] Ibid. 187, 192.

[79] G. Greer, 'Honest Sam. Briscoe', in Robin Myers and Michael Harris (eds.), *A Genius for Letters: Booksellers and Bookselling from the 16th to the 20th Century* (Winchester: St Paul's Bibliographies; Delaware City: Oak Knoll Press, 1995), 33–47. See also G. Greer, *Slip-Shod Sibyls* (London: Viking, 1995), 196; Todd, *Secret Life*, 315–19.

in 1705, and a third edition published as the second volume of the 1718 edition of *Histories and Novels*.[80] The success of Behn's collected novels probably encouraged publishers to market other novelists in a similar way. Several novelists of the early eighteenth century, including Jane Barker, Mary Davys, and Eliza Haywood, were represented by collected editions of their fiction.

Behn's fiction was also transmitted to eighteenth-century readers in other ways. *The History of the Nun*, printed for A. Baskerville in 1689, was never included in the Briscoe collections, but there was a second edition, now very rare, in 1698.[81] Other fiction was more successful. As well as appearing in *Histories and Novels*, *Oroonoko* continued to be published in separate editions right through the eighteenth century; it was also serialized, and translated into French and German. As we have seen, *Oroonoko* was presented in the 'Memoirs' as Behn's most important work, and the biographical dictionaries repeated and deepened this emphasis by treating *Oroonoko* as source material. I discuss the reception of Behn's most famous novel in more detail in Chapter 6. Behn's longest novel, however, which had enormous influence on eighteenth-century novelists, was never included in the collected editions. *Love-Letters between a Nobleman and his Sister*, published serially in three parts from 1684 to 1687, was one of her most popular works, reaching an eighth edition in 1765, and even being turned into heroic couplets in the 1730s. Though the first part was published anonymously, the dedications to the second and third parts were initialled 'A.B.', and Langbaine named Behn as the author in his 1691 *Account*, so it was generally known to be hers.

Love-Letters long survived its original political occasion, and was, more than any other text, instrumental in establishing Behn in the eighteenth-century mind as an erotic novelist. Delarivier Manley and Eliza Haywood, who both wrote scandal-novels, were seen as Behn's successors. James Sterling put the three women together in an encomium poem he wrote for Eliza Haywood in the 1720s, as 'the fair Triumvirate of Wit', a female version of the famous 'Triumvirate of Wit' consisting of Shakespeare, Fletcher, and Jonson.[82] It was only for

[80] Second edition: O'Donnell, *Bibliography*, 204. Third edition: *Seventeen Histories and Novels Written by the Late Ingenious Mrs. Behn, Compleat in Two Volumes* (London: D. Browne et al., 1718).

[81] *The History of the Nun: Or, The Fair Vow-Breaker* (2nd edn.; London: Tho. Chapman, 1698). I am grateful to Mary Ann O'Donnell for this reference.

[82] Eliza Haywood, *Secret Histories, Novels and Poems* (2nd edn.; London: Dan Browne and S. Chapman, 1725), i. sig. A2.

a brief while that the three names were joined together with praise; soon, they were a byword for noxious fiction. While Behn's fiction continued to be read—a popularity that no doubt fuelled the critical reaction against her—it was increasingly defined as the antithesis of what proper fiction should be. In 1739 one pamphleteer ironically recommended a female university in which the novels of Behn and Manley would be studied: 'for the Education of such as have a peculiar Talent for *Novels*, I would have the Works of the learned Authors Mrs *Behn* and Mrs. *Manly* read as the Standard of that Science; and as Impiety and Smut are considerable Branches of it, I would have those Passages, which are the most remarkable for either, particularly inforced to the fair Students.' He painted a traditional picture of the slatternly learned lady, and put Manley's *New Atalantis*, Rochester's poems, and Behn's novels in her library.[83]

If the moralization of the novel set in rather later than the reform of the stage, it was carried out more fervently, drastically, and thoroughly. The beginnings can be seen in the 1720s, when Penelope Aubin made claims for the moral and religious use of her popular novels, explicitly differentiating them from the immoral works of her contemporaries such as Haywood. As Sarah Prescott has shown, these differences were more in the way the fiction was advertised than in the work itself,[84] but it was an indication of the tone novels would soon need to take. The decisive shift came about with the phenomenal success of Richardson's *Pamela* in 1740, and with the critical redefinition of fiction that soon followed; although, as Downie points out, it was only in retrospect that late eighteenth-century commentators named this redefined form the novel.[85] At the time Richardson was at pains to point out that he was not writing novels or romances, forms he lumped together in contradistinction to his own attempt to create 'a new species of writing, that might possibly turn young people into a course of reading different from the pomp and parade of romance-writing, and dismissing the improbable and marvellous, with which novels generally abound, might tend to promote the cause of religion and virtue'.[86] What was new, for Richardson, about his fiction was certainly not its epistolary form but its moral tendency.

[83] *Man Superior to Woman* (London: T. Cooper, 1739), 51–2, 54.
[84] S. Prescott, 'Penelope Aubin and *The Doctrine of Morality*', *Women's Writing*, 1/1 (1994), 99–112.   [85] Downie, 'The Making of the English Novel', 255–6.
[86] Letter to Aaron Hill, early 1741; in *Selected Letters*, ed. Carroll, 41.

Pamela, and later *Clarissa*, were moral replacements for the inflaming and dangerous novels of the previous age.

Behn, Manley, and Haywood, as Ros Ballaster has shown, were given a crucial negative role in the creation of the Richardsonian domestic novel of sentiment that became such a dominant form in the late eighteenth century. Both Richardson and Fielding, the two authors who did most to reconfigure the terrain of fiction in the middle of the century, used elements of the seduction narrative developed by the earlier writers; for all their derision of these female precursors, they were deeply indebted to them.[87] William Warner has expanded on this theme of Richardson's and Fielding's simultaneous use of and denial of the influence of the fair triumvirate, who became a handy trio to be invoked whenever modern fiction needed to distinguish itself from the immorality belonging to a previous age. Richardson's and Fielding's claims to innovation can be seen in this context as an attempt to distance their work from earlier writers, still current and popular rivals in the marketplace. After Richardson's and Fielding's successful efforts to 'elevate' the novel, the works of Behn, Manley, and Haywood appeared immoral by comparison, and were, in Warner's phrase, 'overwritten' by the later novelists using their themes to different purposes. However, he argues, the later novel could never quite escape the influence it sought to deny: 'overwriting the earlier novel involves a paradoxical double relation: the earlier novel becomes an intertextual support and that which is to be superseded, that which is repeated as well as revised, invoked as it is effaced. Thus "the elevation of the novel" is founded in an antagonistic, but never acknowledged or conscious textual interchange with the earlier novel.'[88] The idea of interchange with an unacknowledged precursor informs Warner's readings of Behn and Richardson, and has influenced my own reading of Richardson as Behn's rejecting 'son' in Chapter 3. Warner acknowledges that gender plays some part in this narrative, writing that the novel after 1750 is defined as moral, English, realist, and masculine, as against earlier fiction of amorous intrigue, dismissed as immoral, unrealistic, French-influenced, and feminine, but on the whole he considers that feminist critics have exaggerated the importance of such patterns. My own reading sees gender as more central. While it is true that Behn, Manley, and Haywood's fiction was addressed to both sexes,

[87] Ballaster, *Seductive Forms*, 196–211.   [88] Warner, *Licensing Entertainment*, 193.

and that those who rejected the triumvirate praised other female writers, we cannot conclude from this that the making of the English novel was a process in which ideologies of gender played a negligible role.[89] The femaleness of the fair triumvirate was a large part of its point for admirers and detractors alike. By linking amorous fiction to these three, eighteenth-century novelists and critics implied the existence of a pre-Richardson, pre-Fielding world in which the novel was under the control of unruly female forces. The coming of Richardson and Fielding thus figured as the overturning of an earlier matriarchy, identified by Patricia Parker as one of the two main kinds of creation myth. The 'elevation' of the novel depended in large part on placing male figures at the centre of the novel's history.

This was not simply an attempt to masculinize a genre perceived as feminine. Richardson and Fielding, as many critics have pointed out, took very different lines on the novel's form, significance, and morality. The work of Fielding can be seen as a kind of masculinization. For him, the novel was given its proper place by reference to Aristotelian precepts, and was really a late addition to an ancient epic form. This placed it in a male-dominated tradition in which the unruly amatory fictions of Behn, Manley, and Haywood appeared as no more than recent aberrations. In terms of the creation myths discussed by Parker, Fielding denies any matriarchal past by reaching beyond immediate predecessors to an ancient past and asserting the primacy of a male tradition. This sense of tradition is one source of his confidence, and his references to Behn's fiction are ironic dismissals: in *Tom Jones* her novels are the bedtime reading of the Irishman Mr Macklachlan, who 'had been instructed by a Friend, that he would find no more effectual Method of recommending himself to the Ladies than the improving his Understanding, and filling his Mind with good Literature'.[90] Richardson is much more anxious on this subject. As his letter to Sarah Chapone, quoted earlier, shows, he saw the notorious trio as a bad influence on a modern world threatened with cultural degeneration. As his own lack of a gentleman's education debarred him from taking a comfortably classical position on the novel, he had a stronger need to proclaim the newness of his fiction. For him recent unruly female fiction was a greater

[89] See Warner, *Licensing Entertainment*, 88–92.

[90] *The History of Tom Jones, a Foundling*, ed. Martin C. Battestin and Fred Bowers (Oxford, 1974), ii. 530 (Book X, ch. 2).

threat. His own work was much more dependent on the fiction of amorous intrigue than was Fielding's, and his attempts to deny the connection were therefore more fervent. His fiction does not masculinize the novel, but rather engineers a takeover of feminine territory, in the process attempting to redefine the feminine itself. Crucial to the effect of his fiction is its concentration on the consciousness of the female protagonists. With this minutely detailed inside view of the virtuous female mind, Richardson succeeded in convincing generations of readers that he understood women better than they understood themselves. After Richardson's success, the kinds of femininity described in Behn's novels, which included such characteristics as lust, rapacious selfishness, and murderous violence, seemed not just immoral but inexplicable: unfeminine, unrealistic, and finally incoherent. I discuss Richardson's relation to Behn more fully in the following chapter. Here, it is necessary just to note that Richardson calls on women to provide the virtuous writing that can counteract the effects of female vice. Having established his work as the source for properly moral fiction, he is keen for good women to write in his tradition. Instead of looking to a masculine past to get beyond Behn, Manley, and Haywood, Richardson deals with these 'mothers of the novel' by vilifying them and then denying their significance. Lilith was evil, and didn't exist anyway; and Richardson is happy to give tender advice to Eve.

So successfully was Richardson positioned as the new novelist, the champion of women and creator of virtuous heroines, that not only were the links between his work and that of his female predecessors forgotten for a hundred and fifty years, but the women novelists after him were understood primarily as his imitators, and their own links with earlier fiction were forgotten too. Indeed, they often contributed to this erasure with attacks on or dismissals of women novelists before Richardson. Since proper femininity was increasingly being defined in Richardsonian terms, to admit to being a woman writer in the tradition of Behn was tantamount to a disavowal of femininity.

One of the most striking instances of the attack on Behn is the way that Eliza Haywood, in the post-Richardson years, redefined her own writing and recreated her narrative persona so as to dissociate herself from the other members of the triumvirate and to capture the new moral market. To do this, like Fielding she adopted the tactic of mentioning Behn's fiction within her own. In *The History of Miss Betsy*

Thoughtless (1751), Haywood's most thorough attempt to write a novel in the new mould, with Richardsonian morality and Fieldingesque irony, Behn is invoked in a clearly derogatory context. Flora Mellasin, the heroine's rival and foil, whose truly loose sexual behaviour contrasts with Betsy's foolish but ultimately innocent flirting, sends the hero, Trueworth, with whom she has had a brief affair, a passionate letter upbraiding him with his inconstancy. Thus she places herself in the category of the abandoned mistress, so common a character in Restoration drama and in seventeenth- and early eighteenth-century amorous fiction. Behn had used elements of the abandoned mistress's rhetoric not only in the *Love-Letters between a Nobleman and his Sister*, but in the 'Love-Letters to a Gentlemen', and for the eighteenth-century reader, the abandoned mistress could be understood not only as a typical Behn character but also as a representative of Behn herself. Flora Mellasin appears to read her in this way as she desperately (and, of course, without success) tries to win her lover back by quoting him the words of 'our English Sappho, in one of her amorous epistles'.[91] A few years later, in *The Invisible Spy* (1755), Haywood invokes *Love-Letters between a Nobleman and his Sister* as a dangerous erotic work implicitly contrasted to the didactic story in which it makes a brief appearance. The narrator observes Marcella, a beauty and a public toast, starting an adulterous intrigue with Fillamour. Love-letters are the agent of her illicit affair, and *Love-Letters* its inspiration. After she has written to Fillamour: 'she call'd her chambermaid, and order'd her to send it, as directed, by a trusty porter;—then threw herself upon a couch,—took the novel of Silvia and Philander,—read a little in it,—sigh'd, and seem'd all dissolv'd in the most tender languishment, when her emissary return'd.' The messenger brings a letter from Fillamour arranging a meeting. The narrator leaves the scene, condemning Marcella as a 'fair libertine' and pronouncing himself 'troubled in my mind that a woman, whose beauty had so much attracted my respect, should prove herself so unworthy of it by her conduct'.[92]

---

[91] E. Haywood, *The History of Miss Betsy Thoughtless* (London: T. Gardner, 1751), iii. 77. I have not traced the couplet Haywood quotes, 'Business you feign, but did you love like me, | I should your most important business be', but the sentiments echo Silvia's in the second part of *Love Letters*: 'for those soft minutes thou hast design'd for Love, and hast dedicated to *Silvia, Philander* shou'd dismiss the dull formalities of rigid business', *Works*, ii. 146.

[92] E. Haywood, *The Invisible Spy. By Explorabilis*, 2 vols. (2nd edn., London: T. Gardner, 1759), i. 23, 24.

Behn's position in histories of the novel, then, is very different from her position in histories of drama. Dramatic and stage histories were being produced earlier, at the time that Restoration drama was still prestigious, so that she was given a respectful treatment which continued to influence later accounts even after her work had fallen from favour. Writers of fiction came more slowly to be accorded the canonical treatment given to dramatists; and by the later eighteenth century, when a canon of 'classical' novels was being formed to be reprinted in collections and discussed in critical histories, Behn's fiction was not only out of favour but being widely used as the prime example of the wrong kind of fiction. This should not obscure its place in the earlier, more sporadic attempts of publishers to establish a core of best-known novels, to be marketed in various forms. Behn's work, as we have seen, took part in the earliest moves to canonize fiction when her collected novels were published; and her fiction was among the first to be published in the serial form that could make an established work cheaply available to a wider reading public. *Love-Letters between a Nobleman and his Sister* was published by T. Read in eighteen weekly instalments in 1735 at 4d per instalment, and instalments of the work were also printed in the twopenny periodical the *Oxford Journal: Or The Tradesman's Intelligencer* in 1736. *Oroonoko* was printed in instalments in the *Oxford Magazine: Or Family Companion* in the same year. Behn's fiction seems to have been the main selling-point of these periodicals, since it is prominently mentioned in the advertisements which were scholars' sources for knowledge of these lost magazines.[93] Even in the early 1750s, *Oroonoko* retained enough status to be used as the first in a planned series of novels by 'some of the best Writers of that Class' to be reprinted by 'Jasper Goodwill' in the *Ladies Magazine, or the Universal Entertainer.* It was printed in sixteen parts in 1753.[94]

The projected series of novels after *Oroonoko* never materialized, however, as the magazine folded. There was another attempt to launch a novel collection in the 1770s when the playwright and

[93] For Read's 1735 edition of *Love-Letters* see R. M. Wiles, *Serial Publication in England Before 1750* (Cambridge: Cambridge University Press, 1957), 216–17 and 297. The *Oxford Journal* and the *Oxford Magazine* of 1736 are apparently no longer extant, but advertisements for them in another lost periodical, *Queen Anne's Weekly Journal*, were recorded by Professor James Sutherland (Wiles, 68–9).

[94] R. D. Mayo, *The English Novel in the Magazines 1740–1815* (Evanston, Ill.: Northwestern University Press, 1962), 211, 404–5.

novelist Elizabeth Griffith edited a *Collection of Novels, Selected and Revised* in three volumes. Griffith reprinted English and French fiction, mainly by women, from the seventeenth and eighteenth centuries and included work from Behn and Haywood, carefully altered to render it more suitable for a polite age. The Behn novels chosen were *Oroonoko* and *Agnes de Castro*. However, a much larger and more influential collection, published a few years later, helped establish the later English novelists as the classics of the form. This was Harrison's *Novelist's Magazine* in twenty-three volumes (1779–89). Harrison reprinted *Robinson Crusoe* but no other Defoe novels, *Gulliver's Travels*, and some of the best-known fiction from Spain and France, from Cervantes to Lesage, Marivaux, and Voltaire. The mainstay of the series was English fiction from the middle of the century, including novels by Richardson, Henry and Sarah Fielding, Smollett, Sterne, Johnson, Lennox, and Frances Sheridan. Behn and Manley were not included at all, and only examples of Haywood's later, post-Richardsonian fiction appeared.[95] While the 1780 *Biographia Britannica* described Behn's novels as her most current work, those whose concern was to market and establish a canon of classical novels were now leaving her out altogether. By the time the early nineteenth-century collections of novels consolidated the English fictional canon it was no surprise that Behn was omitted.[96]

While drama was already the subject of critical and historical accounts by the early eighteenth century, histories of English fiction were not attempted until the later part of the century, and even then they were often in the form of remarks on fiction as part of a larger work. Hugh Blair's *Lectures on Rhetoric and Poetry* (1762), for example, included a treatment of 'Fictitious History'. This undertook to clear away the likely objection that romances and novels were 'too insignificant, to deserve that any particular notice should be taken of them' by pointing out fiction's influence over the minds of the young, an influence that should be channelled in a morally useful way. Restoration novels are here dismissed without naming examples as 'trifling', lacking 'the appearance of moral tendency, or useful instruction', and Defoe, Richardson, and Fielding are praised, Richardson the most highly as being the 'most moral of all our novel

---

[95] See May., *English Novel*, 366–7; Downie, 'The Making of the English Novel', 264.

[96] See Brown, *Institutions of the English Novel*, 179–83, for a discussion of the contents of early 19th c. collections of novels.

writers'.[97] Vicessimus Knox wrote an essay 'On Novel Reading', which also mentioned, in a general way, 'that coarse taste, which was introduced in the reign of Charles the Second', and praised Fielding as worthy of 'a high rank among the classics'.[98] James Beattie traced fiction back to Greek and Latin fables in his essay 'On Fable and Romance', published in his *Dissertations Moral and Critical* (1783). Much concerned with categorization, Beattie divided 'Modern prose fable' into 'Allegorical' and 'Poetical' categories, themselves subdivided into 'Historical' and 'Moral', and 'Serious' and 'Comick', respectively. The English writers he finds significant are Bunyan, Swift, Defoe, Richardson, Smollett, and Fielding; but despite appreciations of these he dismisses most fiction as 'unskilfully written . . . tend[ing] to corrupt the heart, and stimulate the passions'.[99] While historians of drama in the late eighteenth century tended still to include mention of Behn, historians of novel and romance were more concerned to justify their chosen form through careful selection of a few good works, and blanket condemnation of the rest. Behn was excluded.

An exception is Clara Reeve, whose *Progress of Romance* (1785) covered works from ancient romance to recently published novels in the form of a series of imaginary conversations between Euphrasia, Hortensius, and Sophronia. Reeve, whose *Old English Baron* (1777) was one of the first gothic novels, took issue with Beattie for ignoring the majority of fictional works: 'Dr Beattie has walked over the ground, and marked out its boundaries, but he has paid little attention to its various produce, whether of flowers, herbs, or weeds; except a very few works of capital merit (some of which he confesses he has not read through) he consigns all the rest to oblivion.'[100] Reeve's own criticism, by contrast, is that of an avowed enthusiast for fiction, despite her typically late eighteenth-century worry over its moral tendency. She treats a number of writers ignored in other contemporary accounts, including Behn, Manley, and Haywood as well as later writers such as Frances Brooke, Elizabeth Griffith, Henry Brooke, and Susanna Minifie. Women writers figure prominently in her canon, and one of her motivations seems to be to make sure that they are given their due in other areas of writing, too. She takes pains to add

[97] Hugh Blair, *Lectures on Rhetoric and Poetry* (1762), in *Novel and Romance: A Documentary Record*, ed. Ioan Williams (London: Routledge, 1970), 249, 250, 251.
[98] Vicessimus Knox, *Essays Moral and Literary* (London: Charles Dilly, 1779), ii. 189, 187.
[99] James Beattie, 'On Fable and Romance' (1783), in *Novel and Romance*, 327.
[100] Clara Reeve, *The Progress of Romance* (Colchester: W. Keymer, 1785), i, p. viii.

to the list of male critics, 'Hurd, Beattie, Warton, Percy and Mallet', 'a name that will not disgrace the list, a writer of my own sex, Mrs *Dobson* the elegant writer of the *History of the Troubadours* and the *Memoirs of Ancient Chivalry*', and she quotes extensively from Elizabeth Rowe's *History of Joseph*, 'a poem not so much known and valued as it deserves to be' (Reeve, *The Progress*, i, pp. xii, xiv). In the body of the text Euphrasia, who can be considered an embodiment of authorial viewpoint, praises Madame de Genlis, whose educational writing deserves 'public honours' (ii. 99).The dialogue form of Reeve's *Progress* is imitated from Madame de Genlis's *Theatre of Education* (i, p. vii), and is designed by Reeve to create female critical authority and to vindicate a woman's fictional tastes. The main participants in the dialogue are Euphrasia and Hortensius. The male figure takes a consciously masculine attitude, suspicious of romance and preferring Fielding to Richardson, a writer who, along with Addison, he claims, writes particularly for women (i. 135). Euphrasia, who is generally allowed to win in this polite debate, argues for a balanced view, granting pre-eminence both to Fielding and Richardson, but her own warmest praise is reserved for Richardson's novels, and for the works of recent sentimental writers like Frances Brooke.

Reeve's is a woman-centred fictional canon, then, but her definition of the properly feminine is a post-Richardsonian one. Behn, Manley, and the earlier Haywood, figure with French and Spanish romances as pernicious influences on female readers of a previous generation, who were without the benefit of Richardson and later female novelists (i. 138). Whereas Manley gets short shrift from Euphrasia, who forbears to mention the scandalous *New Atalantis* and would prefer not to mention its author (i. 119), Behn is given altogether more favourable treatment, despite her licentiousness. Euphrasia insists that:

Among our early Novel-writers we must reckon Mrs *Behn*.—There are strong marks of genius in all this lady's works, but unhappily, there are some parts of them, very improper to be read by, or recommended to virtuous minds, and especially to youth.—She wrote in an age, and to a court of licentious manners, and perhaps we ought to ascribe to these causes the loose turn of her stories.—Let us do justice to her merits, and cast the veil of compassion over her faults.   (i. 117–18)

Hortensius asks suspiciously, 'Are you not partial to the sex of this Genius?— when you excuse in her, what you would not to a man?' Euphrasia admits, 'Perhaps I may, and you must excuse me if I am so, especially as this lady had many fine and admirable qualities, besides her genius for writing' (i. 118). Behn's epitaph is quoted, and Euphrasia adds a reminder that she is the source of Southerne's tragedy: 'it was from her story of that illustrious African, that Mr *Southern* wrote that play, and the most affecting parts of it are taken literally from her' (i. 118–9). However, she stops short of recommending that Hortensius actually read the author she is defending.

Early in the nineteenth century, Anna Letitia Barbauld, writing in the introductory essay to her collection of novels, took up Reeve's point that Behn should be remembered, if only because of Southerne's play,[101] but did not reprint her. John Dunlop included a few remarks on Behn in his *History of Fiction* (1814). He saw her as an immoral Restoration writer, and quoted Richard Steele to the effect that she 'understood the practic part of love better than the speculative'. He singled out *Oroonoko* as her 'most interesting' and unobjectionable work and as Southerne's source.[102] Scott, whose *Lives of the Novelists*, first published as biographical prefaces in *Ballantyne's Novelist's Library* (1821–4), did for fiction writers what Johnson's *Lives of the Poets* had done for poets a generation earlier, did not include Behn in his canon. An interesting light on his thoughts about canonmaking shines from an anecdote he told Lady Louisa Stuart about his great-aunt, Mrs Keith, borrowing Behn's novels from him and then returning them, protesting that she could not get through the first novel (which, assuming the volume she was reading was *Histories and Novels*, would be *Oroonoko*):

'But is it not', she said, 'a very odd thing that I, an old woman of eighty and upwards, sitting alone, feel myself ashamed to read a book which, sixty years ago, I have heard read aloud for the amusement of large circles, consisting of the first and most creditable society in London?' This, of course, was owing to the gradual improvement of the national taste and delicacy.[103]

Scott related this incident in 1826,[104] but it is not clear how long before this Mrs Keith had returned Behn's novels to him. Her 'sixty

[101] A. L. Barbauld, *The British Novelists* [1810], (2nd edn.; London: F. C. and J. Rivington, 1820), i. 35.

[102] John Dunlop, *History of Fiction* (2nd edn.; Edinburgh: James Ballantyne & Co., 1816), iii. 454.

[103] John Gibson Lockhart, *Memoirs of the Life of Sir Walter Scott* (Edinburgh: Robert Cadell, 1842), 466.

[104] *The Letters of Sir Walter Scott*, ed. H. J. C. Grierson (London: Constable and Co., 1936), x. 95.

years ago' may refer to the 1750s or 1760s; at any rate, taken alongside the evidence of new editions of Behn's fiction in those decades,
it suggests that the Richardsonian dismissal of Behn's fiction did not
take immediate effect.

Behn was never accorded a significant place in the early histories
of the novel, except as a negative example of outmoded and immoral
Restoration writing; and this in spite of the fact that there was general agreement that *Oroonoko* was her most significant work. This one
novel was often and favourably mentioned in the late eighteenth century, but was so closely connected in critics' minds with Southerne's
stage version that it was not really considered as part of a tradition of
fiction. By the early nineteenth century Behn was a rarely read,
unperformed, but not forgotten writer. Her drama, though no longer
suitable for the stage, was accorded historical significance, and her
poetry was even beginning a minor renaissance as its lyrical beauties
were noted by some of the Romantics; but her fiction, sharply condemned in the process of establishing the new moral novel, had been
actively written out of the novel's history. Yet it is through her fiction
that she exercised her strongest influence on eighteenth-century writers. It is to the question of Behn as an influence that we turn in the
following chapters.

PART II

Influences

3

The Sons of Behn

APHRA BEHN'S work was certainly a source of inspiration for later writers. In the 1690s traces of her influence can be found in a number of plays. D'Urfey may have been influenced by *The Lucky Chance* when he portrayed a sympathetic adulteress in *Bussy d'Ambois* (1691).[1] Congreve is said to have acknowledged that the astrologer, Foresight, in *Love for Love*, owed a debt to Baliardo in Behn's *Emperor of the Moon*, though the likeness is very general,[2] and Catherine Trotter used Behn's translation of S. B. de Brillac's *Agnes de Castro* for her play of the same name (1696). In the eighteenth century playwrights continued to draw on her work. Edward Young's *The Revenge* (1721), partly based on her *Abdelazer*, became a popular tragedy on the London stage, toured the provinces, went to Dublin, and continued to be performed in the nineteenth century.[3] Novelists drew on her fiction, too, notably Jane Barker, who used *The History of the Nun* in *The Lining of the Patch-Work Screen* (1726). Dramatists were still drawing on Behn in the later years of the century. Her *Young King* was probably the source for part of the plot of John Hoole's *Cleonice, Princess of Bithynia: a Tragedy* (1775). More definitely and extensively, Hannah Cowley based her comedy *A School for Greybeards*, which proved a controversial play at Drury Lane in 1786, on *The Lucky Chance*. Behn's influence also travelled abroad, and Cathrin Brockhaus's current research indicates that she was probably being adapted for performance in Mannheim

[1] Derek Hughes, *English Drama 1660–1700* (Oxford: Clarendon Press, 1996), 373.

[2] Wilkes, *A General View of the Stage*, 59.

[3] It has also been suggested on the basis of very general similarities that Rowe's *The Biter* (1704) was influenced by *The Emperor of the Moon*: see Derek Cohen, 'Nicholas Rowe, Aphra Behn, and the Farcical Muse', *Papers on Language and Literature*, 15/1(1979), 383–95. In some cases Behn's work is one link in a chain of adaptation: Christopher Bullock's *A Woman's Revenge: or, A Match in Newgate* (1715) was an alteration of *The Revenge*, a play that is probably by Behn and which is itself an adaptation of Marston's *The Dutch Courtesans*. The chain lengthened when Bullock's play was turned into *Love and Revenge; or, The Vintner Outwitted: an Opera*, played at the Haymarket in 1729.

in the 1780s.[4] Most significant as an adapter of Behn, however, is the dramatist Thomas Southerne. Behn's fiction provided part of the plot for his *Sir Anthony Love* (1690);[5] and his two most successful plays, *The Fatal Marriage; or the Innocent Adultery* (1694) and *Oroonoko* (1695), were based on stories by her.

Yet Behn is not generally seen as an influential figure in the eighteenth century. In part, this is because the widespread idea of her infamous eighteenth-century reputation has inhibited literary historians from recognizing the continuing life of her works; but there is another, more general reason. Our current ideas of literary influence are still deeply entangled in ancient metaphors of literary genealogy within which women's influence cannot be articulated in the same terms as men's. In the seventeenth and eighteenth centuries, these genealogical metaphors were put to active use in the construction of a national literary tradition, in which women authors were generally placed as peripheral to the significant lines of descent. Because literary genealogies reproduced the patrilineal structures of kinship, naming, and inheritance found in society at large, it was difficult to understand women as possible influences or founders of traditions. The way to become understood as a significant part of the literary tradition was to become known as the father of poetic sons, as Ben Jonson knew well when he encouraged the young poets around him to call themselves 'sons of Ben'. This chapter explores the connections between notions of influence, generation, and genealogy in the construction of literary traditions, and asks: what would it mean to be able, by the addition of the odd 'h', to talk about the sons of Behn?

Undoubtedly Behn was a source to many eighteenth-century writers, but in current thinking this does not make her an influence. Harold Bloom, explaining his own very influential theory of influence, insists that by poetic influences 'I continue *not* to mean the passing on of images and ideas from earlier to later poets'. The relation

---

[4] In the Reiss-Museum Mannheim, there is a ninety-one-page MS of 'Die eheliche Probe. Ein Lustspiel in einem Aufzug nach dem Englischen der Miss Ben' ('The marital test. A comedy in one act after the English of Miss Ben'). The play, an adaptation by Wolfgang von Dahlberg, was produced in Mannheim in 1788 (Cathrin Brockhaus, personal communication, July 1999).

[5] R. Jordan and H. Love, introduction to *Sir Anthony Love*, in *The Works of Thomas Southerne* (Oxford: Clarendon Press, 1988), i. 163–4.

of influence between poets is a more mysterious, less visible affair, not to be pinned down to phrases passed on:

Poetic influence, in the sense I give to it, has almost nothing to do with the verbal resemblances between one poet and another. Hardy, on the surface, scarcely resembles Shelley, his prime precursor, but then Browning, who resembles Shelley even less, was yet more fully Shelley's ephebe than even Hardy was. . . . Poets need not *look* like their fathers.

Clearly poetic fatherhood is here conceived as a spiritual relation, quite distinct from the transmission of mere verbal material. The importance of maintaining this matter–spirit distinction is evident in the contempt Bloom expresses for 'those carrion-eaters of scholarship, the source hunters', whose project may at first seem to resemble his own, but who show by their obsession with matter, and dead matter at that, that they do not understand the living spirit that passes between poets.[6] Bloom's is an extreme position, and few critics dissociate source-matter and influence so sharply. However, his distinction between literary matter and literary spirit remains a familiar one today, and is crucial to an understanding of the way literary genealogies were built up in Behn's time and before.

Several studies have shown that during the Renaissance in England writers were engaged in the construction of a national canon of poets, created through a poetic lineage reaching back to the ancients but founded in England with Sidney, and traceable through Spenser, Jonson, and Milton.[7] In discussions of this lineage, it is often remarked that it is essentially a fiction, and that those creating it did so by suppressing evidence of influence in the material sense, and claiming less visible forms of influence according to desire. John Guillory claims that in terms of 'verbal echoes', Milton was more influenced by Shakespeare than by Spenser, but that he chose to obscure his relations with Shakespeare and to build the fictional line of Spenser to Milton.[8] Raphael Falco emphasizes the fictionality, what he calls the 'forgery', of the line which Renaissance English writers, ignoring Chaucer and Gower, traced back from themselves

---

[6] Harold Bloom, *A Map of Misreading* (New York: Oxford University Press, 1975), 3, 20, 17.

[7] John Guillory, *Poetic Authority: Spenser, Milton and Literary History* (New York: Columbia University Press, 1993); R. Helgerson, *Self-Crowned Laureates: Spenser, Jonson, Milton and the Literary System* (Berkeley: University of California Press, 1983); Raphael Falco, *Conceived Presences: Literary Genealogy in Renaissance England* (Amherst, Mass.: University of Massachusetts Press, 1994).   [8] Guillory, *Poetic Authority*, pp. x, 74.

to the Continental tradition of Dante, Ariosto, and Petrarch. The adoption of these forebears involved, he says, 'the suppression of their legitimate lingual genealogy', or, we might say, of their relation to writers in their mother-tongue.

This forged line, Falco emphasizes, has since been accepted, and 'the myth of literary descent has transformed itself into literary history'.[9] Literary history can then be seen as made up through a line of fathers and sons who are related less by influence in the sense of material transmission, than by the act of claiming relationship. As John Guillory argues, 'the concept of acknowledgement can be usefully distinguished from "influence" in literary history'. What is important is not 'the story of Spenser's influence on Milton, but of their respective acknowledgements. . . . those maneuvers of invocation and recognition by which an author becomes an *auctor*.'[10] These discussions of the willed nature of literary genealogies already suggest that women's place in them, if it exists at all, will be problematic. The father–son trope is not just a side-effect of the male near-monopoly of writing at the time, but affects the way the literary line is understood. Literary fatherhood, like biological fatherhood in the days before DNA testing, is difficult to determine by material signs; it is a matter of claim and acknowledgement.

During the seventeenth century, some writers were concerned to establish their status as fathers in a literary line. In his later years— and after the deaths of his real children—Ben Jonson surrounded himself with a group of poets who identified themselves as the 'Tribe of Ben'. They met in the Apollo Room of the Devil and St Dunstan tavern, where they seem to have enacted rites in which new members were initiated as Jonson's 'sons'. Poems by Jonson, welcoming a new son to the tribe, and by sons thanking him for adopting them, were published. The group of sons, it has been argued, helped Jonson control the interpretation of his works, as part of his 'prolonged, and astonishingly successful, effort to establish a proprietary claim to his own writings', an effort that included his careful supervision of publication and culminated in the appearance of his *Works*.[11] The existence of Jonson's 'sons' played a part in establishing him as a sig-

[9] Falco, *Conceived Presences*, 2, 4.   [10] Guillory, *Poetic Authority*, p. x.

[11] David Riggs, *Ben Jonson: A Life* (Cambridge, Mass., and London: Harvard University Press, 1989), 352. For a discussion of the meetings of the 'Tribe of Ben', and an analysis of Jonson's 'An Epistle Answering to One that Asked to be Sealed of the Tribe of Ben' as an initiation into a cult, see Riggs, 285–7.

nificant author. Although the Tribe of Ben themselves, men like Thomas Randolph, James Howell, Shackerley Marmion, and William Cartwright, did not gain positions of great literary prestige, Jonson's paternal status was extended and generalized after his death, so that the literary-historical line was built up through men identifying themselves as his sons. In Dryden's essay *Of Dramatick Poesie* (1668) he is referred to simply as 'Father *Ben*'.[12]

In the late seventeenth century, this concern for poetic lineage continued with variations. There was a longer sense of the native tradition, not just because it was now further back to Sidney but because of a growing national confidence, expressed and fostered in descriptions of an English canon reaching back to Chaucer, who was rediscovered as a father, and translated for a modern audience by Dryden.[13] There was a particular stress on the trope of the poetic throne. Literary succession and royal succession were repeatedly linked, and the laureateship was seen as the poetic counterpart to the king's crown. Dryden, the key figure in literary succession at this time, was concerned to establish his place both as a son and a father. In his work there is a recurrent worry about proper, legitimate lineal succession and the dangers of its disruption, which has an obvious political resonance in the period of the exclusion crisis and the years following the 1688 revolution. So in 'Mackflecknoe' Dryden mocks Shadwell's pretensions to being one of the sons of Ben Jonson and makes him the son of Flecknoe instead, claiming the title of Jonson's legitimate heir for himself.[14] Years later, in a verse-epistle written as a tribute to William Congreve's comedy, *The Double-Dealer*, he is more concerned with establishing his own succession. Complaining that the offices of poet laureate and historiographer royal, once held by him, have now gone to Nahum Tate and Thomas Rymer respectively, he names Congreve the true son who should have inherited his honours:

---

[12] *The Works of John Dryden* (Berkeley: University of California Press, 1967–89), xvii. 21.

[13] See the discussion of 'The Making of a Modern Canon' in Howard D. Weinbrot, *Britannia's Issue: The Rise of British Literature from Dryden to Ossian* (Cambridge: Cambridge University Press, 1993), 114–41.

[14] See the discussion in Jennifer Brady, 'Dryden and the Negotiations of Literary Succession and Precession', in E. Miner and J. Brady (eds.), *Literary Transmission and Authority: Dryden and Other Writers* (Cambridge: Cambridge University Press, 1993), 27–54.

> Oh that your Brows my Lawrel had sustain'd,
> Well had I been Depos'd, if You had reign'd!
> The Father had descended for the Son;
> For only You are lineal to the Throne.[15]

Dryden acted as the younger writer's mentor and champion, and named him his successor at the age of 23.[16]

That the various literary lines constructed from Sidney's time to Dryden's are based on a patrilineal model of inheritance is so obvious that it has been largely taken for granted in discussions of poetic authority and canon-formation. Yet because this model has had devastating effects on the reception of women writers in the English literary tradition, it is worth drawing out its implications. It assimilates poetic inheritance to the transmission both of name (the surname, or in the poetic line, the poetic name or fame) and property through the father to the son, with the mother considered as a means of transmission, not passing on anything of her own. When poetic identity is understood as a patrilineal inheritance, women writers have no clear place in the line of succession. As April Alliston argues:

In the terms of the patriline model, the original, definitive other, as the very word *patriline* and its cognates inform us, is woman—specifically, woman as (m)other. . . . In this double, synchronic and diachronic representation of literary tradition as patrimony and patrie, women's writings are both exiled and disinherited; they become everywhere and always improper, lacking the real property that establishes proper place.[17]

Alliston's concern is with French and English women's novels of the eighteenth century, but her observations have relevance too for female writers in all genres in the late seventeenth and early eighteenth centuries. It is not that women are not accepted at all as writers, but that they are not seen to inherit and pass on a place in the main literary tradition.

One example of the failure or refusal to incorporate women as creators into literary succession can be seen in a poem by Alexander

---

[15] 'To My Dear Friend Mr Congreve, On His Comedy, call'd, *The Double-Dealer*', *The Works of John Dryden*, iv. 433. James Winn discusses Dryden's attack on Tate and Rymer, and his creation of himself as 'Congreve's poetic father' in this poem in *John Dryden and his World* (New Haven and London: Yale University Press, 1987), 464–7.

[16] Brady, 'Dryden and Negotiations', 49.

[17] April Alliston, *Virtue's Faults* (Stanford, Calif.: Stanford University Press, 1996), 8.

Oldys, 'An Ode, By Way of Elegy, on the Universally Lamented Death of the Incomparable Mr. Dryden'. This poem, published in 1700, was one of many written soon after Dryden's death to mourn his passing and to celebrate and consolidate his position as the next great poet to join a long succession of native writers immortalized by their verse. The souls of dead English poets welcome Dryden into heaven. Their shared poetic identity transcends the political differences that lay between them in earthly life, and helps forge a national identity. Dryden is welcomed into heaven by Waller, Milton (who says his verse atoned for his hideous crime of rebellion, and got him into heaven), Rochester (now a happy convert to the love of God), Buckingham, Orrery, Davenant, Denham, Suckling, Shakespeare, Jonson, Beaumont, Fletcher, Drayton, and —as the culmination of all these—'*Chaucer*, the *Mighty'st Bard* of yo're'. In stanza 6 Dryden's entry into heaven is crowned with Chaucer's paternal greeting. Chaucer

> Caress'd him next whil'st his delighted Eye,
> Express'd his Love, and thus his Tongue his Joy,
>   Was I, when erst Below (said he)
>   In hopes so Great a Bard to see:
> As *Thou my Son*, Adopted into *me*,
> And all this *Godlike Race*, some equal ev'n to Thee!
>   O! tis enough.

It is at this point that the only two women enter the scene, an afterthought or a surplus. They are Katherine Philips and Aphra Behn, the usual two examples of female poetic skill we find in poems at this date:

> Here soft *Orinda* came,
> And Spritely *Afra*. Muses Both on Earth;
> Both Burn'd here with a Bright Poetic flame,
> Which to their happiness *above* gave birth;
> Their Charming Songs, his entertainment close,
> The *mighty Bard* then smiling, Bow'd and 'rose.[18]

This poem has been read as indicating the generous breadth of the English poetic tradition being formed at this time. 'The order of the welcomers suggests the presumed disorder of the ode; but it also

---

[18] Alexander Oldys, *An Ode* (London, 1700; rpr. in *Drydeniana XIV. On the Death of Dryden* (New York and London: Garland Publishing, Inc., 1975)), 6.

suggests the absence of rigid generic or linear distinctions in a chorus rich enough for all great voices';[19] and, we might add, the inclusion of any women at all emphasizes that breadth. However, Afra and Orinda are included on significantly different terms from the men. Just like Milton, they have achieved happiness in heaven on account of their poetry, but their position there is not that of the souls of male poets. That they enter late in the poem, after Chaucer's reference to the 'Godlike Race' surrounding Dryden, implicitly excludes them from that 'Race'. They are muses—inspirations more than creators, characterized by feminine attractions: soft, spritely, charming. They entertain. The last stanza of the ode refers to the empty heavenly thrones awaiting a number of poets still living—Wycherley, Congreve, Southerne, Tate, Garth, Addison, Stepney, Prior, Dennis (but no living women).[20] The effect of all this is implicitly to place women poets out of the running for poetic succession. It is not that Oldys does not mean to honour Afra and Orinda. He attributes literary immortality to them. It is that the readily available terms for honouring female poets do not place them as full members of the poetic race. They are not sons.

The patrilineal model of literary tradition not only made women peripheral to the transmission of name and property, but encouraged a view of the essential masculinity of creative forces. Thinking of writers as fathers, whether of their works or of their literary successors, brought into play people's ideas about the roles of the sexes in reproduction. For a long time these had been dominated by Aristotle's theory that the mother was essentially infertile, contributing only matter to the growth of the embryo. The form and life were provided by the father's semen; he was the true parent. With this theory, Aristotle put forward the hierarchized oppositions between male form and female matter, male spirit and female body, which strongly influenced ideas about sexual characteristics long after his ideas about the reproductive process had been challenged. The main rival theory, up to the sixteenth century, was that of Galen, who held that both male and female contributed seed; but as he characterized the female seed as weaker, his ideas did not disturb the Aristotelian sexual hierarchy. From the sixteenth to the nineteenth centuries, scientific investigations led to a series of new reproductive theories. Most of them agreed in attributing greater reproductive power to the

[19] Howard D. Weinbrot, *Britannia's Issue*, 137.   [20] Oldys, *An Ode*, 8.

male; the exception, the ovist theory in which the embryo existed complete within the ovum, was the object of satire. Some of the new discoveries reinforced the notion that the father's role was spiritual, the mother's only material. William Harvey, in his *De Generatione Animalium* (1651), believed that 'the sperm never reached the uterus physically, but rather acted from afar to determine embryonic development. . . . In metaphoric language he compared the male semen to a magnet that attracts from a distance, like a star that exerts a "spiritual" influence on human beings.'[21]

Throughout the seventeenth century, then, the dominant understanding of fatherhood was that it was the chief life-giving force. The discourse of poetic fatherhood reflects this, crediting the literary father with a transmission of spirit that also reminds us of the religious connotations of this metaphor: the powerful poet passing on his spirit to his sons is analogous to God the Father. William Cartwright thought it unlikely that Jonson's poetic spirit would be passed on to surviving writers: that '*divine* | Free filling *spirit*' of poesy took flight when Jonson died; but he offered his own verse, all its own life owing to Jonson, as a tribute to his godlike mentor:

> *Father* of *Poets*, though *thine* owne great day
> Struck from *thy selfe*, scornes that a weaker *ray*
> Should twine in *lustre* with it: yet my *flame*,
> Kindled from *thine*, flies upwards tow'rds *thy* Name.[22]

Poetic fatherhood, in fact, can be seen as doubly spiritual: if biological fatherhood is spiritual in relation to motherhood, poetic fatherhood, a metaphor founded on mental, not bodily connection, is more spiritual than physical fatherhood. In the construction of literary lineages, biological family connections may play a part; Sir William Davenant certainly felt so when he claimed to be

---

[21] Maryanne Cline Horowitz, 'The "Science" of Embryology Before the Discovery of the Ovum', in Marilyn J. Boxer and Jean H. Quataert (eds.), *Connecting Spheres: Women in the Western World, 1500 to the Present* (New York and Oxford: Oxford University Press, 1987), 90. I am indebted to Horowitz's study for my account of reproductive theories. See also the discussion in Londa Schiebinger, *The Mind Has No Sex? Women in the Origins of Modern Science* (Cambridge, Mass., and London: Harvard University Press, 1989), 178–80. Christine Battersby discusses the implications of the Aristotelian view of reproduction for the gendering of creativity, especially the notion of genius, in *Gender and Genius: Towards a Feminist Aesthetics* (London: Women's Press, 1989), 28–33.

[22] William Cartwright, 'In the memory of the most Worthy Benjamin Jonson' (1638); in D. H. Craig (ed.), *Ben Jonson: The Critical Heritage 1599–1798* (London and New York: Routledge, 1990), 199.

Shakespeare's illegitimate son. Usually, however, it is understood that the real genealogy does not elevate a writer as the chosen, imaginary one does. This can be seen in the difference between Dryden's reactions to the work of his chosen son, Congreve, and to one of his real sons, whose play *The Husband his own Cuckold* 'by Mr. John Dryden jun.' appeared in 1696, three years after Dryden senior had publicly hailed young Congreve as his heir. In his dedication to Sir Robert Howard, his uncle, John Dryden junior claimed a family connection with poetry, but intimated that it was an uneasy one, making him 'unluckily a Poet by descent'.[23] The choice of his uncle, who had been on bad terms with his father, as 'Foster-Father' to his play, may have been unwelcome to Dryden senior, who made it clear in his preface to the play that he had not at first wanted to encourage his son's work: 'being the Essay of a young unexperienc'd Author; to confess the truth, I thought it not worthy of [the stage]'.[24] Howard's patronage, and his revisions, did away with Dryden senior's objections to the play, and James Winn credits this episode with bringing about a reconciliation between Howard and Dryden;[25] but still, Dryden's preface reminded Dryden junior of the superior literary value of the fictional genealogy: 'both my Son and I are extreamly oblig'd to my dear Friend Mr *Congreve*, whose excellent Prologue was one of the greatest ornaments of the Play'.[26]

DAUGHTERS, FATHERS, AND MOTHERS: WOMEN IN THE FAMILY LINE

Faced with a developing patrilineal tradition which excluded them, women writers and their friends and encomiasts had to search for ways of asserting the identity and significance of female creativity. Given the strength of the father–son model of literary inheritance, it is not surprising that they sought to express women's place in literary tradition in genealogical tropes. Like the Renaissance men looking to poets of past ages and other countries to find their fathers, seventeenth-century women writers invented their own lines of inheritance, looking back frequently to Sappho, the Greek proof that women could write. If male writers started out as sons, it seemed to follow that women writers should find their place as daughters, and

[23] John Dryden, jun., 'To the Right Honourable Sir Robert Howard, &c', *The Husband his own Cuckold* (London, 1696), sig. A2ʳ.
[24] 'The Preface of Mr Dryden, to his Son's Play', *The Husband his own Cuckold*, sig. A3ᵛ.
[25] Winn, *John Dryden and His World*, 482.   [26] *The Husband his own Cuckold*, sig. A4ᵛ.

women poets were discussed as the daughters of poetic fathers and poetic mothers, and sometimes even seen as the source of a poetic succession themselves. Such depictions were affected by the association of the mother with matter, and the father with spirit and life; but to some extent, the disabling connotations of these ideas could be overcome by the fictionalization and spiritualization inherent in the metaphor of poetic succession. Even the female might be imagined as spiritual in poetry.

Poems on female poets can often be seen struggling with the mixed spiritual and physical senses of reproduction. One well-known and influential encomium poem, Abraham Cowley's ode to Katherine Philips, tackles head-on the notion of women's inferior reproductive role:

> Woman, as if the Body were their Whole,
>   Did that, and not the Soul
>   Transmit to their posteritie;
>   If in it somtime they conceiv'd,
>   Th'abortive Issue never liv'd.

Philips has changed all this: she transmits the soul to her posterity, here seen as the poems. As the 'mother' of her poems she is compared to Cybele, the 'great Mother' of the 'happy Gods above'. In a new twist on the idea of reproduction as the male cultivation of female earth, Orinda takes on a hermaphrodite role, and tills her own field: a field, moreover, of spirit:

> 'Twere shame and pity, *Orinda*, if in thee
> A Spirit so rich, so noble, and so high
>   Should unmanur'd, or barren lye.
> But thou industriously hast sow'd and till'd
>   The fair, and fruitful field;
> And 'tis a strange increase, that it does yield.

Highly though Orinda is praised, it is always as an exception amongst women. Cowley employs the well-known trope which figures writing a poem as childbirth: applied to a woman poet, the metaphor seems more literal, and Orinda's childbirth also points out her difference from other women because she escapes 'th'ancient curse to Womankind, | Thou bring'st not forth with pain'.[27] In keeping with

---

[27] Abraham Cowley, 'Ode. *On* Orinda's *Poems*', in *The Works of Mr Abraham Cowley* (8th edn.; London: Henry Herringman, 1693), 'Verses written on several occasions', 3.

this, Cowley invokes possible poetic mother-figures for Orinda only to dismiss them: the muses are a fiction; Sappho did not have Orinda's shining virtue. There is the hint, though, that Orinda might transmit an inheritance to later women poets: the Amazons, watching over her from their places in Elysium, hope that the empire of wit will be 'setled in their Sex by her'.[28] It was a hint taken up by many later women writers eager to claim Orinda's inheritance.

Dryden's ode written to commemorate the poet and painter Anne Killigrew looks back to Sappho, but it also takes a different line, seeking to attach Killigrew to poetic tradition as the daughter of her father. Asking where Anne's poetic mind came from, Dryden offers two possible answers: either hers was a reincarnation of a pre-existing soul, or her mind was acquired in the more usual way, by 'Traduction' (derivation from ancestry). If she was a pre-existing soul, she has run through all the Greek and Latin poets and ended as a reincarnation of Sappho: her mind 'was that *Sappho* last, which once it was before'. If she derived her mind from her ancestry then it came from her father, Henry Killigrew: 'Thy Father was transfus'd into thy Blood: | So wert thou born into the tuneful strain'.[29] In these lines Killigrew's poetic inheritance is construed as a bodily inheritance from the Killigrew family. Such a literal inheritance, as we have seen, is not so honourable, in terms of poetic lineage, as the metaphorical inheritance passed from poetic father to poetic son.

Dryden's tribute to Killigrew does allow her some place in that more real because metaphorical poetic kinship. She is akin to the souls of Greek and Latin poets, a reincarnation of Sappho; closer to home she is likened to Orinda; Dryden's phrasing suggests her affinities with Pindar and Cowley.[30] I agree with those who read the ode's intentions 'straight'; the praise is extravagant, according to the conventions of the form he is using, but not deliberately ironic.[31] Nevertheless there is a particular placing of the female poet because of her skewed relation to patrilineal tradition. The invocation of her bodily father overwhelms her poetic identity, making it seem just a function of his 'blood'; the references to a more metaphorical poetic

---

[28] Cowley, 'Verses', 4.
[29] 'To the Pious Memory Of the Accomplisht Young Lady Mrs Anne Killigrew', in *The Works of John Dryden*, iii. 110.   [30] Weinbrot, *Britannia's Issue*, 360.
[31] Arguments against reading Dryden's poem as an ironic attack on its subject can be found in Weinbrot, *Britannia's Issue*, 359–72, and Laura Runge, *Gender and Language in British Literary Criticism, 1660–1790* (Cambridge: Cambridge University Press, 1997), 73–8.

lineage do not entirely redress the balance because she is not seen as the heir to a metaphorical father.

A bolder, more metaphorical use of the father–daughter line is found in Behn's poem to Anne Wharton, 'To Mrs. W. On her excellent Verses (Writ in Praise of some I had made on the Earl of Rochester) Written in a Fit of Sickness'. The familial relation between Wharton and the dead Rochester (Wharton was Rochester's niece) underlies the poem's governing conceit that his soul has been revived in Wharton and his spirit speaks in her verse.

> It [Rochester's phantom/Wharton's poem] did advance,
>   and with a Generous Look,
> To me Addrest, to worthless me it spoke:
> With the same wonted Grace my Muse it prais'd,
> With the same Goodness did my Faults Correct:
> And Careful of the Fame himself first rais'd,
> Obligingly it School'd my loose neglect.
> The soft, the moving Accents soon I knew
> The gentle Voice made up of Harmony;
> Through the known Paths of my glad Soul it flew;
> I knew it straight, it could no others be,
> 'Twas not allied but very very he.

(*Works*, i. 57)

Wharton's poem is seen as a continuation of the kind 'schooling' Behn claims that Rochester offered her. She doesn't mention that any advice Rochester gave was unlikely to have been really in the spirit of Wharton's, which exhorts Behn to 'Scorn meaner Theams, declining low desire, | And bid your Muse maintain a Vestal Fire'.[32] Through this presentation of Rochester as mentor, Behn claims a legacy from him too. As Warren Chernaik has recently argued of this poem, 'both Behn and Wharton are depicted as poetic heirs to Rochester— by conscious discipleship in one case and by a transformative inspiration on the other'.[33] I would add that while the 'transformative inspiration' whereby Rochester appears in Wharton's verse accords her all the obvious glory, as befits her familial relation with him, her social superiority to Behn, and the conventions of encomium verse,

---

[32] Anne Wharton, 'To Mrs. A. Behn, On what she Writ of the Earl of Rochester', in Greer *et al.* (eds.), *Kissing the Rod*, 251.

[33] Warren Chernaik, *Sexual Freedom in Restoration Literature* (Cambridge: Cambridge University Press, 1995), 171.

the putatively humbler 'conscious discipleship' which Behn claims is
much closer to the kind of mentoring relationship being celebrated
between Ben Jonson and his 'sons' and between Dryden and
Congreve. To Wharton's suggestion that Behn should become a new
and moralized Sappho,[34] Behn responds by claiming a place in a
modern, masculine, and unmoral line.

Behn's attempt to be seen as the heir of men is relatively
unusual among women writers. More common is the construction
of an alternative, separate female line of succession, generally
beginning with Sappho for the ancient, and Orinda for the native
modern, ancestor. After Behn's death in 1689, she became (sometimes as 'Afra', sometimes under her poetic pseudonym 'Astrea')
Orinda's usual companion, invoked by the new women writers
emerging in the 1690s. Playwrights like Delarivier Manley and
Catharine Trotter, poets like Sarah Fyge Egerton, and the author
of the *Essay in Defence of the Female Sex* all look back to her as
an example. Male encomiasts collaborated in creating a female
line of succession.

This female genealogy is characterized by great emphasis on the
throne imagery also being used in the male genealogy. This allows for
a few swipes at the French for their 'Salique law' preventing female
participation in royal succession, and an implicit celebration of the
more inclusive English succession laws. It also allows poets to
imagine a rival female empire, established in defiance of or even at
the cost of the male one. In this trope, female poets do not inherit
from men but overthrow them, and their poetry is presented
explicitly as a rebellion against female subordination. An example of
this is Delarivier Manley's poem 'To the Author of Agnes de Castro',
published with Trotter's play in 1696:

> *Orinda,* and the fair *Astrea* gone,
> Not one was found to fill the Vacant Throne:
> Aspiring Man had quite regain'd the Sway,
> Again had Taught us humbly to Obey;
> Till you (Natures third start, in favour of our Kind)
> With stronger Arms, their Empire have disjoyn'd,
> And snatcht a Lawrel which they thought their Prize,
> Thus Conqu'ror, with your Wit, as with your Eyes.
> Fired by the bold Example, I would try

[34] *Kissing the Rod,* 251.

To turn our Sexes weaker Destiny.
O! How I long in the Poetick Race,
To loose the Reins, and give their Glory Chase;
For thus Encourag'd, and thus led by you,
Methinks we might more Crowns than theirs Subdue.[35]

Evidently, a female line of poetic succession is even more of a 'forgery' than Falco claims the male Sidney–Spenser–Jonson one to be. A male line is at least based on the model of inheritance—father to son—operating in the economic sphere. A female line is based on a model which does not transmit name or property in a patrilineal society. There is something radically bogus about claiming Sappho, most of whose work is lost, as the ancestor of a late seventeenth-century poet like Behn, who, with small Latin and less Greek, would not have been able to read it anyway. The fictionality of the model is not an argument against it. As Falco shows, poetic genealogies are necessarily fictions, and the Sappho–Orinda–Astrea line certainly had the definite virtue of making female ancestry and inheritance thinkable. More speculatively, it may have had the virtue for seventeenth-century readers—and certainly should have it for us—of alerting readers to the fictionality of all such lineages. The exclusive masculinity of the canonical Sidney–Spenser–Jonson line is as open to question as the exclusive femininity of this one.

As an alternative to the father–son line of literary genealogy, the notion of female succession held obvious appeal, but it also had its drawbacks. Constructing a separate, entirely female tradition threatened to lock women writers into a literary-historical ghetto. Their relations with and their effect on male writers could be—and often were—discounted at the same time as they were being praised as reincarnations of Sappho. We also need to bear in mind that the female line of succession was not a simple counterpart to the male, and was not imagined in exactly comparable terms. The notion of female inheritance was important, but our interpretations of this should not be unduly coloured by later models of female lineage. We should not conflate the appeals to Sappho and Orinda with the explicit creation of mother–daughter lineages which became a dominant strand in twentieth-century feminist criticism. Feminists

---

[35] Delarivier Manley, 'To the Author of Agnes de Castro', in Catharine Trotter, *Agnes de Castro. A Tragedy. As it is Acted at the Theatre Royal* (London, 1696), sig. A2ᵛ.

looking at eighteenth-century women writers have identified the motherly and the daughterly: Dale Spender has written of the 'Mothers of the Novel' and Marilyn Williamson has constructed two separate traditions of eighteenth-century women writers, the daughters of Aphra Behn versus the daughters of Katherine Philips.[36] This twentieth-century feminist construction of the mother–daughter line was, I think, an entirely necessary fiction of origins, to be compared, maybe, to the Renaissance poet's forging of an English poetic lineage. However, we should not read back this intense feeling about an invented mother–daughter line into the earlier period of female tradition-building. The Sappho–Orinda–Astrea line is invoked many times and in a variety of ways, and of course it depends implicitly on the notion of mother–daughter succession: but the words 'mother' and 'daughter' do not echo through women's poems and prefaces in the way that 'father' and 'son' sound in the works of Jonson and Dryden.

Even those constructing a female lineage in order to legitimate female authorship did not find the generative power of mothers a ready metaphor for poetic succession. Queens passing their thrones to succeeding queens, yes. Ancient poets of almost mythological status, like Sappho, being reincarnated in seventeenth-century women, yes. A professional writer whose audacious pen-name belongs to Astrea, the goddess of justice who left the earth, being invoked after her death by women who hope to revive her in their own work, yes. But daughters claiming to inherit their poetic powers from metaphorical mothers, no. Behn is—very occasionally—seen as a kind of mother. In *The Challenge* (1697), a series of letters purportedly sent in to the *Athenian Mercury*, there is a letter '*Against a* She-Wit' by 'Sir Thomas'. He warns his female correspondent not to try to use the example of women poets as a way of proving anything in women's favour, for 'pray how many *honest Poetesses* can you reckon among ye? From *Granny Sappho*, down to *Mother Behn*?'[37] 'Father Ben' was a title of great honour; 'Mother Behn' was not.

---

[36] Dale Spender, *Mothers of the Novel: 100 Good Women Writers before Jane Austen* (London: Pandora Press, 1986); Marilyn Williamson, *Raising Their Voices: British Women Writers 1650–1750* (Detroit: Wayne State University Press, 1990).

[37] *The Challenge, Sent by a Young lady to Sir Thomas . . . Or, The Female War* (London: E. Whitlock, 1697), 210–11.

The weakness of the concept of maternal inheritance during this period affected the way women were placed in literary history. Women, as we have seen, found ways to add themselves to a literary genealogy. They could see themselves as descended from Sappho, and they could also be seen in daughterly relation to great male poets. But to become truly integrated into and powerful within that genealogy, they would need to take on a generative role themselves. Their power to create, through their writings, models for others to follow would have to be acknowledged; and they would need to wield that power over a wide literary range—it could not be confined to the tiny minority group of female writers. In short, mothers would have to have sons.

So I want to raise the question of the fourth parent–child combination, one that has been given practically no place in literary genealogies: mother–son. This relationship, considered so central by Freud, has been profoundly ignored in literary history. Motherhood, of course, is invoked as a trope for the language the poet must shape; as Henry Hall paid his tribute to Dryden: 'Hail, mighty Master of thy Mother-Tongue'.[38] The mother as muse weeping for the death of her poetic son is also common: Britannia weeps for Dryden's death.[39] Male poets borrow the language of pregnancy and birth to describe the production of their writing. However, the woman as writer is not invoked as the mother to a poetic son. It is important to grasp that this is because of the lack of generative power attributed to motherhood itself, rather than being simply a reflection of the paucity of women poets of sufficient stature to be given a maternal role. The example of Sappho indicates this. In the seventeenth century she is invoked all the time as an ancestor for female poets, but not for male, illustrating that what is at stake is not a demonstrable line of descent but an appropriate line for men and (later) for women. It probably simply did not occur to anyone to include the known women poets of antiquity in the literary genealogy of male poets.

So, what happens when a seventeenth-century woman writer does achieve (and is widely recognized as achieving) enough to be taken

---

[38] Henry Hall, 'To the Memory of John Dryden, Esq'., in *Luctus Britannici* (London, 1700; rpr. in *Drydeniana XIV*), 19.

[39] 'To the Memory of the truly Honoured John Dryden, Esq; By a Young Lady', in *Luctus Britannici*, 15.

notice of? What happens when her work in fiction and in drama (at least) does demonstrably have generative power, inspiring imitations and adaptations by men and by women? What happens, in other words, with Aphra Behn?

A feminist study of writerly authority needs to look at the use of sources, as well as the relations of acknowledgement, because as we have seen, women writers do not receive in the same way that men do those 'maneuvers of invocation and recognition' that elevate a writer's status. When I set out to look for 'the sons of Behn' I do so knowing at the outset that there won't be any, in the sense of the sons of that other Ben—sons who make themselves so by invoking the parent in whose line they want to be counted. In the absence of those acknowledgements by which a spiritual, poetic paternity is created, Behn's literary legacy appears a mundane, material affair. Yet I have kept to the idea of this imaginary group, the sons of Behn, to make two points: that Behn did transmit an inheritance to later writers, one that would have been more readily recognized coming from a male writer; and that this inheritance was not just passed along an (equally imaginary) female line.

Who are Behn's 'sons'? I suggest three men whose relationship to Behn and her work might be understood in filial terms: Thomas Brown, Thomas Southerne, and Samuel Richardson. They represent three groups with different kinds of interest in Behn's work. The first is made up of the friends, writers, and publishers who were left, on her death, with the most literal form of inheritance: her unpublished works. The second group comprises those male dramatists who adapted her work. The 'sons' in the third group denied all relationship to her: they are the male novelists, developing a tradition in which Behn was an important precursor.

Thomas Brown

In the 1680s, Behn formed friendships with a number of young men, including Thomas Creech, Charles Gildon, Thomas Brown, and George Granville. Gildon, Brown, Granville, and an older friend of Behn's, George Jenkins, were all connected in some way with publishing Behn's literary legacies. George Granville published some of her poetry posthumously.[40] George Jenkins brought out her play *The*

[40] See W. J. Cameron, 'George Granville and the "Remaines" of Aphra Behn', *Notes and Queries*, 204 (1959), 88–92.

Widdow Ranter in November 1689, seven months after her death, and it was published in 1690 with his dedication, complaining of the poor acting that had ruined a good play. Charles Gildon had the manuscript of another play, *The Younger Brother*, in his possession, but did not put the play on until 1696, perhaps, as Janet Todd suggests, because Southerne's *Oroonoko* in 1695 had revived interest in Behn.[41] Behn may also have known the publisher, Samuel Briscoe, in her final years, and he brought out the posthumous collection of her fiction, *The Histories and Novels of the late Ingenious Mrs Behn* (1696), prepared for the press by Gildon.

By staging her plays, publishing her work, praising her in prefaces and dedications, and publishing her memoirs, these men between them did their best to exploit Behn's legacy commercially; they also did a great deal to perpetuate Behn's fame, but not in ways that elevated her literary status. In some ways their activities can be compared with those of the sons who guarded Ben Jonson's reputation after his death, or of Congreve, who made it his business to defend Dryden. Gildon had high praise for 'Mrs *Behn*, whose Genius was of that force like *Homer*'s, to maintain its Gayety in the midst of Disappointments, which a Woman of her Sense and Merit, ought never to have met with: But she had a great Strength of Mind, and Command of Thought'. Apart from this comparison to the great epic writer, Gildon usually, as I showed in Chapter 1, described her in terms that helped create her reputation as primarily an amorous writer: 'The Passions, that of Love especially, she was Mistress of, and gave us such nice and tender Touches of them, that without her name we might discover the Author'.[42] Moreover, the strong association built up by the early eighteenth century between Behn and hack writers like Gildon and Brown suggested that she was a hack writer herself.

Charles Gildon's considerable influence on Behn's reception has already been discussed in Chapter 1. Here I am choosing to concentrate on Thomas Brown as Behn's 'son', because with him Behn seems to have had a mentoring relationship in some ways comparable to Jonson's and Dryden's encouragement of younger writers. Born in 1663, the son of a Shropshire farmer, Brown spent some time

---

[41] Todd, *Secret Life*, 336.
[42] 'Epistle Dedicatory', *All the Histories and Novels Written by the Late Ingenious Mrs Behn* (3rd edn.; London: Samuel Briscoe, 1698), sig. A4^v.

studying at Christ Church, Oxford, and then moved to London, where he tried to make a living by writing.[43] He wrote miscellaneous verse and prose, much of it satirical, which was later collected into successive editions of *The Works of Mr. Thomas Brown*. He may have written the short novel *Lindamira* (1702). It would probably be impossible to sort out exactly what he did and did not write. On the one hand, his friend James Drake maintained that 'most of the Anonymous things that took with the Town, were father'd upon him. . . . This, tho' an Injury in Reality to him, is a plain Demonstration of the Universality of his Reputation, when whatever pleas'd from an unknown Hand, was ascrib'd to him.'[44] On the other, he was a notorious forger. On one occasion he attacked Dryden's conversion to Catholicism in pamphlets he wrote as 'Dudley Tomkinson', a made-up name. Another time he signed a commendatory poem to Henry Higden with the name of a contemporary at the Middle Temple, Thomas Palmer, the choice of name 'punningly remarking on his habit of palming his writing off on others'. Later, he acknowledged the poem as his own.[45] Brown was associated with Behn at the start of his writing career. He met her in 1684, when he was 19; they became friends, and Behn included five pieces written by him in her anthology of poems, *Miscellany*. After her death, Brown went on to include works by her—or purportedly by her—in his works. He included an exchange between Behn and the actress Anne Bracegirdle in his *Letters from the Dead to the Living* (1702).[46] After Brown's death in 1704, the connection between Brown and Behn was maintained in his posthumous publications. A poem attributed to Behn, 'A Letter to the Earl of Kildare' was included in Thomas Brown's *Works*, in the edition of 1715, and the *Familiar Letters* of 1718, with their letters and poems under Behn's name, were published together with Brown's *Remains*.

[43] His career is discussed in Benjamin Boyce, *Tom Brown of Facetious Memory* (Cambridge, Mass.: Harvard University Press, 1939).

[44] *The Works of Mr. Thomas Brown, in Prose and Verse; Serious, Moral, and Comical* (London: Sam Briscoe, 1707), i. sig. A8^{r-v}.

[45] D. N. Deluna, 'Mr *Higden*: not a Dryden poem . . . but a Dryden forgery', *Times Literary Supplement*, 4807 (19 May 1995), 13. Deluna gives these and other examples of Brown's forgery, arguing that Brown wrote a poem signed 'J.D.', printed with Henry Higden's *The Wary Widow* (1693), and sometimes ascribed to Dryden.

[46] Janet Todd discusses Behn's help in Brown's career, and describes his composition of the Bracegirdle–Behn correspondence as 'an unkind response to old friendship', in *Secret Life*, 313–14. See also her *The Critical Fortunes*, 29.

Brown perpetuated Behn's fame by putting her name to letters which contributed to the myth of Behn the amorous, bawdy writer. The letter he wrote as 'Anne Bracegirdle' is particularly interesting for the light it throws on the way a woman writer's encouragement of a young male poet is sexualized. A mentoring relationship that between men would be construed in filial terms is seen as a sexual exchange. 'Anne Bracegirdle' describes Behn as simultaneously seducing young men and turning them into poets. Poetry is like the pox, caught through intercourse with an affected woman:

You were the young Poets *Venus*; to you they paid their devotion as a Goddess, and their first Adventure, when they adjourn'd from the University to this Town, was to solicite your Favours; and this advantage you enjoy'd above the rest of your Sex, that if a young Student was but once infected with a Rhiming Itch, you, by a Butter'd Bun, could make him an establish'd Poet at any time; for the Contageon, like that of a worse Distemper, will run a great way, and be often strangely contracted.⁴⁷

Even the attribution of so unspiritual a form of poetic influence to Behn is undermined elsewhere in the letter, where the terms of the exchange are reversed and Behn is described as drawing her own poetry from her sexual partners: 'how could the Spirit of Poesie be otherways than infus'd into you, since you always gain'd by what the Fraternity of the Muses lost in your Embraces?' (*A Continuation*, 171). Her lovers even wrote part of her works: 'the least return, your Versifying Admirers could make you for your Favours, was, first to lend you their assistance, and then oblige you with their Applause; besides, how could you do otherways than produce some Wit to the World, since you were so often Plow'd and Sow'd by the kind Husbandmen of *Apollo*?' (172).

The voice Brown created for 'Aphra Behn' in the exchange with 'Bracegirdle' played on and continued the stereotype of the bawdy woman, scolding the hypocrite prude and hinting at the libertine nature that women hide from men: 'you know 'tis the Custom of our Sex to take all manner of Liberty with one another, and to talk Smuttily and act Waggishly when we are by our selves' (167). This amorous identity was also developed in another of the *Letters from the Dead to the Living*, 'A *Letter of* News from Mr *Joseph Haines*, of Merry Memory, to his Friends at *Will*'s Coffee-House in *Covent-Garden*'.

⁴⁷ Thomas Brown, *A Continuation or Second Part of the Letters from the Dead to the Living* (2nd edn.; London: Benj. Bragge, 1707), 171.

Here, two actors, Haines and Nokes, travel through the underworld visiting various places which correspond to parts of London. In Bedlam they find a trio of women: Dido, Queen of Carthage, 'supported by the Ingenuous Mrs. *Behn* on the one side, and the Learned *Christiana,* Queen of Sweden, on the other'. The exchanges between the men and these three women are all to do with the women's sexual reputations, and Behn is represented as so obsessed with sex that her attempts to support her companions backfire. Dido asks the men not to believe the slanders of Virgil, that she killed herself for love of Aeneas, protesting that she was never alone with Aeneas in the grotto. Haines replies that being alone in a grotto with Aeneas might have been perfectly innocent. Behn angrily intervenes:

How, says Mrs. *Behn,* in a fury, was it not Scandal enough in all Conscience, to say that a Man and a Woman were in a dark blind Cavern by themselves? What tho' there was no such Convenience as a Bed or a Couch in the Room; nay, not so much as a broken-back'd Chair; yet I desire you to tell me, sweet Mr. *Haines,* what other Business can a Man and a Woman have in the dark together, but—. Ay, cries the Queen of *Sweden,* what other Business can a Man and a Woman have in the dark, but, as the Fellow says in the *Moor* of *Venice,* to make the Beast with two Backs?[48]

After Brown's death, the amorous image of Behn that he had helped create was carried further by an anonymous writer who, imitating Brown's own letters from the dead, imagined him meeting Aphra Behn in the shades below and becoming her lover. Again the older writer's relationship to the younger man is interpreted in sexual terms, though the writer does not seem to be aware of their friendship in life. Brown is supposed to write from Westminster Abbey, where, like Behn, he had been buried. Both have joined the immortal company of the poets and Brown is greeted by Chaucer, Spenser, Drayton, Jonson, Cowley, and Dryden. He is, however, far more interested in Behn, who, he reports:

sate down by me, and laid her Head in my Lap, as much as to say she was at my Disposal, and had no manner of Aversion for a Stranger, who she had been told had none for her Sex. I perceived she retain'd the same Passions she had formerly been famous for, though she was not Mistress of the same Beauty. . . .

---

[48] *The Second Volume of the Works of Mr. Tho. Brown, Containing Letters from the Dead to the Living* (London: B. Bragg, 1707), 12, 13.

We have taken an extraordinary liking to one another's Company, and good Conversation is not so overplentiful in these Parts, notwithstanding the great Names before mention'd, as not to make me desirous of hers. Its unspeakable to tell you the Satisfaction I receiv'd in once talking with her, and how a Person so agreeable, sweetens the Discontents I am in for those perishing and fading Pleasures I have left behind me.[49]

The obviously sexual basis for Brown's preference for Behn over the 'great Names' of the other poets serves to diminish both of them: both, it is implied, are too concerned with the flesh to belong in the Abbey with the immortal spirits of poets.

It is possible that Brown also adopted Behn's voice in a much more significant way. Attention has recently been given to the share that he and Charles Gildon may have had in the posthumously published stories that came out under Behn's name in the 1698 and 1700 editions of *Histories and Novels*. As Janet Todd points out, five of the stories in the collected editions, *Oroonoko, The Fair Jilt, Agnes de Castro, The Lucky Mistake*, and *The History of the Nun*, are clearly hers: they were published separately in Behn's lifetime or close to her death, and they are united by psychological realism and an interest in the influence of education. *Memoirs of the Court of the King of Bantam, The Nun, The Adventure of the Black Lady, The Unfortunate Bride, The Dumb Virgin, The Unfortunate Happy Lady, The Wandring Beauty*, and *The Unhappy Mistake*, printed for first time between 1698 and 1700, are much shorter pieces (*Works*, iii, p. vii). It is remarkable that Behn should have left so many as eight unpublished novels, and that they did not emerge until after the success of the 1696 edition had shown how marketable her name was. Germaine Greer considers it 'impossible' that Behn, short of money in her final years, would have left these works without publishing them herself.[50] She points out that if Charles Gildon had indeed inherited these works as part of Behn's papers, he would probably have published them earlier to help him out of financial difficulties; and that Brown, who had given Gildon material for at least one earlier publication, may have been writing 'Behn' stories for the collections Gildon edited and Briscoe published. Briscoe himself drew attention to the doubt people might feel about novels emerging nearly ten years after an author's death, and the explanation he gave for the uncharacteristic style of *Memoirs of the*

---

[49] *A Letter from the Dead Thomas Brown, to the Living Heraclitus* (London, 1704), 9, 11–12.
[50] Germaine Greer, *Slip-Shod Sibyls*, 196.

Court of the King of Bantam—that Behn had taken a wager that she could imitate the style of Paul Scarron, author of the *Roman Comique*—may point towards the involvement of Brown, who was actually engaged in translating Scarron for Briscoe at this time.[51] *The Black Lady* and *The Unfortunate Happy Lady* also seem to Todd candidates for Brown's writing, with 'self-conscious touches' reminiscent of Behn added.[52]

The case is not proven. There is certainly a shift in style from the complex narratives of *Oroonoko* and *The Fair Jilt* to the simpler patterns of the posthumous stories, which are more reliant on common motifs from folk-tales and from intrigue comedy. The narrator in Behn's known novels tends to be carefully individualized, and she introduces her stories as the examples that prove a particular maxim about human nature (as in *The Fair Jilt*, *The History of the Nun*, and the translation of *Agnes de Castro*), or as the fruits of her own first-hand observation and reflection (*Oroonoko*, *The Fair Jilt*). The later novels, in contrast, tend to leap straight into the narrative, with: 'Don *Henrique* was a Person of Great Birth', or '*Frankwit* and *Wildvill* were two young Gentlemen of very considerable Fortunes' (*The Nun*, *Works*, iii. 295; *The Unfortunate Bride*, *Works*, iii. 325). The differences make the idea of a different author plausible, but they could also be explained in terms of Behn's own changing styles, especially if the posthumous stories are thought of as earlier pieces that Behn had put aside. Some internal evidence points to this possibility. *Memoirs of the Court of the King of Bantam* is implicitly set around 1682. Its title refers to an embassy which arrived in London in that year (*Works*, iii, p. x), and the characters go to watch *The London Cuckolds*, first performed in 1682. This seems, though not conclusively, to suggest earlier authorship. It is certainly possible that Brown, an ingenious forger, went to some trouble to introduce details that would give the impression of Behn's authorship, but it is also possible that Behn herself wrote these stories, or, perhaps, left them unfinished, to be taken up and completed by Brown or Gildon later. If Brown was forging Behn stories, I find it surprising that he did not do more to make the stories fit the image of the amorous Behn he and Gildon were building up elsewhere: the posthumous stories are not examples of Behn's erotic writing.

Unless and until new external evidence emerges, or the statistical analysis of linguistic patterns is applied to Behn and Brown (if this

---

[51] Germaine Greer, 'Honest Sam. Briscoe', 36–9.   [52] Todd, *Secret Life*, 317.

method could succeed with an author like Brown, known for adopting other people's styles), I think the question has to remain open. It does seem very possible, though, that some of the stories published as Behn's were not hers at all. If they were passing off their own writing as Behn's, Gildon and Brown were not using her, as literary sons use the father, as a source for their literary identity, but commercially. Instead of building their own names through her, they were cashing in on her name. Instead of literary sons, Behn had hack sons.

Thomas Southerne

Behn also had dramatic followers, as I showed at the beginning of this chapter. The various instances of borrowing from her work should not be overplayed: in a theatrical world where everyone was drawing in some way on their predecessors, it would be odd if she did not supply some details to later playwrights. They are worth mentioning, though, to underline the point that her work participated in the general web of influences that connects eighteenth-century drama, and did not just have effects on the work of women.

The central candidate for Behn's theatrical son is of course Thomas Southerne. Three of his plays, coming out in the years following her death, are based on or take significant elements from her late fiction and drama. *Sir Anthony Love* (1690) takes its plot about the daughters of the French count from her novel *The Lucky Mistake* (1689), while the presentation of its cross-dressing heroine may owe something to Behn's *Widdow Ranter*. A few years later, Southerne's *The Fatal Marriage: or the Innocent Adultery* (1694) is based on Behn's story *The History of the Nun* (1689). The following year his *Oroonoko* transformed Behn's late novel into a tragic drama, while drawing on *The Widdow Ranter* for elements of its comic subplot. These last two were not only Southerne's most successful plays, they were two of the most successful plays of the eighteenth century: they were constantly performed, appeared in numerous editions, and themselves inspired later adaptations. Southerne's career was founded on adapting Behn.

The History of the Nun: Or the Fair Vow-Breaker (1689) is one of those short novels in which Behn's authoritative narrator delivers a cool, witty account of the extremes of behaviour caused by passion. Like other fiction of the time it shows a fascination with the idea of nuns' illicit loves, and of great virtue turning suddenly into great vice. Examining the problems of oath-taking, a subject of concern to Catholic sympathizers like Behn after the exclusion crisis,[53] the story's explicitly stated moral is that Heaven punishes those who break sacred vows, as the heroine, Isabella, does when she runs away from her convent to marry Henault. Yet there is sympathy for the heroine even as she reaches the climax of crime by murdering both husbands together. Put into a convent at the age of 2, encouraged by aunt and father to make her nun's vows in her youth, she shows an early ardour for religion which is later transformed into an even stronger passion for Henault. Their married life is plagued by money worries and childlessness; Henault eventually leaves to make his fortune in the army, and is reported dead in battle. After three years Isabella reluctantly marries a previous admirer, Villenoys, eventually transfers her affections to him, and lives happily until the unexpected return of her first husband. Panicking at the imminent loss of comfort, reputation, and second husband, she smothers Henault in his sleep; she persuades Villenoys to throw the body in the river; then, unable to face carrying on her life with him now that he is aware of her guilt, she compounds it by sewing the sack containing the corpse to the living husband's collar; and the tale turns blackly farcical as Villenoys drowns. Her guilt discovered, Isabella reverts to serene piety on the scaffold.

Southerne took, as he acknowledged, a 'Hint' from this story for his tragedy: 'I have little more than borrowed the Question, how far such a distress was to be carried, upon the Misfortune of a Womans having innocently two Husbands, at the same time'.[54] His drama focuses the action on the second marriage and the first husband's almost immediately subsequent return. Though the broken religious vow is mentioned, the decision to marry a second time is seen as the crucial one. As Jacqueline Pearson shows, Southerne exculpates Isabella at every turn, providing cruel males who are to blame for her fatal decision to take a second husband (here called Villeroy).[55] Her first husband (here Biron) is persecuted by his obdurate father, who has never forgiven him for his marriage; this character is mentioned in Behn's story but is given a central role in the play.

---

[53] Ballaster, *Seductive Forms*, 83–4.

[54] Thomas Southerne, 'Epistle Dedicatory', *The Fatal Marriage: Or, The Innocent Adultery* (London, 1694), A2^r, A2^v.

[55] Pearson, 'The History of *The History of the Nun*,' 235–40.

Not only does he force Biron to seek his fortune elsewhere, he refuses shelter to Isabella and her young son (an addition to the plot), thus driving her into Villeroy's arms. Biron's malicious brother, Carlos (another addition), deceives Isabella into believing Biron dead. Isabella is significant for the paradox that she is both innocent and an adulteress. Though she has a momentary, frenzied thought of killing her returned husband, she is prevented from stabbing him; he is killed by Carlos, Isabella stabs herself, and Villeroy is left alive. The story shifts from a feminocentric study of a woman's crime to one of tragic conflict between father and sons, brother and brother. The repentant father, Baldwin, is left to draw the morals that he started the fraternal rivalry of his sons by not loving them equally, as he ought; and that he should have pardoned Biron's 'only fault' of marrying Isabella.[56]

Southerne also added a comic subplot, in which another erring head of a family, Fernando, is tricked by a drugged, false burial, into repenting of his mistrust of wife Julia and daughter Victoria. Southerne was rather dismissive of this subplot in his dedication to the play, presenting it as a comic part brought in to satisfy the audience; in fact it proved the least popular part of the play, and was excised from later adaptations. What he did not add was that here, too, he had taken a 'hint' from Aphra Behn: this time from her comedy *The Lucky Chance*. *The Lucky Chance* also contains a young wife, also called Julia, whose husband worries about being cuckolded; and Southerne's Julia, like Behn's, teases her husband about it. The exchange between Behn's Sir Cautious and Lady Fulbank: 'How, wou'd, what cuckold me?' . . . 'Yes, if it pleas'd me better than Vertue Sir' (*Works*, vii. 275), is echoed in one between Fernando and Julia: 'run away from your Husband? ha?' . . . 'Ay, and run to another man too; any thing, if my Virtue would permit me' (*The Fatal Marriage*, 79). Behn's Julia eventually does cuckold her husband, being tricked into becoming 'an innocent Adulteress', as her lover puts it (*Works*, vii. 278). Southerne moves this idea to the tragic plot of his play, and echoes the phrase in his subtitle.

In *Oroonoko* Southerne continued the practice of borrowing from Behn, using her fiction for the tragic plot, but also taking hints from her drama. Behn's story of the enslaved African prince and his wife Imoinda, now the most famous of her works, tells of the hero's

---

[56] Southerne, *The Fatal Marriage*, 79.

experiences both in his native Coramantien and as a slave in Surinam. Oroonoko himself tells the romantic story of his Coramantien life to the narrator, who meets him in Surinam. She relates the rest of the story, including the treachery of the white colonists, the diverting 'adventures' in the jungle, Oroonoko's doomed slave rebellion, his killing of Imoinda to prevent her falling into the hands of his enemies, and his cruel and grotesque execution.

Southerne concentrates the action in Surinam. His changes to the plot, which tend to ennoble the hero, have been the subject of much critical discussion. Especially notable is his decision to make Imoinda a white European instead of a black African, giving the play echoes of *Othello*. Her role is made much more passive. She exists mainly as an object of desire, and the governor's lust for her is a motivating force. Instead of being wounded by her arrow as she fights in the slave rebellion, as in the novel, the governor in the play is killed by Oroonoko. Oroonoko himself is spared both the guilt of killing his wife and the ignominy of a shameful execution: he dies heroically by his own hand.[57] Southerne's play included a defence of commercial slavery, and has been read as an attempt to render colonialism more manageable and redeemable than it is seen to be in Behn's work.[58] Behn's late play *The Widdow Ranter* has been identified as another source for Southerne's play. *The Widdow Ranter* also has a colonial setting, and its title-character, the cross-dressing, amorous widow, may have influenced the creation both of Southerne's Widow Lackitt and the cross-dressing Charlotte Welldon, who engages in comic trickery to engineer marriages.[59]

Southerne's *Oroonoko* is discussed in more detail in Chapter 6, together with other adaptations of Behn's novel. Here I am concerned with the way in which Southerne acknowledges her influence on his play. In his dedication, he comes closer than any other male writer to calling himself her follower. Recent discussions of the play suggest, however, that along with this acknowledgement went a

---

[57] See the discussion in Paula Backscheider, *Spectacular Politics* (Baltimore and London: Johns Hopkins University Press, 1993), 93–5. Margaret Ferguson discusses Southerne's reduction of Imoinda's power in 'Transmuting Othello: Aphra Behn's *Oroonoko*', in Marianne Novy (ed.), *Cross-Cultural Performances* (Urbana, Ill., and Chicago: University of Illinois Press, 1993), 15–49.

[58] See the discussions in Suvir Kaul, 'Reading Literary Symptoms: Colonial Pathologies and the *Oroonoko* Fictions of Behn, Southerne, and Hawkesworth', *Eighteenth-Century Life*, 18/3 (1994), 80–96.

[59] See Jordan and Love, Introduction to *Oroonoko*, *The Works of Thomas Southerne*, ii. 93.

severe anxiety—that of being influenced by a female author. If male maturity in this period, as Anthony Fletcher suggests, depended on the sense of becoming free from 'maternal making and maternal influence',[60] a dramatic success based on being influenced by an earlier female author would be hard to accept. Laura Rosenthal suggests that Southerne lays claim to a property in *Oroonoko*, and minimizes Behn's ownership of the story, through complex strategies within the play. Behn's narrator, the authority for the whole in Behn's novel, disappears, but something of her role—a role identified with the author, Aphra Behn, herself—is taken on by the Widow Lackitt and Charlotte Welldon, who reduce the presence of Englishwomen in Surinam from eyewitness recorders to husband-hunting stereotypes. Behn is also identified, in Rosenthal's account, with the newly white Imoinda: pointing to the recurrent hints that Behn had been in love with her noble hero, she argues that Southerne 'illegitimizes Behn's literary property in *Oroonoko*' by making her story seem no more than the story of her own desire.[61] Mary Vermillion similarly reads Southerne's play as an aggressive attack on female authorship, as embodied in the 'mock Behn' which she finds in the character of Charlotte Welldon.[62] She notes the part of the subplot where the Widow Lackitt makes her booby son, Daniel, kneel down and 'repeat her words just as Southerne "repeats" Behn's plots'.[63] Here, indeed, Southerne seems to express an anxiety about having become a son of Behn.

Illuminating though they are, these readings seem to me to overstate the case when they make Southerne's play almost entirely concerned with attacking his female precursor. By attending to the way he acknowledges his debt to Behn, and to the significance of his generic alterations of her work, we can see that Southerne was able to present his use of Behn in a way that greatly alleviated any anxiety of influence, allowing him to give her credit for her work without fearing that he would lose credit for his own.

A number of the changes made to the play can be read as a function of Southerne's change of form, from novel to tragic drama. The

---

[60] Anthony Fletcher, *Gender, Sex and Subordination in England 1500–1800* (New Haven and London: Yale University Press, 1995), 59.

[61] Laura Rosenthal, *Playwrights and Plagiarists in Early Modern England* (Ithaca, NY, and London: Cornell University Press, 1996), 160.

[62] Mary Vermillion, 'Buried Heroism: Critiques of Female Authorship in Southerne's Adaptation of Behn's *Oroonoko*', *Restoration*, 16 (1992), 28–37.   [63] Ibid. 35.

narrator, obviously, is suited for the novel and not the stage. Imoinda's whiteness is perhaps more decorous on a stage where it seems to have been acceptable for men, but not women, to black up, and it heightens an implicit comparison between Oroonoko and Othello. Imoinda's less effective action (instead of shooting the governor, she draws a sword on him but fails to stab him), and her position as focus for male desire, bring her in line with typical tragic heroines of the period. Oroonoko's heroic self-slaughter makes him more like Othello: the horrific 'spectacle of a mangled king' shown in the novel is not staged.

This list suggests some of the reasons Behn had for turning to fiction for some of the experimental work of her final years: she had things to express that stage conventions of the time could not handle. I want to turn now to Southerne's acknowledgement of Behn's influence in *Oroonoko*, both as an example of what Guillory calls the 'invocation and acknowledgement' that makes an *auctor*, as it is applied to a female author; and for what Southerne says about the change from novel to drama.

In his dedication of *Oroonoko* to William, Duke of Devonshire, Southerne writes:

I stand engaged to Mrs. Behn for the occasion of a most passionate distress in my last play [*The Fatal Marriage*]; and in a conscience that I had not made her a sufficient acknowledgement, I have run further into her debt for *Oroonoko*, with a design to oblige me to be honest; and that every one may find me out for ingratitude when I don't say all that's fit for me upon that subject. She had a great command of the stage, and I have often wondered that she would bury her favourite hero in a novel when she might have revived him in the scene. She thought either that no actor could represent him; or she could not bear him represented. And I believe the last, when I remember what I have heard from a friend of hers, that she always told his story more feelingly than she writ it.[64]

This last observation seems now to have become received wisdom about Behn's relation to her story. We should notice, though, the rhetorical work Southerne's claim does here: Behn is unable to give literary expression to the intensity of her feeling, so Southerne, it is implied, has done it for her. Though Southerne expresses his gratitude to Behn, critics of his work from the beginning, and until the recent revisionary wave, have tended to place no significance on his debt to her. This erasure of Behn is connected, I suggest, with what Southerne emphasizes here: the change in form from novel to play.

Acknowledging Behn's command of the stage, Southerne writes that he cannot see why she did not choose to exercise it here: putting Oroonoko in a novel is 'burying' him, putting him in a play is 'reviving' him. So much for Behn's hope, expressed at the end of the novel, that her pen will be enough to make Oroonoko and Imoinda's names live to future ages. In fact, from early on, Southerne, rather than Behn, was credited with making Oroonoko live. Early reactions to the play place Southerne in an honourable male tradition of writing. One poem on Dryden's death describes the muses mourning not only Dryden but Lee, Otway, and Oldham—but not Behn—and says they would mourn Congreve and Southerne if they should die, describing the latter as:

> Southern, who, singing Oroonoko's Flame,
> Has made his own a like Immortal name.[65]

In the eighteenth century, when John Hawkesworth revised Southerne's *Oroonoko* for the tastes of a later age, cutting out its comic scenes, his prologue presented this alteration as the careful preservation of the dramatist's reputation. Southerne must be treated reverently by his son, even (especially) when he is found to be tainted by the immorality of the previous age:

> To mix with *Southern*'s though his Verse aspire,
> He bows with Rev'rence to the hoary Sire:
> With honest Zeal, a Father's Shame he veils . . .[66]

Southerne's modern editors, Jordan and Love, repeat this concern for patrilineal succession when they comment that *The Fatal Marriage* and *Oroonoko* established Southerne as the 'successor to Otway' (not Behn) and 'the leading tragic dramatist of his day'.[67]

It is because Behn wrote novels, and Otway wrote tragic drama, that this lineage works. It depends, that is, on a hierarchy placing form above matter in the discussion of textual transmission and the construction of literary lineages. It is by changing the form of the

---

[65] Robert Gould, 'On the Death of John Dryden Esq.', in *Drydeniana XIV*, 38.

[66] [John Hawkesworth], *Oroonoko, A Tragedy . . . By Thomas Southern. With Alterations* (London: C. Bathurst, 1759), prologue.   [67] *The Works of Thomas Southerne*, i, p. xx.

work imitated that the author lays claim to legitimate ownership of borrowed material: this may mean reshaping within a genre, but a much stronger way of changing the form is generic change. Southerne can acknowledge the plots taken from Behn's fiction because these provide simple matter, which he then shapes into the more prestigious form of tragic drama. Indeed the novel at this time, before it had been been elevated by the efforts of the mid-eighteenth-century novelists, lacked clear definition: and its 'versatility and formal openness constitute a tacit femininity',[68] making it seem particularly suitable for a masculine reconfiguration. In contrast to his acknowledgement of Behn's fiction, Southerne makes no mention of his use of her drama. While this is certainly less central to his plots, it is an element, as we have seen, in *The Fatal Marriage* and *Oroonoko*; and to recognize it might risk placing Southerne, not just as a tragic dramatist in the line of Otway who happens to find a useful source in Behn's fiction, but also as a playwright in the tradition of Behn. Because of the association of matter with femininity and of shaping activity with masculinity, it is likely that when literary matter has been taken from a woman writer, and re-formed by a male writer, the critical tendency to see the shaping as more significant than the original matter is exacerbated. What Southerne does as a masculine 'former' is seen as the essence of his achievement; what he takes in feminine 'matter' is secondary.

The case of Southerne and Behn reveals the need for a feminist reading of influence and reception. Such a reading needs to revalue the subordinate, feminized term of the form–matter dichotomy: to show that it is important to pay attention to the taking of matter. This may be one way of tracing forgotten or repressed female influence on male writers. At the same time, it needs to investigate the dominant, masculinized term of the dichotomy, form, and to ask whether the shaping activity undertaken by women who adapt men's texts has been underestimated because it is not so readily associated with the female writer.

Samuel Richardson

The third group of Behn's 'sons' are the eighteenth-century novelists who repudiate her entirely. Though *Oroonoko* might be seen as a

---

[68] Runge, *Gender and Language*, 83.

founding travel-adventure novel and *Love-Letters between a Nobleman and his Sister* as a founding epistolary novel of amorous and political intrigue, the male novelists of the following century have little good to say of her. As the previous chapter has shown, their treatment of her was part of a process by which the novel gained a new cultural status. Not only Behn, but women novelists of the early eighteenth century, particularly Manley and Haywood, were used in a similar way: they were critically disparaged while elements of their fiction were adopted and revised. There have been some interesting readings of eighteenth-century male novelists' use of their female contemporaries or predecessors. William Warner analyses Defoe's *Roxana* as a rewriting of the novel of amorous intrigue, uneasily caught between an attempt to reform erotic fiction and an exploitation of its appeal.[69] He sees Behn's selfish heroines, especially Silvia of *Love-Letters* and Miranda of *The Fair Jilt*, as precursors of Roxana; but writers on Richardson's precursors in fiction tend to consider the early eighteenth-century novelists, rather than Behn. Margaret Doody has shown how *Clarissa* has similarities with the novels of Eliza Haywood, with their maxims about love, and those of Mary Davys, whose *The Lady's Tale* offers a dramatic realization of 'the theme of filial obedience in conflict with the heart's inclination'.[70] Warner, finding contrasts between Richardson and earlier writers more instructive, reads Haywood's *Fantomina; or, Love in a Maze* as typical of the fiction Richardson is reacting to, and argues that *Pamela*, where disguise is adopted in the service of virtue, adapts elements found in *Fantomina*, where the heroine adopts disguises in pursuit of her selfish desires.[71] I suggest that Behn's *Love-Letters* should be seen as part of the background to *Clarissa*. There are, as I will show, a number of similarities between the early part of *Clarissa* and the first part of *Love-Letters*, and a number of contrasts which could be seen as *Clarissa*'s inversions of the earlier novel. I am not trying to establish that there was necessarily direct influence between Behn's novel and Richardson's. Agreeing with Warner that Richardson need not have read a particular work of fiction in order for his work to be shaped by similar popular elements,[72] I suggest that *Clarissa* is responding to and revising certain patterns in erotic fiction that were

[69] Warner, *Licensing Entertainment*, 149–75.
[70] Margaret Doody, *A Natural Passion* (Oxford: Clarendon Press, 1974) 132.
[71] Warner, *Licensing Entertainment*, 192–9.   [72] Ibid. 192.

popularized by *Love-Letters* and associated with what was understood as a feminine tradition of fiction.

In the case of Richardson, then, I am not looking, as in the case of Southerne, at the male writer's adaptation of a female writer's matter, but at his more general response to a generic tradition perceived to be contaminated by female authority. As Doody points out, in *Clarissa* Richardson was keen to draw attention to his use and revision of dramatic tragedies, from which he frequently quoted, making clear the parallels between his characters' situations and those of characters in English drama;[73] but he did not draw attention to the similarities between his novel and earlier ones. That his wish to 'overwrite' and repudiate earlier fiction is linked to a desire to replace female authority with his own is suggested by a reading of some of the correspondence in which Richardson discusses his writing. Once, writing to Lady Bradshaigh, he recounts a 'bold and saucy thing' he said to 'a Dignitary of Ireland', 'an eminent Pen of that Kingdom', who had questioned the plausibility of Harriet Byron's behaviour in *Sir Charles Grandison*. The source of this eminent pen's authority turns out to be his wife, 'a most excellent Lady, and of fine Parts', who said she could not have been so frank about her affections as Harriet was. The novelist's bold reply was to assert: 'I wrote not *from* Women; but *for* them—In other Words, to give them, not to take from them, an Example'.[74]

In a letter of 1753 to Johannes Stinstra, which is a key source for the story of Richardson's early life, the novelist explained the origins of his writing in a way that suggests that he saw writing '*for*' women—writing for their benefit, and also writing in their place—as being at the root of his practice. The letter first mentions writing in the context of Richardson's apprenticeship to a printer, during which he took every opportunity to improve his mind by corresponding with 'a Gentleman greatly my superior in Degree', who 'was a Master of ye Epistolary Style'. This acknowledged, male authority on letter-writing influenced Richardson in his teens (his apprenticeship began 'at the Age of 15 or 16'), but later in the letter, earlier sources for his writing are mentioned in two anecdotes. One shows that

---

[73] Doody, *A Natural Passion*, 128.

[74] *Selected Letters*, ed. Carroll, 244–5. Richardson's statement is discussed by Tassie Gwilliam, to whose work my treatment of Richardson and female authority is indebted. See *Samuel Richardson's Fictions of Gender* (Stanford, Calif.: Stanford University Press, 1993), 8.

Richardson's 'Love of Letter-writing' began early:

> I was not Eleven Years old, when I wrote, spontaneously, a Letter to a Widow of near Fifty, who, pretending to a Zeal for Religion . . . was continually fomenting Quarrels and Disturbances, by Backbiting and Scandal, among all her Acquaintance. I collected from ye Scripture Texts that made against her. Assuming the Stile and Address of a Person in Years, I exhorted her; I expostulated with her.

Richardson remembered his early letter, then, as an attempt to teach a woman much older than himself, at a time when he himself was still subject to maternal authority. His mother, finding out about the incident, praised his principles but 'chid me for the Freedom taken by such a Boy with a Woman of [the widow's] Years'. The second anecdote concerns an incident from a couple of years later, when Richardson, 'not more than Thirteen', used to read aloud to young women of his neighbourhood, and became a confidant and amanuensis to some of them:

> three of these young Women, unknown to each other, having a high Opinion of my Taciturnity, revealed to me their Love Secrets, in order to induce me to give them Copies to write after, or correct, for Answers to their Lovers Letters: Nor did any of them ever know, that I was Secretary to the others. I have been directed to chide, & even repulse, when an Offence was either taken or given, at the very time that the Heart of the Chider or Repulser was open before me, overflowing with Esteem & Affection.[75]

Here Richardson moves from attempting to teach women to gaining an insight into their hearts which allows him to write on their behalf. As Tassie Gwilliam points out, here and in other letters Richardson is making a claim for a knowledge of women that they do not have themselves: the implication is that 'women require the intervention of a writing man to show them their meaning'. She adds that despite this claim, Richardson's 'identification across the lines of gender . . . is clearly [in his accounts] the source and origin of his writing', and that this 'produces a kind of anxiety about originality that is tinged with anxiety about gender'.[76] Richardson represented his childhood and adolescent writing, then, as designed either to correct women's morality or to write on behalf of women involved in love-affairs. His later novel-writing shares these impulses. Applying these ideas to

[75] Richardson to Johannes Stinstra, 2 June 1753; *Selected Letters*, ed. Carroll, 229, 230, 231.
[76] Gwilliam, *Samuel Richardson's Fictions of Gender*, 7–8, 8.

Richardson's sense of his place in literary tradition, we can see an analogy between, on the one hand, his early attempts to usurp an older woman's authority and to express younger women's feelings for them, and on the other, his later replacement of the older, female-dominated tradition of amatory fiction with his own novels, which he presented as both more moral and truer to the reality of the female heart.

Pamela was such an extraordinary success that its publication in 1740 has long been seen as a turning-point in the English novel's development. As Aaron Hill wrote in a letter that was used to advertise the second edition, 'who could have dreamt, he should find, under the modest Disguise of a *Novel,* all the *Soul* of Religion, Good-breeding, Discretion, Good-nature, Wit, Fancy, Fine Thought, and Morality?'[77] Not everybody, however, was convinced. Fielding's *Shamela* is only the most famous of a series of attacks on Richardson's writing and morality. The subtitle of one of them, *Pamela Censured* (1741), shows how Richardson was accused of the very faults he aimed to correct. This pamphlet claimed to show:

That under the Specious Pretence of Cultivating the Principles of Virtue in the Minds of the Youth of both Sexes, the Most Artful and Alluring Amorous Ideas are convey'd.

And that, instead of being divested of all Images that tend to inflame; her letters abound with Incidents, which must necessarily raise in the unwary Youth that read them, Emotions far distant from the Principles of Virtue.[78]

The details of Pamela's sensations, her descriptions of Mr B———'s assaults on her, and in particular the scene where the reader, a voyeur like Mr B———, watches through the keyhole while Pamela lies in a faint on the floor, made the novel suspect. Fielding's Parson Oliver considered that there were 'many lascivious Images in it, very improper to be laid before the Youth of either Sex',[79] and the author of *Pamela Censured* even thought that some of its scenes were worse than Rochester for giving young readers lewd ideas.[80] In the 1750s Francis Plumer returned to the attack on *Pamela* in terms that made Richardson sound very like Behn, Manley, and Haywood: 'so rich is

[77] Samuel Richardson, *Pamela*, ed. T. C. Duncan Eaves and Ben D. Kimpel (Boston: Houghton Mifflin, 1971), 9.

[78] *Pamela Censured*, quoted in Bernard Kreissman, *Pamela-Shamela* (Lincoln, Nebr.: University of Nebraska Press, 1960), 31.

[79] Henry Fielding, *Shamela*, in *Joseph Andrews and Shamela* (London: Oxford University Press, 1970), 355.   [80] Kreissman, *Pamela-Shamela*, 33.

his Imagination; that he cannot help being perhaps too lively and particular in some Scenes: For he in pleasing Rapture carries us to bed to the blooming Pamela; we clasp her in our Arms; and are almost as happy in Thought as Mr. B—— himself.'[81] This criticism is not very far from the praise offered to Behn in the previous century for her *Voyage to the Island of Love*, where 'In the same Trance with the young pair we lie, | And in their amorous Ecstasies we die'.[82]

In *Clarissa*, one of Richardson's aims was to answer the criticisms *Pamela* had received, and produce a truly virtuous woman—and novel. *Clarissa* is also, as Margaret Doody points out, closer to 'the earlier tales of love and seduction' than *Pamela* had been.[83] It is his most concerted attempt to revise the novel of seduction, by turning it into tragedy. There are some strong resemblances between the early part of *Clarissa*, before the heroine leaves her father's house, and the first part of *Love-Letters between a Nobleman and his Sister*. Both are epistolary narratives dealing with a young woman in conflict with her family over love and marriage. Both Silvia and Clarissa engage in a clandestine correspondence with a potential lover, Philander or Lovelace. In both cases, the heroine's parents want her to marry the man of their choice—in Silvia's case Foscario, in Clarissa's, Solmes, and in both cases fear of being forced into an unwanted marriage prompts the heroine's flight. Sibling rivalry is prominent in both novels. Silvia, of course, is notorious for running away with her elder sister's husband. Richardson's novel contains a shadow of this theme in Bella's sense that she has a prior claim to Lovelace, who was first attracted to the younger sister, Clarissa, while he was understood by the Harlowes to be courting their elder daughter. In both novels, the elder sister tries to come between the heroine and her seducer. Silvia's sister writes a letter imploring her to give up 'this fatal Amour': 'Long foreseeing the misery whereto you must arrive by this fatal correspondence with my unhappy Lord, I have often, with tears and prayers, implor'd you to decline so dangerous a passion; I have never yet acquainted our parents with your misfortunes, but I fear I must at last make use of their Authority for the prevention of your ruine' (*Works*, ii. 74). Clarissa's sister is in league with their parents' authority

[81] *A Candid Examination of the History of Sir Charles Grandison*, quoted in Kreissman, *Pamela-Shamela*, 48.

[82] *Poems Upon Several Occasions*, A8ʳ. For a discussion of Behn, Manley, and Haywood's reputations for arousing and satisfying desire see my *The Rise of the Woman Novelist* (Oxford: Blackwell, 1986), 30, 57–62.   [83] Doody, *A Natural Passion*, 128.

and is, the heroine complains, '[l]et loose upon me' to ridicule her for her affection for Lovelace and to reiterate the demand that she marry Solmes.[84] Both heroines are surrounded by hostile family members. When Silvia describes the terrifying occasion when 'I have been arraign'd and convicted, three Judges, severe as the three infernal ones, sate in condemnation on me, a Father, a Mother, and a Sister' (*Works*, ii. 92), her situation is similar to Clarissa's in many of the scenes she describes. As early as Letter 8 Clarissa is in 'heavy disgrace' with her family, suffering the oppressive weight of their concerted disapproval: 'Such a solemnity in everybody's countenance!—My mamma's eyes were fixed upon the tea-cups . . . My papa sat half-aside in his elbow-chair, that his head might be turned from me . . . My sister sat swelling. My brother looked at me with scorn' (*Clarissa*, 63).

If the heroines' early situations are similar, the contrasts between their feelings and actions are very marked. When Silvia is arraigned by her family she is already guilty of the crime they accuse her of, a love-affair with her sister's husband. In the early part of *Clarissa*, the heroine is guilty only of wanting what the strictest eighteenth-century moralists thought a young woman should be allowed, the right to refuse a husband proposed to her. Her (and Richardson's critics') examination of her other faults—pride, or deceiving herself about the extent of her attraction to Lovelace—demonstrates the great strictness of the moral universe she inhabits. Her correspondence with Lovelace begins with her family's encouragement, and only turns secret under their persecution. Whereas Silvia makes love to Philander in secret assignations under her father's roof, Clarissa is made vulnerable to Lovelace's sexual assaults when she leaves her father's house. Part I of *Love-Letters* concentrates on the correspondence between Silvia and Philander, with only occasional letters from other characters, while in *Clarissa* large numbers of people correspond and Lovelace and Clarissa write very few letters to each other. *Love-Letters* concerns itself with a deliberately erotic build-up of desire, with satisfaction promised and repeatedly delayed before the lovers consummate their passion. *Clarissa* subjects the question of desire to minute rational scrutiny, and never allows desire to be satisfied: the rape brings no satisfaction to Lovelace. Most obvi-

---

[84] Samuel Richardson, *Clarissa*, ed. Angus Ross (London: Penguin, 1985), Letter 42, 192–3.

ously, of course, in the sexual affair which is at the centre of both narratives, Silvia is a willing participant, whereas Clarissa is raped.

Richardson's novel takes the well-established theme of seduction and replaces the erring and desiring heroine with a woman who is as free as possible of sexual sin. His own and his critics' concerns about just how free that is show how important, and difficult, the question of female purity was felt to be. It is as if a single false step by Clarissa, considered within the novel and by many of its readers as a representative of the best possible feminine identity, would turn her into a version of Silvia. The later part of *Clarissa* is very unlike the later parts of *Love-Letters*. After the elopement, Philander and Silvia embark on a fresh set of adventures. Far from being destroyed by her sexual fall, Silvia is merely hardened by her experiences, and the story branches out in new directions, with betrayals, new amours, and the continuation of Philander's political activities. In *Clarissa*, by contrast, the heroine's flight from her father's house, coerced by Lovelace, is a decisive part of the novel's single, tragic action. While Behn's novel ends on an open note, with Silvia and Philander still at large, Richardson's moves inexorably towards tragic closure.

Whether or not *Love-Letters* can be considered a source for *Clarissa*, Richardson's novel responds to the patterns of erotic fiction Behn popularized. The narrative persona she develops in the later parts of *Love-Letters* and in her shorter novels is that of a wise, worldly, often cynical, usually tolerant, sometimes explicitly feminine commentator on life. Richardson's novels replace the authority of such a narrator with other kinds of authority: the epistolary authority of his greatest heroine with her severe, and severely tried, virtue, which he saw as a model for women; and his own didactic commentaries. Aphra Behn stands for a kind of writing, and a kind of femininity, which his novels reject.

Behn's sons, then, are a mixed bunch, and not one of them calls her mother. Nor would it have helped if they had: the discussion of literary genealogies makes it clear that the cultural understanding of motherhood at this time made mothering an inappropriate metaphor for the originary and formative work in which Behn's writings play a part. Yet it is worth imagining the male writers after Behn as her sons, if only to reveal the force of the repression of any such relationship at a time when writers were so keen to find fathers. If it can only ever be a wishful fiction to imagine Aphra Behn as the 'mother' of the novel or any other tradition, to entertain that fiction for a moment makes us look again at the equally fictitious lines from father to son which have been used to create the English literary tradition. Later in the eighteenth century, literary genealogy became less all-pervasive as a way of ordering writing, as the idea of the poet as original genius became more important. Nevertheless writers still looked back to their fathers, especially when they were attempting to raise the novel to literary status. Sir Walter Scott was making a claim for the genre, as well as for his own place as a son, when he called Fielding the 'father of the English Novel'.[85] Patrilineal literary traditions still hold sway in literary history. While critics are aware of their fictionality, they still give them a central place, if only because they have been believed in for so long. Attending to the effects of Aphra Behn's works on later writers shows us the need for a new way of understanding literary history, free from the overworked genealogies which have made influence appear to be the prerogative of men.

[85] Scott, *Lives of the Novelists* (London: J. M. Dent, 1820), 70.

4

Her Wit, without Her Shame: Women Writing after Behn

As early as 1679, Behn was being named as the inspiration and enabling force for the writing of other women. 'Ephelia' addressed a poem 'To Madam *Bhen*':

> Madam! Permit a Muse, that has been long
> Silent with wonder, now to find a Tongue:
> Forgive that Zeal I can no longer hide,
> And pardon a necessitated Pride.

Behn is simultaneously humbling, because of her merit, and enabling, because she makes the speaker so proud 'To see such things flow from a Womans Pen'.[1] Nearly a decade later, an anonymous 'Lady', in one of the miscellany poems published with *Lycidus*, attributed her own attempt at writing entirely to Behn's example:

> Accept, thou much lov'd *Sappho* of our Isle,
> This hearty wish, and grace it with a smile,
> When thou shalt know that thy Harmonious Lire
> Did me, the meanest of thy sex, inspire.
> And that thy own unimitable lays
> Are cause alone that I attempt thy praise.[2]

Anne Wharton, in a poem addressed to Behn in the early 1680s but not published until 1693, praised her elegy to Rochester in terms

---

[1] *Female Poems on Several Occasions* (London: William Downing for James Courtney, 1679), 72.

[2] 'A Pindarick To Mrs. *Behn* on her Poem on the Coronation. Written by a Lady'. *Lycidus: or the Lover in Fashion* (London: Joseph Knight and Francis Saunders, 1688), 'A Miscellany of Poems', 93.

that again situate Behn as the inspiration for another woman's writing:

> It is this Flight of yours excites my Art,
> Weak as it is, to take your Muse's part,
> And pay loud thanks back from my bleeding Heart.

As Wharton's poem continues, however, it shows early signs of the anxiety Behn's reputation aroused in many of the women who were inspired by her writing. Displacing Behn's salacious reputation onto Sappho, who stood at the time as a kind of originary female poet, Wharton exhorts her contemporary to atone for the sins of this erring first mother:

> May yours excel the Matchless *Sappho*'s Name;
> May you have all her Wit, without her Shame:
> Tho' she to Honour gave a fatal Wound,
> Employ your Hand to raise it from the ground.
> Right its wrong'd Cause with your inticing Strain,
> Its ruin'd Temples try to build again.
> Scorn meaner Theams, declining low desire,
> And bid your Muse maintain a Vestal Fire.[3]

Behn signally failed to oblige Wharton by becoming Honour's champion; in fact, her lines disparaging Honour became some of her best-known verses, anthologized in early eighteenth-century poetic manuals. She was not a safe model for a woman attempting to combine writing with respectability. Men who might acknowledge the merits of her work in one context tended to take a very different line when they took on the role of protector or adviser to other women writers. Gilbert Burnet, who tried to get Behn to write in praise of William and Mary in 1689, had in 1682 warned Anne Wharton against associating with 'so abominably vile a woman',[4] while Dryden, who had praised Behn in public, in private wrote to the aspiring poet Elizabeth Thomas that she could become a good poet on certain conditions: 'avoiding (as I know you will) the Licenses which Mrs. Behn allowed herself, of writing loosely, and giving (if I may have leave to say so) some Scandal to the Modesty of her Sex'.[5] Attracted by her writing and the spectacle of her success, warned off by the oppressive protection of their male friends and their own

---

[3] Greer *et al.* (eds.), *Kissing the Rod*, 251.   [4] Ibid. 290.
[5] *The Letters of John Dryden*, ed. C. E. Ward (Durham, NC: Duke University Press, 1942), 127.

worries about feminine modesty, women writers contemporary with Behn wanted to have from her what Wharton had recommended Behn take from Sappho: 'all her Wit, without her Shame'. Throughout the next hundred years, a similar ambivalence underlay the otherwise very divergent reactions of successive generations of women writers to their famous precursor.

Behn's particular significance for women writers has long been recognized. Above and beyond any specific influence her work had on her female successors, she constituted a highly visible demonstration of the possibility of a woman's writing career at a time when women were writing and publishing in unprecedented numbers. Virginia Woolf hailed her as a pioneer on behalf of all women, who led the way in the professional writing that Woolf saw as leading, eventually, to intellectual as well as financial independence: 'All women together', she famously recommended, 'ought to let flowers fall upon the tomb of Aphra Behn . . . for it was she who earned them the right to speak their minds.' At the same time Woolf registered the ambiguity of Behn's legacy to women of a professional role linked in people's minds with sexual immorality in writer and work: 'now that Aphra Behn had done it, girls could go to their parents and say, You need not give me an allowance; I can make money by my pen. Of course the answer for many years to come was, Yes, by living the life of Aphra Behn! Death would be better! and the door was slammed faster than ever.'[6] Not so strong a case for floral tributes, perhaps. Whether Behn's example opened doors or shut them has been a subject for critical discussion in recent years. Paula Backscheider, focusing on the female playwrights of the 1690s, discusses the way Behn was praised and imitated by her successors,[7] while Jeslyn Medoff shows that she could be a stumbling-block even at this early date for women who wanted to write and maintain a respectable reputation.[8] Catherine Gallagher goes further, calling Behn 'a colossal and enduring embarrassment' to later generations of female writers, not only because of her shady image but because her playful treatment of self-representation made it harder for women to put forward a sober image of themselves.[9] Yet however embarrassing, Behn provided her successors with models. Gallagher's own account

---

[6] Virginia Woolf, *A Room of One's Own* (London: Vintage, 1996), 61, 59.
[7] Backscheider, *Spectacular Politics*, 74–80.
[8] Medoff, 'The Daughters of Behn', 40–2.
[9] Catherine Gallagher, 'Who Was That Masked Woman?', 65, 84.

of the female novelist as a fictional 'Nobody' implies that Behn, in her very elusiveness, led the way to the development of authorial personae in the eighteenth century;[10] while Jacqueline Pearson has demonstrated the influence of Behn's work on Jane Barker, a woman anxious not to be identified with her predecessor's personal reputation.[11]

The evidence of eighteenth-century women's literary history shows many different ways of responding to Behn. There is not a simple narrative of rejection, or admiration, or emulation. I have divided consideration of Behn's effect on her female successors into three sections. The first deals with the 1690s, when the recently deceased Astrea is an inescapable point of reference. In the second I focus on the relations between Behn and a number of individual writers in the first half of the eighteenth century, arguing that for Centlivre and Manley, Behn was most significant as a role-model for professional writing, while Jane Barker is influenced in a more complex and troubled way by Behn's work. In the third section I consider women writers' use of Behn in the later eighteenth century. Historical distance and an established female writing role allowed for a new detachment in their attitudes to her, but Hannah Cowley's adaptation from Behn showed that she could still be a significant influence.

ASTREA IN THE 1690S

As Judith Milhous has shown, the division of the United Company left both the patent theatre and the breakaway group short of practised dramatists. They started accepting plays that the United Company had previously rejected, and for the first time in years there was a chance for untried playwrights to get their work performed. Four women were among those who took this opportunity: Catharine Trotter, Delarivier Manley, Mary Pix, and 'Ariadne'. It is worth telling the story of these four women's successive debuts during the volatile 1695–6 season, to show how Behn's name functioned to authorize their attempts, while her work in several cases influenced theirs.

In September 1695, the breakaway company at Lincoln's Inn Fields chose to open the theatrical season with what evidently

[10] Gallagher, *Nobody's Story*, 48.
[11] Pearson, 'The History of *The History of the Nun*', 242–3.

seemed, more than six years after Behn's death, a novelty: a new play
by a living woman writer. *She Ventures, and He Wins*, a comedy, was
advertised as by a 'Young Lady' known only by her pseudonym,
Ariadne. The prologue looked both to Behn and Philips as models for
the woman writer:

> our Author hopes indeed,
> You will not think, though charming *Aphra*'s dead,
> All Wit with her, and with *Orinda*'s fled.[12]

Ariadne has not been identified and we cannot even be certain that
she was indeed a woman, though it seems most likely. What is clear
is that in her work she tried to claim control, authority, and direction
for the female. Taking her pseudonym from the heroine in her
source, a novel by Alexander Oldys called *The Fair Extravagant, or, The
Humorous Bride*, she implicitly claimed as her own the heroine's control over the action. Oldys's Ariadne impersonates a boy to arrange
her own marriage with the man she wants, and after the ceremony
disappears in order to put him through a series of tests, including a
duel and imprisonment for her (fictitious) debts. Eventually satisfied
of his courage and constancy, Ariadne reveals herself as an heiress
and virtuous, loving wife.[13] The dramatic adapter gives these exploits
to a heroine renamed Charlot. Cutting out the duel, she concentrates
on the tests proving the hero's devotion to his elusive and demanding
bride. Whereas Oldys presents his heroine's actions as the result of
unaccountable whimsy, as the words 'extravagant' and 'humorous' in
his title suggest, Ariadne motivates them clearly, in Charlot's desire to
control the courtship relation so that she enters marriage in as
powerful a position as possible. Her hero, Lovewell, demonstrates
love and fidelity to his partner under the most humiliating treatment.
While heroines with a degree of control over the action are a staple
of Shakespearian comedy, and Restoration comic heroines frequently take the initiative, Charlot dominates the action to an
extraordinary degree. Though her actions are framed and justified
within patriarchal conditions—she is trying to find a man to whom
she can safely surrender herself in marriage—the play's action shows
her in control not only of her lover but of the representatives of
social authority. Sir Roger Marwood acts under her directions to

---

[12] *She Ventures, and He Wins* (London: H. Rhodes, J. Harris, and S. Briscoe, 1696), sig. A3^r.

[13] Alexander Oldys, *The Fair Extravagant, or, The Humorous Bride* (London: Charles Blount, 1682).

deceive and imprison Lovewell. Ariadne adds a subplot to the play, repeating this theme of female control: the good wife Urania proves her fidelity and humiliates her would-be seducer.

The element of wish-fulfilment in this unusual play is obvious. In this Ariadne is really rather unlike Behn, whose comedies sometimes offer enterprising heroines, but always set their initiatives clearly in a world generally controlled by men. Nevertheless Ariadne named Behn as her inspiration, writing: 'when our Island enjoyed the Blessing of the Incomparable Mrs *Behn*, even then I had much ado to keep my Muse from shewing her Impertinence; but, since her death, [my Muse] has claimed a kind of Privilege; and, in spite of me, broke from her Confinement' (*She Ventures*, sig. A2ᵛ). Ariadne's venture was not successful. The play failed on the stage, and after this setback the rebel company closed their theatre for some time. Apart from the play's own shortcomings—Ariadne confessed to being 'altogether unacquainted with the Stage and those Dramatic Rules, which others have with so much Art and Success observed' (sig. A2ʳ)—its failure may have been influenced by a rival play, since the prologue refers to the patent company which 'out of spite, | Trump'd up a Play upon us in a Night' (sig. A3ʳ). It is likely too that the play's unusually emphatic 'reversal of sexual roles' failed to captivate its audience.[14]

The next attempt to provide a female dramatic succession was launched at the patent house, and was more successful.[15] Catharine Trotter's *Agnes de Castro: A Tragedy*, produced at Drury Lane in December 1695, launched the 16-year-old's stage career, which was to include four more plays before she abandoned the theatre in the early 1700s. The unsigned dedication in the 1696 edition indicates the shame still attached to a female writer: she refers to herself as 'one who Conceals her Name, to shun that of Poetress'.[16] There were, however, some hints about her identity in the epilogue, which refers to the writer's youth, and Trotter let it be known she came vouched for by a famous male name, publishing her tragedy with 'A Prologue, Written by Mr. *Wycherly* at the Authors request: Design'd to be Spoke' (A3ʳ). The success of her play was sufficiently encouraging for her to

[14] M. E. Novak, 'The Closing of Lincoln's Inn Fields Theatre in 1695', *Restoration and Eighteenth-Century Theatre Research*, 14 (1975), 51–2.

[15] Only one performance is recorded in *The London Stage*, but Gildon's assessment that the play 'met with good Success' implies there were more: see *Lives and Characters*, 179.

[16] *Agnes de Castro*, sig. A2ʳ.

bring out her next work, *The Fatal Friendship*, under her own name in 1698.

Agnes de Castro, like Southerne's *Oroonoko*, takes its source from Behn's fiction, in this case from a translation rather than an original Behn story. Mlle S. B. de Brillac's *Agnes de Castro* (1688) was one of a number of works based on the fourteenth-century life of Ines de Castro, whose mistress, Constanza Manuel, married Pedro, heir to the Portuguese throne. Pedro's love for Ines led to her banishment, but after Constanza's death Pedro brought her back and they lived together until his father had her killed. In de Brillac's version the three protagonists exhibit a delicate sensibility comparable to that of the princess of Cleves in de Lafayette's influential novel. The story, translated into English in two separate versions in 1688, offered Trotter the plot for an unusually female-centred tragedy.[17] She intensified the concentration on the female characters, emphasizing the friendship between Agnes and the princess, and giving the villainess Elvira a more prominent and violent role. That Trotter is using Behn's version, rather than the rival translation by Peter Bellon, is clear from a number of verbal echoes, and from the verses written by the prince about his conflict between love and duty, which are Behn's verses in shortened form.[18] In contrast to Southerne, who was unusually full in acknowledging his debts to Behn, Trotter makes no mention of her source in the printed version of her play. This omission is typical enough of dramatists' practice at the time, and so should not be overinterpreted; but it is striking that the second woman dramatist to emulate Behn on the London stage should use Behn's work without drawing attention to the fact. As a young unmarried woman with a sexual reputation to guard, Trotter may have wanted to avoid being associated with Behn. The epilogue spoken on the performance of her first play confides to the audience that 'Our Poetess is Virtuous, Young, and Fair'.

---

[17] Jacqueline Pearson points out that female characters open the play, dominate the first act, and, exceptionally for a play of this period, speak more than half the lines (*The Prostituted Muse: Images of Women and Women Dramatists 1642–1737* (London: Harvester, 1988), 23).

[18] Compare the verses in Behn (*Works*, iii. 130) with Trotter's version (*Agnes de Castro*, I. i. p. 6):

In Vain, Oh Sacred Duty you oppose,	Fair princess, you to whom my Faith is due,
In Vain your Nuptial tye you plead,	Pardon the Destiny that drags me on,
These forc'd devoirs Love overthrows,	'Tis not my fault my Hearts untrue,
And breaks the Vows he never made.	I am compell'd to be undone.

Though Trotter avoids Ariadne's invocation of Behn's example, her play was printed with an encomium poem that drew the comparison for her. A page of the first edition, opposite Wycherley's prologue, is devoted to Delarivier Manley's poem, 'To the Author of Agnes de Castro', hailing Trotter as the writer to fill the 'Vacant Throne' that had been left after the deaths of Orinda and Astrea. Rewriting the 1689 elegy on Behn's death (which may have been hers originally) in a newly martial and optimistic mood, Manley finds that Astrea can be replaced after all.[19] Her poem deliberately, and selectively, fashions a female dramatic tradition, pointedly ignoring Ariadne's very recent play at the rival theatre in order to portray Trotter as the third woman writer to take to the stage. This is not just a female tradition but a female Drury Lane tradition: Manley's own first two plays, *The Lost Lover* and *The Royal Mischief*, were in preparation at the time this was written, and both were intended for Drury Lane.[20] In fact the poem is as much to do with promoting Manley as praising Trotter, following up four lines in praise of Trotter's overthrow of men's empire with four lines giving a broad hint of Manley's intention to follow her into the 'Poetic Race'.[21] It is signed '*Dela Manley*', making Manley's the only woman writer's name published in the first edition of *Agnes de Castro*, since the author herself was identified only as a 'Young Lady'.

Manley soon kept her promise. *The Lost Lover* was put on at Drury Lane early in 1696, probably in March, a few weeks after the posthumous mangling of Behn's *The Younger Brother*. It is an intrigue comedy with one plot concerning Wildman's attempt to cuckold the Turkey-merchant Smyrna, and the other concerning Wilmore's pursuit of Marina while avoiding the attempts of his ex-mistress, Belira, to marry him off to Marina's mother, Lady Young-Love. The hero's name recalls Behn's Willmore, and his situation, when faced with the reproaches of an abandoned mistress, echoes Willmore's. Belira criticizes her false lover rather more sharply than Angellica does

---

[19] *Agnes de Castro*, sig. A2ᵛ; see the discussion in Ch. 3, above.

[20] *Letters Written by Mrs Manley* (London, 1696), advertises Manley's plays in the Epistle Dedicatory. 'J.H.' builds up expectation about her by suggesting that the two theatres are competing for her work: '*Sir* Thomas Skipworth *and Mr* Betterton *are eagerly contending, who shall first bring you upon the Stage, and which shall be more applauded, your Tragick or Comick Strain*' (A2ʳ⁻ᵛ). *The Lost Lover* was staged at Drury Lane and *The Royal Mischief* rehearsed there, but after disputes with the actors Manley moved in to the rival company at Lincoln's Inn Fields.

[21] R. Foxton, 'Delariviere Manley and "Astrea's Vacant Throne" ', *Notes and Queries*, NS 33 (1986), 41–2.

Willmore,[22] but the overall effect is not so sympathetic to the mistress, or as derogatory to the hero's dignity, as the effect of *The Rover.* Where Behn shows the love-scenes between Willmore and Angellica, making her later anger at his infidelity understandable, Manley's Belira has been cast off before the action begins and is seen rather as a nuisance to the hero. Wilmore is not so much blamed for his desertion of Belira as praised for what is presented as almost excessive generosity when he refuses to foil her plans by telling everyone about his affair with her, which would destroy her reputation and credibility.

While the Wilmore–Belira plot contains Manley's homage to the 'fair Astrea', the other precursor she had invoked in her poem to Trotter receives strange treatment in the play. One of Manley's characters is 'Orinda, an Affected Poetess': a dangerous choice of satiric butt for a starting woman writer.[23] Despite the use of her soubriquet, the portrait of Orinda bears little resemblance to the general image people held at the time of Katherine Philips.[24] She is rather a stereotyped picture of a silly female writer, whose main characteristics are the use of comically vulgar expressions like 'O Gud', 'O Jesu', and 'Lard' (II. i, pp. 12–13), and a propensity to fall in love and write about it, crying: 'O I can't hold my Muse! Muse go Lament the Misfortune' (IV. i, p. 25). At the same time there are hints, never fully developed, of a more sympathetic treatment for Orinda, to whom Wildman is attracted by the end of the play. The contrast between Manley's glorification of female solidarity in her poem to Trotter, and the uneasily belittling portrait of a woman writer within her first play, indicates that the question of how to take up a position as a woman playwright was far from being resolved.

The Lost Lover failed badly on the stage, but Manley's tragedy, *The Royal Mischief,* followed very soon after, at Lincoln's Inn Fields in April 1696. It was rather more successful; the author of *A Comparison Between the Two Stages,* disparaging as he is to Manley's work, admits that it 'made a shift to live half a dozen Days', which was a reasonable run.[25] A heroic tragedy of lust and violence, its treatment of the

[22] Todd, in *Works,* v. 450.

[23] D. Manley, *The Lost Lover* (London: R. Bently, F. Saunders, J. Knapton and R. Wellington, 1696), sig. B2ᵛ.

[24] Backscheider suggests that Manley is responding here to Philips as 'author-function' (*Spectacular Politics,* 73, 76), implying that Manley is rejecting the limiting role encouraged by the praise of Philips for modesty and decorum. However, Manley's Orinda does not reflect this image of Philips. Philips was famously 'chaste Orinda', while Manley's Orinda is mocked for being amorous.   [25] *A Comparison Between the Two Stages* (London, 1702), 31.

violent clash between personal desire and public order makes it, in Derek Hughes's recent assessment, one of the better tragedies of the 1690s, with something of the 'moral subtlety and scepticism of Behn'.[26] On its publication Catharine Trotter and Mary Pix provided poems hailing Manley as a female champion. Trotter, returning the compliment of Manley's verse to her, wrote:

> For us you've vanquisht, though the toil was yours,
> You were our Champion, and the Glory ours.
> Well you've maintain'd our equal right in Fame,
> To which vain Man had quite engrost the claim.

Mary Pix contributed a poem invoking the usual female precursors: Manley, she wrote, was

> Like *Sappho* Charming, like *Afra* Eloquent,
> Like Chast *Orinda*, sweetly *Innocent*. [27]

Pix, the last of the season's four new women dramatists, brought out her first play, *Ibrahim*, at Drury Lane in May or June 1696. Like Manley, she brought out two plays in quick succession, following her heroic tragedy with a farce, *The Spanish Wives*, at Drury Lane, shortly afterwards. Unlike Manley's, her work pleased on the stage. Gildon noted the success of its pathos: 'the Distress of *Morena* never fail'd to bring Tears into the Eyes of the Audience; which few Plays, if any since *Otway*'s, have done'.[28]

Pix's first plays do not respond to Behn's work as clearly as *Agnes de Castro* and *The Lost Lover* do. *Ibrahim* is a Fletcherian tragedy with an Eastern setting, and has little in common with Behn's work. Pix is more reminiscent of Behn in some of her comedies of unsatisfactory marriage. *The Spanish Wives* has echoes of *The Lucky Chance*. The Governor of Barcelona, an old man dotingly fond of his wife, sounds like Behn's Sir Feeble Fainwould as he sings about his desires,[29] and elsewhere in the play there is an echo of Sir Feeble's situation. Elenora, unhappily married to the marquess, was contracted before

---

[26] Hughes, *English Drama 1660–1700*, 446.
[27] *The Royal Mischief* (London, 1696), A3ᵛ.   [28] [Gildon], *Lives and Characters*, 111.
[29] Compare the Governor's song in II. vi: 'I'll rouse ye, and mouse ye, and touse ye as long as I can, | Till squeaking I make ye confess: | There's heat in a vigorous Old Man, | When he loves to excess, when he loves to excess' (*The Spanish Wives* (London: R. Wellington, 1696) 26), with Sir Feeble's boast of the way he used to treat the young wenches: '[I] would rouse 'em, and touse 'em, and blowse 'em'. Sir Feeble also sings a song to indicate his desire and virility (*The Lucky Chance*, I. iii; *Works*, vii. 230).

to Camillus, who comes to get her from her jealous husband—a situation rather similar to that of Leticia, Bellmour, and Sir Feeble Fainwould in Behn's comedy. Divorce easily solves the dilemma. When Elenora worries about her marriage Camillus replies briskly: 'No more o'that; the Cardinal's my Friend, and has promis'd a Divorce immediately' (III. v, p. 46); and there is nothing, in this light-hearted farce, corresponding to *The Lucky Chance*'s treatment of Julia, trapped in an unhappy marriage. In *The Deceiver Deceived* (1697) Pix has a more serious treatment of a similar theme: Olivia has to dismiss the gallant with whom she was in love before her marriage, and is left looking towards widowhood as her best hope.

Though she compared Manley to 'Afra', Pix did not invoke Behn as her own precursor. References to Astrea and Orinda belonged in the martial constructions of female authorship employed by Manley and Trotter, whereas Pix's self-presentation was very different. Her refusal of female tradition held a potential advantage, freeing her to position herself (as, in fact, Behn had done) in the larger tradition of her male forebears; and certainly in *Queen Catharine* (1698) the prologue makes the bold move of referring to Shakespeare's English history plays as her model. This is undercut, though, by the way it is done: she does not simply express a personal diffidence about putting herself in his tradition, but sees it as one closed to all women: 'But how shall Woman after him succeed [?]' The answer is that the woman writer can write a feminine version of a history play, concentrating on the love and grief of the female characters: a solution which could become either a narrowing of scope or the springboard for developing a woman's difference of view.[30] Pix is typically apologetic about her work and female authorship in general. In complete contrast to Manley's self-presentation as the next in a line of female champions, she described her first drama as a 'harmless, modest Play', and its epilogue assured the audience that:

> The Author on her weakness, not her strength relies,
> And from your Justice to your Mercy flies.

When she published it, it was with a dedication that treated female authorship as a shameful weakness revealed in her text: 'I am often told, and always pleased when I hear it, that the Works not mine: but oh I fear your Closet view will soon find out the Woman, the

---

[30] Mary Pix, *Queen Catharine* (London: William Turner and Richard Basset, 1698), sig. A3ʳ.

imperfect Woman there', and a preface that attempted to forestall criticism by admitting: 'I am very sensible those that will be so unkind to Criticize upon what falls from a Womans Pen, may soon find more faults than I am ever able to answer'.[31]

By the end of the 1695–6 season, then, four new women playwrights had had six new plays performed between them. Even given the failure of two of the plays and the modest success of the others, this was an extraordinary event and drew attention to the fact of women's writing for the stage in a very striking way. It is not surprising that the following season saw the production of *The Female Wits*, an anonymous satire which, like Buckingham's *The Rehearsal*, mocks writerly pretensions by showing them displayed at rehearsals. While Buckingham mocked Bays (Dryden) as a writer, however, the 'female wits' (Manley, Pix, and Trotter—Ariadne had dropped out of sight, too insignificant to be included) are derided mainly on sexual grounds.[32] No subsequent season repeated the concentration of woman's plays found in 1695–6, but female playwrights became an established feature of the London theatres. Manley moved on to the political satire that was her greatest success, though she did write two more plays, performed in 1707 and 1717. Trotter wrote four more plays between 1698 and 1707, but her later works were philosophical and religious. Of the three it was Mary Pix, in her apologetic public stance the least Behn-like of the new women playwrights, who most closely followed Behn in the success of her stage career, producing twelve plays between 1696 and 1706.

Behn was used in different ways by the women dramatists of the 1690s, but a recurring theme is the use of her name as a banner to authorize women's ventures into writing. This use of her spread beyond the drama. The feminist potential of the appeal to Behn was exploited by the anonymous author of *An Essay in Defence of the Female Sex* in 1696. Unlike Mary Astell, the best-known of seventeenth-century feminist writers, who grounded her criticisms of women's social role in a Christian scorn for worldly arrangements, and who recommended a religious academy to give gentlewomen a nobler view of their purpose in life, the author of *Defence* was keen to encourage women to take an active part in social and public life. Women's writing seemed to her an emblem of this participation.

[31] Mary Pix, *Ibrahim* (London: John Harding and Richard Wilkin, 1696), p. 42, sig. A2^r, sig. A3^r.   [32] Hughes, *English Drama* 1660–1700, 448–9.

Untroubled by the reputed frivolity or immorality of literary reading, she saw it as an advantage to young girls that they often read 'Books, such as *Romances, Novels, Plays* and *Poems;* which though they read carelessly only for Diversion, yet unawares to them, give 'em very early a considerable Command both of Words and Sense', and she wanted them to put this experience to use in writing. It was because they did not appreciate the extent of their own abilities, she insisted, that women, 'who are commonly charged with talking too much, are Guilty of Writing so little', and she used famous names to try to rouse them: 'I wish they would shake of[f] this lazy Despondence, and let the noble examples of the deservedly celebrated Mrs. *Philips,* and the incomparable Mrs *Behn* rouse their Courages, and shew Mankind the great injustice of their Contempt'. An encomium poem prefaced to her work compared her to both these women, claiming that she had extended their work by turning women's writing from poetry to polemic:

> Long have we sung the Fam'd *Orinda*'s praise,
> And own'd *Astrea*'s Title to the Bays,
> We to their Wit have paid the Tribute due,
> But shou'd be Bankrupt, before just to you.
> Sweet flowing Numbers, and fine Thoughts they writ;
> But you Eternal Truths, as well as Wit.
>
> ('To the most Ingenious Mrs. — o[n] her
> Admirable Defence of Her Sex'). [33]

Behn, then, was generally an enabling model throughout the 1690s. There were certainly references to her undesirable morality, but in some ways this seems to have helped her successors rather than embarrassing them. When Elizabeth Singer's *Poems on Several Occasions. By Philomela* were published in 1696, Elizabeth Johnson cited Behn among a number of female worthies in proof of female ability: 'we have not only *Bunduca*'s [*sic*] and *Zenobia*'s, but *Sappho*'s, and *Behn*'s, and *Schurman*'s, and *Orinda*'s, who have *humbled* the most haughty of our Antagonists'. While some poetesses had spoiled their reputations by indulging in forbidden love, Johnson added, this only set Singer's virtue in strong relief. An anonymous encomium poem continued the theme, proclaiming Singer a virtuous version of two of her three predecessors:

---

[33] *An Essay in Defence of the Female Sex* (London: A Roper and E. Wilkinson, and R. Clavel, 1696), 57, 56, 56, B3ʳ.

> Sappho *and* Behn reform'd, *in thee revive,*
> *In thee we see the* Chast Orinda *live.* [34]

Praise of Trotter claimed that she outshone both Behn and Philips. An encomium poem printed with her tragedy *The Fatal Friendship* in 1698 looked back to '*Charles*'s days' when Orinda and Astrea were writing:

> And we suppos'd Wit cou'd no higher rise,
> Till you succeeding, Tear from them the Prize.[35]

A few years later, Lady Sarah Piers developed this idea in a poem published with Trotter's *The Unhappy Penitent* (1701), which compared Orinda to a faint dawn whose 'slight Charms but warm us at the most'. Though a 'Champion for her Sex' Orinda had been too 'Conscious of Female weakness' to take the bays from men. The poem presents Astrea as stronger than Orinda, but flawed:

> Next gay *Astrea* briskly won the Prize,
> Yet left a spacious room to Criticise.[36]

Finally Trotter herself, the full sun outshining Orinda's morning star, receives the bays from Apollo. Behn's faults, in these examples, prove very useful: they allow new writers to be seen to surpass their predecessor, and help to create the sense of an improving female poetic tradition.

THE EARLY EIGHTEENTH CENTURY

During this period, an accepted role for women writers was gradually consolidated, with the emphases on morality, domesticity, and sentimentality becoming more pronounced. Responses to women's writing concentrated more than ever on what was seen as specifically feminine about it. The feminine writer was being constructed, with all the gains in market opportunity and social authority, and the losses in freedom of range and expression, that this implied. In this process Aphra Behn, the professional precursor, changed her significance. She was still cited, especially in the earlier years, as a positive

[34] *Poems on Several Occasions. Written by Philomela* (London: John Dunton, 1696), sig. A3ᵛ, A7ʳ.
[35] 'To the Author of Fatal-Friendship', in Trotter, *Fatal Friendship* (London: Francis Saunders, 1698), sig. A4ᵛ.
[36] *The Unhappy Penitent: A Tragedy.* (London: William Turner and John Nutt, 1701), sig. A4ᵛ.

role model, but this image of her became gradually displaced by the more negative ones that had coexisted with her praise from the start. By the middle of the century she was mentioned much less often, but she was an implicit presence in the work of some women who still needed, however covertly, to build their own authorial identity in opposition to hers.

Anne Finch and 'The Circuit of Apollo'

Anne Kingsmill Finch, later the Countess of Winchilsea, was one of a number of women who began writing poetry in Behn's lifetime. As a well-born woman, intimate with court circles as one of the maids of honour to Mary of Modena, she lived in a very different world from Behn. During the seventeenth century her poetry circulated in manuscript, free of the commercial pressures that shaped Behn's œuvre, and her literary contacts were not professional playwrights and Grub Street hacks but other court poets like Anne Killigrew, another of the maids of honour.

Despite the huge social gulf between the Countess of Winchilsea and Aphra Behn, the two writers had a number of points in common. Both were pro-Stuart writers, and Finch wrote Jacobite poetry that looked back to Behn's political poetry.[37] There was also a geographic connection between the two, since Kent, where Heneage and Anne Finch lived on their estate after their banishment from court, was Behn's birthplace. This connection is central to 'The Circuit of Apollo', a poem not published in Finch's lifetime but circulated in manuscript. In this poem Finch rewrites the seventeenth-century tradition of the competition for the bays, in which Apollo is depicted judging the pretensions of a number of competitors, usually depicted satirically. As we have seen, Behn had appeared in such poems, a fact which (however satirical her portrait) attested to the extent to which she was understood as part of the literary scene.

Finch's poem constructs an entirely female competition for the bays. Surveying Kent, Apollo finds that there aren't many poets in the county and most of them are women. Four women answer his summons: Alinda, Laura, Valeria, and finally Ardelia (Finch herself). Each is required to prove her poetic merits. We can read the contest

---

[37] Carol Barash, *English Women's Poetry, 1649–1714* (Oxford: Clarendon Press, 1996), 270.

as helping to construct that sense of the specifically feminine concerns of women's poetry that was to become a commonplace of eighteenth-century critical thought. The themes introduced by the first three contestants are respectively love, praise of Orinda, and fear of public exposure. Alinda sings of love, and is praised for her appeal to the emotions: 'So easy the Verse, yett compos'd with such art, | That not one expression, fell short of the heart'.[38] Apollo is moved to accompany her on his lyre. Before he can crown her, however, Laura intervenes by reading her 'paper' praising Orinda, thus establishing the importance of female poetic tradition. While Apollo remains undecided between these two he is taken aside by Valeria, who gives him a paper which she insists he read in private. What Valeria has written is not revealed, though it delights Apollo; so her intervention represents the problem of reconciling poetry with the feminine wariness of publicity also expressed, in less extreme form, by Finch herself. Apollo reproves Valeria, considering her insistence on privacy a misuse of her gift: he 'told her withall | If she kept itt still close, he'd the Talent recall' (Folger, 44). Ardelia comes last 'as expecting least praise', for she writes to please herself and not for fame. There is of course biblical precedence for the idea that the last shall be first, and Ardelia's meekness seems calculated to inherit the earthly success she disparages. Finch, recognizing this, provides Apollo with a telling retort to her own stance, articulated not only here but throughout her poetry, as the poet of retreat and retirement:

> But Appollo reply'd, tho' so carelesse she seem'd,
> Yett the Bays, if her share, wou'd be hig[h]ly esteem'd.

(Folger, 45)

Instead of crowning Ardelia/Finch, as her position in the group may have led the reader to expect, Apollo ends the poem on that note of comic inconclusiveness common to many poems of this type. As he is about to make an oration he remembers that no woman can bear to have another preferred before her, and decides to award the prize to all, but this does not please the contenders either. Apollo has to refer the question to the muses, since no man—or male immortal—would dare to antagonize three out of the four women.

[38] Folger MS N.b.3, 44. The poem is printed in *Poems of Anne Countess of Winchilsea*, ed. Myra Reynolds (Chicago: University of Chicago Press, 1904). I am grateful to Carol Barash for enabling me to consult the Folger MS version, and to Germaine Greer for discussing the MS readings with me.

This light ending, while undermining the pretensions of all four contenders, highlights by contrast the more elegiac tone of the early part of the poem, which identifies Behn as the lost woman poet against whom, it is implied, Apollo will judge her successors. Apollo's sorrow that Kent can only provide him with four women poets is directly linked to his sorrow for the loss of one who surpassed them all:

> A summons sent out, was obey'd but by four,
> When Ph[o]ebus, afflicted, to meet with no more,
> And standing, where sadly, he now might descry,
> From the banks of the Stowre the desolate Wye,
> He lamented for Behn, o're that place of her birth,
> And said amongst [females][39] was not on the earth,
> Her superior in fancy, in language, or witt,
> Yett own'd that a little too loosly she writt;
> Since the art of the Muse, is to stirr up soft thoughts,
> Yett to make all hearts beat, without blushes, or faults.

(Folger, 43)

This is an extraordinary tribute. While Laura praises Orinda, the model of virtuous writing, Apollo himself mourns for Behn, and not as 'Astrea', the convenient goddess of Manley's martial encomia, but under her own name and firmly located in her Kentish birthplace. That Finch, in a marginal note to this poem, was keen to specify Behn's social place as a barber's daughter and no gentlewoman, only underscores her determination to commemorate a real poet rather than an artificially perfect precursor. The final lines of this passage, containing Apollo's admission of Behn's shortcomings, should be read in this context, not as the later poet's rejection of Behn in the name of virtue, but as her admiring and troubled response to a predecessor who is as yet unmatched. Behn, who wrote so publicly and so 'loosly', is not an easy model for Ardelia and her friends and rivals, who are trying to write movingly yet chastely, and to be as removed from public gaze as is consistent with entering the poetic contest at all. That none of them can, in Apollo's judgement, surpass their untrammelled predecessor, indicates that Finch was aware how problematic was the opposite ideal to which she herself was drawn, that

---

[39] Myra Reynolds renders this as 'Femens': see *Poems of Anne Countess of Winchilsea*, 92. In the Folger MS the word is originally 'Women'; this has been crossed out and another word, 'femeles' or 'females', substituted above.

of the chastely circumscribed feminine poet. Behn has left Finch with a difficult task: her aim, recorded in 'The Circuit of Apollo', is to write poetry as stirring as Behn's while remaining within the confines of feminine modesty.

Susanna Centlivre, Delarivier Manley, and Eliza Haywood

When the Countess of Winchilsea aimed to write without becoming disgraced, she did so with the advantages of her social status and the fact that she need not write for money. Other women writers were following Behn into the world of commercial writing. Delarivier Manley and Eliza Haywood were Behn's two most prominent female successors in the early eighteenth-century fictional market, while Susanna Centlivre was by far the most successful of the eighteenth-century women who wrote for the stage as a living. While all three of these writers were influenced by Behn's work, perhaps her greatest significance for them was as a model for a woman's writing career. Another novelist, Mary Hearne, took Behn's *Love-Letters* as a model for her own fiction.

    In December 1709, the popular periodical the *Female Tatler* ran a number advertising *The Man's Bewitch'd; or, The Devil to do about her*, the latest comedy by a well-known playwright. 'Emilia', one of the fictional 'Society of Ladies' who supposedly edited the paper, reported that 'This Evening the *Ingenious* Mrs. *Centlivre* did me the Favour of a *Visit*, . . . her Business then was chiefly to have my Opinion of her *New Comedy*, for that she *spy'd* me out the first Night in the *Box* . . . the whole Company *Congratulated* her on the *Success* of her *Performance*, and were rejoyc'd to see the inimitable Mrs. *Bhen* so nearly reviv'd in Mrs. *Centlivre*'. The new play was praised as 'a genteel, Easy and Diverting Comedy', with 'a better Plot, and as many Turns in it' as the same author's famous *The Busy Body*. At the same time the paper was careful to point out that Centlivre had not offended the ladies of the audience: 'The *Ladies* highly commended the *Author*, as what cou'd they expect less from one of their own *Sex*, for the Care she had taken not to Offend the *nicest Ear*, with the least *Double Entendre*'.[40] Though the contrast with the inimitable Behn, who had reputedly annoyed the ladies with the bawdry of *The Lucky Chance*, was not

---

[40] *Female Tatler*, 69 (Mon. 12 Dec.–Wed. 14 Dec. 1709). *The Man's Bewitch'd* was first performed on 12 Dec., and there was a second performance on 14 Dec.

explicitly drawn, it is evident that the *Female Tatler* was trying to place Centlivre as a new Behn for a new age.

If Susanna Centlivre herself was the author of this puff for her play (a charge she vehemently denied),[41] it is a rare example of her making the link between herself and her predecessor which earlier women writers had been so keen to exploit.[42] In general Centlivre avoided the martial imagery used by Manley and Trotter for women's writing, though she did supply Sarah Fyge Egerton with an encomium poem, addressing her as 'Champion for our Sex' and exhorting her to 'go on and show | Ambitious Man what Womankind can do'.[43] She arrived on the London literary scene a few years later than Manley, Pix, and Trotter, first coming to notice around 1700 when her first play, *The Perjur'd Husband,* was performed at Drury Lane.[44] While the earlier women had used Behn's name to make their own way into the theatre, Carroll, later Centlivre, did not. By this time, female playwrights were less of a novelty, and the new emphasis on pleasing the ladies with moral writing offered an alternative way of claiming female authority. For Centlivre in particular, who identified early with the Whig cause and consistently supported Whig policies in her plays, the famously Tory Behn was not the best of role models.

Nevertheless, she was the one who inherited Behn's position as most successful and popular female playwright of her generation. She wrote nineteen plays, three of which, *The Busy Body, A Bold Stroke for a Wife,* and *The Wonder,* were among the most successful comedies of the century, and continued to entertain audiences into the nineteenth century. Centlivre in fact outstrips all women dramatists of 1660–1800, Behn included, in the number of performances of her plays.[45] Centlivre pleased audiences by her clever use of intrigue and

---

[41] The *Female Tatler* article quoted Centlivre's strong complaints about the behaviour of the actors. In her preface to the first edition of the play Centlivre denied having written this, pointing out that it could only damage the run of her play, and that it would have been folly to have written so openly about herself. The case for Centlivre's authorship of this and a number of the *Female Tatler* papers is made by Paul Bunyan Anderson in 'Innocence and Artifice: or, Mrs. Centlivre and *The Female Tatler*', *Philological Quarterly*, 16/4 (1937), 358–75.

[42] The two writers are implicitly linked in letters published as between Susanna Carroll (later Centlivre) and George Farquhar, in which she sometimes signs herself 'Astrea' and he calls himself 'Celadon'; but it is not clear if the letters are genuine. See *Familiar Letters of Love, Gallantry, and Several Occasions,* ii. 277–91.

[43] *Poems on Several Occasions, together with a Pastoral. By Mrs. S.F.* (London: J. Nutt (1703?)) (A7ʳ). [44] Bowyer, *The Celebrated Mrs Centlivre,* 25–6, 32.

[45] Judith Stanton, 'This New-Found Path Attempting', in M. A. Schofield and C. Macheski (eds.), *Curtain Calls* (Athens, Oh.: Ohio University Press, 1991), 334–5.

her creation of new comic characters such as Marplot, the amiable bungler of *The Busy Body*. In many ways, her career echoes Behn's. Like Behn's her origins are obscure, and our ideas of them coloured by fanciful biographies.[46] Like Behn, she had to negotiate her position as a woman author: she faced criticisms of her first play for indecent expressions, as Behn had done in *The Lucky Chance*, and like Behn she justified the language she used as suited to the characters she had created, and complained that 'the *Beaus*' were more apt to criticize a woman writer than a man.[47] Like Behn, in the early stages of her career she alternated between presenting her work implicitly as a man's, and making a point of its female authorship; and like Behn, she faced disparagement of her work as a woman's, in her case most famously from the actor Robert Wilks, who was said to have thrown his part in *The Busy Body* in the pit as a 'woeful thing writ by a Woman'.[48]

Like Behn, Centlivre laid claim to entertainment rather than to classical rules, as a way of making the stage seem accessible to a woman. But where Behn also showed, in other moods, the extent of her ambition for 'my masculine part the poet in me', it is likely that Centlivre was the more acceptable as an author because she laid no claim to belonging in a prestigious male tradition.[49] She was praised in limiting terms. Elizabeth Inchbald, summing up her achievements in the early nineteenth century, defends her theatrical achievements while distinguishing them from those of poetic authorship. Centlivre, she writes, is not to be compared as an author to Congreve, but 'as plays are productions that depend on action, and require talents of a nature, in which writing has, perhaps, the smallest share, Mrs Centlivre has . . . been more attractive on the stage than the great poet whom her success offended'.[50]

Centlivre, then, squarely based her version of the writing woman on her skill as a professional entertainer. How did she use that earlier professional entertainer, Aphra Behn? It is not always easy to distinguish specific Behn influence from the general similarities shared by two playwrights using the conventions of comic intrigue, and

[46] James R. Sutherland, 'The Progress of Error: Mrs. Centlivre and the Biographers', *RES* 18 (1942), 167–82.

[47] Preface to *The Perjur'd Husband*, in *The Dramatic Works of the Celebrated Mrs. Centlivre* (London: John Pearson, 1872), i. sig. B2^r.   [48] Bowyer, *The Celebrated Mrs. Centlivre*, 89.

[49] See Rosenthal, *Playwrights and Plagiarists*, 206.

[50] Inchbald, *The British Theatre*, xi, 'Remarks', prefaced to *The Wonder*, 3–4.

sometimes a similarity of names misleads critics who are keen to see the later woman's work reflecting the earlier's.[51] Nevertheless, Behn's work does find echoes in Centlivre's. Centlivre's reference to a rakish male character as a 'Rover' suggests a consciousness of Behn's popular comedy,[52] and her early plays, in particular, indicate how pervasive Behn's presence was. In *The Perjur'd Husband* characters refer casually to Behn's poetry, clearly indicating its fashionable nature: the maid Lucy reports that she found Ludovico 'in his study, reading the Lover's Watch, which he swears does not at all agree with his Constitution' (II. i, *Dramatic Works*, i. 18–19), and later, offering to smuggle Ludovico into Lady Pizalto's chamber, she promises: 'if you dare take me for your Pilot, I'll warrant you success in your Voyage— I'll set you safe in the Island of Love' (III. iii, *Dramatic Works*, i. 35). In *The Beau's Duel* (1702), the two-couple comedy is very reminiscent of *The Rover*. When Emilia teases Clarinda with questions about her lover, their exchange, beginning with Clarinda's 'Dear *Emilia*, you ask so many Questions, pr'thee have some Pity, and spare me a little' (I. ii, *Dramatic Works*, i. 72), closely echoes Florinda's with Hellena, beginning 'What an Impertinent thing is a Young girl bred in a Nunnery? How full of Questions? Prithee no more' (*The Rover*, I. i, *Works*, v. 455). Mrs Plotwell offers an interesting variant on the cast-mistress character: now that she has a fortune she is no longer interested in her old lover, Bellmein, and is enjoying the opportunity for a life of virtue. Her machinations and clever use of disguise drive the comedy forward. Comparing this with Behn's treatment of the cast mistress in Angellica it is easy to see how the later and gentler comedy offers female characters stage-power on condition of their virtue.

After *The Beau's Duel* Centlivre does not draw so extensively on Behn's work again, though it forms part of the background to her

---

[51] Rosenthal (*Playwrights and Plagiarists*, 47) reads Angelica in *The Gamester* as a variant on the Angellica of *The Rover*, though Centlivre's Angelica, a cross-dressing heroine who reforms her lover by outwitting him, is a different character-type from Behn's, and derives rather from the Angelique of Centlivre's source-plays, Jean-François Regnard's *Le Joueur* and Charles du Fresnoy's *Le Chevalier Joueur*. See J. M. Cameron, 'Centlivre, not Shirley', *Notes and Queries*, NS 43/3 (1996), 292–6.

[52] See e.g. the song in II. ei of *The Platonick Lady* (1707):

> Ask him who most affects the Rover's Part,
> Caressing every fair that will be kind,
> If some one Woman reigns not in his Heart;
> And is the sovereign Mistress of his Mind (*Dramatic Works*, ii. 213).

comedies as does the more contemporary work of Farquhar. As her work matures she develops her more original situations and roles, less directly influenced by other playwrights. Behn is significant to Centlivre, then, not so much as somebody whose work she is revising and extending, but as an enabling model for the role of the woman dramatist as successful entertainer.

Before Centlivre began writing for the stage, Delarivier Manley had called on the 'fair Astrea' in her attempt to authorize a new female dramatic tradition, but it was in her prose fiction that she herself most successfully followed Behn's example. Her most famous work, *The New Atalantis* (1709), and the *Memoirs of Europe* (1710),[53] drawing on the French tradition of the *chronique scandaleuse* and especially on the work of Marie d'Aulnoy,[54] also showed the influence of Behn's *Love-Letters* in their attacks on political figures through exposure of their love-lives. Like Anne Finch, Delarivier Manley could look back to Behn as a political precursor. Their methods and effects were very different, however. It is difficult to extract a clear partisan political message from the later parts of *Love-Letters*, in which Behn begins to articulate a dark vision of all political engagement.[55] Manley, by contrast, wrote her political fictions as direct pieces of propaganda with the clear intention of influencing current events. *The New Atalantis* and *Memoirs of Europe* attacked leading Whig figures at a time when this would prove helpful to Robert Harley, who engineered the Tory rise to power in 1710.[56] In keeping with this clear political purpose, Manley favours an unambiguous narrative style. *The New Atalantis* recounts numerous episodes of Whig perfidy, treachery in love, as in *Love-Letters*, matching wrongdoing in state affairs. Names are disguised but broad hints to identities are given (a key was also published), and the episodes are framed by explanations and comments from a trio of female deities—Virtue, her daughter Astrea, goddess of justice, and Lady Intelligence, who brings them their information.

The Astrea of *The New Atalantis* may contain, as Ballaster argues, a reference to the pen-name by which Manley had celebrated Behn

---

[53] *The Secret History of Queen Zarah and the Zarazians* (1705) has also been ascribed to Manley, but there is no clear evidence that it was hers.

[54] See Ballaster, *Seductive Forms*, 123–31, for a discussion of Manley's debt to d'Aulnoy.

[55] See Todd, *Secret Life*, 388–91.

[56] Ballaster, introduction to *The New Atalantis* (London: Penguin, 1992), pp. xvi–xvii.

thirteen years previously;[57] but no sustained comparison of Manley's Astrea to Behn's poetic persona can be made. It is as goddess of justice that this Astrea has her main significance. Her return to earth has a political motive: she is on earth to guide a young scion of the House of Hanover so that he shall become, in time, a good British ruler.[58] Her pronouncements on the dire moral state of Atalantis/Britain, in which the only gods revered are Bacchus and Venus 'in their most criminal rites' (*New Atalantis*, 11); her firm understanding of feminine passivity in erotic affairs in which women 'seldom are, and never ought to be, the aggressors' (81); and her desire to have her prince 'renowned for his chastity' (81) and to introduce severe penalties for forbidden love (228), all fit her role as the prim, shockable, otherworldly visitor, speaking for justice in a corrupt age. A narrative voice descended from Behn is found not in Astrea but rather in the stories of erotic misdemeanour told by Intelligence, who quotes Rochester to illustrate the force of love, and whose worldly-wise comments on passion recall the narrator of *The Fair Jilt* and *The History of the Nun*: 'The god of Love finds little more difficulty in subduing the grave than the gay, the desires he gives are alike ubiquitary, and, if he sometimes reign more potently, 'tis in the heart of those to whom nature has given the largest portion of understanding' (193). Manley's fiction, then, takes from Behn in two ways: in her development of a narrative authority based on a woman's knowledge, especially of love, and in her deployment of that authority in political fiction.

Mary Hearne, the author of two short novels, *The Lover's Week* (1718) and *The Female Deserters* (1719), took both Behn and Manley as models for her epistolary love-stories. Having no premonition of the critical reaction to come, she considered that Delarivier Manley's 'NAME prefix'd to any thing of LOVE, who have carry'd that Passion to the most elegant Height in your own Writings, is enough to protect any Author who attempts to follow in that mysterious Path'.[59] An encomium poem, signed Joseph Gay, complimented the writer on her erotic style in terms very familiar from the praises heaped on Behn as poet of love. In this poem there was no anxiety about

---

[57] Ballaster, *Seductive Forms*, 114–15.

[58] See *The New Atalantis*, 8, for Astrea's explanation of her mission, to which she refers on occasion throughout the novel. Ballaster's notes, 270, identify Astrea's young prince with the future George II.

[59] Mary Hearne, *The Lover's Week: or, the Six Days Adventures of Philander and Amaryllis* (2nd edn., London: E. Curll and R. Francklin, 1718), dedication.

dividing women writers by morality: Hearne was encouraged to 'rival our ORINDA in Applause', and 'Let BEHN and MANLEY not eclipse thy Name'.[60] Hearne's hero is named after Behn's Philander, and he reads 'the famous Mrs. *Behn's* Novels', as a prelude to seducing the heroine (*The Lover's Week*, p. 17). The novel ends with the lovers happily secluded together in a rural retreat.

Eliza Haywood published her first novel shortly after Hearne's. *Love in Excess* (1719) also took seduction and attempted seduction as its theme, though it did not treat them so lightly as Hearne's novel did. Haywood was also hailed as an erotic writer, and as we saw in Chapter 2, she was identified, first in panegyric but quickly, and more persistently, in detraction, as the heir to both Behn and Manley. This extraordinarily prolific and popular writer, whose novels are the reason why the 1720s was a more productive decade for fiction than the ones preceding or the one following it, went even further than Behn in founding her narrative authority on a feminine viewpoint on love. Though she did write some political scandal somewhat in Manley's vein—*The Adventures of Eovaii* (1736) is an attack on Walpole—most of Haywood's novels offer amatory fiction without party-political allegory.[61] Her writing career is an index of the growing commercial opportunities opening up for the writer of short amatory novels.[62] Haywood's novel-writing career spanned the period of moralization and sentimentalization of the form, and her later novels implicitly renounce her place in the Behn–Manley–Haywood triumvirate. Placed by Reeve as an unfortunate erring heroine herself, 'seduced' by Behn's and Manley's example into writing wicked novels but proving her redemption through her later moral narratives,[63] Haywood was mythologized for the later eighteenth century as an exemplary instance of the woman novelist's escape from the corrupting influence of Behn.

Jane Barker, Aphra Behn, and the writing nun

If Centlivre, Manley, and, for all her later repudiation, Haywood, are Behn's followers because her example helped them develop their pro-

---

[60] 'To the Fair and Ingenious Author', in *The Lover's Week*.

[61] Ballaster, *Seductive Forms*, 153–6.

[62] For a discussion of Haywood's career and her exploitation of the image of amorous writer see Sarah Prescott, 'British Women Writers of the 1720s: Feminist Literary History and the Early Eighteenth-Century Novel', Ph.D. thesis (Exeter, 1997), 61–94.

[63] Clara Reeve, *The Progress of Romance*, i. 120–1.

fessional role, Behn's writing has a more complex influence on one writer who was adamant that she did not want to follow Behn's example. During the 1720s, when Haywood was still building on her legacy from Behn, Jane Barker was already attempting to extricate herself from an influence she felt to be dangerous. Up to this time women writers had either praised Behn or mingled admiration with uneasiness about her 'warmth' and 'looseness', but Barker broke decisively with these responses, and her one direct reference to Behn is emphatic in its condemnation. She depicts the semi-autobiographical Galesia, narrator of *Love Intrigues* (1713) and the central figure in *A Patch-Work Screen for the Ladies* (1723) and *The Lining of the Patch-Work Screen* (1726), rejecting the whole tradition of combining in '*Orinda*'s Judgment, and *Astrea*'s Fire' a valued legacy from both famous seventeenth-century precursors.[64] Katherine Philips figures prominently in her work as the poet to whose achievement she most aspires, while Aphra Behn is rejected. In *A Patch-Work Screen* Galesia describes her own awkward efforts to join in London literary conversation: 'One ask'd me, If I lik'd Mrs. *Philips*, or Mrs. *Behn* best? To whom I reply'd, with a blunt Indignation, That *they ought not to be nam'd together:* And so, in an unthinking, unmannerly Way, reproach'd the Lady that endeavour'd to divert and entertain me; she having that Moment been pleased to couple them.'[65] The revulsion from Behn is palpable, but so is the sense of blunder in her expression of it. Galesia's social ineptitude (contrasting sharply with the conversational brilliance frequently attributed to Behn) is linked to her rejection of the predecessor who 'endeavour'd to divert and entertain' her readers as Galesia's hapless companion tries to entertain her.

We can read, in this, Barker's coded expression of her own resistance to the role of popular author, whose works sold as *The Entertaining Novels of Mrs. Jane Barker.* Her early work is poetry, from the pastoral verse published in the 1680s to the Jacobite poetry written in exile after the 1688 revolution. In politics, like Anne Finch, she was close to Behn, but even more than Finch she wanted to dissociate herself from the amorous voice of Behn's verse. Back in London in the early 1700s, Barker turned to the literary market to enhance her income, and was published and promoted by Edmund Curll as one

---

[64] '*To Mrs. S.F. on her Poems*', *Poems on Several Occasions, together with a Pastoral. By Mrs. S.F.* (London: J. Nutt (1703?)), sig. A5ʳ.

[65] *The Galesia Trilogy*, ed. C. S. Wilson (New York: Oxford University Press, 1997), 108.

of his popular amorous writers, so that the unusual story of a heroine who achieves a virgin life dedicated to poetry and medicine was marketed as *Love Intrigues: or the Amours of Bosvil and Galesia*. Her homages to Orinda, a chaste model for the female poet, and her rejection of Behn, are connected to her wish to avoid the identity of commercial novelist and to retain that of a pastoral poet free of the degradations of the literary market.[66]

Barker's revulsion from Behn's example was coupled with a fascination with her work, in particular the plots of her novels. Her last two publications, *A Patch-Work Screen* and *The Lining*, contain stories loosely held together by a framework in which Galesia recounts her adventures and exchanges stories with a group of ladies. Various characters narrate inset stories, and these borrow in a number of places from Behn's novels. The new impulse to moralize fiction is starkly present in Barker's use of her originals. Stories with an ambiguous moral or with no explicit moralizing at all are modified in the direction of crude didacticism. For example, the interlinked tales 'The History of the Lady Gypsie' and 'The Story of Tangerine, The Gentleman Gypsie', draw on 'The Wandring Beauty', one of the stories published in the 1700 edition of Behn's *Histories and Novels*. The story of a young woman who leaves home to avoid an arranged marriage and manages, while concealing her birth and quality, to secure the love of a rich and worthy husband, is modified by Barker to include clear narrative condemnation of the heroine's disobedience and independence of spirit—qualities the original narrative tended to endorse.[67]

Where Barker's imagination was most fired, and most troubled, by Behn's work was in her stories of nuns. In their frequent references to nuns both writers were drawing on a fictional tradition of the nun both as sexual transgressor and as writer. The nun, supposedly dedicated to God and to chastity, provided a particularly potent image for the exploration of religious and sexual transgression. She is a frequent figure in pornographic literature, but also appears in more mainstream literature. The letters of the nun Héloïse to her lover Abelard became particularly important to eighteenth-century readers through Pope's poem. More influential in Behn's time was a set of letters from a fictional nun: the *Lettres Portugaises* (1669), purporting to

---

[66] See Prescott, 'British Women Novelists', 204–14.
[67] Pearson, 'The History of *The History of the Nun*', 243.

be the letters of a Portuguese nun to her unfaithful lover, were translated into English by Sir Roger de l'Estrange as *Five Love-Letters from a Nun to a Cavalier* (1678), and Behn used this work in her own development of an epistolary voice. The Portuguese nun's letters are presented as the despairing cries of an abandoned woman. It is central to the effect that there are no replies from the lover: her unanswered calls constitute a display of feminine vulnerability, passion, and defeat. Behn's own 'Love-Letters to a Gentleman' aim for something of the same effect in recording the voice of a passionate woman, but complicate it with the resilience of a speaker who, far from brooding on her lover in the loneliness of the cloister, suffers love in the midst of a busy urban life. Her lover's visits, her own visits to friends, and above all the references to her other, professional writing, which remind the reader that this is not her only voice, both add a sense of reality to her passion by contextualizing it, and refuse to confine her within that passion. Behn's *Love-Letters*, especially Part I, also draw on the epistolary tradition of the Portuguese nun, though with a twist: both lovers write and their letters chart the progress towards consummation rather than the process of loss and abandonment.

In both these works, the methods of the Portuguese nun are used to express the passion of female speakers who are emphatically not nuns. Elsewhere in her fiction, Behn focuses directly on the figure of the passionate nun, but instead of providing her with an epistolary voice, she places her within third-person narratives which chart the progress of her passion. Behn's nuns, active in the pursuit of their transgressive desires, become criminals, and these heroines prove particularly influential on Barker's work. Three of the stories published in Behn's collected novels deal prominently with the desiring nun. In *The Fair Jilt* Miranda belongs to the Beguines, an order of nuns who make temporary vows, and so occupy the borderline between worldly life and dedication to God. Miranda's lust for the young friar combines religious and sexual transgression, and these lead as if by natural progression to her later crimes, when she enlists her page and her husband Tarquin in a plan to murder her sister. In *The History of the Nun*, which has the most direct bearing on Barker's work, the heroine's violation of her holy vows when she runs away from the convent with her lover is seen as the source of her later sensational crime as the murderer of two husbands. *The Nun: or, the Perjur'd Beauty*, one of the posthumous stories, reprises the theme: Ardelia takes the veil during a fit of depression when her love for

Henrique appears hopeless, and later plans to escape with him, but everything goes wrong when she falls in love with Don Sebastian.

The nuns of Behn's stories act out forbidden desires, instead of expressing hopeless passion, but like the Portuguese nun, they bear a metaphorical relationship to the figure of the writing woman. The narrator of Behn's stories is never given a name, but the remarks she drops about her travels and her writing implicitly identify her as a version of Aphra Behn the writer. This narrator tells the stories of nuns in the third person, but she confides to the reader her sense of kinship with these heroines. 'I once was design'd an humble Votary in the House of Devotion', she announces in *The History of the Nun*, 'but fancying my self not endu'd with an obstinacy of Mind, great enough to secure me from the Efforts and Vanities of the World, I rather chose to deny my self that Content I could not certainly prom- ise my self, than to languish (as I have seen some do) in a certain Affliction' (*Works*, iii. 212). This 'Behn' avoided the mistakes of her fic- tional nuns by choosing the world and writing, and the influential 'Memoirs' underlined this sense of her alternative, worldly vocation by describing her life after Antwerp as 'entirely dedicated to Pleasure and Poetry'.[68] 'Behn' has escaped from the convent.

For Barker, the writing and desiring nun is a particularly prob- lematic figure. The Portuguese nun links women's writing with for- bidden desire: she writes because she loves, and if she were true to her vows she would be silent. Barker, a Catholic convert who repeat- edly links her writing vocation with fidelity to God, to James II, and to a virgin life, wants to reverse the meaning of the nun's writing. Writing shall no longer signify the forbidden, but the achievement of a virgin identity beyond desire. Through the persona of Galesia, her fiction attempts to rework the story of the abandoned Portuguese nun. *Love Intrigues* deals with the familiar story of a lover's perfidy and his lady's grief, while renouncing the passionate despair of the Portuguese nun. Galesia does not write passionate missives to her faithless lover, Bosvil; instead, she recounts their story to a friend after the event, concentrating on an attempt to rationalize Bosvil's way- ward behaviour, to analyse her own feelings, and to celebrate the way they have been overcome. *A Patch-Work Screen* and *The Lining* continue the story of Galesia's unfortunate life, dedicated to serving an exiled king and writing in the cause of virtue. In Galesia and in Fidelia, the

---

[68] *Histories and Novels* (London: S. Briscoe, 1696), sig. C2ᵛ.

speaker of her poems, Barker recreates the figure of the writing nun. This time she writes because she is true to her vows, not because she is perjured.

Where Behn's fiction presents the cloister as a confinement against which the desiring subject rebels and which the writing subject has escaped, Barker locates the writing subject in various scenes in which a wicked world is rejected. At the same time she makes Galesia ambivalent about her muse, who is both the 'gentle *Muse*' who provides her with a welcome retreat from the world into her garret closet, 'a kind of Paradise; where I thought I met with my old Acquaintance as we hope to do in the other World' (*A Patch-Work Screen*, in *The Galesia Trilogy*, 122), and, simultaneously, a dangerous force that 'again took Possession of me: Poetry being one of those subtle Devils, that if driven out by never so many firm Purposes . . . yet it will always return and find a Passage to the Heart, Brain, and whole Interior' (124). Barker wants to conceive of writing as a nun's vocation, yet is troubled by the sense that it may be something less holy. It follows that Behn's stories of desiring nuns are particularly fascinating and troublesome to her.

Barker fits three different stories of nuns into *A Patch-Work Screen* and *The Lining*. The first is told in *A Patch-Work Screen* by one of the passengers in Galesia's stage-coach. This is a tale of desire overcoming devotion, as in Behn's similar stories, but here the story is made as safe as possible. The lovers meet legitimately, and only insufficient fortune forbids their marriage; the young lady enters the convent in an attempt to overcome her passion, and she has not taken her final vows at the time when her lover returns, rich and able to marry her. Even so, her letters from the cloister are full of her sense of the guilt represented by writing: 'My Thoughts, Words, Writings, on this Occasion, are Faults! The very Corresponding with the young Lady you placed here, is a Fault!' (69). The situation is resolved when she comes to the altar to take her final vows, and declares she will take vows to marry her lover instead. Not only does she secure her parents' and the Church's agreement, but the young Huguenot page employed by her lover to correspond with her confesses at the same time to being really a girl in love with the chevalier, and since he is about to marry another, she begs to be allowed to take the veil herself. With this swap the Church is satisfied: 'the Nuns received the Hugonot; the Couple was married; and Things were brought to a happy Conclusion' (71).

The other stories of desiring nuns do not end so happily. In *The Lining*, Galesia meets an old acquaintance, Philinda, who tells the assembled company a story 'from her old Book': this is a much shortened and simplified version of Behn's *The History of the Nun*. Behn's novel resists easy moral interpretation. Though it begins with an unequivocal condemnation of violated vows, which are the root cause of the heroine's later crimes, much of the story is given over to a detailed rendering, in Behn's erotic vein, of the progress of Isabella's passion for Henault. The narrator's commentary is more sympathetic than ironic as the heroine gives up the struggle for virtue:

She had try'd Fasting long, Praying fervently, rigid Penances and Pains, severe Disciplines, all the Mortification, almost to the destruction of Life itself, to conquer the unruly Flame; but still it burnt and rag'd but the more; so, at last, she was forc'd to permit that to conquer her, she could not conquer, and submitted to her Fate, as a thing destin'd her by Heaven itself; and, after all this opposition, she fancy'd it was resisting even Divine Providence, to struggle any longer with her Heart (*Works*, iii. 235).

In contrast, Barker's nun, without any inner conflict, simply 'enter'd into an Intrigue with a Cavalier' and plans to run away with him, which is easily done: 'she that could suffer her self to consent to the Temptation of the Flesh, the Devil was at hand to help her through, and found a means for her Escape, to the utter breach of her Solemn Religious Vow of Chastity' (*The Lining*, in *The Galesia Trilogy*, 214–15). In Behn's novel the relationship with Villenoys, Isabella's second husband, is also rendered in detail, from his early unrequited love for her to their later meeting, after she believes Henault to be dead. Behn, while sympathizing more with the vow-breaker, also makes her more guilty: she kills Henault and deliberately causes Villenoys's death. She evades suspicion with a plausible tale, and is only incriminated later when an old friend of Henault's comes to the town. She then repents as stylishly and eloquently as she had earlier concealed her crimes, and dies 'generally Lamented' (*Works*, iii. 258). In contrast, Barker's curt tale strips the glamour from guilt. She makes her nun kill the first husband deliberately but the second by accident; and she is immediately suspected, confesses, and is punished, with her epitaph an anticlimactic proverb '*Marry in haste, and Repent at leisure*' (*The Galesia Trilogy*, 217).

A few pages later another lady relates a story about 'the *Portuguese*

Nun, whose amorous Letters have been the Entertainment of all the World' (222–3). The object of Barker's revision here is not a particular Behn story but the identity of the erotic woman writer, figured by the Portugese nun and by Behn herself, another famous writer who entertains with amorous letters. Barker's technique here is to take from the Portuguese nun the epistolary voice that makes her attractive. Her narrator turns resolutely from everything about the Portuguese nun that had fascinated readers: 'We will not pretend to know or guess, by what steps of Fancy or Cogitation they climb'd up to an extream Passion, such as her printed Letters demonstrate, or how they first discover'd their amorous Sentiments each to other' (224). This nun, instead of being abandoned and writing in her grief, uses her correspondence with her lover (mentioned but never rendered in the narrative) to plan an escape that is made as wicked as possible. Literalizing the common metaphor of passion as fire, she conceals her escape by burning the body of another nun in her own bed, taking the risk that the convent may burn down altogether. The nuns survive, she marries and has children, but on her husband's untimely death she falls into convulsions, confesses, and dies; and her children are left likely to lose their inheritance because their parents' marriage is null. The Portuguese nun's voice is recorded not in her passion but only as the confession of a dying criminal: 'How was it possible, I say, to break all Laws Divine and Human, and to become so great a Monster as to hazard the burning of so stately an Edifice, and in so doing, murder so many excellent pious Persons!' (226) Through her moralized versions of the traditional tales of desiring nuns, Barker attempted to exorcise the influence of the erotic woman writer, most strongly represented for her by the entertaining novelist Aphra Behn, and to establish a way of being a commercial novelist that would be compatible with being a religious writer.

THE LATER EIGHTEENTH CENTURY

In the middle of the eighteenth century, as the image of the virtuous woman writer grew in dominance, Behn's significance as a precursor changed. While her novels and plays continued to sell, she was more and more often referred to as a bad example for women writers. Particularly in the novel, the genre most concerned with the rejection of Behn, women writers needed to differentiate themselves from

Behn. This is implicit in the work of Sarah Fielding, which claims moral authority for the truth-telling female author in unspoken contrast to the scandal-mongering of earlier writers like Behn and Manley.[69] In Eliza Haywood's later novels, as we saw in Chapter 2, Behn's *Love-Letters* are used to stand for the erotic tradition which is now to be transformed into new, moral fiction. In the discourse surrounding female authorship, women writers' respectability was being assured by divesting them of the rakishness associated with Behn. Thomas Birch, for example, presented Catharine Trotter (later Cockburn) as 'a model woman writer . . . an exemplary, self-sacrificing wife and mother' in his 1751 biography.[70] Explicit references to Behn in the context of a female tradition of writing were now negative ones, made by men who wanted to establish the virtue of the new woman writer: John Duncombe praised female geniuses by contrast with 'modern Manley, Centlivre and Behn'.[71]

By the later eighteenth century, women writers no longer needed to define themselves in relation to Behn. Now less read and rarely performed, she was not the dominating presence she had been at the beginning of the century. Women writers had come to an accommodation with patriarchal society whereby they were granted a feminine authority on condition that they kept to feminine proprieties, so Behn was less needed either as an authorizing model or as a negative example. In these conditions it was possible for women writers to show a new detachment in their attitudes to Behn, who nevertheless remained an important figure for many of them, especially the new generation of women critics and editors who were turning their attention to writers of the past. While mid-century writers such as Sarah Fielding, Charlotte Lennox, and Frances Sheridan tended not to make direct reference to Behn, as if their moral authority would be better established by avoiding the thought of her, later in the century women secure in their respectable authorship turned their attention back to her. Elizabeth Griffith chose two of Behn's novels, *Oroonoko* and *Agnes de Castro*, for inclusion in her 1777 *Collection of Novels*. She treated Behn as a valuable but old-fashioned author, whose Restoration tone needed to be altered to suit a later generation, but whose faults could be explained historically, so that there

---

[69] See my 'Women Writers and the Eighteenth-Century Novel', in John Richetti (ed.), *The Cambridge Companion to the Eighteenth-Century Novel* (Cambridge: Cambridge University Press, 1996), 218.

[70] Medoff, 'The Daughters of Behn', 46.   [71] *The Feminiad* (London, 1754), 15.

was no danger of her contaminating the new generation of women writers. Clara Reeve treated her in a similar way in *The Progress of Romance*, carefully noting her faults but also implying that once Eliza Haywood had freed herself from the clutches of Behn's immorality, women novelists were out of danger, so that her impeccably moral spokeswoman Euphrasia is free to admit to having a partiality for Behn, as a writer of her own sex.[72]

Hannah Cowley's School for Greybeards

Late in the eighteenth century Behn's continued influence on the drama was evident in one remarkable instance. Hannah Cowley adapted the plot of *The Lucky Chance* for her comedy *A School for Greybeards*, performed at Drury Lane in November 1786. The play was far from being one of Cowley's successes—in fact, it caused an audience uproar, and had to be withdrawn and altered before it could run a second night—but for that very reason, it provides an insight into the limits placed on the popular dramatist, particularly the female dramatist, in the more refined and conformist Georgian theatre. The use of one of Behn's plays that had offended some part of the audience even on first representation tested and discovered those limits.

Cowley's decision to use Behn was a bold one because in the context of the late-century theatre, women writers had not quite achieved the same security of respectable identity and clear separation from the image of Behn as they had in the novel. Writers on theatre, as we have seen, had never turned against Behn so decisively as novelists had done. The promotion of the moral woman novelist, begun in the 1720s and intensified in the 1740s and 1750s, had changed expectations about the genre. By the 1780s discussions of the novel had successfully suppressed the memory of Behn, and women novelists were likely to be judged against Sarah Fielding, Charlotte Lennox, Frances Sheridan, or Frances Burney, women who were taken to have the impeccable moral credentials now required of the female author. In the theatre a similar process of establishing a new kind of respectable woman writer took place a few years later than in the novel. From the 1750s onwards, David Garrick was particularly influential as a supporter and sponsor of new women playwrights.

[72] Reeve, *The Progress of Romance*, i. 118.

He established a new role for the theatre manager as respectable fatherly patron of the woman dramatist, who took up a position as a literary daughter, protected within the public world of the theatre.[73] Elizabeth Griffith, Charlotte Lennox, Hannah Cowley, and Hannah More were among the women who received his encouragement and advice. Significantly, this mentoring of new women playwrights went hand-in-hand with rejection of the work of Aphra Behn, the unruly female predecessor who appeared from this viewpoint as a woman who had operated without proper benevolent male control. Garrick avoided staging Behn, though her works were still occasionally put on by other managers at this date. Just as Richardson and Fielding encouraged a select few moral women novelists while disparaging Behn, Garrick contributed to Behn's disappearance from the London stage while encouraging his own theatrical daughters. Consciously or not, the care of the 'good' father was being substituted for the dangerous example of the 'bad' mother. Ellen Donkin has shown how badly this relation of dependence on and gratitude to the theatre manager affected women dramatists' self-confidence and suggests that to succeed in the longer term, they needed to separate psychologically from the male mentor.[74] For Cowley, I suggest, part of this process involved looking back to Aphra Behn and rewriting her work.

Cowley's first great success in the theatre in fact came in 1780, the year after Garrick's death. *The Belle's Stratagem,* an instantly and enduringly popular comedy, showed her laying claim to the tradition of Restoration comedy. It was clearly, if loosely, modelled on Etherege's *The Man of Mode,* and its title paid tribute to Farquhar's *The Beaux' Stratagem.* The play made Cowley's name, and was called by one reviewer 'the best dramatic production of a female pen which has appeared since the days of Centlivre, to whom Mrs. Cowley is at least equal in fable and character, and far superior in easy dialogue and purity of diction'.[75] This concern with purity of language is telling: Centlivre, by this time, needed purifying for the stage. Of course Cowley, like any dramatist of her time, had taken care to purge her Restoration source materials of indecency, but the point remains that she could be associated with Etherege, Farquhar,

---

[73] Ellen Donkin, *Getting into the Act: Women Playwrights in London,* 1776–1829 (London and New York: Routledge, 1995), 25–31.   [74] Ibid. 27, 57–76.

[75] *Critical Review* (1782), quoted in Joyce East, 'The Dramatic Works of Hannah Cowley', Ph.D. thesis (University of Kansas, 1979), 91.

Centlivre, and perhaps even Wycherley, with honour.[76] Aphra Behn, however, was a different matter. In the year after *The Belle's Stratagem*, Cowley's *The World as it Goes* was severely criticized in the reviews. One damning notice threw Behn's name at her as the final insult. Cowley's play was judged 'by far the most despicable composition that ever insulted a British audience under the appellation of a Comedy. Fable . . . it has none: in point of characters, it is quite deficient: its incidents are of too extravagant and vulgar cast even for the regions of farce; and as to the language, it exceeds in gross ribaldry, the productions of the notorious Mrs. Behn.'[77] It is not surprising, then, that when Cowley decided to adapt *The Lucky Chance* a few years later, she was vague about her source, writing in her preface to the published version that she had taken merely an 'idea' from 'an obsolete Comedy, the work of a poet of the drama, once highly celebrated'.[78] The stage historian John Genest later criticized her for this reticence, noting that on the play's first night he had recognized the elements from *The Lucky Chance*: 'as Mrs. Behn's play, tho' a very good one, is too indecent to be ever represented again, Mrs. Cowley might without any disgrace to herself have borrowed whatever she pleased; provided she had made a proper acknowledgement'.[79] Genest here misses the point of the female playwright's particular problems with borrowing. She needed to ensure, not only that her source was 'obsolete' and therefore a legitimate target, but also that it was morally safe. The 'disgrace to herself' would come not just from borrowing from a current competitor but from being associated with the 'indecent' work of Behn.

Wary though she was of being associated with her predecessor, Cowley took the risk of modelling her plot closely on that of *The Lucky Chance*. What attracted her to Behn's play was the way it allows one of the heroines to escape from her marriage, but she was to learn that 'An event which had in the last century been stampt with the highest applause . . . was found in this, to be ill-conceived' (*A School for Greybeards*, p. viii). *The Lucky Chance* is set in contemporary London and has two main love-triangles: one, City knight Sir Feeble

[76] See East, 'Hannah Cowley', 99–116.

[77] *Morning Herald*, 26 Feb. 1781; quoted in East, 'Hannah Cowley', 121–2.

[78] Hannah Cowley, *A School for Greybeards; or, the Mourning Bride* (London: G. G. J and J. Robinson, 1786), Preface, p. vii.

[79] John Genest, *Some Account of the English Stage from the Restoration in 1660 to 1830* (Bath: Carrington, 1832), v. 427.

Fainwould, his bride Leticia, and her former betrothed, Belmour; the other, another rich alderman, Sir Cautious Fulbank, his young wife Julia, and her impoverished lover, Charles Gayman. The action involves various tricks and disguises as the young couples pursue their desires. Belmour practises various tricks to prevent Sir Feeble consummating his marriage to Leticia. At the end Leticia's marriage is set aside in favour of her earlier betrothal. Julia is not similarly free to marry Gayman, but she announces her intention of separating from her husband's bed. In a subsidiary action, Sir Feeble's daughter Diana evades a planned marriage to Sir Cautious's nephew Bearjest, and marries Leticia's brother Bredwell instead; and Bearjest is tricked into ratifying a former betrothal to the lady's maid, Pert.

Like a number of Restoration comedies, then, the play depicts the cuckolding of an older City man by a young rake about town, but whereas Restoration comedies of the 1670s tended to see cuckolding as a comic solution, *The Lucky Chance* treats Lady Fulbank's unhappy marriage as a serious problem which is not amenable to easy solutions. The two main triangles of *The Lucky Chance* offer different messages about marriage: in the first triangle, the apparently radical implications of Sir Feeble's being robbed of his bride are offset by the revelation that the most sacred marital vows are those that preceded his marriage to Leticia. In the second triangle, there is no way to reconcile Julia and Gayman's desires with law, unless we count the uneasy expedient suggested at the end: that they should hang around waiting for Sir Cautious to die, when he will bequeath his wife to Gayman. In the meantime, perhaps their affair will continue, but if so this is a less than satisfactory solution to a woman who has claimed, 'I prize my Honour more than Life',[80] and who expresses anger at having been made the subject of a bargain between husband and lover. The play thus opens up questions about a system which offers no accessible divorce. It is poised between Restoration sex-comedy and turn-of-century marriage-problem play.

When *The Lucky Chance* was criticized for being bawdy in 1686, the issue seems to have been sexually suggestive language and stage action.[81] In the eighteenth century, however, the plot itself was a problem for potential performances of *The Lucky Chance*. Cowley starts by changing the setting to a vaguely realized Portugal, so that the topicality, realism, and vulgarity of Behn's play are swallowed up

---

[80] *The Lucky Chance*, I. ii, *Works*, vii. 227.   [81] See Behn's preface, *Works*, vii. 215–17.

in the ideal gentility of an imagined location; and then makes crucial changes to the plot. The first triangle remains much as it was. Sir Feeble, Leticia, and Belmour become Don Gasper, Donna Antonia, and Don Henry. Like Leticia, Antonia has married an older man because she has been led to believe her betrothed lover is dead; like Belmour, Henry has been exiled after a fatal duel and returns in disguise to obtain his pardon and trick his rival out of the lady before the marriage can be consummated. The second triangle, however, is greatly altered, in order to eliminate the figure of the adulterous young lover. Sir Cautious, Julia, and Gayman become Don Alexis, Seraphina, and Octavio. Seraphina not only remains faithful to her husband, she is not even tempted by Octavio, who corresponds to Behn's Bearjest rather than to Gayman. He courts her by mistake for her stepdaughter Viola (corresponding to Behn's Diana) and she encourages him only in order to facilitate Viola's elopement with Sebastian (Bredwell). In this way, the unhappy young wife, a troubling and problematic figure in *The Lucky Chance*, is transformed into a sprightly lady who gets what she wants without wanting anything too challenging. By creating the lively Seraphina, Cowley transformed *The Lucky Chance*'s greatest liability (from an eighteenth-century perspective) into the greatest asset for *A School for Greybeards*.

She was then free, she thought, to concentrate on the other main plot: the Leticia–Belmour–Sir Feeble (now Antonia–Henry–Gasper) triangle. This was the aspect of *The Lucky Chance* which, she says in her preface to the 1786 edition of her play, first attracted her: 'The circumstance which most particularly interested me, and fixed itself in my mind, was that of snatching a young woman from a hateful marriage, the moment before that marriage became valid—that is to say, after the ceremony' (pp. vii–viii). Leticia is married, but her marriage has not been consummated; and in 1687, it was easy for the dramatist to show such a marriage being put aside. Leticia and Belmour rest their legal case against the marriage on the grounds of pre-contract. In the seventeenth century in England marriage was still legally governed by the ecclesiastical courts, and what did and did not constitute a valid marriage was a complicated affair; but the essence of the contract was mutual consent, and a church ceremony was not necessary. If a couple exchanged vows of marriage 'in words of the present tense'; then whether consummated or not the union would be upheld in the courts against a subsequent marriage of one of the partners, even if the second marriage had taken place in church, was of long standing, and had produced children.[82] Young lovers in comedy of course always oppose the authority of older men. In the case of Leticia and Belmour they do so in a very Tory fashion—challenging the authority vested in a City magistrate, in the name of the authority of the ecclesiastical courts. Implicitly, their story tells against those seventeenth-century republicans who wanted to bring marriage under civil regulations. Belmour may put a libertine gloss on his behaviour, referring in an anti-clerical jibe to 'Those Vows that tye us faster than dull Priests' (II. ii, *Works*, vii. 239), but the Church in fact would support his views.

However, what was unexceptionable to a Restoration audience had a very different effect on the late eighteenth-century one. Lord Hardwicke's Marriage Act of 1754 had brought marriage under civil regulations, and had among other things made privately formed contracts like Belmour and Leticia's invalid. Marriages now had to be solemnized either in church or by special licence. Cowley evidently anticipated that this would make what for her was the central circumstance of the play, difficult for her audience to grasp. She tried to get around this by setting her play in a Catholic country where ecclesiastical courts still governed and where her audience would expect different customs to obtain; and by explaining and stressing the nature of the contract, something that is largely taken for granted in *The Lucky Chance*.

The manuscript of *A School for Greybeards* in the Larpent collection represents the play as first performed. Here, Antonia's situation is closely modelled on Leticia's. Her wedding to Don Gasper has just taken place and the wedding party has returned from church; there are several references to the ceremony. As in *The Lucky Chance*, the old husband's young rival schemes to prevent the consummation of the marriage, interrupting the couple as they are about to retire to bed with a story about imminent riots which the husband must help to put down. Antonia's exclamation, '''Tis not a Marriage since my Henry lives','[83] echoes Leticia's '''Tis not a Marriage, since my *Belmour* lives' (II. ii, *Works*, vii. 239). Both Henry and Antonia provide explanatory references to the pre-contract, emphasizing (as Belmour and Leticia do not) that it was a betrothal ceremony held before witnesses. When Henry first hears that Antonia is at church giving her

---

[82] G. E. Howard, *A History of Matrimonial Institutions* (Chicago: University of Chicago Press, 1904), i. 335–7.   [83] Larpent MS 748, p. 13.

vows to Gasper, he exclaims: 'In the face of Heaven and before Witnesses, they are mine—if she has given them to another they cannot be Valid—but by my Assent—I'll fly instantly to the House, the Marriage may be Solemniz'd but shall never be Compleated' (Larpent MS, p. 7). In the final scene, Henry even produces a document from the episcopal court, 'acquitting [Antonia] of her vows—and declaring the Marriage illegal; being founded on falsehood, and deception' (Larpent MS, p. 18).

It was not enough. When *A School for Greybeards* was played at Drury Lane on Saturday 25 November 1786, some of the audience objected to it. The immediate motives for the attack were probably to do with theatrical rivalry, but the pretext for it was a general one that would be applied to any late eighteenth-century comedy, and especially one by a woman: Cowley, like Behn before her, was accused of indecency. The charge was seen as reasonable even by the critic who objected to the concerted malice against the playwright. Most of all, the audience objected to Antonia's marriage to Don Gasper being set aside. By the time *A School for Greybeards* was performed again, on Thursday 7 December, Cowley had revised the play. According to a rather awkward new contrivance invented to explain the setting of the action in Gasper's house, it is the custom in Portugal for a bride to go to her bridegroom's home before the ceremony on her wedding day. It is the wedding ceremony, rather than the consummation, which Henry and Antonia now scheme to avoid. With this alteration, the play was well received and praised in the reviews. The published text of the play, dated 1786, prints the altered version, with a defensive preface from the author, who was evidently unhappy with the changes she had been forced to make. Like Behn and Centlivre before her, Cowley had to mount an argument for a woman's right to write realistic dialogue for stage characters: 'in my case it seems resolved that the point to be considered, is not whether that *dotard*, or that *pretender*, or that *coquet*, would so have given their feelings, but whether Mrs. *Cowley* ought so to have expressed herself' (p. vi). From the evidence of the early reception of Cowley's play, it is clear that, while it is a much more decorous work than *The Lucky Chance*, it should not be seen as a watered-down, innocuous revision of Behn's originally challenging play. The first version, which aroused such strong objection, was obviously a challenge to the audience's views. Cowley, in fact, was contesting some of the same issues Behn had done. She was claiming freedom of expression for the female playwright, and exploring the problem for women of being trapped in unsuitable marriages.

Cowley's challenge to accepted views is not surprisingly situated very differently from Behn's. Accepted views of marriage—and, therefore, ways of challenging conventional mores—had changed in the intervening years. What attracted Cowley in the Leticia–Sir Feeble plot was the fact that, just as it seems inevitable that Leticia will be trapped in this hateful marriage, the comedy finds a way out. In *The Lucky Chance*, this is actually the more conservative plot of the comedy, and it was in the Julia–Sir Cautious plot that the real challenge to marriage customs was situated. In *A School for Greybeards* this pattern is reversed. The Antonia–Don Gasper plot has become a challenge to the late eighteenth-century view of marriage as an indissoluble civil contract. Cowley's critique of marriage should not be exaggerated: she is, after all, here and in her other plays, primarily one of its sentimental supporters; but her sentimental commitment to happy marriage does include a willingness to question the institution. The audience was revolted by the annulment of Antonia's marriage because, in the post-1754 context of civil marriage, this dissolution looked uncomfortably like divorce. A plot that had once affirmed the sanctity of marriage vows now undermined it. Cowley defiantly underlined that point, even as she capitulated to audience pressure. When she announced the change to the Antonia–Gasper relationship, she did so in terms that echoed the very action she had been forced to cut: 'I did not, however, dispute the decision of my Critics—and the marriage has been in course *dissolved*' (Preface, p. viii; my italics).

In the Seraphina–Alexis plot, Cowley radically alters her source and makes of it something far less challenging. By doing that, however, she gives herself scope to make Seraphina a much more dominant figure in the dramatic action than Behn's Julia. In *The Lucky Chance* Behn shows women forced into relatively passive roles. Julia is the object of exchange between husband and lover, while Leticia just waits around until Belmour rescues her. In *A School for Greybeards* Cowley alters the balance between the roles. In *The Lucky Chance*, Belmour and Leticia, renewing their vows to each other, are interrupted by Sir Feeble and company. Belmour's quick wits save the day: he catches her in his arms and pretends that she has fainted. In a similar scene in *A School for Greybeards*, Henry can think of nothing, and it is Antonia who gets the pair out of an awkward situation by loudly repeating her vows so that to Gasper it sounds as if they are vows of her love for *him*. Most importantly, Cowley makes Seraphina into the play's leading role. She orchestrates the action, deliberately encouraging Octavio in his mistake so that Viola can marry Sebastian; in her flirtation with Octavio she is tricking him all along; and she controls her own unmasking in the final scene. She is outspoken: Julia has a few references to her husband's unsatisfactory sexual performance, but Seraphina frequently and merrily teases her husband that she might cuckold him. Seraphina's power rests of course on the absolute impregnability of her 'virtue'. We might sum up the effect of Julia and of Seraphina by characteristic quotations from their speeches to their husbands about desire and fidelity. Julia openly admits that she desires another man; she can't help her desires, but she can, she says, control her actions, 'I can keep my Vertue Sir intire' (v. iv, *Works*, vii. 275). It is a problematic statement because, either before or after this scene depending on your reading of the first assignation with Gayman, Julia loses what is usually called her 'virtue' to her lover. We could read her as hypocritical; as sincere, but unable to keep her vow through Gayman's trick and her own treacherous desire; or even as reaching for a statement about feminine self-worth in which 'virtue' might mean something other than chastity. The corresponding statement from Seraphina is simpler in its effect. Sure of herself and her self-control, she tells her husband: 'It is due to my own feelings to be chaste—I don't condescend to think of yours in the affair' (*A School for Greybeards*, 19). Her sauciness gives her dramatic dominance, but is based on her thorough internalization of the standard of feminine virtue.

Cowley's Seraphina and her own writing career attest to the ascendancy of a new kind of female authority in English culture—one that could be both publicly visible and accorded widespread respect and attention. It was also one which, as Cowley discovered to her cost, depended on a denial or submerging of female sexual desire and a curbing of female freedom of expression. Part of Behn's achievement, in fact, had to be repressed; but for Cowley she was still a champion of women whose message should be adapted for and absorbed into the new age. After *A School for Greybeards*, Behn's work was not used by women in this detailed way again, as both source-text and a source for writing authority. By the end of the eighteenth century, women writers were working—some happily, some not—within new boundaries for female expression. Some, like Mary

Wollstonecraft, were offering a new feminist challenge to those boundaries. From our perspective it is easy to see a kind of parallel between Behn and Wollstonecraft: both were challenging the limits on women's cultural role imposed in their time. It is not surprising, though, that the radical women of the 1790s did not see a royalist Restoration playwright as their precursor. Mary Hays, including 'Aphara Behn' in her compilation *Female Biography* in 1803, simply derived her entry from the usual sources, without giving her the special significance she had held a century earlier. Women writers were no longer looking back to Behn.

PART III

Receptions

5

The Rover

WE saw in Chapter 1 that *The Rover* rapidly became Behn's most successful comedy, the play by which she was most frequently known, and that more than any of her other comedies it proved adaptable to the eighteenth-century stage. Its popularity grew in the early years of the century and reached a peak in the late 1720s and early 1730s, those years just before the Licensing Act when there was flourishing competition among a growing number of London theatres. In April 1730 it would have been possible for a theatregoer to see the play in three different productions: at Drury Lane, with the veteran Robert Wilks playing the title role he had first taken on twenty-seven years earlier; at Lincoln's Inn Fields, with the younger Lacy Ryan as Willmore; and at the new theatre in Goodman's Fields, with Giffard as the rover. From the late 1730s its popularity declined and, as we have seen, it was increasingly felt to need alteration and adaptation to fit it for a modern audience. This chapter traces the history of *The Rover* in eighteenth-century performance, a history that we can reconstruct patchily but in some detail from a number of sources, including contemporary playbills, comments and criticisms, a promptbook copy of the text, and two altered editions.

Before considering the eighteenth-century changes in detail, we need to ask why it was worth going to the trouble of altering this particular Restoration comedy to ensure its continued popularity. What was *The Rover*'s appeal? Since the late 1970s the play has received great and growing critical interest, and widely diverging interpretations. One of the earliest of these sees it as a royalist's celebration of cavalier life: 'What lads we were; how clever, how brave, how irresistible.'[1] While this is very far from being the final word on the play, it is a good guide to its original appeal to Restoration audiences. A carnivalesque intrigue comedy set in Naples during the Interregnum,

---

[1] Duffy, *The Passionate Shepherdess*, 145.

pitting exiled English royalists against Spanish noblemen, and allowing the English heroes to win the Spanish heiresses, *The Rover* flattered the Restoration court with a nostalgic image of its cavalier past. An English fool, Blunt, failing in the games his fellow-countrymen won, provided a foil to the hero and the broad humour of farcical scenes. In Hellena the play offered a cross-dressing heroine who engaged in the witty duels with her lover that were becoming a popular convention; and in Angellica, an unusually sympathetic portrait of a stock figure, the cast-off mistress, whose life as a courtesan was taken seriously enough to add depth and a satiric edge to the comedy. Much of this appeal remained in the eighteenth century, and was not overshadowed by the changes in political situation and social mores that curtailed the stage-lives of some of Behn's other plays.

The play was not, like Behn's early 1680s comedies, *The City-Heiress* and *The Roundheads*, tied to a particular Tory moment and message. Willmore, 'a Rover of Fortune, | Yet a Prince, aboard his little wooden World' (v. i, *Works,* v. 518), was certainly linked to the roving Charles, the exiled Stuart who 'Reigns still Lord of the watry Element' (I. ii. *Works,* v. 460), and whose 'Buffe' (leather military coat) he wears (II. i. *Works,* v. 466); but his political significance proved very flexible.[2] In the early 1690s, certainly, this image of the king in exile took on dangerously Jacobite connotations, and the Jacobite actor William Smith was booed off the stage when he entered as Willmore in his first performance after the abdication of James II.[3] Nevertheless, the play was also successfully performed at the court of William and Mary, and in later times, its royalism could easily shade into a kind of general patriotism perfectly well suited to the years of Whig ascendancy. The hero changed colour to suit the times. During the early eighteenth century he left off the buff leather of a seventeenth-century cavalier and wore the red coat that indicated an eighteenth-

---

[2] For the 'doubling' between Willmore and Charles II see Elin Diamond, '*Gestus* and Signature in *The Rover*', in J. Todd (ed.), *Aphra Behn: Contemporary Critical Essays* (Basingstoke: Macmillan, 1999), 32–56. For the story that the fleeing Charles disguised himself in buff see also Susan Staves, *Players' Scepters: Fictions of Authority in the Restoration* (Lincoln, Nebr., 1979), 2.

[3] The incident is described by Chetwood in *A General History of the Stage*, 96–7: Smith had served as a volunteer in James's army and returned to the stage in 1691 or 1692. 'The first Character he chose to appear in, was that of *Wilmore* in the *Rover*, . . . but, being informed that he should be maltreated on account of his Principles, he gave Orders for the Curtain to drop, if any Disturbance should come from the Audience. Accordingly the Play began in the utmost Tranquillity, but when Mr *Smith* entered in the first Act, the Storm began . . . Mr *Smith* gave the Signal, the Curtain dropp'd, and the Audience dismiss'd.' Smith did not return to the stage until 1695.

century English soldier,[4] and towards the end of the century he changed services, dressed in blue, and joined the newly glorious British navy.[5]

If Willmore's political connotations were malleable, his sexual adventures, for all Steele's disapproval, were more excusable than those of some other rake–heroes. Crucially, they did not involve adultery. His affair with the courtesan Angellica Bianca makes no man a cuckold, and in his venture with Hellena on 'the storms of the marriage bed' he affirms, however ruefully, the institution he has earlier mocked. This was much easier for respectable theatregoers to accept than the sympathetically treated adultery of *The Lucky Chance*, which as we have seen, had only one eighteenth-century revival. It was also more acceptable than the cuckolding of Wycherley's *The Country Wife* or the conclusion of Etherege's *Man of Mode*, which leaves open to doubt the questions of the hero's marriage and the ending of his affair with Bellinda. So, although *The Rover*'s sexual content was, as we shall see, the main focus of eighteenth-century anxiety and alteration, it was not a complete bar to its success on the stage. Willmore was ripe for transformation into an eighteenth-century reformed rake.

These are negative reasons for the play's longevity: it was not too narrowly political, not too extremely libertine. Positive reasons include the treatment of the two main female roles, Angellica Bianca and Hellena. Angellica is not the figure of fun that a woman in her position—seduced by the hero and later discarded in favour of the virginal heroine—would be in most Restoration comedy. Her blank-verse scenes with Willmore invest her love for him with serious significance, and her later realization of the impossibility of her position, longing for romantic love when she has lost the virginal status that is required for it, is rendered with pathos. Considered as one of the sex-comedies of the 1670s, Behn's play was considerably 'softer' in its attitudes, anticipating a more sympathetic treatment of women found in the comedies and the pathetic tragedies of the 1690s and after. While this acts as a disturbance to comic tone, it is a

---

[4] In the prompt copy of the play references in Act II scene i to Willmore's 'Buffe' are deleted and the word 'Red' substituted. See the copy of the first edition of *The Rover* in the University of London Library (Durning-Laurence Library (XVII) Bc (Behn)), 16, 23.

[5] See *Love in Many Masks* (London: T. and J. Egerton, 1790), where the references to buff are altered to 'blue' (14, 19), and the description of Willmore as a rover of fortune becomes: 'though a private man, yet every Captain in the British navy is himself a King aboard his little wooden world' (71).

complication that is likely to have added to the attractions of the play in the early years of the eighteenth century, when the 'fallen' woman was the focus of interest as tragic heroine. Calista, the heroine of Nicholas Rowe's *The Fair Penitent* (1703), sounds rather similar to Angellica when she delivers her famous lament, 'How hard is the Condition of our Sex',[6] and this female complaint about feminine victimhood was a popular feature of the early eighteenth-century stage. Productions of the play are likely to have emphasized the pathos of Angellica's position during this period, when she was played by famous tragic actresses, including Mary Porter and Elizabeth Barry; and when Barry played the role, her fame made Angellica the star attraction of the play.[7]

Hellena's role, however, was in most cases treated as equally important with, or more important than, Angellica's;[8] and in the middle and later years of the century attention seems to have shifted decisively to her. Breeches parts enjoyed a vogue in the middle of the century, with Margaret Woffington famous not only for playing cross-dressing heroines but for taking on male roles. She made her name, as Robert Wilks had done before her, as Sir Harry Wildair in *The Constant Couple*, and was considered to have eclipsed her male rival in the role.[9] In 1741, when she played Hellena opposite Lacy Ryan at Covent Garden, their two names appeared together (his first) at the top of the bill, and she was given strong promotion in the advertising campaign that preceded the run.[10] In 1790 Hellena was played by

---

[6] Nicholas Rowe, *The Fair Penitent. A Tragedy* (London: Jacob Tonson, 1703), III. i, p. 26.

[7] Cast-lists usually placed the men first, followed by the women. Barry had the rare distinction of being able to disrupt this order and take first place, and though the usual pattern was sometimes maintained when she played in *The Rover*, her name headed the bill on at least one occasion, when she played Angellica opposite Wilks at the Queen's Theatre on 29 Oct. 1709. Anne Oldfield, playing Hellena, was listed with the other actresses, after the actors. For Mary Porter's long stint as Angellica (she played the role over forty times between 1715 and 1730) see Ben R. Schneider, 'The Coquette-Prude as an Actress's Line in Restoration Comedy During the Time of Mrs Oldfield', *Theatre Notebook*, 22 (1967), 143–56, table 1.

[8] Again, the evidence of cast-lists can help. Anne Oldfield, playing Hellena, frequently came near the top of the bill (but after Willmore). On one occasion, at Queen's on 31 Dec. 1709, Willmore (Wilks), Angellica (Barry), Hellena (Oldfield), and Blunt (Estcourt) were distinguished—in that order— as the only actors named on the bill.

[9] She played Sir Harry Wildair at Covent Garden 'night after night, for weeks, and Wilks was forgotten'. J. Doran, *Their Majesties Servants* (2nd edn.; London: W. H. Allen and Co., 1865), 209.

[10] See *London Daily Post and General Advertiser*, no. 1995, Monday 16 Mar. 1741, for the cast-list; no. 1989, Monday 9 Mar. 1741, for a letter singling out for praise the character of Hellena, 'which I am positive Mrs Woffington must appear amiable in'.

Dorothy Jordan, another actress famous in breeches roles, and again Hellena's part was clearly considered much more important than Angellica's, which was taken by a little-known actress, Sarah Ward. A contemporary reviewer thought that the play had been revived 'for the purpose of exhibiting that fascinating favourite of the town, Mrs. Jordan'.[11] Just as Angellica had particular appeal when pathetic tragedy was in vogue, Hellena suited a period when the sprightly heroine had a strong position on the comic stage.

However, while Behn's witty heroine and her complex courtesan may both have appealed to actresses (Elizabeth Barry played both), they were not usually in a position to dictate the repertoire. It was the play's provision of an attractive male lead that was decisive in making it one commonly chosen for eighteenth-century performance. Robert Wilks, as one of the managers of Drury Lane, had a good deal of control over the repertoire, and his success in the role of Willmore meant that the play was frequently chosen. At Covent Garden Lacy Ryan did not exert comparable control, but he too made Willmore a long-running role, and went to some pains to promote the play. The century's last incarnation of Willmore was developed by John Philip Kemble, then the manager at Drury Lane, who both altered the text and played the lead. *The Rover*'s long stage success was bound up with the opportunities its leading male role offered to these and other actors; and eighteenth-century discussions of the play make it clear that it was viewed very much as the story of its men.[12] Though the treatment of Willmore changed over the century, its core attraction for male stars was an enduring one. The basis of this attraction, I will argue, is that they were able to shine in a role that allowed for the combination of rakish power and glamour with developing notions of the charms of gentlemanly behaviour.

The versions of Willmore that we can construct from the evidence we have about eighteenth-century performance differ enormously

---

[11] *English Review*, 15 (1790), 386.

[12] See e.g. the plot-summary given in a popular compendium telling the stories of a range of stock plays: *A Companion to the Theatre: or, a View of our most celebrated Dramatic Pieces*, 2 vols. (London: J. Nourse, 1747), II. 244–58. Though the play, notably, opens on an all-female exchange, the plot-summary begins with Belvile and his companions, and consistently writes the story from the point of view of the male characters. The writer of this has been identified as Eliza Haywood, whose record as a feminocentric novelist might suggest she would approach *The Rover* more as the story of Hellena, Florinda, and Angellica. See Christine Blouch, 'Eliza Haywood and the Romance of Obscurity', *Studies in English Literature*, 31 (1991), 535–52.

(but not surprisingly) from the sinister and violent rake who is at the centre of some recent discussions of the play. *The Rover* has been presented as an analysis of patriarchal power in which Willmore 'acts not only as the rover but as signifier for the play's phallic logic', and whose theft of Angellica's picture is a defining moment, revealing that the economy of the play (and the theatre) is one in which women are inescapably commodities for male consumption.[13] Several critics have pointed out that rape is a central theme of the play, and that it is given unusually serious treatment. The heroine's sister, Florinda, faces the threat of rape at almost every turn. Blunt threatens her with rape in direct revenge for the humiliation he has endured at the hands of another woman, and such violence is not only offered by the play's fool, but by his companion Frederick. Worse, this scene echoes an earlier one in which the hero, meeting Florinda on her way to meet her lover Belvile, assumes she is sexually available and subjects her to physical coercion while simultaneously arguing that because of her provocative behaviour, no violence from him could be properly judged as rape. As the man who expresses this 'patriarchal logic', the hero is revealed 'less as a libertine exception than as the most extreme representation of a particular ideal of manliness'. The world of the play is revealed as a 'rape culture' in which men are defined by their power over women and other men, and women are unable to escape being defined by men's view of their sexuality.[14] There is much in the text to support this dark view of the play, and that it stands among 'producible interpretations' has been well demonstrated by productions in the 1990s.[15] However, it renders the comic ending, with Willmore's marriage to Hellena, extremely problematic, and generally works against the comedy which was the basis of the play's appeal to its eighteenth-century audience: as Anita Pacheco puts it, the 'critique of patriarchy' has to 'break through the comic smoke-screen' to be realized.[16] When this happens, as it cer-

---

[13] Diamond, 41.

[14] Anita Pacheco, 'Rape and the Female Subject in Aphra Behn's *The Rover*', *ELH* 65 (1998), 341–42. See also discussions of the rape theme in Jones DeRitter, 'The Gypsy, *The Rover*, and the Wanderer: Aphra Behn's Revision of Thomas Killigrew', *Restoration*, 10/2 (1986) 82–92; Elaine Hobby, *Virtue of Necessity: English Women's Writing, 1640–89* (London: Virago, 1988), 122–7; and Jacqueline Pearson, *The Prostituted Muse*, 153–4.

[15] See e.g. Susan Carlson's discussion of JoAnne Akalatis's 1994 production for the Guthrie Theatre in 'Cannibalizing and Carnivalizing: Reviving Aphra Behn's *The Rover*', *Theatre Journal*, 47 (1995), 517–39, and my own discussion of Nesta Jones's 1991 production in Aphra Behn, *The Rover and Other Plays*, p. xx.

[16] Pacheco, 'Rape and the Female Subject', 328.

tainly does in Jules Wright's Women's Playhouse Trust production of 1994, recorded on video for the Open University, the effect can be to take the play altogether out of the realms of comedy.[17]

This is not to argue that a serious reading of the rape theme is not valid, or that the true interpretations are the ones offered by pre-twentieth-century productions. Indeed, it is quite possible that by highlighting an issue that was, as we shall see, toned down in eighteenth-century productions, recent interpretations of the play are giving expression to something that some members of Behn's earlier audiences felt: as Lizbeth Goodman reminds us, 'Perhaps the "truth" for women in Behn's audiences differed from that of men.'[18] As we trace the tangible evidence of earlier audiences' tastes, we need to remember that it is never the whole picture, and that the unrecorded tastes of the subordinate may have differed from those of the dominant group. Nevertheless, it is clear that to understand the reasons for *The Rover*'s continuing popularity, especially its use as a vehicle for leading actors, the key is not its critique of patriarchy but the extent to which this was (or could be made to be) subsumed into a comic mode in which Willmore's activities move laughter, not outrage.

Other interpretations see the play as critical of Willmore in a rather different way: rather than emphasizing his power, they note how the jokes work against him in a number of places. When he attacks Florinda he is being given a role that belonged to the fool in Behn's source-text, and he is repeatedly revealed as a blunderer and buffoon.[19] This line of approach has the advantage that it allows for the possibility of social critique working with rather than against the comic form, and in my view it identifies more accurately Behn's specific contribution to the treatment of the rake–hero. Jacqueline Pearson has argued that during the late seventeenth and early eighteenth centuries, some of the strongest feminist themes in drama, defined as direct protest about injustices to women, are to be found in the work of male playwrights such as D'Urfey and Southerne,

[17] For discussions of this production see Lizbeth Goodman's account in W. R. Owens, and Lizbeth Goodman (eds.), *Shakespeare, Aphra Behn and the Canon* (London: Routledge in association with the Open University, 1996), 175–91, and the less favourable view from Bob Owens in the same volume, complaining of 'the seeming lack of recognition that the play was supposed to be a *comedy*', 173.   [18] Goodman, ibid. 190.

[19] See Arthur Gewirtz, *Restoration Adaptations of 17th Century Comedies* (Washington: University Press of America, 1982), 96–7; DeRitter, 'The Gypsy', 82–92; Pearson, *The Prostituted Muse*, 152–4.

while women dramatists are distinguished instead by their irreverence towards male characters: '[w]omen are more likely to mock men, even their nominal heroes'.[20] Whether Behn's comic attacks on her hero's dignity were conveyed in the heyday of the play's performance is another matter. As we will see, there is some evidence that the late eighteenth-century version of the play, at least, acknowledged the force of elements mocking the hero by cutting them.

The significance of those elements of the play that can be read as mockery of Willmore is all the greater because they can be shown to be among Behn's own contributions to a play whose ownership has always been in dispute. In order to make sense of the way Behn's work was subject to alteration, we need to raise the question of *The Rover* as itself a work of alteration. If Southerne is a son of Behn, Behn is certainly a daughter of Killigrew, whose ten-act closet drama *Thomaso, or, The Wanderer* provided the basis for many of the characters and incidents, and much of the language of her play.[21] That the first-ever play by a woman to achieve the distinction of becoming a long-running stock piece on the London stage owes so much to a male source demands comment and analysis. Predictably, early reaction to Behn's borrowing was to accuse her of plagiarism and declare that *The Rover* did not really belong to her. Among the tokens by which Gerard Langbaine distinguished legitimate borrowings from illegitimate theft were proper acknowledgement and credit of the source, and improvement of the original.[22] While in general he condoned Behn's practices since 'whatever she borrows she improves', in the case of *The Rover* he considered that she had failed on both counts of acknowledgement and improvement: 'These [*The Rover*, Parts I and II] are the only Comedies, for the Theft of which I condemn this ingenious Authoress; they being so excellent in their Original, that 'tis pity they should have been altered . . . what she has omitted of worth in her first part, she has taken into the second; and therefore could not justly call these Plays her own.'[23]

[20] Pearson, *The Prostituted Muse*, 254.

[21] Thomas Killigrew, *Thomaso, or, The Wanderer: A Comedy . . . In Two Parts* (London: Henry Herringman, 1663). The play was written in 1654 when Killigrew, like his hero, was a cavalier living in exile.

[22] Langbaine, Gerard, *Momus Triumphans: or, the Plagiaries of the English Stage* (London: N.C. for Sam Holford, 1688), sig. A1r–A1v.

[23] Langbaine, *An Account of the Dramatick Poets*, 18, 21.

Langbaine was particularly concerned that the language of a play should be new;[24] Behn's close adoption, sometimes verbatim quotation, of lines from Killigrew's text was another reason to deny her ownership of *The Rover*. As we saw in Chapter 2, however, ideas about the status of borrowed material and what counts as improving it are strongly marked by gendered assumptions about source-matter and influence. The numerous close verbal echoes of Killigrew in Behn's text show that he provided a great deal of her material, that 'feminine' matter which, when taken and shaped by a male writer, is understood as 'mere' matter, subordinate to the work done by 'the shaping spirit of imagination'. When a woman writer takes matter from a man, however, there is a tendency for critics to read this as a different kind of transaction. His matter is spiritualized: her work is seen as the transmission of his. This tendency is still found in modern criticism, as when Gewirtz, while noticing that Behn changes Killigrew's hero into a 'buffoon', remarks that on the whole she is 'faithful' to the 'spirit' of Killigrew.[25] Behn's adaptation from Killigrew should rather be approached as her claim to the masculine privilege of taking and shaping another's material. John Dryden argued in the preface to *An Evening's Love* that the materials a poet borrows from others 'are the least part of that which gives the value: The price lies wholly in the workmanship'.[26] David B. Kramer has shown how Dryden's theory of borrowing aligns it with invasion and conquest, justifying 'this imperial practice with arguments similar to his justifications for national conquest. . . . Appropriating others' work without comment is plagiarism; glorying in such depradations is peculiar to the imperial poet.'[27] This heroic masculine idiom was not available to Behn, but if she does not openly glory in her depradations she does not pass them by silently either. As Greer points out, she made no attempt to disguise the verbal echoes of *Thomaso*.[28] The extent of her blatant borrowings, and the lack of any evidence that Killigrew (who, as proprietor of the rival theatre company and master of the Revels, was in a powerful position) ever objected to Behn's use of his work, suggests that she may well have

---

[24] Paulina Kewes, 'Between the "Triumvirate of Wit" and the Bard', in Cedric C. Brown and Arthur F. Marotti (eds.), *Texts and Cultural Change in Early Modern England* (London: Macmillan, 1997), 215.   [25] Gewirtz, *Restoration Adaptations*, 99.
[26] *The Works of John Dryden*, x. 212.
[27] David B. Kramer, 'Onely Victory in Him: The Imperial Dryden', in Miner and Brady (eds.), *Literary Transmission and Authority*, 55.   [28] Greer, *Slip-Shod Sibyls*, 205.

had his permission. It has even been speculated that she acted at some point as an amanuensis for Killigrew.[29] If so, *The Rover* would stand, among other things, as her declaration of independence: she is no longer simply transmitting another's work. In her famous defensive postscript to *The Rover*, she certainly played down the extent of her debt when she claimed that Angellica was 'the only stolen object', but she also explicitly calls for a comparison between the original and her adaptation: 'I will only say the Plot and Bus'ness (not to boast on't) is my own: as for the Words and Characters, I leave the Reader to judge and compare 'em with *Thomaso*, to whom I recommend the great Entertainment of reading it.' Whether or not we read as ironic her reference to the 'Entertainment' of Killigrew's long-winded comedy, which she had sharpened and fitted for performance, it is worth taking up her challenge. Her claim, like Dryden's, is to have used another's material and given it a higher 'price' by her 'workmanship'. By using Killigrew's speeches and actions but assigning them to different kinds of character, so that the heroine is given the words of rakish males and the hero the exploits of the fool, Behn creates a new play enriched by its critical dialogue with its source.

Some of the most fruitful recent approaches to Behn's use of Killigrew come from critics who have analysed *The Rover* as a woman's radical revision of a play centred on a potent male fantasy.[30] Thomaso is a wishful self-portrait of the exiled cavalier author Thomas Killigrew, who wrote the play in the 1650s. He triumphs in fights against the Spaniards and by winning the affections of various women: he has affairs with Angellica Bianca and Saretta during the course of the action, while Paulina remembers him as her first lover. At the end of the action he reforms, leaving his wandering life for marriage to Serulina, whom he protects from attempted rape by the fool Edwardo. By swapping round some of the main actions of the male characters, Behn undercuts Killigrew's self-indulgent vision of an ever-successful, yet fundamentally honourable, rake. Serulina becomes Florinda, loved by Willmore's friend Belvile, who takes over the hero's romantic traits. Willmore, instead of rescuing Florinda from attack, is her drunken attacker: both violent and foolish, he is

[29] Greer, *Slip-Shod Sibyls*, 197–213.
[30] See esp. DeRitter, 'The Gypsy', 82–92, and Heidi Hutner, 'Revisioning the Female Body: Aphra Behn's *The Rover*, Parts I and II', in Hutner (ed.), *Rereading Aphra Behn: History, Theory and Criticism* (Charlottesville, Va., and London: University Press of Virginia, 1993), 102–20.

robbed of most of Thomaso's abundant heroic dignity. In Killigrew's play Angellica Bianca is certainly depicted with sympathy and her cutting speeches against the sexual double standard give voice to a feminist complaint, but in the dramatic action she is 'the good-natured whore writ large'.[31] After an abortive attempt to revenge herself on the unfaithful wanderer by preventing his marriage to Serulina, she flees the country, leaving behind her plea for forgiveness since 'all my crimes were but so many loves of him'.[32] Behn's Angellica, by contrast, leaves the hero looking foolish, even though she does not carry out her threat to shoot him.

Most original of Behn's characters is Hellena. The witty heroine, brought in to play verbal duels with the hero and at least to begin to redress the balance of dramatic power between the sexes in the play, takes her name from a minor character in *Thomaso*, Helena, 'an old decayed blind, out of Fashion whore', who is so humiliated in the source-play as to provide an epitome of female abjection. Her only positive identity has been as an object of desire. Having lost her youth and beauty she has nothing, and her one plea is to have these restored. This she asks the mountebank, Lopes, to do, but she is tricked by his wife into taking the wrong restorative bath and instead of becoming a young woman she is given the body of the rogue Scarramucha. She is last heard of horrified at her beard and breeches—her female identity taken away and only a travesty of masculinity being given her in its place. Behn, as Heidi Hutner puts it, 'rescues' Hellena from the treatment Killigrew gives her.[33] Restoring youth and beauty and turning her into the heroine, she makes Hellena assertive and dramatically dominant, giving her smutty lines from one of the male characters in *Thomaso* and from the servant Callis, allowing her to reduce her arrogant brother to inarticulate anger, letting her witness and comment on Willmore's activities. She offers, perhaps, the fantasy of a powerful heroine to counteract the fantasy of the all-powerful rake offered by Killigrew.

De Ritter's reading of the popularity of *The Rover* as evidence that the theatregoing public in general was concerned by the issues Behn raised, and shared her critique of Willmore, is less convincing.[34] The play seems to me rather to contain an example of a woman's mockery of male pretension that gets by with audiences because it is

[31] DeRitter, 'The Gypsy', 88. [32] *Thomaso*, Part II, v. vi, p. 453.
[33] Hutner, 'Revisioning the Female Body', 105. [34] DeRitter, 'The Gypsy', 91.

lightly done and contained within a comic plot that reinstates the dominant order. The mockery is there, but it does not have to be noticed. The ending marries Willmore to Hellena and the fortune that is clearly part of her attraction, and leaves Angellica, with her romantic and hopeless vision of another basis for sexual relationships, returning defeated to her courtesan's trade.

As several critics have noted, this was not Behn's most radical reshaping of Killigrew's material. Several years after the success of *The Rover* she returned to *Thomaso,* putting further elements from the long play—the mountebank and the giantesses—to service in a rerun of Willmore's adventures. In a cool comment on the 'happy ending' she had given Hellena, she makes Willmore recount with mock-sorrow his wife's death after a month of marriage. His revelation that Hellena died 'with a fit of kindness, poor soul—she would to Sea with me and in a Storm—far from Land she gave up the Ghost' retrospectively adds a chilling meaning to the 'Storms o'th' Marriage Bed' so lightly invoked in *The Rover*.[35] Marriage has killed the lively heroine. In the action of *The second part of the Rover*, there is another contest between a courtesan and a rich virgin for Willmore's love. This time, not only does the courtesan, La Nuche, win, she enters not marriage but a free union with Willmore. The conclusion goes beyond other contemporary critiques of marriage, in which the freedoms offered by libertinism were presented from a male perspective as freedom for (male) rakes. This radical vision never held the appeal for audiences that the first *Rover* had, and it was not revived during the eighteenth century.

In both parts of *The Rover*, then, Behn took as her basis a powerful male fantasy rendered by Killigrew in especially self-indulgent form, and reshaped it with a woman's critical 'difference of view'. That difference is what most interests us about the plays today, and no doubt had its appeal for some part of the early audiences, who appreciated the challenge of Restoration comedy's satirical edge. However, it was the presence of the male fantasy itself, I believe, that did most to ensure *The Rover*'s continuing popularity. While *The second part of the Rover* was quietly dropped, the first part carried on entertaining audiences who were increasingly encouraged to identify with Willmore rather than criticize or laugh at him. In *The Rover* we see a man's

---

[35] *The second part of the Rover* (London: Jacob Tonson, 1681), I. i. p. 5; *The Rover*, v. i, *Works*, v. 519.

celebration of the male rake transformed by a woman's viewpoint; and in the performance history of the play up to 1790 we see the reappropriation of the rake–hero for a sentimentalized, but still masculinist, view. In the hands of male actors and managers, Willmore charmed the town.

There is evidence that from an early date, the part of Willmore was being softened in production. A recurrent note in comments on the various actors who played Willmore is praise of gentlemanly acting. As early as 1690, the rake was being reformed by William Mountfort. Colley Cibber's *Apology* describes Mountfort's acting style:

In Comedy, he gave the truest Life to what we call the *Fine Gentleman*; his Spirit shone the brighter for being polish'd with Decency . . . The *agreeable* was so natural to him, that ev'en [*sic*] in that dissolute Character of the *Rover* he seem'd to wash off the guilt from Vice, and gave it Charms and Merit. For tho' it may be a Reproach to the Poet, to draw such Characters, not only unpunish'd, but rewarded; the Actor may still be allow'd his due Praise in his excellent Performance. And this is a Distinction which, when this Comedy was acted at *Whitehall*, King *William*'s Queen *Mary* was pleas'd to make in favour of *Monfort*, notwithstanding her Disapprobation of the Play.[36]

From this it is clear that Mountfort's performance emphasized neither the sexual violence nor the foolishness that Behn had added to the hero's character. Neither, of course, did it tally with the uncomplicated acceptance of libertine behaviour found in Killigrew's play. For a moralizing age, the male fantasy of the powerful rake had to be modified. Cibber's conception of Willmore takes no account of the possibility of satirical treatment, which would invite the audience to view with critical amusement the spectacle of vice rewarded. For him comedy should be exemplary, and if Willmore is not properly punished Behn is to blame, while the hero himself is redeemable through agreeable performance. This simultaneous blame of the author and praise of the actor may hold a clue to the way *The Rover*'s popularity coincided with a strong vein of detraction of its author: the men playing the leading part could be given the credit for what was good about the play.

This gentlemanly interpretation of Willmore was adopted by Robert Wilks, who, playing the character more often than any other actor, defined the role as it was understood in the eighteenth century.

[36] Colley Cibber, *An Apology for the Life of Mr. Colley Cibber* (London: John Watts, 1740), 76–7.

Cibber notes that 'Wilks, from his first setting out, certainly formed his acting on the model of Mountfort'. Like Mountfort, who was 'tall, well made, fair, and of an agreeable Aspect', Wilks was an attractive man, and was said to be especially popular with women in the audience.[37] He first made his name as Sir Harry Wildair in *The Constant Couple*, 'in which, by a Vivacity in the Performance, proportionably extravagant to the writing of that Character, he obtained universal, deserved Applause'.[38] In *A Rhapsody on the Stage* (1746) it was claimed that:

> Wilks with genteel and unaffected air
> In gay Sir Harry Charm'd th'attentive fair.[39]

Both vivacity and gentility were frequently mentioned as his distinguishing characteristics: while Cibber thought he had 'sometimes too violent a Vivacity',[40] the author of *Tyranny Triumphant* called him 'the genteelest Actor of his time'.[41] The two qualities together suggest his ability to convey the high spirits of Behn's rake in a manner acceptable to polite audiences. It seems likely, in fact, that his Willmore was influenced by his Wildair, Farquhar's softened version of a libertine, the newer comedy exerting its pull on interpretations of the older one.

Less is known about the acting style of Lacy Ryan, who for many years was a rival Willmore, playing at Lincoln's Inn Fields while Wilks played at Drury Lane. According to *Biographia Dramatica*, 'In his person he was genteel and well made; his judgment was critical and correct; his understanding of an author's sense most accurately just', though his voice was not his strong point.[42] It is likely he and Wilks offered similar interpretations of the role; Ryan's main advantage

---

[37] Cibber, *An Apology*, 75. Steele commented on his performance in John Banks's tragedy *The Unhappy Favourite, or the Earl of Essex*: 'the person and behaviour of Mr Wilks has no small share in conducing to the popularity of the play; and when a handsome fellow is going to a more coarse exit than beheading, his shape and countenance make every tender one reprieve him with all her heart' (*Tatler*, 11 May 1709).

[38] Victor, *The History of the Theatres of London and Dublin*, ii. 53.

[39] Quoted in Highfill, Burnim, and Langhans (eds.), *A Biographical Dictionary of Actors* (Carbondale and Edwardsville, Ill.: Southern Illinois University Press, 1973–87), xvi. 20.

[40] *An Apology for the Life of Mr. Colley Cibber, Comedian, and Late Patentee of the Theatre-Royal* (London: John Watts, 1740), 337.

[41] Quoted in Highfill, Burnim, and Langhans (eds.), *A Biographical Dictionary of Actors*, xvi. 20.

[42] Baker, *Biographia Dramatica* (London: Longman, Hurst, Rees, Orme and Brown, 1812), i. 614.

may have been youth. He was around 30 when he began to play the part, at a time when Wilks was still playing the rover at the age of 60. When *The Rover* was revived at Covent Garden in 1757, acting styles were changing, but gentlemanliness was still crucial to the portrayal of Willmore. The actor playing him in 1757 was in fact known as 'Gentleman' Smith, and according to one nineteenth-century stage history: 'the stage . . . had no more perfect gentleman than Smith. In gay comedy lay his strength . . . Smith was indefatigable in his profession, and proud of his own position in it, congratulating himself on never having had to act in a farce, or sink through a trap.'[43] The parallels between Willmore and Blunt would not have been brought out in his performance.

The long gap between this Covent Garden production and the performance of *Love in Many Masks* in 1790 meant that any sense of the role of Willmore as a 'line', passed down between actors who would model their performance on earlier interpretations, was lost. Kemble had to recreate the role; and given that he was known as a stately actor, most famous for his tragic roles, the vivacity Wilks had brought to Willmore was probably not a key feature of his performance. Although, as we will see, his version of the play emphasizes the hero's role, Kemble's Willmore does not seem to have made a strong impression. *Love in Many Masks* had a good first season, being performed eight times, and was revived once the following season; but its popularity was more due to Dorothy Jordan's acting than Kemble's.[44] Willmore had lost his charm, and *The Rover* was not performed again till the late twentieth century.

A series of charming actors, then, did a great deal to fit Behn's play for the eighteenth-century stage; but handsome faces and genteel airs were not enough on their own. The text itself was significantly altered for performance from the early eighteenth century. We can trace this through three different kinds of altered text. The first of these is a prompt copy of the first edition of *The Rover*, now in the University of London library. Edward Langhans has described it in detail, and in his more recent work suggests that it was prepared for

[43] Doran, *Their Majesties Servants*, 335–6.

[44] After publication, the play was reviewed without enthusiasm in the *Monthly Review* (NS 2, 1790, 356), and in the *English Review*, which considered the piece 'ill-suited to the present improved state of the English theatre', and considered Jordan its only attraction: 'as long as the town continues to be enchanted by Mrs Jordan, 'Love in many Masks' will live'. *English Review*, 15 (1790), 386.

a Covent Garden production of the play in 1740. The changes it records, however, probably date from performances in the play's most popular decade, the 1720s: Langhans considers that the prompter was likely to be working from an older prompt copy, perhaps one prepared by John Stede for Lincoln's Inn Fields.[45] The alterations are mainly cuts, and demonstrate that the comedy was being toned down for performance by 1740 at the latest, and most likely by the 1720s. The second is the 1757 edition of the play, printed 'With the Alterations, As it is now reviv'd and Acting at the Theatre-Royal in Covent-Garden'. While there were probably alterations not recorded in the printed version—which may have printed in full scenes that were cut in performance—this edition does give plenty of evidence of change, indicating that by this date the play was considered old-fashioned enough to need updating. Someone has taken the trouble to make a large number of minor verbal changes, often to the detriment of Behn's rhythmic prose. The intention seems to be to modernize the language-use, clearing up possible obscurities and correcting the diction. The changes are more numerous at the beginning, as though the adapter lost steam as the work went on. The third is Kemble's *Love in Many Masks*, which despite the new title is an alteration of the Behn text rather than a new play based on it. Kemble cuts a good deal of the original text, and adds about thirty lines of his own. The result extends the bowdlerization begun earlier in the century, and significantly alters the emphasis of the play. From the evidence of these texts, together with eighteenth-century comment on performances (notably the 1741 advertising campaign and the hostile newspaper reaction to the 1757 production) we can build up a pattern of *The Rover*'s fortunes in the eighteenth century.

Looking first at Willmore's role, it seems that though there were some textual changes, his behaviour—before 1790—was altered more by the actor's nuances than by actual cuts. The gentlemanly actors were still playing a drunken, violent rake. In III. v, Florinda enters the garden at night, intending to elope from her brother's house with Belvile. When she unlocks the garden door she leaves her-

---

[45] A full description of the copy is in Edward A. Langhans, 'Three Early Eighteenth-Century Promptbooks', *Theatre Notebook*, 20 (1966), 142–50. Here it is conjectured that the promptbook was used for a Drury Lane performance in the 1720s. Langhans reconsiders this promptbook in *Eighteenth Century British and Irish Promptbooks: A Descriptive Bibliography* (New York and London: Greenwood Press, 1987), suggesting that the notes were made by Richard Cross at Covent Garden between 1739 and 1741.

self open to Willmore's entry and his wild misreading of her actions. The drunken Willmore considers all women the same and all equally attractive: 'what has God sent us here!— a Female!—by this Light a Woman!—I'm a Dog if it be not a very Wench!' When she, in alarm, asks who he is and where he comes from, his befuddled reply is 'prithee Child—not so many hard questions', which he follows up with an immediate sexual proposition, promising the only inducement he expects her to need, secrecy: 'I'll not boast who 'twas oblig'd me, not I—for hang me if I know thy name.' All this was left untouched in the promptbook, with only the omission of his invitation to 'come hither,—'tis a delicate shining Wench—by this hand she's perfum'd, and smells like any Nosegay'.[46] Florinda's threat to cry 'Murder! Rape! or any thing!' and his victim-blaming response— 'A Rape! Come, come, you lye . . . why at this time of Night was your Cobweb Door set open dear Spider—but to catch Flyes?'—remain, as do his threat to become 'damnably angry', his offer of money, and their physical struggle, interrupted only when Belvile's arrival saves Florinda (1677: III. v, pp. 42–3; *Works*, v. 487). However, his libertine arguments in favour of sex without vows are expunged. In this passage I have enclosed in square brackets the section that was cut in the promptbook:

FLOR. Heavens! what a filthy Beast is this?

WILL. I am so, and thou ought'st the sooner to lye with me for that reason— [for look you Child, there will be no sin in't, because 'twas neither design'd nor premeditated. 'Tis pure Accident on both sides—that's a certain thing now—indeed shou'd I make Love to you, and vow you fidelity—and swear and lye till you believ'd and yielded—that were to make it wilful Fornication—the crying Sin of the Nation—thou art therefore (as thou art a good Christian) oblig'd in Conscience to deny me nothing. Now—come be kind without any more idle prating.

FLOR. Oh I am ruin'd—Wicked Man unhand me.

WILL. Wicked!—Egad Child a Judge were he young and vigorous, and saw those Eyes of thine, wou'd know 'twas they gave the first blow—the first provocation—come prithee let's lose no time, I say—this is a fine convenient place.]

FLOR. Sir, let me go, I conjure you, or I'll call out.

(1677: III. v, p. 42; *Works*, v. 486–7)

---

[46] *The Rover: or, The Banish't Cavaliers. As it is Acted at His Royal Highness The Duke's Theatre* (London: John Amery, 1677), III. v, pp. 41–2; *Works*, v. 486).

Willmore's irreligious tone is clearly the important target here. The cuts also—perhaps incidentally—reduce his threatening behaviour simply by shortening the scene. What this suggests is that while there was a concern to cut the anti-Christian slant of Restoration libertinism, the attack on Florinda was not seen as problematic in itself. Given what we know of the acting styles, it seems likely that during the early eighteenth century this scene (whether or not played with the cuts in this promptbook) was still considered a comic one, with Wilks's vivacity making light work of Willmore's sexual advances. In 1757, when 'Gentleman' Smith played the part, there is no textual evidence that Willmore's attack was considered a problem: indeed, it seems that the passage previously cut was restored. The 1757 edition omits only the phrase 'that were to make it wilful Fornication—the crying Sin of the Nation'; and in this text is following cuts made in earlier editions, rather than representing an alteration made for the 1757 performance.[47]

By the time of Kemble's revival in 1790 a very different Willmore appeared (the stage directions make him only '*a little drunk*'). Florinda's struggle with Willmore is drastically shortened and toned down. The entire exchange between them, before Belvile's arrival, reads:

WILL. . . .—By this light, a woman!—I'm a dog, if it be not a very wench! —

FLOR. He's come!—Ha!—who's there?

WILL. Sweet soul! let me salute thy shoe-string.

FLOR. 'Tis not my Belville.—Good Heavens! I know him not—Who are you, and from whence come you?

WILL. Prithee—prithee, child—not so many hard questions—let it suffice I am here, child.

FLOR. Good Heav'n! what luck is mine!

WILL. Only good luck, child, parlous good luck—come hither—'tis a delicate shining wench.—I'll be very secret. I'll not boast who 'twas obliged me, not I—for, hang me, if I know thy name.

FLOR. Sir, can you think—

WILL. Madam, I think you're a beautiful creature; and that's all the thinking I care for just now—so come to my arms—why, what a work's here—in good time—come, no struggling.   [*She struggles with him*

(*Love in Many Masks*, III. iv, p. 37)

---

[47] Both the 1702 and 1724 collected editions of Behn's plays omit the quoted phrase.

Willmore has no libertine arguments, the word rape is not mentioned, he does not offer Florinda money, and he is a good deal less threatening and more polite (he had not called her 'Madam' before). By this time it was clearly problematic for the hero to treat a lady as though she were a whore.

The drastic alterations to the 1790 Willmore indicate that the whole conception of the character had become difficult to present on stage. This pattern holds for other elements of the play, too: the promptbook shows minor excisions where 1790 makes drastic cuts. However, when we look at some of these other elements it is clear that many changes were made in the promptbook. Willmore might need little change for early eighteenth-century consumption, but other characters needed more.

Another scene of sexual violence that has been the focus of recent comment is Blunt's attack on Florinda in Act IV. Again, Florinda discovers that as soon as she leaves her brother's house she is treated as sexual prey. She arrives at Blunt's house, asking him for protection, at the moment when he has just vowed revenge on all womankind for the humiliation visited on him by Lucetta in Act III. He threatens to rape and beat Florinda, and Frederick, who arrives in the middle of the scene, is initially quite willing to join in, only changing his mind once he suspects that her social status is too high for her to be raped with impunity. The scene—based on a similar incident in *Thomaso*—is a chilling one, revealing the ugliness of the power-relations behind the façade of gentlemen's gallantry, and depriving sexual violence of the rakish glamour sometimes invested in it in Restoration comedy. It was considerably toned down in some eighteenth-century performances. In the promptbook a number of cuts were made to Blunt's threats. In the examples cited below, words deleted in the promptbook are placed in square brackets. When Blunt insults Florinda and 'pulls her rudely', she cries, 'Dare you be so cruel?' He replies:

Cruel, adsheartlikins as a Galley-slave, or a *Spanish*-Whore: [Cruel, yes, I will kiss and beat thee all over; kiss, and see thee all over; thou shalt lye with me too, not that I care for the injoyment, but to let thee see I have ta'en deliberated Malice to thee, and will be reveng'd on one Whore for the sins of another;] I will smile and deceive thee, flatter thee, and beat thee, kiss and swear, and lye to thee, imbrace thee and rob thee, as she did me, fawn on thee, and strip thee stark naked, then hang thee out at my window by the heels, with a Paper of scurvy Verses fasten'd to thy breast, in praise of damnable women—Come, come along. (1677: IV. v, p. 65; *Works*, v. 505)

In the promptbook, Frederick's initial reaction to Florinda's plight is still to mock her—'What's this, a Person of Quality too, who is upon the ramble to supply the defects of some grave impotent Husband?'—but his nastiest comment is cut:

BLUNT. No, no, Gentlewoman, come along, adsheartlikins we must be better acquainted—[we'l both lye with her, and then let me alone to bang her.
FRED. I'm ready to serve you in matters of Revenge that has a double pleasure in't.
BLUNT. Well said. You hear, little one, how you are condemn'd by public Vote to the Bed within,] there's no resisting your Destiny, sweet heart.

(1677: IV. v, p. 66; *Works*, v. 506)

The 1757 production, however, seems again to have stuck closer to the original than the one served by the promptbook. Blunt's threats to Florinda are almost untouched in the 1757 edition, and this does not seem to be a case of printing unaltered a scene that was cut in performance, because there are enough minor verbal changes to suggest that the text is taking account of alterations made for performance.

In 1790 great changes were made to this scene for *Love in Many Masks*. The alterations go far beyond those in the promptbook. The scene (now placed in Act V) is considerably shortened. Blunt's threats to Florinda are carefully unspecified. When she asks, 'Can you be so cruel as to—' he replies, 'Cruel! Adsheartlikins, as a galley-slave.— Come along—or I shall—'. The remainder of the two passages quoted above is omitted. Frederick's participation in the scene is given an altogether new colouring. He immediately ranges himself with Florinda against Blunt, telling her, 'Fear nothing, Madam' (V. iv, p. 58). This is one of many indications of sentimentalization of all the young lovers' roles. Blunt is a comic butt and as such can be allowed to retain his threats, though their expression has to be obscured; but Frederick is to marry Valeria, Florinda's cousin, and by 1790 it is quite inappropriate for him to threaten a lady.

The pattern that emerges from the three altered versions is of uneven change: excisions and toning down in the promptbook, the restoration of contentious elements in 1757, and a new, much more thorough bowdlerization in 1790. Assuming that the promptbook can be taken, not as the text always used but as representative of the kinds of change being made in the 1720s, 1730s and 1740s, this suggests that the play secured its eighteenth-century popularity through a general softening of its hard edges. The version of 1757 stands out as an anomaly. Its alterations work in the direction of greater clarity, not greater decency. Not only does it preserve boldness and bawdy, at times it even embellishes them in the interests of explicit meaning. For instance, one of the speeches that identifies Hellena as an aggressive heroine in the first scene of the play is her expression of revulsion from Don Vincentio, the older man being proposed as a husband for her sister. The promptbook cut down her remarks on the disgusting husband waiting in bed for his wife, as indicated by the square brackets in the following quotation:

the Gyant stretches itself; yawns and sighs [a Belch or two, loud as a Musket, throws himself into Bed, and expects you in his foul sheets], and e're you can get your self undrest, call's you with a Snore or two—and are not these fine Blessings to a young Lady? (I. i, p. 4; *Works*, v. 457)[48]

The 1757 edition not only restored the cut but added a phrase to emphasize Vincentio's impotence: he now calls to his bride 'with a Snore or two *but nothing else*'.[49] In the light of this and other evidence for the bawdy nature of the 1757 production, the severe criticism which it received can be better understood. It was not a case of elements acceptable in the earlier part of the century becoming suddenly outrageous in the 1750s. Rather, an earlier tradition of canny modification had been lost, and the play offered at Covent Garden in the 1750s was coarser and bolder than the one that had held the boards up to the 1740s.

This pattern can be most clearly seen in the fortunes of the character that caused most offence to eighteenth-century audiences: Ned Blunt. The booby who is tricked and humiliated by the 'jilting wench' Lucetta, and later tries to take his revenge by raping and beating Florinda, was billed as a comic attraction;[50] but he was also the focus

---

[48] It might be argued that the prompter was only continuing a process of bowdlerization begun by Behn herself. The corresponding remarks in *Thomaso* read 'the Gyant stretches himself, yawns and sighs a belch or two, stales in your pot, farts as loud as a Musket' (Part II, Act II. ii, p. 400). In Killigrew's play, however, these lines are spoken not by the heroine but by Harrigo, one of the hero's male friends, to Serulina. *The Rover*'s boldness is not just a matter of what is said but who says it.

[49] *The Rover* (London, 1757) I. i, p. 6, my italics.

[50] e.g. the bill for the August 1710 performance at the new theatre in Greenwich, played for the benefit of the comedian Penkethman, gave pride of place to 'Ned Blunt—by the famous true Comedian Mr Cave Underhill, to oblige Mr Penkethman's Friends'.

of most comments on the play's indecency. Though his attack on Florinda was, as we have seen, toned down in the promptbook, it was not the main problem he posed. The scene that caused most out-raged comment was the scene in Lucetta's chamber, when he strips to his shirt and drawers onstage, before moving towards her bed, and falling through a trapdoor. The following scene has him '*creeping out of a Common-Shoar, his face, &c. all dirty*', and cursing Lucetta for her trick and himself for his gullibility (1677: III. iv, p. 40). The two scenes together combined the titillating (if unkept) promise of sexual display, the broad reference to imminent sexual activity, and the coarse dis-play of the actor dirtied in the sewer, which eighteenth-century critics found disgusting. Steele, writing disdainfully of Behn as 'an Author of the [female] Sex, who, in the *Rover*, makes a Country Squire strip to his Holland Drawers', set the tone for subsequent cri-ticism.[51] This incident became notorious, and the 1741 production was carefully planned to reduce the offence caused. The 1757 pro-duction, on the other hand, restored the stripping, and as a result became subject to fierce critical attack. In 1790, there was no undress-ing at all: Blunt simply placed '*his sword, hat, watch, purse etc. on table*', and he was not tipped into the sewer.[52]

Blunt's undressing and dipping in the sewer are worth investigat-ing in detail, because they show what was found most objectionable in Behn's work. The focus of objection is the affront to the ladies involved in his on-stage undressing; but the performance details and an analysis of some of the criticism suggest that another cause for concern was the staging of Blunt's humiliation.

In these two consecutive scenes, both problematic for eighteenth-century audiences, Behn first has Blunt display (or part-display) him-self by stripping to his drawers, and then shows him in a discovery scene, revealed in the abject position of crawling out of the sewer. The second of these scenes is one of Behn's own touches: in *Thomaso*, Blunt's counterpart, Edwardo, is tricked by Lucetta but he is not tipped in the sewer, and he has his revenge by getting his bravoes to cut Lucetta's face. It was an early casualty of eighteenth-century per-formance: the entire scene was ruled around in the promptbook, indicating that it was to be omitted. Economy as well as decency may have been a motive: the omission saves one scene-change in a

---

[51] *The Spectator*, no. 51, Saturday 28 Apr. 1711; ed. Bond, i. 218.
[52] *Love in Many Masks*, III. iii, p. 35.

crowded act. It is also, significantly, the scene in which the fool is most graphically humiliated by the whore.

Meanwhile the on-stage undressing that had annoyed Steele continued to be played, the stage-direction left intact in the promptbook; but it too, was the focus of revision towards the middle of the century. A couple of weeks before the play was revived at Covent Garden in 1741, it was the subject of a campaign in the *London Daily Post and General Advertiser*, evidently organized by Lacy Ryan, who had chosen the play for his benefit night. On 3 March and 5 March, notice was given that the play was to be revived on Monday 16 March, and that tickets were available from Ryan's lodgings in Great Queen-Street. On 9 March the paper published a letter addressed to Ryan from an anonymous gentleman who reported that he had defended the play's merits against the objections of some ladies of his acquaintance. In this gendered debate over the play's decency, Ned Blunt's undressing is the central problem for ladies whose feminine delicacy is established by their very reluctance to mention the incident:

after some hesitation [the ladies] told me, tho' they allowed the Play to be full of Spirit, Wit and Humour, yet the scene of Ned Blunt's undressing was rather too loose; an Incident [which] however diverting to the Upper Gallery, was Indecent, and not fit for the Company that frequent the Boxes. As this may be easily remov'd or alter'd (by his retiring when he undresses) I thought proper to give you this Notice, which will oblige the Company that then remark'd it, and I don't doubt a great many more of the Female Part of your Audience.[53]

The 'Female Part' of the audience is thus seen as guardian of public decency, not only on behalf of their sex but on behalf of the genteel classes, who want to avoid the coarseness that delights the lower orders in the cheap upper gallery. I am sure that this very constructive critic, who is careful to mention that he has bought tickets for the performance and who offers a solution to the play's one difficulty, is Ryan himself, creating his own opportunity for the reply which the paper published the following day. This revealed that Ryan had, in fact, all along intended the very alteration the helpful gentleman suggested. Ryan's pronouns give the game away:

Sir, I saw a Letter in your Paper of Yesterday directed to me, and think myself oblig'd to the Gentleman for giving myself the opportunity of

---

[53] *London Daily Post and General Advertiser*, no. 1989, Monday 9 Mar. 1741.

making publick my Intent (which I have already communicated to several Ladies, who made the same Objection) of omitting the Indecency of Ned Blunt's undressing himself before the Audience . . .

Ryan went on to argue that it was necessary for Blunt to appear in shirt and drawers, ready to fall through the trapdoor to the sewer: it was only the act of undressing that was to be avoided, and even this was a problem not so much in itself as because it encouraged ribaldry in the audience: 'It has indeed been often thought a very great Error, that, for the sake of a ridiculous Clamour, occasion'd by Ned Blunt's undressing himself, so good a Comedy shou'd be render'd incapable of being an Entertainment to the only valuable Part of the Fair Sex.'[54]

Sending Blunt off-stage to undress was a key part of Ryan's strategy to gentrify *The Rover*, and with this alteration the comedy played twice in the 1740–1 season, and continued on the boards for the next three seasons. The care he took over the 1741 revival shows that the role of Willmore was valuable enough for him to pay close attention to cleaning up the whole play, and that the drive was to make *The Rover* into a moral comedy that would appeal to the more genteel part of the audience. The revival of 1757 was a very different story. The concern to correct and clarify the text was not matched by a comparable sense of what the gentry wanted. The scene where Blunt crawls out of the sewer was printed in the edition and may have been performed; and the notorious on-stage undressing was restored. Far from being unpopular, this bold revival had a long run of ten performances between February and May, and played again three or four times in each of the next three seasons. In fact, it was its very popularity with audiences that enraged the critic in the *London Chronicle*, who conducted a single-handed campaign against the play for three weeks in 1757. After an initial bad review, this writer noted subsequent performances of '*The Rover* again' with increasing exasperation. After a particularly angry piece in the issue of 10–12 March, the critic claimed the credit when the play was dropped in favour of Cibber's *The Refusal* (in fact, *The Rover* was back again a month later).[55]

The instance of the 1757 *Rover* suggests that the stage history of Restoration plays in the later eighteenth century should not be

---

[54] *London Daily Post and General Advertiser*, no. 1990, Tuesday 10 Mar. 1741.

[55] *London Chronicle: or, Universal Evening Post*, 22–4 Feb. 1757; 26 Feb.–1 Mar. 1757; 3–5 Mar. 1757; 5–8 Mar. 1757; 10–12 Mar. 1757; and 12–15 Mar 1757.

simply interpreted as the result of changing audience tastes overall. Those changes were being affected by pressure from a developing base of newspaper criticism. The late-century refinement of the stage was the work of a newly dominant cultural group including critics and the more genteel part of the theatre audience: theatre-managers played a crucial part, but they had to balance the move towards refinement with the need to retain audiences who were by no means entirely refined themselves. Eventually, though, the lower orders had their tastes mocked and their amusements withdrawn.

The *London Chronicle*'s objections to *The Rover* centred on Ned Blunt, or more precisely, on his effect on the audience:

One of the Personages of the Drama takes off his breeches in the sight of the Audience, whose Diversion is of a complicated nature on the Occasion. The Ladies are first alarmed; then the Men stare: The Women put up their fans.—'My Lady Betty, what is the Man about?'—'Lady Mary, sure he is not in earnest!'—Then peep thro' their Fans—'Well, I vow, the He-Creature is taking off his odious Breeches—He—he—Po!—is that all?—The Man has Drawers on.'—Then, like *Mrs* Cadwallader in the new Farce,—'Well, to be sure, I never saw any *Thing* in the Shape of it.'—Mean time, the Delight of the Male Part of the Audience is occasioned by the various Operations of this Phaenomenon on the Female Mind.—'This is rare Fun, d——n me—Jack, Tom, Bob, did you ever see any thing like this?—Look at that Lady yonder—See, in the Stage Box—how she looks half averted,' &c &c. It is a Matter of Wonder that the Upper Gallery don't call for a Hornpipe, or 'Down with the drawers', according to their usual Custom of insisting upon as much as they can get for their Money. But to be a little serious, it should be remembered by all Managers that this play was written in the dissolute Days of Charles the Second; and that Decency at least is, or ought to be, demanded at present.[56]

According to this critic, the men respond to the spectacle of Blunt by turning their gaze instead on the women in the audience, making their embarrassment into the spectacle. The class dimension to their aggressive mockery—'Jack, Tom, Bob' looking from the pit or the gallery towards the higher-ranking lady in the stage-box—shows once again that the ladies are seen as the representatives and guardians of gentility. To protect them, as Ryan did by his alterations and the *London Chronicle* writer claims to do by his criticisms, is to raise the social status of the theatre. The passage is complicated, however,

[56] *London Chronicle*, 22–4 Feb. 1757.

by the critic's ambivalent attitude to the ladies. Jack, Bob, and Tom may be deceived when they attribute the lady's averted gaze to discomfort. Lady Mary and Lady Betty, peeping through their fans to be disappointed that only Blunt's underwear is on display, are not so far removed from the vulgar crowd in the upper gallery after all. The critic's call for decency in the name of the ladies almost founders on the fear that it is not really what they want, though 'Decency . . . *ought to be*' demanded. His concerns illuminate the way Behn's treatment of Blunt can work to undermine male dignity. The undressing in order to join Lucetta in bed raises the idea of a display of potency, but instead only Blunt's underwear is shown, without 'any *Thing* in the shape of it': what is staged is Blunt's lack of phallic power. The *London Chronicle*'s uneasy response hints that a scene which 'ought' to embarrass the ladies might also work to direct a female gaze onto male inadequacy. Behn's propensity for discovery scenes that display the acting body to the spectators has been noticed by critics and seen as an instance of the commodification of the female body on the Restoration stage;[57] but less attention has been given to the fact that she also stages the display of the male, and in a way that undermines the notion that male self-display connotes power. A play's comic butt is always there to be humiliated, but when a female author displays him there may be a new consciousness of the scene as the humiliation of the male as such; and Blunt's undressing seemed especially indecent because planned by a female author.[58]

Eighteenth-century criticisms and revisions, then, were directed not only at indecency as such but at elements that could undermine traditional gender relations. This can also be seen in the treatment of the two main female roles during the period. As we have seen, Hellena and Angellica are both strong roles developed by rethinking the relationships in *Thomaso*. Killigrew's play centres on the adventures of the rake–hero who dominates the action, and his satellites include the strongly drawn courtesan Angellica and the less interesting heroine Serulina, his prize at the end. Behn focused on this triangle, eliminating Thomaso's other partners, and remodelled it to create a delicate balance among three strong roles: the lively,

[57] Diamond, '*Gestus* and Signature', 47–8.

[58] Steele's criticism of Blunt's undressing is part of a discussion of the particular lewdness of the 'Poetesses of the Age' exemplified by Pix and Behn. *The Spectator*, no. 51, Sat. 28 Apr. 1711; ed. Bond, i. 218.

thoughtless Willmore, the near-tragic Angellica, and the witty heroine Hellena. Both Hellena and Angellica challenge the expectations
placed on them in the social world of the play, or to put it another
way, both challenge the conventions of representation governing
their character types. Angellica steps out of the courtesan's role by
offering a free and passionate love, and the convention of the laugh-
able cast-off mistress is twisted when the play is shaped so as to present her distress seriously. Her unhappiness qualifies the comic
delight of the ending, and may in performance make the audience
question the happiness of Hellena's success in obtaining Willmore.
Hellena herself, the witty heroine who pursues her man in successive disguises, as gypsy and boy, challenges her social role by her outspoken, often bawdy language. During the eighteenth century the
carefully balanced equilateral triangle of roles created by Behn was
pulled out of shape by the emphases of different performances, and
the roles of both Hellena and Angellica were simplified in the process
of turning the play into eighteenth-century comedy.

The balance among the three roles was probably most nearly pre-
served in the early productions, when, as we have seen, Angellica's
role was played by leading tragediennes and sometimes given prominence in the playbills. The promptbook version, however, shows that
there was some reduction of her role in the 1720s. In Act IV scene ii,
a scene not based on any counterpart in Killigrew, Willmore is pursued by both Angellica, reproaching him for infidelity, and Hellena,
who interrupts their exchange by appearing in boys' clothes, pretending to bring a message from another lady who loves Willmore
and has been deceived by him. Comic misunderstandings and
revelations follow. Willmore, deceived by Hellena's disguise, is
delighted at the idea that there is yet another woman interested in
him. Then he recognizes her, and the balance of dramatic power
shifts as he teases her with the threat to expose her disguise. At the
end of the scene Angellica is left alone on stage, and there is a return
to the serious idiom of her disappointed love.

WILL. Yes, you can spare me now,—farewel, till you're in better Humour—
[*aside*] I'm glad of this release—Now for my Gipsie:
For tho' to worse we change, yet still we find
New Joys, new Charms, in a new Miss that's kind.

[*Ex. Willmore*

ANG. He's gone, and in this Ague of my Soul
The Shivering fit returns;

Oh with what willing haste, he took his leave,
As if the long'd-for Minute, were arriv'd
Of some blest assignation.
In vain I have Consulted all my Charms,
In vain this Beauty priz'd, in vain believ'd,
My Eyes cou'd kindle any lasting fires;
I had forgot my Name, my Infamie,
And the reproach that Honour lays on those
That dare pretend a sober passion here.
Nice reputation, tho' it leave behind
More vertues than inhabit where that dwells;
Yet that once gone, those Vertues shine no more.
—Then since I am not fit to be belov'd,
I am resolv'd to think on a revenge
On him that sooth'd me thus to my undoing.

(1677: IV. ii, p. 60; *Works*, v. 501)

The promptbook records a considerable alteration to the close of the scene. Angellica's exit comes immediately after she dismisses Willmore, so he, not she, is the one left holding the stage at the end of the scene. Her soliloquy disappears, and the emphasis of the ending is on Willmore's cheerful closing couplet. This cut tends towards a simplification of the comedy's emotional effect. Up to this point the scene has been exploiting the comic potential of Willmore's infidelity, which makes him temporarily embarrassed by the simultaneous attentions of both women. The shift of tone involved in Angellica's final speech complicates the comedy. Getting rid of her speech makes for a lighter, simpler scene, more clearly centred on the comically beleaguered but ultimately triumphant hero.

As Angellica's distress was toned down, there was a corresponding increase in concentration on Hellena. We have already seen that her role was emphasized in publicity, with Ryan's campaign for the 1741 production making a feature of Woffington's role as Hellena. However, it was Hellena's virtue rather than her cheek that was brought into prominence. Ryan's defence of the moral tendency of the play depended on a simplified view of the relations between Willmore, Angellica, and Hellena. The affair with Angellica, he contended, demonstrates: 'that Vice, however adorn'd with Charms, has not Force enough to fix the Rover's Mind, which the Spirit, Wit, and Virtue of Hellen[a]'s Character Compleats, without the Knowledge of her Birth or Fortune.'[59] This reduction of Angellica and Hellena to vice and virtue glosses over the more challenging nuances of the play (such as the clear indication that the revelation of Hellena's fortune does make quite a difference to the rover's attitude). Even before this date, the simplification, and toning down, of Hellena can be traced in the promptbook version of the play. We have seen that her remarks about Vincentio in Act I scene i were cut; other elements in the scene, indicative of her sexual boldness, were also cut. In those performances regulated by the promptbook the heroine no longer referred to her 'Vigour desirable', exclaimed 'Marry *Don Vincentio*! hang me such a Wedlock would be worse than Adultery with another Man', or remarked in sardonic aside to the audience: 'a Nun! yes I am like to make a fine Nun! I have an excellent humour for a Grate: no, I'le have a *Saint* of my own to pray to shortly, if I like any that dares venture on me' (1677: I. i, pp. 2, 4, 5; *Works*, v. 456, 457, 458).

This taming of the challenge offered by the two main female characters was most thoroughly done in Kemble's revised version. This production, a last attempt to turn Behn's comedy into something that could fit the refined stage of the late eighteenth century, had a much softer Angellica, a more refined Hellena, and a greatly reformed Willmore. The relationships between the three main characters were so altered that *Love in Many Masks* becomes a different kind of play from *The Rover*, needing some separate consideration.

Angellica's relationship with Willmore, her situation as a courtesan, and the sharp reflections on a whore's life offered by her bawd, Moretta, were all problematic on the late eighteenth-century stage. This can be seen in the changes made to II. ii, one of those naughty Restoration scenes in which, when characters leave the stage, it is evident that they are about to go to bed together. In Behn's original text, the scene ends like this:

ANG. The pay, I mean, is but thy Love for mine.
— Can you give that?
WILL. Intirely—come, let's withdraw! where I'll renew my Vows—and breath 'em with such Ardour thou shalt not doubt my zeal.
ANG. Thou hast a Pow'r too strong to be resisted.

              [*Ex. Will. and Angellica*

MORET. Now my Curse go with you—is all our Project fallen to this? to love the only Enemy to our Trade? nay, to love such a Shameroone, a very

---

[59] *London Daily Post and General Advertiser*, no. 1990, Tues. 10 Mar. 1741.

Beggar, nay a Pyrate Beggar, whose business is to rifle, and be gone, a no Purchase, no Pay Taterdemalion, and *English* Piccaroon. A Rogue that fights for daily drink, and takes a Pride in being Loyally Lousie—Oh I cou'd curse now, if I durst.—This is the Fate of most Whores.

> *Trophies, which from believing Fops we win,*
> *Are Spoils to those who couzen us agen.*

(1677: II. ii, pp. 28–9; *Works*, v. 476)

The passage had already received a few alterations in the prompt-book, which omitted Angellica's 'Thou hast a Pow'r too strong to be resisted', and substituted the euphemism 'of our Proffession' for the word 'Whores'. In 1790, however, Kemble completely altered the scene's ending. Moretta's speech was omitted altogether, and instead of the coarse bawd, Angellica closes the act, with a new speech by Kemble.

ANG. The pay I mean, is but thy love for mine.—Can you give that?

WILL. Intirely.

ANG. Then I receive you as my future servant.

WILL. Madam—

ANG. But mark me, Sir—my birth, my breeding and pride raise me far above the coarse interchange of mere convenient pleasures—I offer my heart for your's: Yet how depend on men for constancy!

WILL. Depend!—may I depend upon your's?

ANG. Ah! this is one of the virtues you always blame the want of in us, though you never practise it yourselves.

> Virgins or wives, from us our tyrants claim
> A strict performance of the task of fame;
> Yet to themselves indulgently allow
> The breach of honour and the marriage-vow.
> No more let man our weaker sex condemn
> For faults, originally taught by them;
> Since, if from Virtue's holy path we stray,
> We only follow where you point the way.

(1790: II. ii, pp. 23–4)

Angellica's explicit acceptance of Willmore, followed by a quick exit towards the bedroom, are replaced by the haughty diction of a romance heroine ('my future servant', 'mere convenient pleasures'), and the couple's imminent love-making (though it is still supposed to occur) is obscured by the moralizing vein adopted by the lady. Her new, generalizing couplets present Angellica as the typical victim of seduction beloved of late eighteenth-century sentimentalists. Her plight is taken as representative of all women's, and her speech excuses her own (and other women's) sexual behaviour by blaming men for all lapses from 'virtue'.

In stressing the pathos of Angellica as victim here, Kemble is echoing some of the concerns of Killigrew's *Thomaso*. Despite the great differences between Killigrew's libertine romp and Kemble's carefully sanitized version of Behn, the two men share a tendency to present Angellica as a victim and to see her loss of virginity as the source of her pathos. Here they both differ from Behn, who uses the more rebellious side of Killigrew's Angellica, the side of her that questions the concept of honour and the sexual double standard, and does not incorporate the more abject side of her as a woman lamenting and excusing her lost purity.[60] In *Thomaso*, Part I, Act II scene iv, the basis for Behn's II. ii, Killigrew's Angellica describes how she was sold into prostitution, begging Thomaso to 'forget and forgive my faults that are past, which are crimes of the Nation, not mine; sold by a Mother, oppress'd with misery when I knew no better than to obey her'. She wishes: 'that such a stream [of her tears] could make me as pure a Virgin as I am now a perfect Lover; then I would beg to be thy wife; but that must not be; for love bids me not ask that which honour forbids thee to grant; yet you may be my friend' (*Thomaso*, Part I, Act II scene iv, p. 341). Killigrew's and Kemble's texts both in their different ways make the fact of Angellica's being a courtesan the focus of their sympathetic treatment of her. Behn's text is distinctive in its attempt to see Angellica positively, as a sexually experienced woman who offers free love. The problem is not her profession, but Willmore's inability to appreciate the importance of her offer to renounce it.

While Kemble gave Angellica extra lines in II. ii to align her with the seduced victims of sentimental writing, on the whole he reduced her part, throwing more of the emphasis on Willmore and Hellena.[61] In his version Hellena is absorbed into the late eighteenth-century

---

[60] In a later scene, IV. ii, Angellica in soliloquy does lament that she is 'not fit to be belov'd' because of her loss of honour, but here the focus is on an attack on honour for obscuring the importance of virtues other than chastity.

[61] A similar point is made by Paula Backscheider: 'By grinding down both the most romantic and the most mercenary aspects of Angellica, Kemble produces a female character who competes less with Hellena and who is easily experienced as part of a patriarchal plot pattern' (*Spectacular Politics*, 99).

tradition of the sprightly heroine, whose dramatic dominance is based on her combination of spirit with carefully emphasized purity. Kemble makes explicit in the text the theme of the rake reformed by feminine virtue that Ryan had earlier made a part of his interpretation. Act IV scene ii, which had originally ended on the abandoned Angellica's soliloquy and had been altered in the promptbook to end on Willmore's breezy declaration in favour of new mistresses, is altered again in *Love in Many Masks*. Again Angellica's soliloquy is cut, but Willmore's closing remarks are replaced by a new couplet which indicates that in his heart he is already the virtuous Hellena's captive:

> Now for my gipsy:
> For though I wildly rove from fair to fair,
> I feel she holds unrivall'd empire here.

> (*Love in Many Masks*, 53)

While Willmore's feelings for Hellena are simplified and sentimentalized, the 'gipsy' herself is softened by cuts. Though the heroine's lively charm, as conveyed by Dorothy Jordan, was considered the main attraction of Kemble's production, it had to be confined within stricter limits than had applied to Hellena in earlier versions of Behn's play. Ryan had seen Hellena as the victorious heroine because of her 'Spirit', Wit, and Virtue';[62] Kemble's Hellena has all the virtue, but less of the spirit and wit. In his text she is deprived of nearly all the sauciness that originally characterized her. The exchanges with Don Pedro in the first scene, which as we have seen were toned down in the promptbook, are drastically cut in Kemble's version. Hellena no longer remarks that Florinda's rich but feeble suitor 'may perhaps encrease her Baggs, but not her Family'; she no longer overwhelms her brother with a long description of Don Vincentio in the bedchamber, belching, snoring and having to be kissed by a reluctant bride who must 'nuzel through his Beard to find his Lips', and she no longer refers to adultery. In the new, shortened scene it becomes rather puzzling that Don Pedro should refer to the heroine as a 'Wild Cat'. (I. i, pp. 3–5; *Works*, v. 456–8; *Love in Many Masks*, 4). Her scenes with Willmore, too, are marked less by witty repartee than by her maidenly retreats. In *The Rover*, when the two first meet, he demands access to her: 'thy Lodging, sweetheart, thy Lodging! Or I'm a dead Man!' and her retort, 'Why must we be either guilty of

---

[62] *London Daily Post and General Advertiser*, no. 1990, Tues. 10 Mar. 1741.

Fornication or Murder if we converse with you Men' exposes his lover's rhetoric as a cover for lust (I. ii, p. 12; *Works*, v. 463). In the same scene in Kemble's version, she makes no reply and simply runs away.

Willmore himself is also greatly altered. From his first appearance, he is less of a rover than Behn's original character. His lewd remarks to the courtesan in Act I scene ii are omitted. He no longer says there is only one way for a woman to oblige him, or longs to have his arms full of 'soft, white, kind—Woman!' (1677: II. i, p. 16). He does go to bed with Angellica, but all references to his taking money from her are taken out. His love for Hellena is cleared of its mercenary taint. Hellena's fortune is still mentioned, but Willmore is shown to be more interested in her gentility than her money. His love for Hellena is clearly his real love, and his desire for Angellica just a temporary aberration. He still makes a speech to Angellica about virtue being an infirmity in woman, but it's clear he doesn't mean it. The ending of the play shows a thoroughly reformed and sententious hero. The original Willmore teases Hellena about their imminent marriage: 'Have you no trembling at the near approach?' She replies 'No more than you have in an Engagement or a Tempest', and his rejoinder closes the play:

> WILL. Egad thou'rt a brave Girle, and I admire thy Love and Courage.
>   Lead on, no other Dangers they can dread,
>   Who Venture in the Storms o' th' Marriage Bed.
>
> (v. i, p. 83; *Works*, v. 519)

In *Love in Many Masks*, this final exchange is converted from a contemplation of marriage as a battle to a discussion of a rake's reform—that favourite subject of late eighteenth-century sentimental drama. Willmore closes the play with a new set of couplets:

> WILL. Thou'rt a brave girl!—I admire thy love and courage, and will give thee as little cause as I can to repent 'em.
>   Henceforth no other pleasures can I know,
>   Than those of fond fidelity to you;
>   Your pow'r my captive heart in chains shall bind,
>   Sweet as the graces of your face and mind:-
>   Blest in my friends, and doubly blest in love,
>   My joy's complete indeed—if you approve.
>
> (*Love in Many Masks*, v. iv, p. 73)

The need to chasten both Willmore's role and Angellica's makes it difficult to present a coherent version of their relationship. On the one hand Angellica is detached as far as possible from her life as a courtesan, and made a representative female victim of male seduction. On the other hand her seducer is also absolved as far as possible from blame: he didn't really mean it, and he gives up roving as soon as he can for the love of a good woman. Hellena emerges as the winner, in the name of virtuous woman; but in the process she has lost the sauciness that made her a heroine fit to match with the rover.

While both female parts lose out in certain ways, Willmore gains in dignity what he loses in libertine speech. Unlike Behn's original hero, he is never made to look foolish where money is concerned. Killigrew's Thomaso had boasted of winning not only Angellica but her money; then, towards the end of the play, he sends the money back with a sententious speech:

> The *Angellica* shall have her thousand crowns again, 'twas the first money I ever got by the sex; and I cannot but wonder at their narrow minds, as well as their fortunes that can be so poorly spirited as to design farther then the kindness of a woman. I have bought many in my time, but never yet either ask'd or got more of a woman than her flesh.   (*Thomaso*, Part II 5.v. vii, p. 459).

Behn transformed this incident by making Willmore offer the money to Angellica in person during the scene when she threatens him with a pistol. Saying that he cannot offer constant love, he offers her a purse instead: 'I'l pay you back your Charity, | And be oblig'd for nothing but for Love.' Scornfully rejecting the offer and the 'mean . . . thought of me' it reveals, she continues to pursue him across the stage while he backs away '*still amaz'd*' (v. i, p. 76; *Works*, v. 514). Where Thomaso is made to look superior, Willmore is made to look lame. Kemble dealt with the threat to the hero's dignity in this incident by removing it altogether: his Willmore never lowers himself to take money from Angellica in the first place. Kemble also omits Behn's hints of the dependence of masculine identity on mercenary power. Her Willmore's virility is threatened by his lack of money, so that when he first hears of Angellica's prohibitive price he remarks ruefully, 'The very thought of it quenches all manner of Fire in me' (I. ii, p. 15; *Works*, v. 466). In Kemble's version, it is simply desire Willmore feels: 'The very thought of her makes me mad' (I. ii, p. 13). Kemble is also concerned to moderate Willmore's unheroic behaviour in fight-scenes. In Act III scene vi, Willmore (still suffering from drink) draws on Antonio, wounds him, and '*reels out*' when he hears someone say that Antonio is killed: 'How! a Man kill'd! then I'l go home to sleep' (III. vi, p. 46; *Works*, v. 489). Belvile is left to take the blame. Kemble kept the incident, necessary as it is to the plot, but softened it first by making Willmore give Antonio proper warning by calling on him to draw his sword, and secondly by making him say that he hopes his antagonist has not been killed (III. v, p. 40). Behn's hero is decidedly short on such elements of the heroic masculine ideal as courage, dignity, and gallantry; Kemble's revisions attempt to deliver a more manly man. Despite the differences between late eighteenth-century ideals of masculinity and Restoration ones, he is returning to the dynamics of Killigrew's original play, with its affirmation of the hero's centrality, worth, and importance.

Throughout the eighteenth century, then, male actors, managers, and adapters delivered a male-centred *Rover*, softening Behn's mocking view of her hero. Kemble's version was the culmination of this process but also marks the point where the story of Willmore lost its wide appeal: Kemble was trying to make Willmore a sentimental reformed rake, but he did not add enough to do this convincingly. He cut much of the original humour without adding new, and the production was criticized as tame: if Kemble had got rid of Behn's obscenity, one reviewer remarked, he had also got rid of the play's comic appeal.[63] After this, Behn's play was not revived until the late twentieth century, when it has been interpreted in widely differing ways. While some productions, inspired by a feminist reading of the play, have concentrated on and developed the critical attitude to Willmore, *The Rover* has also been presented in a new adaptation that, tellingly, goes back to Killigrew for some of its details. John Barton's RSC version of 1986–7 centred, like the successful productions of the eighteenth century, on the attractions of Willmore, played by Jeremy Irons as a lovable roisterer.[64]

The different possibilities for Willmore indicate a tension at the core of this remarkable play. Aphra Behn wrote the first play by a

---

[63] *Town and Country Magazine*, 22 (1790), 279.

[64] For critical accounts of the Barton production see Nancy Copeland, 'Re-Producing *The Rover*: John Barton's *Rover* at the Swan', *Essays in Theatre*, 9 (1990), 45–60; Jessica Munns, 'Barton and Behn's *The Rover*: or, the Text Transpos'd', *Restoration and Eighteenth-Century Theatre Research*, 2nd ser. 3/2 (1988), 11–22; Susan Carlson, 'Cannibalizing and Carnivalizing', 520–2.

woman to appeal to successive generations of London actors, managers, and theatregoers by adopting and to an extent pandering to a recognizable male fantasy; but she complicated and enriched the work by a mocking vein that proved troublesome in the eighteenth-century theatre, and was carefully modified. Yet without at least some of that bite, the play lost its entertainment value. *The Rover*'s long but chequered stage history provides us with a detailed view of the processes by which a woman author becomes a popular force within a male-dominated theatrical world.

6

Oroonoko

THE part that *Oroonoko*, now the most famous of Aphra Behn's works, played in her eighteenth-century afterlife had two major aspects: its contribution to the formation of her biography and her reputation as woman and author; and its influence on the abolitionist movement. We have already seen how the novel's narrative claims, taken as autobiographical, gave the early biographers details that apparently substantiated their vision of a gentlewoman of Kent. In the account of the novel found in the biographical tradition, the position of the narrator is central to the story, and the story of her friendship with the African prince is used as a way of building up a romanticized or titillating picture of her. Southerne's adaptation, with its praise of Behn and its transformation of Imoinda into a white woman, also played a part in creating the myth of Behn. When Thomas Brown and Aphra Behn were imagined meeting after death in their burial-place in Westminster Abbey, their conversation turned to her literary work. 'Brown' reported:

I gave her to understand, her Novel of *Oroonoko* had been christen'd into a Play since her Death, by one Mr. *Southern,* who had done her Justice as to the Drammatical part of it in such a manner, as to make her *Imoinda,* not of the Complexion belonging to the Country she came from, but so very beautiful, as to give us a valuable Idea of the Fair Person that gave Being to her Character.[1]

The beautiful heroine is a reminder of the author, mythologized as Oroonoko's lover rather than as his creator. As the century went on, *Oroonoko,* in translation and in dramatic adaptation, took on new meanings, and the image of the author herself became less important. The hero's fame was such that 'Oroonoko' seems even to have

---

[1] *A Letter from the Dead Thomas Brown,* 10.

passed into common currency as a name to be used in contexts far removed from the novel itself or its adaptations.[2] Much more significantly, though, *Oroonoko* took on new cultural life as a story of slavery, the more poignant because it was understood to be true. As Wylie Sypher's pioneering study of British anti-slavery literature showed, Oroonoko moved out of his original context to become 'the Oroonoko legend', whose influence can be traced in poems, plays, and novels which organized anti-slavery sentiment around the vision of the 'noble Negro'.[3]

Sypher was scathing about the sentimental falsity of this tradition, but its contribution to the attack on slavery has to be recognized. In his history of the trade, Hugh Thomas sees Behn as one of the inspirations of the abolitionists: 'Aphra Behn's contribution to the preparation for the abolitionist movement can scarcely be exaggerated. She helped to prepare literary people's minds for a change on humanitarian grounds. She was more influential than popes and missionaries.'[4] The seeming hyperbole of this judgement is moderated in context: one of Thomas's recurrent themes is the little notice that was taken of successive papal edicts condemning the trade.[5] The parliamentary campaign against the trade, begun in the 1780s, was kindled by growing opposition to slavery, especially among nonconformist groups interested in other forms of religious and political reform, but spreading to include large sections of the public of all classes.[6] A burgeoning anti-slavery culture expressed itself in poetry, newspapers, pictures, and artefacts like Wedgewood's famous medallion whose kneeling slave demanded 'Am I not a man and a brother?' Among these influential works was the story of Oroonoko in the var-

[2] Late in the 18th c., the name was used in a satirical poem about Anglo-Irish affairs, *An Heroic Epistle, from Kitty Cut-A-Dash to Oroonoko* (Dublin, 1778). Oroonoko seems to be named for his dark complexion, mentioned in the poem; there is no other indication of the name's significance.

[3] Wylie Sypher, *Guinea's Captive Kings: British Anti-Slavery Literature of the XVIIIth Century* (1942; rpr. New York: Octagon Books, 1969), 108.

[4] Hugh Thomas, *The Slave Trade: The History of the Atlantic Slave Trade: 1440–1870* (London: Picador, 1997), 452.   [5] See ibid. 9, 12, 71–2, 582.

[6] See e.g. discussions of the British abolitionist movement in James Walvin, 'The Public Campaign in England against Slavery, 1787–1834', in David Eltis and James Walvin (eds.), *The Abolition of the Atlantic Slave Trade: Origins and Effects in Europe, Africa, and the Americas* (Madison, Wis.: University of Wisconsin Press, 1981), 63–79; James Walvin, *England, Slaves and Freedom, 1776–1838* (Basingstoke: Macmillan, 1986); David Turley, *The Culture of English Antislavery, 1780–1860* (London and New York: Routledge, 1991); and Clare Midgley, *Women Against Slavery: The British Campaigns, 1780–1870* (London and New York: Routledge, 1992).

ious forms, narrative and theatrical, in which it was presented to the public in England and France. Co-opted for the abolitionist movement, Behn's African prince became a powerful emblem of the evils of slavery.

The relation of this abolitionist use of the story to Behn's original work is a complex one. Most recent discussions of the novel are united in finding that the narrative condemns not slavery *per se*, but the enslaving of a prince. The captain who invites prince Oroonoko to a feast on his slave-ship and then takes him and his followers prisoner is excoriated for treachery, not for being a slaver. That Oroonoko has previously sold slaves to this man himself, and that later, in Surinam, he attempts to bargain for his freedom with the promise of sending slaves in the future, might have been the focus of ironical reflections in the hands of an anti-slavery writer, but Behn's narrative seems to take these points for granted. They do not detract from Oroonoko's heroic status; rather, they underline the contrast between European perfidy and the African prince's honour. Oroonoko, who joins with the narrator in condemning the execution of Charles I, and who bears in captivity the same name—Caesar— which Behn used to address both Charles II and James II,[7] has been seen as a figure for Stuart royalty, and the plight of the prince, his wife Imoinda, and their unborn child has been compared to that of the beleaguered James and Mary at the time the novel was written.[8]

However, the presence of Anglocentric political references does not rule out concern with the slaves' experience in its own right. The vivid description of the brutality of Oroonoko's execution parallels contemporary and later accounts of the treatment of West Indian slaves.[9] In Behn's time some few writers, especially among Quakers, were beginning to show a humanitarian concern about the cruelties of the slave-trade and slave system. One writer voicing humanitarian concerns was Behn's friend Thomas Tryon, for whose *The Way to Health, Long Life, and Happiness* (1682) she wrote a commendatory poem (*Works*, i. 179–80). She probably knew his *Friendly Advice to the Gentlemen-Planters* (1684), which contained an early attack on colonial slavery. In a section called 'The Complaints of the Negro-Slaves

[7] Laura Brown, *Ends of Empire: Women and Ideology in Early Eighteenth-Century English Literature* (Ithaca, NY, and London: Cornell University Press, 1993), 56–7.

[8] See George Guffey, 'Aphra Behn's *Oroonoko*: Occasion and Accomplishment', in *Two English Novelists: Aphra Behn and Anthony Trollope* (Los Angeles: Clark Library, 1975), 3–41.

[9] Brown, *Ends of Empire*, 60–1.

against the hard Usages and barbarous Cruelties inflicted upon them', Tryon gives voice to the slaves. Their complaints detail their living conditions, the poor diet, gruelling work, the punishments inflicted on them, and the fact that women are allowed no rest for childbirth.[10] Blacks are declared to be equal in nature to whites, and slaves who attempt to escape are said to be only following the law of nature.[11] The colonists' cruelty is a recurrent theme. Compassion and charity are:

Plants that scarce grow in these Islands; nothing thrives here so fast as *poysonous Tobacco* and *furious Pride, sweet Sugar* and most *bitter ill Nature:* a false conceit of *Interest* has blinded their Eyes and stopt their Ears, and rendred their Hearts harder than *Rocks of Adament,* more Remorseless than hungry *Bears* or *Tygers* in the *Hercanian Wilderness:* To *Sigh* they interpret to *Rebell,* and if we do in the least complain, 'tis with them a sufficient cause for addition of *Stripes,* and encrease of ill Usage   (*Friendly Advice,* 77).

The slaves point out the inconsistency of the planters' behaviour with their professed religion:

when our strength fails us, the inconsiderate and unmerciful Overseers make nothing to Whip and Beat us, and the best words they can afford us, are *damn'd Doggs, Black ugly Devils, idle Sons of Ethiopean Whores,* and the like.
    Alas! We expected another sort of Treatment from the Christians, who boast themselves the Sons and favourites of the God of Love and Goodness   (85–6).

Oroonoko, too, is given impassioned eloquence in his speech to the slaves, when he

made an harangue to 'em of the Miseries, and Ignominies of Slavery; counting up all their Toyls and Sufferings, under such Loads, Burdens, and Drudgeries, as were fitter for Beasts than Men; Senseless Brutes, than Humane Souls . . . Men, Villanous, senseless Men, such as they, Toyl'd on all the tedious Week till Black *Friday*; and then, whether they Work'd or not, whether they were Faulty or Meriting, they promiscuously, the Innocent with the Guilty, suffer'd the infamous Whip, the sordid Stripes, from their Fellow *Slaves* till their Blood trickled from all Parts of their Body; Blood, whose every drop ought to be Reveng'd with a Life of some of those Tyrants, that impose it   (*Works,* iii. 105).

At the same time, Oroonoko compares traditional slavery favourably with the European slave-trade, asking his fellow slaves: '*Have they Won*

---

[10] *Friendly Advice to the Gentlemen-Planters of the East and West Indies. By* Philotheos Physiologus (n.p.: Printed by Andrew Sowle, 1684), 87–104.   [11] *Friendly Advice,* 114–15, 111.

us in Honourable Battel? And are we, by chance of War, become their Slaves?
This would not anger a Noble heart . . . *no, but we are Bought and Sold like Apes,*
or Monkeys, to be the Sport of Women, Fools and Cowards' (Works, iii. 105).
The relatively new commercialization of slavery is sharply distinguished from the ancient practice of enslaving those conquered in
battle, suggesting the focus of Behn's interest in the question of colonial trade and custom. The novel expresses mixed attitudes on this:
the narrator's fascination with the New World as a source of exotic
commodities, and her regret that such a valuable colony was ceded
to the Dutch, mingle with her picture of the brutality of the slave-
owners and the sharp contrast between Christian treachery and
pagan honour.

The novel's most direct criticisms are focused on the practice of
colonial government under William Byam. If the novel is partly
shaped by the occasion of its 1680s composition, it seems more
strongly, if in some ways still mysteriously, marked by memories of the
occasion of its setting. The authenticity of Behn's stay in Surinam,
long a bone of contention, is now generally accepted, and she writes
with first-hand knowledge of a colonial society which contemporary
records show to have been as full of conflict, confusion, and violence
as the scenes of her novel. It is well known that Behn includes in her
story real-life characters such as William Byam, deputy governor of
the colony, and Trefry, an agent of Lord Willoughby and opponent of
Byam. Though no direct historical parallels for Oroonoko and
Imoinda are known, slave rebellions were common in the West Indies
during this period and in the eighteenth century, and were often led by
people from Coramantien, given as Oroonoko's home country.[12]
Groups of escaped slaves, known as maroons, from the Surinam
plantations, took up residence in the interior of the continent, where
their descendants still live.[13] Behn's knowledge of Surinam included a
divided colonial government marked by violent internal disputes, and
knowledge if not direct experience of slave rebellion and escape.
Through her reflection of this semi-anarchic state of affairs, the
novel, for all the narrator's allegiance to the absent Lord Willoughby,
problematizes the colonial project.

[12] Brown, *Ends of Empire*, 46. For the description of Coramantines as fierce and stoical
'Heroes', see David Brion Davis, *The Problem of Slavery in Western Culture* (New York and
Oxford: Oxford University Press, 1988), 477.
[13] Robin Blackburn, *The Making of New World Slavery* (London and New York: Verso,
1997), 212–13, 501.

As Laura Brown observes, the novel offers an account of slavery that is 'neither coherent nor fully critical'.[14] It seems to me that the incoherence arises because the depiction of colonial Surinam is motivated less by direct interest in the issue of slavery than by Behn's attempt to stamp her own authority on an account of internal rivalries among the colonists. Behn's political and personal alliances during the time she was in Surinam are obscure, and the novel gives mixed messages about English politics. The later strongly Tory writer seems at this time to have been involved with the republican William Scot; and the narrator of *Oroonoko* refers favourably to Parliamentarians in a way radically different from the hostile treatment of them in the rest of Behn's writing.[15] As Warren Chernaik argues, the critique of slavery in *Oroonoko* has similarities to the republican attack on the institution voiced by Milton and others.[16] At the same time, Behn makes her hero express his 'Abhorrence' of the execution of Charles I (*Works*, iii. 62), and there is much praise for royalist principles. If Behn's villain, Byam, was royalist, so too were Trefry, for whom the narrator offers fiercely partisan support, and of course, the supposedly benign governor, Lord Willoughby. Neither royalism versus republicanism, nor support for versus attack on the colonial slave-system, seem to be the central issues for the narrator of *Oroonoko*. Rather, she is concerned to vindicate one group of colonists, including Trefry and Martin, and criticize another—the acting Governor, Byam, and his council 'who . . . consisted of such notorious Villains as *Newgate* never transported; and possibly originally were such, who understood neither the Laws of *God* or *Man*; and had no sort of Principles to make 'em worthy the Name of Men' (*Works*, iii. 112). She presumably reflects the hostile judgement made by the young Aphra Johnson, about whose visit to the plantation little is known for certain. Whatever her capacity in Surinam, however, it was not the high-status one she claimed in the novel's dedication, where she writes '*I had none above me in that Country*' (*Works*, iii. 56). *Oroonoko* seems, among other things, to be an attempt to rewrite the events of this colonial visit, of personal importance to the author, but

---

[14] Brown, *Ends of Empire*, 49.

[15] She praises Colonel George Martin as 'an English Gentleman, brother to *Harry Martin*, the great *Oliverian*' (*Works*, iii. 97).

[16] 'Captains and Slaves: Aphra Behn and the Rhetoric of Republicanism', paper given at the British Society for Eighteenth-Century Studies Annual Conference, 1999. I am grateful to Warren Chernaik for allowing me to consult this paper before its publication.

now very shadowy to us; and to rewrite them in such a way as to claim a higher status and authority for herself than she enjoyed at the time.

Recent criticism of *Oroonoko* has focused on the complex and conflicting relations between the white narrator and the royal African slaves whose story she takes it on herself to relate. The narrator, presented within the text as a version of Behn herself, claims to befriend Oroonoko and Imoinda but reveals herself as a spy on the hero's actions, working on behalf of the colonists who are feeding him 'from Day to Day with Promises' of his freedom, but who prove treacherous (*Works*, iii. 93). The narrator, vacillating between claims of friendship and trust between herself and the hero and fear of his violence when he begins the rebellion, and between boasts of her high position in Surinam society and claims of powerlessness when her countrymen trick, torture, and eventually dismember Oroonoko, is as duplicitous as the rest of the European society she both represents and condemns. Attempting to deny her own complicity in the events she describes, she claims for her 'Female Pen' the position of moral observer.[17]

We can interpret this claim of female authority as a challenge to the male authority of her fellow European settlers. By dividing European male authority into good-but-absent (the governor, Willoughby) and unworthy present (the deputy governor, Byam), Behn legitimizes her own criticism of it. Contemporary documents show Byam to have been involved in bitter dispute with some of his fellow settlers. The novel suggests some rivalry, in Behn's mind if nowhere else, between her authority and that of Byam. The narrator's claim to be the daughter of the man who would, had he not 'dy'd at Sea, and never arriv'd to possess the Honour design'd him', have been 'Lieutenant-General of Six and thirty Islands, besides the Continent of *Surinam*' (iii. 95), works to imply that Byam holds a position which ought to belong to her family. The narrative sets up two examples of legitimate, benevolent, but absent male authority—the dead father and the never-arriving Willoughby—and depicts power

---

[17] See esp. Susan Z. Andrade, 'White Skin, Black Masks: Colonialism and the Sexual Politics of *Oroonoko*', *Cultural Critique*, 27 (1994), 189–214; Stephanie Athey and Daniel Cooper Alarcón, '*Oroonoko*'s Gendered Economies of Honor/Horror: Reframing Colonial Discourse Studies in the Americas', *American Literature*, 65/3 (1993), 415–43; and Joyce Green MacDonald, 'The Disappearing African Woman: Imoinda in *Oroonoko* after Behn', *ELH* 66 (1999), 71–86.

passing instead to an unworthy male, while it remains unclear what status and influence the worthy man's daughter can inherit. The relation of all this to Behn's life is obscure, and we should read it as a fable about female relation to authority rather than a piece of biography. However, the story may also represent in part Behn's struggle with Byam for specifically authorial authority. As Janet Todd has shown, *Oroonoko* may include a response to a pamphlet Byam himself wrote. Published in 1665, the short pamphlet gives an account of a settler called John Allin, who quarrelled with other colonists, was accused of blasphemy, and committed suicide after attempting to assassinate Lord Willoughby. These events probably occurred shortly after Behn's departure from the colony. After Allin's death his body was mutilated in a way very similar to the dismemberment of the hero Behn describes in *Oroonoko*. There are some suggestive verbal echoes of Byam in Behn's novel: her conclusion that 'Thus Dy'd this Great Man' may be a deliberate reworking of his that 'Thus died this Atheist'.[18] If Behn is taking some ideas from John Allin's life and death for her creation of Oroonoko, her rivalry with Byam is evident. The white atheist and rebel so scornfully treated in Byam's pamphlet is transformed into a black hero, on whom Aphra Behn is the authority. By making her hero an African slave (even as she honours him as a prince) she is able to claim authority as a white woman to interpret him for white society. Byam himself is, of course, made into the villain.

As Anita Pacheco has shown, the novel plays out a conflict within white society between aristocratic values of honour and dishonourable commercial values, a conflict through which the female narrator attempts to claim her own authority to record and interpret.[19] Several critics have argued that this white authority is developed in particular in relation to the black heroine of the novel. An implicit rivalry between the narrator and Imoinda, Oroonoko's wife, has been suggested, and it results in a division of female identities between the two women.[20] In the Surinam part of the narrative Imoinda is increasingly described in terms of her body while being

[18] Janet Todd, *Gender, Art, and Death* (Cambridge: Polity Press, 1993), 44–9.

[19] Anita Pacheco, 'Royalism and Honor in Aphra Behn's *Oroonoko*', *SEL* 34 (1994), 491–506.

[20] Margaret Ferguson, 'Juggling the Categories of Race, Class and Gender', in M. Hendricks and P. Parker (ed.), *Women, 'Race' and Writing in the Early Modern Period* (London: Routledge, 1994), 220.

deprived of a voice; the narrator, on the other hand, dominates not only as the recorder of events but in her verbal relationship with the hero.[21] Onto the black woman is projected the submissiveness and self-sacrifice belonging to female subordination, while the white narrator asserts her own importance and takes good care not to get her own throat cut. This relationship can be seen as a paradigm for the way white women's writing in the century following Behn built up a sense of a civilized female authority in contradistinction to a subordinated, 'savage' female position associated with non-European cultures.[22]

Certainly there is evidence that Imoinda was understood as a figure of female subordination. Her willingness to die at Oroonoko's hands, presented by the narrator as an example of the extreme husband-worship practised in Coramantien society, was remarked on by early readers. *The Challenge*, made up of letters supposedly sent to the *Athenian Mercury*, was full of those exchanges between misogynist and feminist viewpoints that were fashionable in the late seventeenth century. Imoinda was invoked in a letter by 'Mr Bexford' as an example of the beauty of black women, 'the *humblest*, dociblest [*sic*] most *obedient Creatures*'. Every 'English *Lady-wife*' ought to 'often look upon *Behn's Imoinda*' as an example to emulate: 'When I wonder, shall we see one of you so *meekly*, so *gently* hold out your *Necks*, like innocent *Lambs*, when your *Lord* and *Husband* intimates his will and pleasure, that you shou'd *resign* your *Lives* to his *Disposal*?' The reply, written under the pseudonym 'Sapho', indicating a conscious claim on behalf of female authority, replaced Bexford's misogyny with racism, attempting to defend 'women' by sarcastic remarks on black ones. White women would not follow Imoinda's example, however much Mr Bexford tried to 'persuade us there's a wonderful *Virtue* in planting *Tobacco*, and having our *Throats* cut'.[23] Like Behn's own narrator, this unknown letter-writer bases a female authority and defence of white women on the construction of black women as the savage and submissive other. This is a simplification of the relation between Imoinda and the narrator in Behn's text. Imoinda is not a constant figure of female submission but is one of the most active of the

---

[21] Andrade, 'White Skin, Black Masks', 202.
[22] See Felicity Nussbaum, *Torrid Zones: Maternity, Sexuality and Empire in Eighteenth-Century English Narratives* (Baltimore and London: Johns Hopkins University Press, 1995).
[23] *The Challenge, Sent by a Young lady to Sir Thomas . . . Or, The Female War* (London: E. Whitlock, 1697), 105, 110.

rebels, and the most nearly effective in her attack on Byam during the slave rebellion. Her arrow-shot at him parallels the rhetorical attack performed by the narrator, as if Imoinda here is a fantasy substitute for the heroic action the narrator cannot take. The split between the two women expresses anxieties about narrative position: to take on a narrator's authority, it seems, is also to accept a position on the fringes of the action, unable to intervene.

Behn's *Oroonoko*, then, is a troubled and opaque text, full of anxious claims and obscure quarrels. It is not a clear attack on the institution and practices of slavery, but the sympathetic treatment of Oroonoko and Imoinda, the descriptions of white cruelty, and even the narrator's very inconsistencies and divided position, have the effect of presenting a disturbing picture of colonial life, and provide the germ for the later, abolitionist development of Oroonoko's story.

However, the first reinterpretation of Behn's work moved in the opposite direction. Southerne's dramatic adaptation of *Oroonoko* was not designed to make a slaving nation uncomfortable. Southerne's hero actually defends the Europeans for the very reason that Behn's condemns them, because they have purchased their slaves. When Aboan tries to persuade him to lead the slaves in rebellion, he argues:

> If we are slaves, they did not make us slaves,
> But bought us in an honest way of trade
> As we have done before 'em, bought and sold
> Many a wretch and never thought it wrong.
> They paid our price for us and we are now
> Their property, a part of their estate,
> To manage as they please.[24]

Southerne's view is not surprising, given that at this time he was probably seeking patronage from Christopher Codrington, one of the richest West Indian slave-owners.[25] Yet, as the novel went through its many early eighteenth-century editions, and the play made Southerne's reputation, the story of Oroonoko began to take on new significance. At first its sentimental appeal grew and was underlined in commentary; and gradually the sentimental pleasure of sympathizing with a betrayed prince or with a noble pair of distressed

[24] Thomas Southerne, *Oroonoko*, ed. Maximilian E. Novak and David Stuart Rodes (London: Edward Arnold, 1977), III. ii, p. 64.
[25] Robert Jordan and Harold Love, introduction to *Oroonoko* in *The Works of Thomas Southerne* (Oxford: Clarendon Press, 1988), ii. 95.

lovers became mixed with concern about the slave system that was at the root of their troubles. In this chapter I trace the metamorphosis of *Oroonoko* into a vehicle for anti-slavery sentiment, showing how this change coincided with a tendency to play down the significance of Behn as narrator and as author. Abolitionists had very little to say about Behn herself, and that little was not favourable; and the complex relationship between the black hero and the white woman who takes it on herself to tell his story was dropped from later versions.

The afterlife of *Oroonoko* is intimately bound up with historical developments in racial and sexual attitudes that bear upon the kind of narrative authority Behn claims. In general terms the woman writer's voice as moral arbiter becomes more established in British culture. At the same time, Behn's personal claim to that authority is challenged. In different versions and descriptions of the story of Oroonoko, the relationship between the narrator and her hero and heroine, which in the novel establish her authority, are transformed in ways that alter and generally diminish it. The dramatic versions of the story cut out the narrator and displace her story of the relationship between a black man and white woman onto the figures of Oroonoko and Imoinda, who is transformed into a white European. In Southerne's original play the white narrator is also, as we have seen, displaced onto the husband-hunting white women who figure in the comic scenes. Meanwhile the influential French translation of the novel keeps 'Madame Behn' as the narrator, and teams her with a white Imoinda, daughter of a European general.[26] In fact, apart from literal translations, no version of the novel after Behn has kept her depiction of a relationship between a black woman and a white one.[27] This may suggest, as well as the obvious influence of *Othello*, a mixed racial and sexual prejudice to the effect that a white actress, unlike an actor, could not take on a black part while maintaining both

---

[26] Imoinda's mother is not mentioned, and it has been suggested that this Imoinda is of mixed race: see Jürgen von Stackelberg, tr. Geneviève Roche, 'Oroonoko et l'abolition de l'esclavage: le rôle du traducteur', *Revue de littérature comparée* 63/2 (1989), 247. However, as Imoinda is said to have been already a few months old when her father moved to Coramantien, presumably from Europe, I think the more likely inference is that she is of white parentage. See Pierre-Antoine de la Place, *Oronoko traduit de l'anglois, de Madame Behn* (Amsterdam, 1745), 13–14.

[27] 'Biyi Bandele's new adaptation of *Oroonoko*, playing in Stratford and London in 1999, is the first dramatic adaptation of the novel to have a black Imoinda. It has no white women, and the part the novel's narrator takes as the hero's white friend/betrayer is given to a white man, Trefry. See 'Biyi Bandele, *Aphra Behn's Oroonoko* (Oxford: Amber Lane Press, 1999).

dignity and desirability. Whatever the reasons for the whitening of Imoinda, one of its effects is to cut out the relationship which is now seen as central to the narrative's construction of white female authority.[28] This is not to say that adaptations of Behn's story are engaged in a deliberate attempt to undermine that authority. What I think the adaptations do show is a concern to depict alternative, less disturbing kinds of female authority. Behn's implicit rivalry with male authority (tolerated as a convention of literary compliment, but more worrying if seriously intended) and her (half-conscious?) foundation of her own authority in the contrast between herself and the black heroine, dropped out of sight as her work was adapted to new times.

Southerne's *Oroonoko* was the most influential of the adaptations of Behn's novel. We have already seen in Chapter 3 how its transformations, especially its splitting of the white narrator's role among the play's female characters, were part of his strategy for dealing with the anxieties of his situation as a 'son of Behn'. Here I want to concentrate on the way the tragedy of Oroonoko and Imoinda came to function in the early eighteenth century as an expression and encouragement of feminine feeling. Composed in the mixed tragicomic form that violated neo-classical standards but was popular in the late seventeenth century, the play was originally presented as an entertainment to suit all moods:

> We weep and laugh, join mirth and grief together,
> Like rain and sunshine mixed in April weather.
> Your different tastes divide our poet's cares:
> One foot the sock, t'other the buskin wears.[29]

It opened—rather like *The Rover* —with a comic scene between two assertive young women looking for husbands. Charlotte and Lucy Welldon are sisters visiting Surinam in the hope of making their fortunes by marriage. Charlotte, dressed as a man, passes for Lucy's brother. During the course of the play she manages to arrange her sister's marriage to the stupid but rich Daniel Lackitt, while herself tricking Daniel's mother, the Widow Lackitt, into a supposed marriage. When she reveals her true identity the widow agrees to marry

---

[28] For an excellent discussion of the 'enforced invisibility of the black female subject' in Southerne's play see Joyce Green MacDonald, 'Race, Women and the Sentimental in Thomas Southerne's *Oroonoko*', *Criticism*, 40 no. 4 (1998), 555–70.

[29] 'Epilogue, Writtten by Mr. Congreve, and spoken by Mrs. Verbruggen'. Thomas Southerne, *Oroonoko*, ed. Novak and Rodes, 125.

Jack Stanmore while Charlotte herself marries his brother. This is a plot typical of Restoration comedy, chiefly remarkable for the active roles given the female characters; but intermingled with its scenes are the more tragic notes of the African prince's story. The second scene introduces the slaves just landed and ready to be sold, and the story of how Oroonoko (here the prince of Angola, not Coramantien) was tricked into slavery. Lucy exclaims about the 'miserable fortune' of all the slaves, but Blanford (a sympathetically treated planter, whose role corresponds to Trefry's in the novel) expresses a narrower view: 'Most of 'em know no better; they were born so and only change their masters. But a prince, born only to command, betrayed and sold! My heart drops blood for him' (I. ii, p. 30). When Oroonoko appears, his blank-verse speeches about trust, honour, and nobility move the action onto a heroic plane. He embraces his friends, telling them:

> Now we are fellow-slaves. This last farewell.
> Be sure of one thing that will comfort us:
> Whatever world we next are thrown upon
> Cannot be worse than this.[30]

(I. ii, p. 31)

The next act opens on Charlotte Welldon's comic ploys to trap Daniel Lackitt into marriage with Lucy, a union that Lucy herself views with cool cynicism: 'I am for anything that will deliver me from a reputation, which I begin to find impossible to preserve' (II. i, pp. 37–8). In sharp contrast, the next scene depicts Oroonoko's mourning for the loss of the wife he adores; and the third scene reveals Imoinda as the fair slave Clemene, struggling to preserve not reputation, but her honour from the Lieutenant Governor's advances. The reconciliation between husband and wife, following Oroonoko's heroic defence of the planters from an Indian attack, closes the act.

As the play continues, the tragic plot takes up a greater proportion of the action. It dominates the third act, in which Oroonoko, originally reluctant to listen to Aboan's talk of rebellion, fires up at the thought that the returning Governor, 'Luxurious, passionate, and amorous', may take his wife from him (III. ii, p. 67). His heroic rant at

---

[30] Cf. Behn's Oroonoko's speech on arrival in Surinam: 'Come, my Fellow-Slaves; let us descend, and see if we can meet with more Honour and Honesty in the next World we shall touch upon', *Works*, iii. 86.

this point, beginning 'Ha! Thou hast roused | The lion in his den' became some of the play's most famous lines, epitomizing Oroonoko as Restoration hero, mighty in anger, motivated by love. The third act closes on the rebellion plan, and the hint that it will be betrayed by Hottman; the fourth act returns to Welldon's intrigues, which are followed by the failed slave rebellion, Oroonoko's surrender on promise of fair treatment, and the Lieutenant Governor's treachery. Imoinda and Oroonoko are taken prisoner and forced apart.

The last act begins by tying up the ends of the comic plot: identities are revealed, marriages are made. After this the Welldons take on a new role somewhat reminiscent of the role of Behn's narrator: they are sympathizers with Oroonoko and helpless witnesses to his suffering. Until the second scene of Act V there has been little contact between the comic and heroic characters. They start to come together when Blanford, shocked by the Lieutenant Governor's treatment of Oroonoko, tries to raise sympathy for the hero:

> So, Stanmore, you, I know, the women too,
> Will join with me.
> [*To the women*] 'Tis Oroonoko's cause,
> A lover's cause, a wretched woman's cause,
> That will become your intercession.
>
> (v. ii, p. 103)

The women—Charlotte, Lucy, and the Widow Lackitt—respond to this plea and all beg for gentle treatment of Oroonoko. The next scenes show them joining Blanford and Stanmore in a visit to the imprisoned hero, and then attempting to find Imoinda and rescue her from the Governor. He sends them away with false assurances, and they leave the stage, their part in the play finished. It is left to the heroic characters to conclude the action, with Imoinda assisting Oroonoko to kill her, and Oroonoko stabbing the Governor and then himself.

This mixed form certainly proved popular with audiences. The play was one of the most frequently performed of all London dramas in the first half of the eighteenth century, and survived into the nineteenth. It went to Ireland, toured the English provinces, and in the late eighteenth century crossed the Atlantic to North America.[31]

---

[31] *Oroonoko* was played in New York and in Baltimore in 1783. Philadelphia, Charlestown, and Boston 'also saw the play during the last decade of the eighteenth century.' John Wendell Dodds, *Thomas Southerne, Dramatist* (New Haven: Yale University Press, 1933), 162.

However, from an early date there were strong criticisms of the mingling of comic and tragic elements, and it was considered that 'the Comick Part is below that Author's usual Genius'. The same work identified *Oroonoko* as 'the favourite of the Ladies'.[32] It seems that the ladies—at least, as they are represented in contemporary accounts—responded to the lovers' tragedy rather than to the exploits of Charlotte Welldon. The action of the play transforms this cynical and contriving comic heroine into a woman of feeling, last seen trying in vain to help Imoinda and Oroonoko. It was this manifestation of femininity that contemporaries recommended to ladies of the audience. Just as the Welldons, and even the comic Widow, become feeling women by sympathizing with Oroonoko, women in the audience were seen to prove their feminine feeling by weeping at his tragic end. By the 1730s there was even a poem in praise of a weeping female spectator of the play. John Whaley's 'On a Young Lady's weeping at Oroonooko [*sic*]' depicted the female spectator's pity as a manifestation of romantic attraction to the hero, an attraction he is seen to reciprocate:

> At Fate's approach whilst ORoONOOKO Groans,
> *Imoinda's* Fate, undaunted at his own;
> Dropping a gen'rous Tear *Lucretia* Sighs,
> And views the heroe with *Imoinda's* Eyes.
> When the prince strikes who envy's not the Deed?
> To be so Wept, who wou'd not wish to Bleed?[33]

By her feeling response to the distressed hero, 'Lucretia' makes herself attractive to him and to the poet. This response, of course, is not in itself a manifestation of anti-slavery sentiment. A similar sentimental response was evoked by other pathetic tragedies in the period. In fact Whaley made something of a minor genre of the weeping theatregoer poem, writing another piece 'On a Young Lady's weeping at The Fair Penitent'.[34]

During the early years of the century, then—the years of its greatest popularity—Southerne's play functioned not as a protest against slavery but as a display of love and heroism calculated to let the ladies show their fine sympathetic feelings. In time, however, those feelings became more closely connected with an awareness of

---

[32] *A Comparison Between the Two Stages,* 19.

[33] John Whaley, *A Collection of Poems* (London: John Willis and Joseph Boddington, 1732), 92–3.   [34] Ibid. 157–9.

the slave-trade. At one performance in 1749, theatregoers were moved by the spectacle of a real African prince, in the box watching the play, weeping at the representation of a misfortune similar to his own. William Unsah Sessarakoo, son of a Fante chief of Annamaboe, had been sent with a companion to receive a European education. The Liverpool slave-trading captain under whose protection he had been placed sold the two men into slavery in the Barbados in 1744. After protests from Sessarakoo's father they were ransomed and taken to London, where they were looked after by the Earl of Halifax, President of the Board of Trade and Plantations. The performance of *Oroonoko* at Covent Garden on 1 February 1749 was put on for their entertainment, and their emotional response was very gratifying. The *Gentleman's Magazine* reported:

They were received with a loud clap of applause, which they acknowledged with a very genteel bow, and took their seats in a box. The seeing persons of their own colour on the stage, apparently in the same distress from which they had been so lately delivered, the tender interview between *Imoinda* and *Oroonoko*, who was betrayed by the treachery of a captain, the account of his sufferings, and the repeated abuse of his placability and confidence, strongly affected them with that generous grief which pure nature always feels, and which art had not yet taught them to suppress; the young prince was so far overcome, that he was obliged to retire at the end of the fourth act. His companion remained, but wept the whole time; a circumstance which affected the audience yet more than the play, and doubled the tears which were shed for *Oroonoko* and *Imoinda*.[35]

The President of the Board of Trade and Plantations, who took these men under his protection, was responding to treachery against a prince, not to man's inhumanity to man—displaying the older social attitude that class hierarchies were of greater importance than racial differences, in contrast to the Liverpool captain who, displaying the racism that was growing with the Atlantic slave-trade, had ignored social distinctions among Africans.

Indeed, the pleasures of sympathizing with a distressed African prince could be enjoyed without criticizing the colonial practices that caused his problems. Further sentimental capital was made of the prince of Annamaboe when William Dodd wrote two poems based on

[35] *Gentleman's Magazine*, 19 (Feb. 1749), 89–90. Accounts of William Unsah Sessarakoo are found in *Oroonoko*, ed. Lipking, 154–5, and Thomas, *The Slave Trade*, 465–6. The prince and his companion later returned home. His story was recorded in *The Royal African: or, Memoirs of the Young Prince of Annamaboe* (1749 or 1750).

his story, 'The African Prince, when in England, MDCCXLIX. To Zara at his Father's Court', and 'Zara, at the Court of Annamaboe, to the African Prince, when in England'. Mixing up Indians and Africans in a way typical of primitivist literature, 'The African Prince' describes the prince's visit to the theatre to see *Oroonoko*:

> O! Zara, here, a story like my own,
> With mimic skill, in borrow'd names, was shown;
> An Indian chief, like me, by fraud betray'd,
> And, partner in his woes, an Indian maid.

Far from criticizing the British slave-trade, which had expanded enormously since Behn's time, Dodd made his poem an occasion for praising British generosity and love of liberty. Only the treacherous captain is criticized: everyone else behaves well, and Britain's king is credited with saving his country's honour by rescuing a fellow prince:

> The gen'rous crew their port in safety gain,
> And tell my mournful tale, nor tell in vain;
> The king, with horror of th'atrocious deed,
> In haste commanded, and the slave was freed.
> No more Britannia's cheek the blush of shame
> Burns for my wrongs, her king restores her fame:
> Propitious gales, to freedom's happy shore,
> Waft me triumphant, and the prince restore.[36]

Dodd's prince is favourably impressed with Britain's economy, culture, and religion, even intending to go back home to teach his countrymen Christianity. This is a poem of national, sentimental self-congratulation, ignoring the realities of the slave-trade. Behn had allowed her Africans to throw into question her own country's values; Dodd's poems use the African to underline British Christianity, fine feeling, and honourable behaviour.

Not everyone who witnessed the prince of Annamaboe viewed him so complacently, however. The juxtaposition of a fictional hero with a real African sufferer struck a chord with those who were beginning to question the morality of the slave-trade. Horace Walpole, who wrote a letter describing how the prince retired weeping after watching a scene between Oroonoko and Imoinda,[37] was among these. In 1750 he wrote to Sir Horace Mann:

---

[36] *Poems, by Dr. Dodd* (London: Dryden Leach, 1767), 13, 12.
[37] Quoted in Thomas, *The Slave Trade*, 466.

we, the British Senate, that temple of liberty, and bulwark of Protestant Christianity, have this fortnight been pondering methods to make more effectual that horrid traffic of selling negroes. It has appeared to us that six-and-forty thousand of these wretches are sold every year to our plantations alone!—it chills one's blood. I would not have to say that I voted for it for the continent of America![38]

Walpole's opposition to the slave-trade (he later became a firm abolitionist) was influenced by Montesquieu, whose *L'Esprit des lois* (1748) containing a sarcastic reflection on the unchristianity of the trade, began a strong French tradition of anti-slavery philosophical writing.[39] In the same letter he told Mann: 'I despise your *literati* enormously for their opinion of Montesquieu's book. Bid them read that glorious chapter on the subject I have been mentioning, the selling of African slaves.'[40] By the middle of the eighteenth century, then, at least some members of the audience for Southerne's *Oroonoko* were beginning to read it against the grain, finding food in it for the anti-slavery thought that was being developed elsewhere.

Meanwhile Behn's original novel continued to be reprinted, as we have seen. It also began to spread its influence in other languages. There was a German translation in 1709, which also introduced a version of Behn's life-story, taken from the 'Memoirs', to a German readership.[41] Towards the end of the century Southerne's version of *Oroonoko* was also translated into German.[42] *Oroonoko* travelled as far as Russia.[43] The most influential translation, however, was the French adaptation of the novel by Pierre-Antoine de la Place, published in 1745 and going through seven eighteenth-century editions. It became one of the most popular English novels in mid-eighteenth-century France, and from contemporary reviews discussing the moral questions raised by the story, it is clear that it did play a part in making slavery a topic of discussion for the French public.[44] Behn's hero

[38] Quoted in Sypher, *Guinea's Captive Kings*, 13.

[39] Montesquieu's influence, and the development of anti-slavery as a reform programme from the intellectual tradition of anti-slavery writing he began, are discussed in Walvin, *England, Slaves and Freedom 1776–1838*, 98–100.

[40] Quoted in Sypher, *Guinea's Captive Kings*, 14.

[41] M. V**, *Lebens- und Liebes-Geschichte des Königlichen Sclaven Oroonoko* (Hamburg, 1709).

[42] *Oronoko: ein Trauerspiel*. In *Deutsche Schaubühne* (Augsburg, 1789).

[43] It was published in 2 vols. as *Pokhozhdenie Oronoka Kniazia Afrikanskago* (St Petersburg: [Tipografii Akademii Nauk], 1796). I am grateful to Mary Ann O'Donnell for this reference.

[44] Edward D. Seeber, '*Oroonoko* in France in the XVIIIth Century', *PMLA* 51 (1936), 954–5.

influenced the black heroes of Mme de Stael's *Mirza*, La Vallée's *Le Negre comme il y a peu des blancs*, and Saint-Lambert's *Ziméo*, a novel which was used as the basis for an important argument against slavery in the *Ephémerides du citoyen* in 1771.[45]

Any use of La Place's translation for anti-slavery purposes had to run counter to the text. Unlike the German translation, which closely matches the original paragraph for paragraph, the French translation is an adaptation, some parts following the original closely but others freely improvised. La Place explained that it was necessary to alter the story for a French audience.[46] However, these changes were not in the direction of anti-slavery argument. The hero is given some reference to liberty and the feelings of freeborn men, when he tells Jamoan to stir the slaves to rebellion: 'Ranime en eux, ces sentimens naturels a tout homme né libre!'[47] On the whole, though, as Jürgen von Stackelberg has demonstrated, La Place's translation aims not so much to argue against slavery as to turn *Oroonoko* into a classical French novel.[48] It has a happy ending—the only one in all the various versions of the story. This involves leaving a radically different impression of colonial government. While Behn upheld, in theory, the proper government of Lord Willoughby, his chief function in her text is to fail to arrive in time to save Oroonoko. In practice, colonial government under Byam is violent, split, unjust, and on the verge of descending into anarchy. In the French translation, on the other hand, Byam dies, and the Lord Governor returns and keeps his promise to send Oroonoko back to his home country—where the old king obligingly abdicates in his favour. The proper order of things is restored, and slavery is an accepted part of that order. Oroonoko is sent home on the first available trading vessel—evidently another slaving ship—and sends back presents. In a revised version of his translation published in 1769, La Place specifies that Oroonoko gives the captain who takes him back home a payment of 300 slaves.[49]

Upholding things as they are, the translation concentrates on the romance between Imoinda and Oroonoko. Imoinda is altered to conform to a heroine's standards of femininity. Instead of Behn's 'black Venus' whose body is covered with exotic carvings, this white Imoinda is merely described in general terms as beautiful and

---

[45] Ibid. 956–9.   [46] *Oronoko traduit de l'anglois*, 'Preface du Traducteur', p. viii.
[47] *Oronoko*, Part II, 70.
[48] 'Oronooko et l'abolition de l'esclavage: le rôle du traducteur', 237–48.
[49] *Oronoko, ou le prince nègre* (London and Paris: Vente, 1769), 211.

charming. Like Southerne, La Place emphasizes Imoinda's position as the focus of male desire. Behn had treated the rivalry between Oroonoko and his grandfather for possession of Imoinda, and had made Trefry initially lust after her, but Southerne had made sexual rivalry central to the tragedy by making the Governor's desire for Imoinda a strong motivating force. La Place adopted this idea, and added another rival in Jamoan, a defeated enemy who has become Oroonoko's faithful servant, and whose part in the translation is greatly expanded from the brief mention in the original. In La Place's version, Jamoan confesses to Oroonoko that he too loves Imoinda. The translator also took pains to make Imoinda conform better to the norms of heroinely behaviour. In his version, unlike Southerne's, she does retain her active role in the slave rebellion, wounding Byam among others (*Oronoko*, Part II, 90), and she also attacks Byam in an earlier incident; but this is in defence of her honour rather than in battle, and when Jamoan, rescuing her, is about to kill Byam, she orders that the Governor's life be spared. This is presented as a mistake, but one that reveals her essential generosity (Part II, 63–5). Like Southerne, La Place avoids Oroonoko's killing of Imoinda: but where Southerne got round the problem by having Imoinda assist him, so that the act is effectively suicide, La Place manages to avoid Imoinda's death altogether. As in the original novel, Oroonoko intends to kill Imoinda before taking his revenge on Byam. After several attempts he throws the knife away, but his resolve is hardened when she shows him a letter from Byam, saying that Oroonoko will be executed unless Imoinda yields to Byam. He is about to kill her when they are interrupted by Byam himself. Imoinda is left wounded, while Oroonoko and Byam fight. When Trefry enters the forest to bring back the wounded Oroonoko, Imoinda has disappeared.

The sequel to this event is told in the 'Histoire d'Imoinda', an addition to the narrative by La Place. As the narrative approaches resolution, Imoinda is revealed—in typical romance fashion—in the disguise of the new servant Oroonoko has brought back from a visit to the Indian village. She explains that after she was wounded she was taken to the Indian village by Jamoan. There she gave birth to her son and resisted Jamoan's plans to tie her to the village—and to a relationship with him—by accepting a place for her baby as the future leader of the Indians. The reunited couple are able to return with their son to Coramantien.

This new focus on romance and happy ending alters the narrator's position in the story. As Imoinda is given the romance heroine's centrality and the privilege of a voice in the text (she narrates the twenty-seven-page 'Histoire' of her adventures), the narrator's importance correspondingly diminishes. Her role is also simpler and less ambiguous. As in the original, she promises Oroonoko his freedom when the Lord Governor returns, and then spends some time spying on his actions; but she is carefully exonerated from the charges of deception that have been laid against Behn's original narrator. Together she and Trefry try to persuade Byam to release Oroonoko before the Lord Governor arrives, offering to take responsibility for the action, but Byam refuses. Later they raise a force of servants to rescue Oroonoko, and indirectly they cause the death of Byam, who expires in a fit of rage over the hero's escape. At the end, instead of the narrator giving a dead hero all he can now receive, fame, the last act is King Oroonoko's: he sends presents to the Lord Governor, to Trefry, and to 'Madame Behn' herself.

La Place's translation, then, is designed to smooth out those awkward points of the novel that made colonial government, and the narrator's place in it, problematic. Female narrative authority, so important an issue in the original novel, is not central for La Place: he allows it to the narrator simply and without examination, and he also gives it to Imoinda as a romance heroine. Because this translation was the main channel of Behn's work to a French readership, this presentation of the narrator is an important strand in her afterlife. In the translator's preface, Behn is given favourable treatment, and compared to the famous French romance-writers Villedieu and Scudéry. The story of her life is taken from the 'Memoirs', and includes a reference to her reputed desire for her own hero: her lively, interesting writing is seen as a reason to believe she was in love with him.[50] Behn's story of colonial slavery became the occasion to present the novelist herself to a French readership in simplified form, as a celebrated writer and a woman of feeling.

While this translation spread the influence of Behn's novel in late eighteenth-century France, in England the dramatic adaptation was becoming the best-known version of *Oroonoko*. After great popularity

---

[50] 'La manière vive & intéressante, dont il est écrit, a fait croire à plusieurs personnes, que la jeune Astrea n'avoit pas été insensible au mérite de son Héros' (Preface du Traducteur, xii).

in the first half of the century, the play was beginning to decline, though most seasons in the 1750s saw at least two or three performances. Then a new wave of adaptation focused interest on the play again. Around 1760, at just the time when other seventeenth-century plays were receiving the attentions of adapters and revisers, Southerne's play was revised in three different versions within a short period. The best-known of these, John Hawkesworth's, was premiered at Drury Lane on 1 December 1759. Another version by Francis Gentleman was performed at Edinburgh in 1760, and several years later, in 1768, moved to London. There was also an anonymously altered version published in 1760, which was not staged. These adaptations represent a turning-point in the history of the Oroonoko story. Up until this time, adaptations had been moving in the opposite direction from popular feeling on slavery, with the odd result that versions which in themselves were less critical of slavery than Behn's original sometimes prompted anti-slavery sentiments among an audience and readership much more willing to entertain them than Behn's first readers had been. From Hawkesworth on, however, a tendency towards anti-slavery feeling began to make itself felt in successive adaptations.

The three versions of 1759–60 share one of their main features: all three cut out the comic subplot and turn Oroonoko into an unmixed tragedy. Even early reactions, as we have seen, were unfavourable to the comic part of Southerne's play; and as the late eighteenth-century refinement of the stage developed, what were seen as the absurdities and obscenities of the parts involving the Stanmores, Welldons, and Lackitts were ripe for revision. In 1752 a writer in the *Gentleman's Magazine*, possibly John Hawkesworth himself, had set forth the case for a new version.[51] Similar arguments were put forward in Hawkesworth's preface. While the tragic plot and the scenes between Oroonoko and Imoinda were universally admired, he wrote, 'these Scenes were degraded by a Connexion with some of the most loose and contemptible that have ever disgraced our Language and our Theatre'.[52] Getting rid of these, he announced his intention to turn the play into 'a regular Tragedy of five acts' ([Hawkesworth],

---

[51] John Lawrence Abbott, *John Hawkesworth: Eighteenth-Century Man of Letters* (Madison, Wis., and London: University of Wisconsin Press, 1982), 78.

[52] [Hawkesworth], *Oroonoko, A Tragedy . . . By Thomas Southern. With Alterations* (London: C. Bathurst, 1759), p. v.

Oroonoko, p. v), altering the tragic parts as little as possible, but lengthening them by the addition of new action. The additions were intended to give more logical development and consistent motivation to the tragic plot. To this purpose the parts of Oroonoko's faithful servant Aboan, and the treacherous fellow-slave Hotman, were enlarged. Southerne, Hawkesworth pointed out, had made both Oroonoko and Aboan act oddly: both suspect Hotman of treachery, yet they still let him know the plan of the rebellion and the time of the rendezvous, thus laying themselves open to his betrayal (p. vii). Hawkesworth's additions account for their actions: Aboan is deceived into trusting Hotman, while Oroonoko, who does suspect Hotman, acts more sensibly by concealing the time of the rendezvous from him. That he leaves Hotman alive and able, in the event, to betray him, becomes a proof of his honour (p. viii).

Hawkesworth presented his adaptation, then, in aesthetic terms: he wanted to produce a clearer tragedy. His notion of heroism for both Oroonoko and Imoinda shows the influence of eighteenth-century sentimentalism. He criticizes Southerne's Oroonoko for resolving to strike first, thus becoming in Hawkesworth's view responsible for the tragedy; this, he argues 'renders him somewhat less worthy both of Reverence and Pity, than if his Misfortunes had arisen from the Fault of another' (p. viii). His own Oroonoko is the victim of events: he is meant to arouse pity, not the mingled admiration and fear that were appropriate responses to the ranting, violent hero of Restoration tragedy. Similarly, his Imoinda is softened by the addition of some 'tender Expostulations' against the Governor's seduction attempts, indicating her 'refined Sensibility' (p. vi).

Though Hawkesworth did not present his revision as an anti-slavery argument, the changes he made did affect the impression of slavery given in the text. The first act is extensively altered, with a new opening scene focusing on the West Indian planters, whose callous talk serves to highlight the cruelty of the slave system and indirectly to introduce the notion of the right to freedom. The first planter complains:

every time a Ship comes in, my money goes for a great raw-boned negroe Fellow, that has the Impudence to think he is my Fellow-creature, with as much Right to Liberty as I have, and so grows sullen and refuses to work; or for a young Wench, who will howl Night and day after a Brat or a Lover forsooth, which nothing can drive out of her Head but a Cat-o'nine tails; and if Recourse be had to that Remedy, 'tis ten to one but she takes the next Opportunity to pick my Pocket by hanging herself.   (I. i, p. 2)

The second scene, following Southerne apart from cutting out the comic characters (some of the Widow Lackitt's remarks as a slave-owner are kept, and attributed simply to a 'Woman') introduces Oroonoko. The third scene is another new one, beginning with Aboan's soliloquy mourning for his lost liberty, and moving on to a scene between him and the more experienced slaves, who warn him of the overseer's whip. Their exchange, punctuated by the off-stage cries of beaten slaves, turns on his attempt to rouse them from their 'patient Drudgery' by promising, in Oroonoko, 'a mighty Prince' to lead them to freedom (I. iii, p. 10). As J. R. Oldfield argues, this revised first act served to 'reorientate' the following action, so that the slave system, not just the enslaving of a prince, was made a target.[53] Further additions break down the distinction made in previous versions between wrongfully enslaved prince and naturally slavish multitude. The ordinary slaves are sympathetically, if condescendingly, treated as men and women of feeling. The manuscript submitted to the censors shows that great care was taken with stage directions to depict the slaves' emotions. During an exchange between Hotman and Aboan, the other slaves:

retire to ye back of the Stage, and during the Scene . . . they give significant looks at each other and nod in Approbation of what is said; during the detection of Hotman too in the subsequent Scene their looks & Actions shou'd express wonder & Anxiety & Expectation as hearing only part of what passes between Aboan and Oroonoko, at the same time marking their great Earnestness & Emotion.[54]

Their feelings were also highlighted in the new songs in the play, replacing Southerne's conventional pastoral airs with verses addressing the desire for freedom. An actor and actress representing a black man and woman sing of the impossibility of their love under slavery:

> WOM. In vain the Song and Dance invite
>   To lose Reflection in Delight;
>   Thy Voice, thy anxious Heart belies,

[53] 'The "Ties of Soft Humanity"': Slavery and Race in British Drama, 1760–1800', *Huntington Library Quarterly*, 56 (1993), 3.

[54] [Hawkesworth], *Oroonoko*, Larpent MS 162, p. 20. (Scene III. iv in MS, corresponding to III. iii in the printed version). These directions did not appear in the printed version but were presumably used in performance.

> I read thy Bondage in thy Eyes:
> Does not thy Heart with mine agree?
> MAN. —Yes, Love and Joy must both be free.

(I. i, p. 19)

The long, favourable account of this version that appeared in the *Critical Review* was probably written by Samuel Johnson, a close friend of Hawkesworth.[55] Johnson's own opposition to slavery has become famous from remarks recorded as eccentricities by James Boswell, himself a firm supporter of the slave-trade. The review does not directly discuss the issue of slavery, concentrating as Hawkesworth's preface had done on aesthetic issues, but Johnson's choice of passages for citation makes the most of the play's new anti-slavery slant. He quotes extensively from the first scene, including the slaves' song, Aboan's soliloquy, and the exchanges between him and the other slaves; and he quotes approvingly Hawkesworth's explanation that the slaves' songs 'should, though amorous, be plaintive, the expression of beings at once capable of love, and conscious of a condition in which all its delicacies must become the instruments of pain'. His concluding remarks seem obliquely to hint at an apology on Hawkesworth's behalf for not making a more radical alteration of Southerne:

> If there be any who looks into this performance, with a desire of finding faults, let him first consider how few opportunities of excellence the re-formation of a play affords. The characters are already settled . . . The events of the play are fixed; . . . even sentiments are very little in the reformer's power; for the necessary connection of the new scenes with the old, confines the writer to a certain line of transition, from which he cannot pass aside, whatever treasures of sentiment might reward his deviations. There is, likewise, a necessity of yet greater constraint, by conforming the diction and thoughts to those of the first author, that no apparent dissimili-tude may discover what is original, and what is additional.[56]

Johnson, we might infer, would have liked Hawkesworth to go further. Nevertheless his play uses sentimental discourse to present black slaves as fully human by virtue of their finer feelings, and its additions to Southerne move the work in the direction of anti-slavery argument.

In taking this view I differ from some recent discussions of Hawkesworth's and other adaptations of Southerne, which argue

---

[55] Abbott, *John Hawkesworth*, 81.   [56] *Critical Review*, 8 (1759), 485–6.

that the *Oroonoko* plays, including the later adaptations, domesticate and universalize slavery and work 'in the service of naturalizing colonialism and its economic reliance on the slave trade'.[57] This is true enough of Southerne's play, but the revisions made in the later years of the century seem to me to work against the acceptance of slavery as natural and inevitable. While I agree with Suvir Kaul about the complacent patriotism of later versions, written at a time when British colonization has advanced and 'aristocratic and absolutist conceptions of imperial right are giving way to more seamless, more rational, accounts of English superiority and cultural and material authority',[58] I would add that this very patriotism was capable of being co-opted in the service of abolitionism. Howard Temperley's analysis of the reasons for the late eighteenth-century attack on slavery rejects both the abolitionist account of a heroic struggle towards enlightenment, and the later economic analysis, according to which slavery was only abandoned when no longer viable.[59] He argues that some Britons began actively to organize against slavery, as opposed to merely regretting it, when they began to see their own society thriving on a free-labour system (though that system was underpinned by slavery in the colonies). Believing that it was possible to have a society without slavery allowed the moral objections to slavery to take on new urgency. Their views were opposed by those who were directly dependent on the slave-trade and slave-labour, and 'the attack on slavery can be seen as an attempt by a dominant metropolitan ideology to impose its values on the soci-

[57] MacDonald, 'The Disappearing African Woman', 76. MacDonald discusses Southerne's play, the Hawkesworth version, and the later adaptation by John Ferriar. See also Kaul, 'Reading Literary Symptoms', 80–96. Kaul claims to discuss Behn's, Southerne's, and Hawkesworth's versions of the Oroonoko story, but this essay is marred by an error of attribution: the play cited as Hawkesworth's is in fact the very different, unperformed, and anonymous revision of Southerne published in 1760, so the criticisms being made of Hawkesworth do not apply to him. A more favourable interpretation of the tendencies of the Southerne revisions is found in J. R. Oldfield, 'The Ties of Soft Humanity', 1–14, to which my own discussion is indebted. Oldfield discusses all three of the 1759–60 revisions of Southerne, but not the later Ferriar version.

[58] Kaul, 'Reading Literary Symptoms', 91.

[59] Howard Temperley, 'The Ideology of Antislavery', in Eltis and Walvin, *The Abolition of the Atlantic Slave Trade*, 21–35. For the view that slavery was abolished only when it was no longer economically viable see Eric Williams, *Capitalism and Slavery* (1944; New York: Russell, 1961); for the opposing view that abolition worked against British economic interests see Seymour Drescher, *Econocide: British Slavery in the Era of Abolition* (Pittsburgh: University of Pittsburgh Press, 1977).

eties of the economic periphery'.[60] This analysis suggests an alternative way of looking at the alterations of Southerne, with their resolute excision of his comic plot. Kaul sees this excision as a repression: Southerne could at least obliquely acknowledge the economic and social relations of colonial society by putting them into a comic subplot in which marriage becomes a cynical barter with ironic parallels to the slave-trade, but to turn his play into a simple tragedy was to obscure those relations, and to 'emphasize the redeeming possibilities of sympathy without seriously questioning the structure and function of slavery'.[61] This implies that Britain's economic dependence on slavery was a guilty secret which the adapters suppressed in the interests of supporting the status quo. However, as the issue of the slave-trade moved into open debate in the second half of the century, pro-slavery writers were quite explicit about the economic importance of slavery: it was considered the vital argument in favour of the system. The opponents of slavery were the ones who wanted to move the argument away from economic to religious and moral concerns. In the context of late eighteenth-century England, turning Southerne's work into sentimental tragedy, however much it prettified reality, was a way of questioning the necessity of the slave-trade, not naturalizing it.

Francis Gentleman's revision of *Oroonoko* was close in time to Hawkesworth's. Performed in Edinburgh and kindly received there, he reported, despite 'some lamentable deficiencies in the representation', it was published in 1760.[62] Both adapters were attempting to rescue Southerne from the immodesty of his era by getting rid of the mixed tragi-comic form which showed, in the words of Hawkesworth's prologue, that the dramatist was 'Slave to Custom', and in those of Gentleman's, that he was forced to 'prostitute his genius to the Age'.[63] Gentleman claimed that Southerne himself had declared, 'in his latter days, that he most heartily regretted his complying with licentious taste, by writing anything so offensive to modesty, as the comic part of his works; especially that which was so unnaturally joined to the tragedy of this play' (Advertisement (A2ʳ)). Like Hawkesworth, too, Gentleman aimed to clarify the motivation for the tragic plot, in his case by introducing two new characters,

---

[60] Temperley, 'The Ideology of Antislavery', 29.
[61] Kaul, 'Reading Literary Symptoms', 93.
[62] Gentleman, *Oroonoko*, Advertisement [A2ʳ].
[63] Hawkesworth, *Oroonoko*, Prologue, n.p.; Gentleman, *Oroonoko*, Prologue, A4ʳ.

Massingano and his accomplice Zinzo, in place of Hotman. Massingano, Oroonoko's old battle-enemy, shot the poisoned arrow that killed Imoinda's father; and in the play's action he betrays the slave rebellion. All this suggests he is the stereotypical black villain, the counterpart to the 'noble Negro', but he is more complex than that. His plan of revenge is given credible and in fact sympathetic motivation: Oroonoko has, in the past, killed Massingano's brother, conquered his country, and sold Massingano himself into slavery. As Massingano plans to betray Oroonoko, his villain's soliloquy is given an ironic twist that reflects not on his wickedness, but on the deceitfulness of Christians:

> I must become a Christian in my scheme,
> Invert my nature, bend my stubborn heart,
> And work, by stratagem, to gain my end.
>
> (I. i, p. 25)

Behn's original sarcasms directed at the European assumption of religious and moral superiority are adopted and expanded in this text. Oroonoko tells Blandford that Africa's 'unletter'd shores' contain 'brighter virtues' than those of Christian countries (I. i, p. 19), and Blandford himself has an anti-slavery speech attacking the slaver Captain Driver as 'the sordid Buccaneer' who carries out a 'savage trade'. Driver is:

> Without one human feeling in his breast;
> Yet vaunts, that, as a Christian, he has right
> To make the most of infidels.
>
> (I. i, p. 12)

Massingano's own opening speech, a flowery meditation on his homesickness for 'Africk's golden shores', detailing his loss of 'freedom', 'rejoicing friends', 'martial fame', and the 'milder beauties of domestic bliss' (I. i, p. 21), is clearly meant to be taken as a genuine and affecting evocation of the hardships of slavery, and has much in common with the sentimental anti-slavery poems of the later eighteenth century.

Gentleman makes no clear abolitionist statement: his advertisement and the prologue show that he is writing to appeal to men and women of feeling, but take no clear stand on the issue of slavery. His dedication, indeed, is to James Boswell, who was to become an emphatic spokesman in defence of the slave-trade. His depictions of the evils of slavery are suffused with a sentimental self-indulgence. Blandford (who remains a slave-owner, despite his scornful view of the trade) is allowed to defend the white planters—and appeal to the white audience—by claiming the virtues of fine feeling:

> We are not monsters all;
> Some here the touch of melting pity know,
> Our eyes have tears for merit in distress;
> Our hearts are form'd to sympathize in woe.
>
> (I. i, p. 18)[64]

Imoinda is equally sentimentalized in this version. As in Southerne's version, she is subjected to the Governor's sexual assaults, but instead of drawing a sword on him, as she does in Southerne, she responds to him only with a heroine's elevated diction ('Where, tyrant, hast thou plac'd my helpless lord?', v. ii, p. 75). New exchanges between her and Oroonoko, emphasizing her charms and the strength of love, are added. Her own lament against her slavery is not about injustice, cruelty, or the loss of freedom, but the power of love:

> Tho' pity's hand has kindly loos'd my chains,
> Smooth'd stern captivity to gentle smiles,
> And try'd all means to flatter female pride,
> My widow'd heart, that mourns its absent mate,
> Shuns the fond service of officious care . . .
>
> (II. ii, p. 30)

Gentleman's *Oroonoko* does not have Hawkesworth's degree of attention to the feelings of the ordinary slaves as distinct from the noble protagonists, but its revisions of Southerne, for all their complacent sentimentality, do show a movement in the direction of anti-slavery opinion.

The issue of white female authority, which made its troubling effects apparent in Southerne's text as well as his discussion of the play, is not so prominent in the Hawkesworth and Gentleman revisions. When they discuss their versions of *Oroonoko* their point of reference is Southerne, not Behn. As the comic subplot disappears so do the Welldon sisters and Widow Lackitt. The only named female character is Imoinda, and her authority is of the kind eighteenth-century

---

[64] The first line of this quotation comes from Southerne; the following lines are Gentleman's additions.

England found acceptable in women: an authority of tender feeling, wifely devotion, and virtuous resistance to seduction. On the question of women and race, however, Hawkesworth adds a complex touch. Though he follows Southerne in making Imoinda white, he represents some of the planters as unconvinced by her colour. Discussing the black slaves in the first scene, one planter thinks that 'the Women are worse than the Men' and brings Imoinda into the discussion as a slave 'that they say is not of their Complexion'. One of his companions replies: 'So they say; but she's of the Breed, I'll warrant her—she's one of the sulky ones—the Lieutenant-Governor has taken a Fancy to her; and yet, wou'd you believe it, she gives herself airs and will scarce speak to him.' Another planter calls her 'a mongrel Succabus [*sic*], which for aught we know may be half Sister to the Devil' (I. ii, p. 10). The African woman has not quite disappeared in this version of Imoinda: in the minds of Hawkesworth's unsympathetic planters, at least, her resistance casts doubt on her race and links her to a 'devilish' blackness.

The third of the revised versions, the anonymous *Oroonoko* of 1760, brings female characters and female authority much more strongly to the fore. It also engages in much more open discussion of the question of slavery than previous versions, though its presentation of the issue is not consistent: anti-slavery arguments added by the reviser sit oddly alongside the speech originally given to the hero by Southerne, in which dealing for slaves is presented as 'an honest Way of Trade'.[65] This version has two new characters, Heartwell, 'President of the Council' in Surinam, and Maria, sister to the Lord Governor, who is engaged to Blandford. The creation of Heartwell counters the picture of the cruel and lustful Lieutenant Governor with a benevolent representative of British colonial authority, and is a key element in this patriotic version, with its many references to the humanity and fairness of Britain. So concerned is this adapter to present British power as generally beneficent, and the Lieutenant Governor's cruelty as an aberration, that the tragic ending is made to seem unwarranted. It is not at all clear why Imoinda, having been rescued from the Lieutenant Governor by Blandford and Heartfree, having expressed her gratitude to these representatives of a country 'for sympathizing feeling fam'd' (v. v, p. 57), and having set off with them to free her husband, should suddenly revert to Southerne's text

---

[65] Anon., *Oroonoko*, III. ii, p. 28.

in the following scene, enter into Oroonoko's despair, and be ready to die.

The patriotism expressed in this version seems designed to flatter an audience into opposing slavery on the grounds that the British must be too full of sympathy to tolerate it. For the first time in the *Oroonoko* plays, there is an attempt to dramatize the pro- and anti-slavery arguments that were being exchanged in mid-century Britain. The play's chief exponents of anti-slavery arguments are the two women. It is striking that this version reverts to the pattern of Southerne's play by opening on a scene between two women: but instead of these being husband-hunting comic heroines, they are Imoinda and Maria, two sentimental friends, discussing Imoinda's griefs. Imoinda praises Maria's 'more than manly Friendship' which has comforted her in slavery (I. i, p. 1). This female intimacy provides the context for a speech that goes beyond simply deploring the existence of slavery, to become a direct criticism of British policy. Imoinda asks:

> Is't possible?
> A Nation thus distinguish'd, by the Ties,
> Of soft Humanity, shou'd give its Sanction,
> To its *dependant* States, to exercise,
> This more than savage Right, of thus disposing,
> Like th' marketable Brute, their Fellow-Creatures Blood?

'Too just the Charge—too closely urg'd', admits Maria, claiming to be too ignorant of 'the hidden Paths of States' to be able to reply. Yet she tries to persuade Imoinda that 'the Justice, Equity, | With Wisdom blended, of the sage Rulers, | Of my Parent Country' could provide good reasons for continuing with the slave-trade (I. i, pp. 5–6). In a later exchange with Blandford she takes the opposite view, mentioning that Imoinda holds slavery 'in just Disdain'. Blandford, who himself has lofty ideals of liberty, which even peasants—so long as they are British peasants—hold 'Inviolate and sacred', also wishes for a more 'humane Expedient' for colonial plantations than slavery, but counters Maria's objections with a standard pro-slavery argument, that slaves are originally captives in war and would be even worse off if not bought and shipped from Africa (IV. ii, p. 42).

Whether or not this anonymous reviser went back to Behn's text as well as Southerne, he or she showed an interest in the white woman's relation to colonial power that recalls Behn's work. Maria is in important ways closer to Behn's original narrator than any characters in previous dramatic versions. As the Lieutenant Governor's sister she is—like Behn's narrator, though in a different way—close to the representatives of power. She is the play's reflective moralist, uncomfortably caught between allegiance to her country's values and her sympathies for Oroonoko and Imoinda. The relationship between a female colonist and the slaves she tries to befriend is explored here as it had not been since Behn's novel. However, the differences between the novel and this version of the play are equally striking. Maria's relationship with the slaves is mainly her friendship with Imoinda, who is of course white. The hint of attraction between white narrator and black hero is replaced by sentimental friendship between two white women. Anti-slavery opinions are therefore linked here to the authority of sentimental femininity. Reason is invoked on both sides of the slavery argument, with Blandord reasoning with Maria that slavery is not the worst option, and Imoinda maintaining that the slaves' intelligence and abilities prove them 'the equal Work of Reason's God' (I. i, p. 6); but feeling gives a clearer message: Maria's reply to Blandford is that his 'Reasoning will not weigh with those, who feel | Th' Oppression' (IV. ii, p. 42). In the interval between Behn's novel and this 1760 revision of Southerne, female cultural authority has become more acceptable, less ambiguous, and strongly associated with humanitarian feeling. Its invocation in this version of the Oroonoko story looks forward to its use in the abolitionist campaigns of later years.

These three revised versions of *Oroonoko*, then, demonstrate not only the new demands of the period of stage refinement, but a new focus on slavery as an issue that was now in public debate. Though the anonymous version does not seem to have been performed, Hawkesworth's and Gentleman's both had some success on the stage. Hawkesworth's was revived in several seasons during the 1760s and 1770s. Gentleman's moved from Edinburgh to London in March 1769, and also played four times in the 1769–70 season.[66] In addition, a version called *The Royal Captive*, 'A new Tragedy altered from

[66] The records in *The London Stage* do not index the different versions of the play by the revisers' names, but it is possible for most entries to determine which version is being played. Cast-lists for Hawkesworth's version omit the comic characters and include reference to the 'Dance of Slaves', while Gentleman's version is once identified as his under the title *The Royal Slave*, so that I have taken other performances at the same theatre under that title as his.

Southern's Oroonoko', was performed in September 1767 at the Haymarket.[67] However, the revisions of Southerne did not replace the original play on the stage. During the 1760s Hawkesworth's version played at Drury Lane while Southerne's original continued at Covent Garden, and in the 1770s and 1780s Southerne's version became once more the one most regularly performed. New editions published in these years show that it was usually played with cuts, but the much-derided comic plot was still there, if in softened form. It was still being played, though much less frequently, in the 1790s, and continued to be played at intervals in the early nineteenth century.

While slavery was debated in Britain throughout the second half of the century, it was not until the 1780s that a concerted effort to get rid of the slave-trade began. The Society for the Abolition of the Slave Trade was founded in 1787, and the long parliamentary campaign against the trade began. During the late 1780s anti-slavery propaganda played an important role in mobilizing support for the campaign. The role played by *Oroonoko* in these events is a complex one. In general, the play was actually much less popular in these years than it had been earlier. *The London Stage* records no performances in the 1786–7 season, one only in 1787–8, none in 1788–9, and two in 1789–90. Those performances that were staged in these years were the unrevised Southerne text. While the revised versions of 1759–60 may have contributed in a general way to the growth of abolitionist feeling in the 1760s and 1770s, then, they had no direct role in the abolitionist campaign. Meanwhile the reduced popularity of Southerne's original play coincided with a growth of definitely abolitionist writing in poetry and fiction—some of it inspired by the Oroonoko story. *Oroonoko* was being replaced by the Oroonoko myth.

Though the play was not written nor (with one exception) deliberately staged as an abolitionist drama, that is how people were beginning to remember it. Hannah More, who corresponded with

---

[67] *The London Stage*, Part 4 vol. 2. I have not located a copy of this play (John Maxwell's *The Royal Captive. A Tragedy*, published in York in 1745, is a different play, not related to *Oroonoko*). It is possible that the play performed as *The Royal Captive* in 1767 was Gentleman's version of Southerne under another title, or the anonymous 1760 version retitled; but it may equally well represent a separate, fourth revision of Southerne. D. E. Baker had suggested in 1764 that he wished to see a new revision of Hawkesworth's version, and thought that: 'by interweaving with its present Texture, such additional Incidents as Mrs. *Behn's* extensive Novel might very amply furnish . . . the whole might be render'd equally interesting, and the Piece become entitled to that Immortality its Merit is entitled to'. Baker, *The Companion to the Play-House*, i, entry on *Oroonoko*.

Clarkson and Wilberforce and was heavily involved in the early abolitionist campaign, wrote an anti-slavery poem in 1787 with an
appeal to the powers of 'plaintive Southerne'. She shares his feelings,
she writes, but directs them differently: to the real African slaves, not
a fictional African prince:

> For no fictitious ills these numbers flow,
> But living anguish, and substantial woe;
> No individual griefs my bosom melt,
> For millions feel what Oronoko [*sic*] felt:
> Fir'd by no single wrongs, the countless host
> I mourn, by rapine dragg'd from Afric's coast.[68]

Some time later she suggested to one of her correspondents, Lady
Middleton, that it would be a good idea to get *Oroonoko* staged:

I know of no place but the play-house, where three thousand people meet
every night. Many people go to a play who never go to church, and if they
do go to church, few preachers except the Bishop of Chester and Mr.
Ramsay will vindicate the rights of slaves. Now I was thinking if we could
get the manager of Drury Lane to act the affecting tragedy of 'Oroonoko,
or the Royal Slave', which, you know, exhibits in a most touching manner
the captivity of a black prince, by the treachery of Christians, falsely so
called—this on condition that they will leave out the comic part, which is
indecent and disgusting. Then if we could get some good poet to write an
affecting prologue, descriptive of the miseries of these wretched negroes,
and what a glory would accrue to this land from their redemption.[69]

More's suggestion was not acted upon—the 1789–90 Drury Lane
performances contained the comic scenes, and there is no indication
that they had an anti-slavery prologue. However, she was not the only
one to think of Southerne's play as potential abolitionist propaganda.
It was claimed that *Oroonoko* was rarely or never performed in
Liverpool because that slaving port would find its message unwelcome, and there is an anecdote that John Philip Kemble once insulted a rioting Liverpool audience by comparing it to Captain Driver in
the play.[70] The change, it would seem, was not so much in what was
staged as in how it was interpreted. Tears themselves were being

---

[68] Hannah More, *Slavery: A Poem* (London: T. Cadell, 1788), 4.

[69] Georgiana Chatterton, *Memorials, Personal and Historical of Admiral Lord Gambier, G.C.B.*,
2 vols. (London: Hurst and Blackett, 1861), i. 169–70. Letter from Hannah More to Lady
Middleton, from Cowslip Green, dated 10 Sept.; editoral note adds 'Probably 1788' (i. 167).

[70] J. D. Broadbent, *Annals of the Liverpool Stage* (Liverpool: Edward Howell, 1908), 72.

reread: they no longer meant just the pleasures of weeping, but the proof of anti-slavery feeling.

There was one occasion when *Oroonoko* was revised and performed as a deliberate attempt to create abolitionist propaganda. This was in 1787, when John Ferriar's new version of the play was produced at Manchester's Theatre Royal. Ferriar, a Unitarian physician, was a member of the Manchester Literature and Philosophical Society and had a prominent role in the 'culture of reform' that made the city a leader in the progressive social movements of this period.[71] He wrote papers linking typhus outbreaks to poor living conditions, instituted reforms in the treatment of patients at the Lunatic Hospital, and criticized the city's entrepreneurs for the unhealthy conditions in the cotton mills.[72] Among his miscellaneous literary efforts, mainly essays and verses, was this one dramatic venture, undertaken, as he explained, not from any literary ambition but for the good of the abolitionist cause.[73] The *Monthly* reviewer, taking the point without supporting the cause, treated the play not as a theatrical production but a 'political pamphlet'.[74] Ferriar wrote that:

When the attempt to abolish the African Slave Trade commenced in *Manchester*, some active friends of the cause imagined, that by assembling a few of the principal topics, in a dramatic form, an impression might be made, on persons negligent of simple reasoning. The magnitude of a crime, by dispersing our perceptions, sometimes leaves nothing in the mind but a cold sense of disapprobation. We talk of the destruction of millions, with . . . little emotion . . . But when those who hear with Serenity, of depopulated Coasts, and exhausted Nations, are led by tales of domestic misery, to the sources of public evil, their feelings act with not less violence for being kindled by a single spark. . . . nature will rise up within them, and own her relation to the sufferers.   (Preface, p. i)

The story of Oroonoko and Imoinda thus became the example of individual suffering that could bring home the evils of the slave-trade to an English audience. It was part of the emotive propaganda needed to supplement rational arguments against the trade.

The Society for the Abolition of the Slave Trade, at first mainly made up of Quakers, had been founded in early 1787. By the autumn

[71] Turley, *The Culture of English Antislavery*, 119.

[72] Edward M. Brockbank, *John Ferriar: Public Health Work, Tristram Shandy, Other Essays and Verses* (London: William Heinemann, 1950), 11–14; Turley, *The Culture of English Antislavery*, 119–20.   [73] Ferriar, *The Prince of Angola*, preface, p. vii.

[74] *Monthly Review*, 78 (1788), 522.

of that year the city of Manchester was beginning to organize the first of the many petitions that made Parliament begin to consider measures against the trade. By the end of May 1788 there had been over a hundred petitions against the slave-trade, the one from Manchester bearing over 10,000 signatures.[75] John Ferriar was active from the beginning in the Manchester campaign, and was one of the thirty men appointed to a new committee for the city's Society for the Purpose of effecting the Abolition of the Slave Trade in December 1787.[76] His version of *Oroonoko* was produced as part of the highly successful campaign to get the citizens of Manchester to sign the petition. Its performance and publication were given prominent publicity in the *Manchester Mercury*, a weekly paper that devoted a good deal of space to campaigning against the slave-trade. The play was performed on 28 November 1787, and was advertised as 'The TRAGEDY of OROONOKO; or, The Royal Slave. Carefully revised and altered from Southern'.[77] Its new prologue, printed in the following week's issue of the *Manchester Mercury*, was explicitly abolitionist, taking the hero as a spokesman for his race:

> To-night, reviv'd, sad Oroonoko pleads,
> For each poor African that toils and bleeds.

Its sentimental rhetoric used feeling as the guarantor of common humanity: 'MIND has no COLOUR—ev'ry Heart can feel'. The spectators were exhorted to think of the victims of the slave trade, 'And hear Compassion tell you—THESE ARE MEN.'[78] A few weeks after the performance, the *Manchester Mercury* began to advertise the play's forthcoming publication under the title *The Prince of Angola*.[79] It was published in February 1788[80] with a subtitle announcing that it was 'Adapted to the Circumstances of the Present Times', and a preface praising the people of Manchester for their opposition to the slave-trade and expressing the hope that the British Parliament would soon introduce anti-slavery legislation (pp. viii–ix).

Joyce MacDonald, one of the few critics to give any attention to *The Prince of Angola*, argues that it plays down the significance of

---

[75] Walvin, *England, Slaves and Freedom*, 107, 110.

[76] *Manchester Mercury*, Tues. 15 Jan. 1788.   [77] *Manchester Mercury*, Tues. 27 Nov. 1787.

[78] *Manchester Mercury*, Tues. 4 Dec. 1787; *The Prince of Angola*, Prologue, p. 1.

[79] *Manchester Mercury*, Tues. 25 Dec. 1787.

[80] It was advertised as 'This day is published' in the *Manchester Mercury*, 12 Feb. 1788.

race.[81] In its 1780s context, however, Ferriar's emphasis on the shared feelings and experiences of different races should be seen as part of the humanitarian appeal that was central to the development of the abolition movement. It is certainly true that his preface, with its reference to 'the Mumbo Jumbo' as 'an African's highest religious mystery', shows him to have little appreciation for the culture of the people whose cause he is taking up (*The Prince of Angola*, p. v), but on the whole it is remarkable how thoughtfully this version of *Oroonoko* deals with the transformation of a heroic tragedy into a piece of political theatre. Ferriar was the first of the revisers to attack Southerne's pro-slavery bias, and he found Hawkesworth's adaptation (on which his own drew extensively in matters of structure) disappointing on this issue as well. In the preface he noted that:

> Although the incidents appeared even to invite sentiments adverse to slavery, yet Southern, not contented with refusing them, delivered by the medium of his Hero, a grovelling apology for slave-holders, which Hawkesworth has retained; and an illiberal contempt of the unhappy Negroes is so entwined with the fabric of the Piece, that it was impossible to separate it, without making large encroachments on the Author's design   (p. ii).

Accordingly he was careful to weave into the play many of the new sentiments which Johnson had thought it so difficult for an adapter to create.

He does not introduce new characters, mainly following Hawkesworth's alterations to the plot, but he alters the sentiments of existing characters. Blandford is made an opponent of the slave-trade, who counters the Lieutenant Governor's use of Southerne's original pro-slavery argument ('don't we buy them fairly?') with abolitionist reason: 'But does the seller get them fairly, Sir? Don't tell me that you are not obliged to scrutinize his right to dispose of them . . . by supporting the demand for them, you encourage the worst villainies that the heart of man can devise'. Like the eighteenth-century abolitionists who made a strategic decision to attack the slave-trade first, before attempting to abolish slavery itself, Blandford believes that without a supply of new slaves planters would at least have to treat existing slaves more humanely. He himself has slaves and hopes that his 'mild treatment' of them will allow him to 'preserve my negroes without a fresh importation' (I. i, pp. 1–2).

---

[81] Macdonald, 'The Disappearing African Woman', 81.

Oroonoko himself is no slave-trader in this version: where Southerne's Captain declares, 'I have formerly had dealings with [the enslaved prince] for slaves which he took prisoner, and have got pretty roundly by him' (II. ii, p. 28), Ferrier's has simply 'dealt for slaves thereabouts [in Angola]' (I. i, p. 4).

Opposition to slavery as a system, as well as to the trade, is a motivating force in this version, and a new sense of Oroonoko's fellowship with ordinary, non-royal slaves is created. In Act III scene ii, where Aboan persuades Oroonoko into rebellion, there are considerable changes of emphasis. Oroonoko no longer defends the planters for buying slaves 'in an honest way of trade' or refers to his own slavery as relatively light (Southerne, *Oroonoko*, III. ii, p. 64). Instead of appealing to Oroonoko as a 'prince' whose 'god-like office' is to free the oppressed (Southerne, *Oroonoko*, III. ii, p. 65), Ferrier's Aboan argues on humanitarian grounds. When he urges:

> If any cause can fire the gen'rous breast,
> If any wrong provoke to retribution,
> 'Tis the poor harrass'd slave's. With honesty!
> With praise, you may, you must attempt our rescue,
>
> (*The Prince of Angola*, III. ii, p. 28)

his words are a direct appeal to the Manchester audience as well as to the hero. Oroonoko, as in Southerne, is still swayed, in the end, by his horror at the thought of his own children becoming slaves. Yet in the following scene, when he speaks to his fellow-slaves, he makes a different claim:

> No private sufferings urge me to your side—
> You've known me honour'd, courted here, and soon
> Would see me publicly restored to freedom,
> And royal rights. But never should my ear
> Forget the bondman's cry; still should I droop,
> For my sad brethren left in slavery.
> Let us be jointly free, or jointly perish.
>
> (III. iii, p. 31)

If the adapter has here (perhaps inadvertently) put his hero's sincerity in question, the speech he has added affirms a common humanity, transcending differences of rank, which would make Oroonoko (and should make the audience) feel even in freedom for the suffering of the enslaved.

As Ferriar had noted, it was difficult to get rid of the 'illiberal contempt of the unhappy Negroes' expressed by Southerne's Oroonoko,
since the plot requires the majority of the slaves to abandon the
rebellion and leave the hero and his close companions exposed to
their enemies. His revisions to this scene were ingenious. For
Southerne's Oroonoko, his countrymen's surrender shows them to be
'by nature slaves—wretches designed | To be their masters' dogs and
lick their feet' (Southerne, *Oroonoko*, IV. ii, pp. 90–1), creatures who
have forfeited their humanity:

> Why should they look like men who are not so?
> When they put off their noble natures for
> The grovelling qualities of downcast beasts,
> I wish they had their tails.

> (IV. ii, p. 91)

Ferriar's twist on this bitter speech makes use of the progressive ideas
of his milieu, soon to be formulated in William Godwin's declaration
that 'the characters of men originate in their external circumstances'.[82] Speaking like a late eighteenth-century radical, his
Oroonoko cries:

> And is it thus? Is this to be a Slave,
> To be a man no more in ought but shape?
> Now, Tyrants, I perceive your lashes cut,
> Ev'n deeper than I knew; they mark the soul.

> (IV. i, p. 37)

The blame reverts from the slaves to the slave-holders who are
responsible for degrading their victims. Later, when Blandford and
Stanmore argue that the Lieutenant Governor should keep his word
and let Oroonoko live, the racism of the slave-holders is explicitly
condemned. The Lieutenant Governor asks 'Whom . . . have I
deceived? | . . . Whom but a negro? Not so good a creature, | (Not
half so docile) as my horse or dog', and Blandford replies: 'What
insolence! To strip the injured negro | Of his last privilege, the rank
of man!' (V. i, pp. 41–2). Fear of the returning Governor forces the
Lieutenant Governor to agree to let Blandford free Oroonoko, thus
vindicating colonial authority to some extent. However, the effect is

---

[82] The title of Book I, ch. iv of *Political Justice* (1793). See William Godwin, *Enquiry Concerning Political Justice*, ed. Isaac Kramnick (Harmondsworth: Penguin, 1976), 96.

very different from that of the La Place translation of the story, in which the true Governor is portrayed as benign because he sets free the royal slave. Ferriar's Blandford recognizes, as previous ones had not, that it is not enough to free the 'royal pair':

> With the same breath, would I had power to offer
> Relief to ev'ry drooping African
> That now must envy their deliverance!

> (V. iii, p. 46)

Ferriar's more passive, less heroic Imoinda does not, as Southerne's does, help her reluctant husband to stab her. Oroonoko kills her, an action that is almost immediately shown to have been unnecessary as Blandford and Stanmore rush in, just too late, to free the couple. Where Southerne's Oroonoko, acting according to a heroic code, takes the consequences of his action on himself, proclaiming 'The deed was mine' (*Oroonoko*, V. v, p. 123), Ferriar's blames Blandford, taking him now for a representative of the whites: 'You are a white man . . . Look there—[*Looks at Imoinda's body*] You forc'd me to it.' After Oroonoko's suicide Blandford sums up: 'the guilt is ours; | For deeds like these are slav'ry's fruit' (*The Prince of Angola*, V. iv, p. 52).

The Prince of Angola, then, is the first version of Oroonoko's story to give an explicit analysis of the tragedy as the result of colonial slavery. Its use of female authority is tailored to that purpose. Where Southerne's play, and in a different way the anonymous 1760 version, had replaced Behn's female narrator with female characters who took on certain kinds of authority within the action, Ferriar's reduces female engagement in the action. His Imoinda is a softer creature than previous ones, and women in the play are mainly important as victims to arouse the audience's pity: Oroonoko, rousing his fellow-slaves to rebellion, is given additional lines emphasizing that the female slaves have suffered as wives and mothers (III. iii, p. 32). As for the authority of the writer of the original novel, some acknowledgement was originally offered. The prologue printed with the newspaper report of the first performance of Ferriar's play invoked Behn as the guarantor of the story's authenticity and thus its power to move the audience's pity:

> No stale poetic tricks delude the Ear,
> Nor fancy'd Woes beguile you of a Tear;
> From Aphra's Pen the faithful Records move,
> Of ruin'd Majesty and injur'd Love.

A footnote explained that 'Aphra's Pen' referred to 'Mrs. Behn'.[83] However, Ferriar's reliance on Behn's authority was strictly limited. Where she could be portrayed as a woman of feeling, recording the truth and raising a tear, she was to be honoured, but in his preface he reacted scornfully to what he saw as an outrageous lack of realism in her novel. In a footnote, Southerne was criticized for the 'injudicious fidelity' he showed to Behn's work by using Oroonoko's speech about setting the woods on fire, and Behn herself was mocked for the tall tale of the tiger found with 'seven musket-balls in the heart . . . the wounds . . . very neatly *seam'd up!*' (*The Prince of Angola*, p. iii). Thus the female writer was granted, not the authority she claimed to describe and comment on a whole society, but only the power to appeal to the heart; and even this limited acknowledgement disappeared from the published version of the play, for which the prologue was altered to omit the reference to Aphra's pen.[84]

For Ferriar, the true location of female authority is neither in authorship nor in represented action, but in the audience. The play's prologue flatters the ladies of the audience as slavery's natural opponents from the tenderness of their hearts:

> Our better Hopes within this Circle Rest:
> Here Pity lives in ev'ry gentle Breast.
> Folly may scoff, or Avarice may hate,
> Since Beauty comes the Negroe's Advocate
>
> .   .   .   .
>
> YOU check Oppression's lash, protect the Slave,
> And, First to charm, are still the First to save.

A footnote glossed the reference to 'this Circle': 'The LADIES of MANCHESTER have distinguished themselves very honourably in this Cause.'[85] As Clare Midgeley has shown, this was quite true. Women were not asked to sign the city's petition, this being considered the privilege of adult males, but they formed nearly a quarter of the subscribers to Manchester's abolition society, a far higher female proportion than in other such societies, and they provided nearly a

---

[83] 'Prologue to the Tragedy of Oroonoko, Spoken at the Manchester Theatre, November 28, 1787', *Manchester Mercury*, 4 Dec. 1787.

[84] The lines are revised to read: 'No stale poetic Tricks delude the ear, | Nor fancy'd Woes beguile you of a Tear. | Alas! Too just the faithful Records prove, | Of ruin'd Majesty, and injur'd Love.' *The Prince of Angola*, 1.

[85] 'Prologue to the Tragedy of Oroonoko', *Manchester Mercury*, 4 Dec. 1787. These lines also appear in the published version: see *The Prince of Angola*, 2.

quarter of the money that was raised to start the city's anti-slavery campaign in 1787–8.[86] Abolitionists tapped into a growing belief in the moral authority of sentimental womanhood, and the 'moral qualities on which abolitionist commitment was based were ... identified as especially "feminine" in nature'.[87] In the same month that *The Prince of Angola* was performed, the *Manchester Mercury* invited women to subscribe to the abolitionist cause as a public duty compatible with femininity:

if any public Interference will at any Time become the Fair Sex; if their Names are ever to be mentioned with Honour beyond the Boundaries of their Family, and the Circle of their Connections, it can only be, when a public Opportunity is given for the Exertion of those Qualities which are peculiarly expected in, and particularly possessed by that most amiable Part of the Creation—the Qualities of Humanity, benevolence, and Compassion.[88]

Ferriar's work joined a wide stream of late eighteenth-century writing that was attributing to women a moral authority and, to some extent, a public role, on the basis of a feminine compassion that should be devoted to humanitarian causes. Cultural authority was being extended to a much wider group of women, but on very special and restrictive terms.

The Prince of Angola was one of a long line of works that built a myth out of Behn's story of the African prince. *Oroonoko* stood in Behn's œuvre as a late short novel, in which she drew on her own past experience as well as her wide reading to establish the cosmopolitan authority of her female pen. In the century after her death it was taken up in a myriad ways, contributing to the mythologizing of its author, and becoming caught up in an abolitionist movement that she did not foresee. It became the work that did most to carry Behn's reputation forward, and today it is the subject of new critical interpretations and dramatic adaptation. *Oroonoko* got away from her, and took on a life of its own.

---

[86] Midgeley, *Women Against Slavery*, 18–19, 23.
[87] Ibid. 20.
[88] *Manchester Mercury*, 4 Nov. 1787.

Conclusion

Behn was a significant influence on eighteenth-century literature and theatre. As the author of one of the most popular Restoration comedies, she was influential in British theatre, and as the originator of the powerful Oroonoko myth, she had a much wider-reaching impact. In part that impact must be attributed to her deliberate emphasis on 'my Masculine Part the Poet in me' (*Works*, vii. 217). Taking on a masculine poetic tradition—in the sense of adopting it but also in some respects, as we have seen, in the sense of tackling it as critic and opponent—she achieved her greatest fame with heroes, the comic Willmore and the tragic Oroonoko, rather than with heroines. Her refusal to be confined to feminine subjects or styles was crucial to her achievement. She entered, took part in, and made her distinct contribution to, traditions of writing that had been predominantly masculine; and she influenced the men, as well as the women, who followed her.

However, the critical assumptions of the eighteenth century—many of them, too, very influential, even now—militated against granting Behn a full place in the national literary tradition. The understanding of generative power as a male force has made her influence hard to recognize. The tendency to place women writers in a class apart, whether as disruptive elements to be expelled or as charming decorations to be prized, has made it difficult to see her work as central to any canon or historical process. She was most easily granted recognition in early discussions of the drama by those who were happy to be discussing theatre as entertainment, and could afford a matter-of-fact acceptance of the contribution of female entertainers alongside male. In discussions of the novel, where the genre's claims for morality, respectability, even spiritual authority, were being made, Behn's work received a very hostile reaction. In discussions of poetry, the high cultural status of the writing meant that her contributions were recognized, if at all, as secondary.

The development of her reputation shows the cultural insistence on defining the woman writer in limiting and sexualized terms. Praise and disparagement alike turned on the assumption of a seamless connection between her erotic femininity and her writing. Because she was one of the earliest women to be considered part of the emergent literary canon, she was defined as a representative of womankind. To be a literary mother, as we have seen, has never carried the honour granted to literary fathers, and if Behn was sometimes seen as a kind of mother, she was our first mother, Eve. During her lifetime the association was made obliquely in a poem in the miscellany printed with *Lycidus*, 'A Pindarick to Mrs. *Behn* on her Poem on the Coronation. Written by a Lady.' This commendatory poem hailed her as 'sole Empress of the Land of wit', claiming that her writing:

> did at once a Masculine wit express
> And all the softness of a Femal tenderness,

and that she was the woman poet who would depose men:

> No more shall men their fancy'd Empire hold,
> Since thou *Astrea* form'd of finer mould,
> By nature temper'd more with humid cold,
> Doth man excel—
> Not in soft strokes alone, but even in the bold.

The poem ends, however, by naming its subject the winner in an all-female competition:

> The femal Writers thou hast all excell'd,
> Since the first mother of mankind rebell'd.[1]

With revisionary feminist intent, the writer manages to praise Behn while associating her with Eve, whose rebellion is implicitly seen as the source for female writing. Nevertheless, the weight of the traditional understanding of Eve's sinfulness and secondary, subordinate status lies heavy on these lines. To be associated with the first mother of mankind was to be associated with her Fall. It was also, by the time this poem to Behn appeared, to be associated with a particular, influential version of Eve: the one created by Milton in *Paradise Lost*. As we have seen, in the eighteenth century the idea of Behn as

---

[1] 'A Miscellany of Poems', 89, 90, 94. In *Lycidus: or the Lover in Fashion . . . Together with a Miscellany of New Poems By Several Hands* (London: Joseph Knight, 1688).

Eve surfaced again, and the saucy Restoration poet was compared to Milton's Eve in her fallen and sexualized state, while Rochester was imagined carrying her away as Adam carried Eve to the myrtle bower.[2]

The link made between Aphra Behn and Milton's Eve illuminates the formation and masculinization of the English literary canon during the eighteenth century. It is only one example of the recurrent definition of her in terms of the sinful and sexual body as opposed to the heaven-seeking and spiritual mind of the male genius. Milton was a key figure in the sublime and spiritual national literature raised to pre-eminence in the Enlightenment. Marcus Walsh contends that 'no poet seemed closer to the divine than Milton, and no poem seemed closer to the sacred Scripture than *Paradise Lost*', which even before the beginning of the eighteenth century 'had become established as the great central work of the nascent literary canon'.[3] Even while his republicanism was criticized, Milton grew in fame as a sublime poet. His choice of heavenly subject made the poet himself appear a spiritual figure, rising heavenwards:

> No vulgar heroe can his Muse ingage;
> Nor earth's wide scene confine his hallow'd rage,
> See! See, he upward springs, and tow'ring high
> Spurns the dull province of mortality.[4]

The contrast between this image and that of Behn, with her familiar, worldly-wise poetic persona and fictional narrator, her discussion of sex, political intrigue, and other mundane matters, and her choice of comedy and irony, could hardly be greater. If Milton was a quasi-divine creator, Behn seemed less akin to him than to his version of sinful female creation.

If any poet did indeed seem 'closer to the divine' than Milton it was Shakespeare, in his case elevated not so much by his subject-matter as by his godlike facility for creating so many great and memorable characters. Michael Dobson goes so far as to say that Shakespeare was 'recognized as occupying a position in British life directly analogous to God the father'.[5] In 1769 a Jubilee was held

---

[2] *The Connoisseur*, 69 (Thur. 22 May 1755), 413.

[3] Marcus Walsh, *Shakespeare, Milton and Eighteenth-Century Literary Editing: The Beginnings of Interpretative Scholarship* (Cambridge: Cambridge University Press, 1997), 53.

[4] Addison, 'An Account of the Greatest English Poets', 1694; quoted in John T. Shawcross (ed.), *John Milton: The Critical Heritage* (London: Routledge, 1995), 105.

[5] Dobson, *The Making of the National Poet*, 7.

which ratified Shakespeare's birthplace as 'a site of secular pilgrim-age';[6] here David Garrick, referring to the Bard, adapted Juliet's words to Romeo, and called him 'the god of our idolatry', mingling suggestions of an erotic feminized response to a male lover and human worship of the divine.

During the eighteenth century these two almost sacred poets came to have a 'central symbolic importance for a sense of English literary identity and English literary history'.[7] Meanwhile Behn, as if to provide the necessary counterpoint to such masculine sublimity, was seen as the female body writing its desires. The familiar hierarchized dualisms of mind–body, spirit–matter, male–female, were reproduced in the construction of the literary canon. It was, of course, difficult enough for male poets to follow in the footsteps of Shakespeare or Milton. Far easier, like Garrick, to become known for interpreting Shakespeare than for imitating him. Male poets were, though, understood to partake—even if to a much lesser degree—of creative genius, a quality that as the century went on became increasingly understood as the essence of poetry. Women's poetry was seen as different in kind. While male poets were revered as creators, then, Behn was understood much more as creation, and was imagined through the feminine characters appearing in the work of the poets she wanted to be her brothers. Shakespeare, as well as Milton, provided images used in the interpretation of Behn. The Othello–Desdemona relationship not only influenced Southerne's rendering of Oroonoko and Imoinda, but began to influence the understanding of Behn's own relationship to her hero, within the biographical tradition that made so much more of her femininity and sexuality than of her creativity.

Despite critical disparagement, Behn held for some time a recognized place in canons of poetic and theatrical writing; and we have seen how her reception differed within different generic traditions, reflecting the disparate interests of those constructing canons of poetry, drama, and the novel. Within all of these very different traditions, however, we can see that there were points at which new advances in the construction of a national tradition were accompanied by gestures repudiating Behn. The writer of 'The Apotheosis of Milton' imagined Milton's triumphant entry into Westminster

⁶ Dobson, *The Making of the National Poet*, 3.
⁷ Walsh, *Shakespeare, Milton, and Eighteenth-Century Literary Editing*, 111.

Abbey as accompanied and somehow ratified by her expulsion: an expulsion that also signified the rejection of the bodily (for her body, unlike his, lay in the Abbey) in favour of the spiritual presence. At a later date, the theatrical world which had given her the most recognition and honour also turned away from her, if not so harshly. Here again, her loss of status was associated with the apotheosis of a great man. The canonization of Shakespeare in the eighteenth-century theatre was consolidated most notably by the efforts of David Garrick. At the opening of Drury Lane in 1747, Garrick spoke a prologue written by Samuel Johnson, which looked ironically forward to a time when low entertainment might replace Shakespeare:

> But who the coming Changes can presage,
> And mark the future periods of the Stage?—
> Perhaps if Skill could distant times explore,
> New Behns, new Durfeys, yet remain in Store.
> Perhaps, where Lear has rav'd, and Hamlet dy'd,
> On Flying Cars new Sorcerers may ride.[8]

Despite the protestations of one of her defenders that the 'author cannot be well acquainted with Mrs. Behn's works, who makes a comparison between them and the productions of Durfey. There are marks of a fine understanding in the most unfinished piece of Mrs. Behn, and the very worst of this lady's compositions are preferable to Durfey's best',[9] the association of Behn with poor reputations and pantomimes stuck. Garrick, as Johnson well knew, wished to purge the stage of such low amusements, and we have seen how his tenure at Drury Lane coincided with that theatre's dropping of Aphra Behn's work. Within the novel, too, the move to refine, moralize, and spiritualize was performed through the expulsion of Behn and the kind of femininity she was understood to represent. Richardson eclipsed Behn, and later ages have named him rather than her as first English novelist; but equally striking here is that Aphra Behn, understood as a kind of feminine character, was eclipsed by Richardson's creation. The establishment of his heroine Clarissa as the epitome of feminine virtue was achieved through the suppression of the less spiritual feminine qualities embodied in Behn's notorious heroines; and the process made those heroines, and

---

[8] Quoted in Sheffey, *The Literary Reputation of Aphra Behn*, 110–11.
[9] T. Cibber, *Lives of the Poets*, iii. 27.

the woman who created them, seem not only immoral and unfeminine, but even unrealistic and unbelievable, to later generations of readers.

In Shakespeare and Milton, the English national tradition had its quasi-divine heroes and its fathers. If Behn was, for a time, seen as its mother, she was Eve: defined in terms of her sexual difference, her bodily and not spiritual existence, her sinfulness, her subordination, her secondariness; and, too, in terms of a female rebelliousness that needed to be suppressed to make way for the incorporation into that tradition of the authority of sentimental femininity.

Bibliography

PRIMARY SOURCES

Manuscripts

British Library Harleian 7317, fol. 58
Folger Shakespeare Library, Nb 3
Huntington Library Larpent MS 162
Huntington Library Larpent MS 748

Printed Sources

ADDISON, JOSEPH, and STEELE, RICHARD, *The Spectator*, ed. D. F. Bond, 5 vols. (Oxford: Clarendon Press, 1965).

AMES, RICHARD, *The Pleasures of Love and Marriage, A Poem in Praise of the Fair Sex. In Requital for the Folly of Love, and Some other late Satyrs on Women* (London: R. Baldwin, 1691).

[AMORY, THOMAS], *Memoirs of Several Ladies of Great Britain* (London: John Noon, 1755).

ARBUTHNOTT, JOHN, *et al.*, *Memoirs of the Extraordinary Life, Works, and Discoveries of Martinus Scriblerus. Written in Collaboration by the Members of the Scriblerus Club*, ed. Charles Kerby-Miller (1950; rpr. New York and Oxford: Oxford University Press, 1988).

'ARIADNE' (pseud.), *She Ventures, and He Wins. A Comedy, Acted at the new Theatre, in Little Lincoln's-Inn-Fields, By his Majesty's Servants. Written by a Young Lady* (London: Hen. Rhodes, J. Harris, Sam Briscoe, 1696).

Athenian Mercury, 5/13, Tuesday 12 January 1691/2.

Athenian Mercury 15/25, Tuesday 27 November 1694.

AUDEN, W. H., *Collected Shorter Poems 1927–1957* (London and Boston: Faber and Faber Ltd., 1981).

BAKER, DAVID ERSKINE, *The Companion to the Play-House*, 2 vols. (London: T. Becket and P. A. De Hondt, 1764).

—— [continued by Isaac Reed] *Biographia Dramatica, or, A Companion to the Playhouse*, 2 vols. (London: Mess. Rivingtons, *et al.*, 1782).

—— [continued by Stephen Jones] *Biographia Dramatica: or, A Companion to the Playhouse*, 3 vols. (London: Longman, Hurst, Rees, Orme, and Brown, 1812).

BANDELE, 'BIYI, *Aphra Behn's Oroonoko in a New Adaptation* (Oxford: Amber Lane Press, 1999).

BARBAULD, ANNA LETITIA (ed.), *The British Novelists; with an Essay, and Prefaces Biographical and Critical*, vol. i (London: F. C. and J. Rivington, 1820).

BARKER, JANE, *A Patch-Work Screen for the Ladies; or, Love and Virtue Recommended: In a Collection of Instructive Novels* (London: E. Curll, 1723).

——— *The Lining of the Patch-Work Screen; Design'd for the Farther Entertainment of the Ladies* (London: A. Bettesworth, 1726).

——— *The Galesia Trilogy*, ed. C. S. Wilson (New York: Oxford University Press, 1997).

BEDFORD, ARTHUR, *The Evil and Danger of Stage-Plays* (Bristol: W. Bonny, 1706).

——— *A Serious Remonstrance In Behalf of the Christian Religion* (London: John Darby for Henry Hammond, *et al.*, 1719).

[BEHN, APHRA], *Covent Garden Drolery, or a Collection, Of all the Choice Songs, Poems, Prologues, and Epilogues, (Sung and Spoken at Courts and Theaters) Never in Print Before. Written by the refined'st Witts of the Age. And Collected by A.B.* (London: James Magnes, 1672).

BEHN, APHRA, *The Rover: or, The Banish't Cavaliers. As it is Acted at His Royal Highness The Duke's Theatre* (London: John Amery, 1677).

——— *Love-Letters between a Noble-man and his Sister* (London: Randal Taylor, 1684).

——— *Poems Upon Several Occasions: With a Voyage to the Island of Love. By Mrs. A. Behn* (London: R. and J. Tonson, 1684).

——— *Love Letters from a Nobleman to his Sister: Mixt with the History of their Adventures. The Second Part* (London, 1685).

——— *La Montre: or the Lovers Watch. By Mrs A. Behn* (London: R.H. for W. Canning, 1686).

——— *The Amours of Philander and Silvia: Being the Third and Last Part of the Love-Letters Between a Nobleman and his Sister* (London, 1687).

——— *The Emperor of the Moon: A Farce. As it is Acted by Their Majesties Servants, at the Queens Theatre* (London: R. Holt, 1687).

——— *The Emperor of the Moon: A Farce. As it is Acted by Their Majesties Servants, at the Queens Theatre* (2nd edn., London: R. Holt, 1688).

——— *Lycidus: or the Lover in Fashion . . . Together with a Miscellany of New Poems By Several Hands* (London: Joseph Knight, 1688).

——— *Oroonoko: or, The Royal Slave* (London: Will. Canning, 1688).

——— *Agnes de Castro: or, The Force of Generous Love. Written in French by a Lady of Quality. Made English by Mrs. Behn* (London: William Canning, 1688).

——— *The Forc'd Marriage, or the Jealous Bridegroom: A Tragi-Comedy, As it is Acted by His Majesties Servants at the Queens Theatre* (2nd edn., London: James Knapton, 1688).

——— *The History of the Nun: Or, the Fair Vow-Breaker* (London: A. Baskerville, 1689).

——— *The Lucky Mistake, A New Novel, By Mrs. A Behn* (London: Richard Bentley, 1689).

—— *The Younger Brother: or, the Amorous Jilt. A Comedy, Acted at the Theatre Royal, By His Majesty's Servants. Written by the late Ingenious Mrs. A Behn* (London: J. Harris, 1696).

——*The Histories and Novels Of the Late Ingenious Mrs. Behn: In One Volume . . . Together with The Life and Memoirs of Mrs. Behn. Written by One of the Fair Sex* (London: S. Briscoe, 1696).

—— *Poems Upon Several Occasions; with a Voyage to the Island of Love. Also The Lover in Fashion, being an Account from Lycidus to Lysander, of his Voyage from the Island of Love. By Mrs. A. Behn. To which is added a Miscellany of New Poems and Songs, by several Hands* (2nd edn., London: Francis Saunders, 1697).

—— *The Rover: or, The Banish't Cavaliers. As it was Acted by His Majesty's Servants, at the Theatre in Little-Lincolns-Inn-Fields* (2nd edn., London: J. Orme for Richard Wellington, 1697).

—— *All the Histories and Novels Written by the Late Ingenious Mrs Behn, Entire in One Volume. The Third Edition, with Large Additions* (London: Samuel Briscoe,1698).

—— *The City-Heiress: or, Sir Timothy Treat-all. A Comedy, As it is Acted at his Royal Highness his Theatre* (2nd edn., London: R. Wellington, 1698).

—— *The Roundheads: or, The Good Old Cause, A Comedy, As it is Acted at the Duke's Theatre* (2nd edn., London: R. Wellington, 1698).

—— *The Young King: or, the Mistake. As it is Acted at the Duke's Theatre* (2nd edn., London: R. Wellington, 1698).

—— *All the Histories and Novels Written by the Late Ingenious Mrs. Behn, Entire in One Volume. The Fourth Edition, with Large Additions* (London: R. Wellington, 1700).

—— *Histories, Novels, and Translations, Written by the most Ingenious Mrs. Behn; The Second Volume* (London: W.O. for S.B., 1700).

—— *Plays Written by the late Ingenious Mrs. Behn*, 2 vols. (London: Jacob Tonson, 1702).

—— *Plays Written by the late Ingenious Mrs. Behn*, 2 vols. (London: printed for M.W. and sold by W. Meadows, 1716).

—— [revised by unknown hand], *The Land of Love. A Poem* (London: H. Meere and A. Bettesworth, 1717).

—— *Seventeen Histories and Novels Written by the Late Ingenious Mrs. Behn*, 2 vols. (London: D. Browne *et al.*, 1718).

—— *Plays Written by the late Ingenious Mrs. Behn*, 4 vols. (London: Mary Poulson, 1724).

—— [adapted by an unknown hand], *Love-Letters Between a Nobleman and his Sister: Viz. F——d Lord Gr——y of Werk, and the Lady Henrietta Berk——ley, Under the Borrow'd Names of Philander and Silvia. Done into Verse, by the Author of the Letters from a Nun to a Cavalier* (2nd edn., London: Charles Corbett, 1734).

—— *All the Histories and Novels Written by the Late Ingenious Mrs. Behn*, 2 vols. (8th edn., London: W. Feales *et al.*, 1735).

BEHN, APHRA, *All the Histories and Novels Written by the Late Ingenious Mrs. Behn*, 2 vols. (9th edn., London: T. Longman *et al.*, 1751).

—— *The Emperor of the Moon. As now Acting with Applause at the Theatre-Royal in Smock-Alley* (Dublin: James Rudd, 1757).

—— *The Rover: or, the Banish'd Cavaliers. A Comedy, With the Alterations, As it is now Reviv'd and Acting at the Theatre-Royal in Covent Garden* (London, 1757).

—— *The History of Oroonoko; or, the Royal Slave. A Novel. Containing a Variety of Entertaining Passages. Published by Charles Gildon. The Ninth Edition corrected* (Doncaster: C. Plummer, 1759).

—— [translated by an unknown hand], *Histoire d'Agnès de Castro*, in *Romans traduits de l'anglois* (Amsterdam, 1761).

—— [translated by an unknown hand], *Histoire d'Agnès de Castro, traduite de l'anglois*, in *Mélanges de littérature*, 6 (Amsterdam, 1775).

—— *The Emperor of the Moon. A Dialogue-Pantomime . . . As performed at The Patagonian Theatre* (London: T. Sherlock, 1777).

—— *Oroonoko*, ed. E. Griffith, in *A Collection of Novels, Selected and Revised by Mrs Griffith*, vol. i (London: G. Kearsley, 1777).

—— *English Nights Entertainments. The History of Oroonoko; or, The Royal Slave. Written originally By Mrs. Behn, and revised by Mrs Griffiths* (London: T. Maiden for Ann Lemoine, 1800).

—— *The Works of Aphra Behn*, ed. Montague Summers, 6 vols. (London: William Heinemann, 1916).

—— *The Emperor of the Moon*, in Leo Hughes and A. H. Scouten (eds.), *Ten English Farces* (Austin, Tex.: University of Austin, 1948).

—— *Selected Writings of the Ingenious Mrs. Aphra Behn*, ed. R. Phelps (New York: Grove Press, 1950).

—— *The Works of Aphra Behn*, ed. Janet Todd, 7 vols. (London: William Pickering and Chatto; Columbus, Oh.: Ohio State University Press, 1992–6).

—— *The Rover and Other Plays*, ed. Jane Spencer (Oxford: Oxford University Press, 1995).

—— *Oroonoko*, ed. Joanna Lipking (New York and London: W. W. Norton, 1997).

[BELLON, PETER], *The Fatal Beauty of Agnes de Castro; Taken out of the History of Portugal. Made English out of French By P.B.G.* (London: R. Bentley, 1688), bound in *Modern Novels*, vol. v (London: R. Bentley, 1692).

BETHAM, MATILDA, *A Biographical Dictionary of the Celebrated Woman of Every Age and Country* (London: B. Crosby and Co., 1804).

Biographia Britannica; or, the Lives of the Most Eminent Persons Who have Flourished in Great Britain and Ireland, 1 (London: W. Innys *et al.*, 1747).

Biographia Britannica: or, the Lives of the Most Eminent Persons who have Flourished in Great Britain and Ireland. By Andrew Kippis . . . With the Assistance of the rev. Joseph Towers, LL.D. And other Gentlemen, 2 (London: W. and A. Strahan, 1780).

BLACKMORE, A., *Luck at Last; or, the Happy Unfortunate*, in W. H. McBurney (ed.), *Four before Richardson: Selected English Novels, 1720–1727* (Lincoln, Nebr.: University of Nebraska Press, 1963).

BLOUNT, SIR THOMAS POPE, *De Re Poetica* (London: R. Everingham for R. Bently, 1694).

BOADEN, JAMES, *Memoirs of the Life of John Philip Kemble, Esq. Including a History of the Stage, from the Time of Garrick to the Present Period*, 2 vols. (London: Longman, Hurst, Rees, Orme, Brown and Green, 1825).

—— *Memoirs of Mrs. Inchbald*, 2 vols. (London: Richard Bentley, 1833).

BROWN, THOMAS, *The Works of Mr. Thomas Brown, in Prose and Verse; Serious, Moral, and Comical*, 2 vols. (London: Sam Briscoe, 1707).

—— *The Second Volume of the Works of Mr Tho. Brown, Containing Letters from the Dead to the Living . . . The Third Part (by Mr. Tho. Brown) Never before Printed* (London: B. Bragg, 1707).

—— *A Continuation or Second Part of the Letters from the Dead to the Living, By Mr. Thomas Brown, Capt. Ayloff, Mr Henry Barker, etc.* (2nd edn., London: Benj. Bragg, 1707).

—— *The Third Volume of the Works of Mr. Thomas Brown, Containing, Amusements Serious and Comical, Calculated for the Meridian of London* (London: Printed for S.B. and sold by B. Bragg, 1708).

—— *The Lover's Secretary: or, The Adventures of Lindamira, a Lady of Quality. Written to her Friend in the Country. In XXIV Letters. Revis'd and Corrected by Mr. Tho. Brown* (2nd edn., London: R. Wellington, 1713).

—— *Amusements Serious and Comical, and Other Works*, ed. Arthur L. Hayward (London: George Routledge and Sons, Ltd., 1927).

BULLOCK, C., *A Woman's Revenge: or, a Match in Newgate. A Comedy. As it is acted at the New Theatre in Lincoln's Inn Fields* (London: E. Curll and J. Pemberton, and J. Brown and W. Meers, 1715).

BUTLER, REV. WEEDEN (trans.), *Zimao, the African* (London: Vernor and Hood, 1800).

BYSSHE, EDWARD, *The Art of English Poetry* (London: H. Knap, E. Castle and B. Tooke, 1702).

CARROLL, S., *The Perjur'd Husband: or, the Adventures of Venice. A Tragedy. As 'twas Acted at the Theatre-Royal in Drury-Lane, By His Majesty's Servants* (London: Bennet Banbury, 1700).

CENTLIVRE, S., *The Gamester. A Comedy. As it is Acted at the New-Theatre in Lincoln's-Inn-Fields, by Her Majesty's Servants* (London: W. Turner and W. Davis *et al.*, 1705).

—— *The Platonick Lady. A Comedy. As it is Acted at the Queen's Theatre in the Hay-Market* (London: J. Knapton and Egbert Sanger *et al.*, 1707).

—— *The Man's Bewitch'd: Or, the Devil to Do about Her. A Comedy: As it is Acted at the New Theatre in the Hay-Market, By her Majesty's Servants* (London: B. Lintot *et al.*, 1709).

—— *The Perplex'd Lovers. A Comedy. As it is Acted at the Theatre Royal in Drury Lane By Her Majesty's Servants* (London: Owen Lloyd *et al.*, 1712).

CENTLIVRE, S., *The Busy Body, The Wonder, A Bold Stroke for a Wife*, in *The British Theatre; or, A Collection of Plays . . . With Biographical and Critical Remarks*, by Mrs. Inchbald, vol. xi (London: Longman, Hurst, Rees and Orme, 1808).

—— *The Dramatic Works of the Celebrated Mrs. Centlivre, with A New Account of her Life*, 3 vols. (London: John Pearson, 1872).

—— *A Bold Stroke for a Wife*, ed. Thalia Stubbs (London: Edward Arnold, 1969).

The Challenge, Sent by a Young Lady to Sir Thomas . . . Or, the Female War (London: E. Whitlock, 1697).

CHETWOOD, W. R., *A General History of the Stage, from its Origin in Greece down to the Present Time* (London: W. Owen, 1749).

—— *The British Theatre. Containing The Lives of the English Dramatic Poets; with An Account of all their Plays* (Dublin: Peter Wilson, 1750).

CIBBER, COLLEY, *An Apology for the Life of Mr. Colley Cibber, Comedian, and Late Patentee of the Theatre-Royal* (London: John Watts, 1740).

—— *An Apology for the Life of Mr Colley Cibber, Comedian, and Late Patentee of the Theatre-Royal* (2nd edn., London: John Watts, 1740).

—— *Three Sentimental Comedies*, ed. Maureen Sullivan (New Haven and London: Yale University Press, 1973).

CIBBER, THEOPHILUS, *The Lives of the Poets of Great Britain and Ireland*, 4 vols. (London: R. Griffiths, 1753).

COLLIER, JEREMY, *A Short View of the Immorality, and Profaneness of the English Stage* (London: S. Keble, R. Dare, and H. Hindmarsh, 1698).

[COLMAN, GEORGE, and THORNTON, BONNELL], *The Connoisseur. By Mr. Town, Critic, and Censor-General*, 2 vols. (London: R. Baldwin, 1755–6).

A Companion to the Theatre, 2 vols. (London: J. Nourse, 1747).

A Companion to the Theatre (Dublin: Peter Wilson and Sam Price, 1756).

A Comparison Between the Two Stages, ed. Staring B. Wells (Princeton: Princeton University Press, 1942).

CONGREVE, WILLIAM, *Love for Love*, ed. Emmett L. Avery (London: Edward Arnold, 1966).

—— *The Complete Plays of William Congreve*, ed. Herbert Davies (Chicago and London: University of Chicago Press, 1967).

—— *The Double Dealer*, ed. J. C. Ross (London: Ernest Benn Ltd., 1981).

C[ONSET], H., *The Practice of the Spiritual or Ecclesiastical Courts* (London: T. Basset, 1685).

COOPER, ELIZABETH, *The Muses Library; Or a Series of English Poetry, from the Saxons, to the Reign of King Charles II*, vol. i (London: J. Wilcox, T. Green, J. Brindley and T. Osborn, 1737).

COWLEY, ABRAHAM, *The Works of Mr Abraham Cowley* (8th edn., London: Henry Herringman, 1693).

COWLEY, HANNAH, *A School for Greybeards; or, the Mourning Bride* (London: G. G. J. and J. Robinson, 1786).

DAVIES, THOMAS, *Dramatic Miscellanies*, 3 vols. (London: Printed for the Author, 1784).

[DAY, THOMAS], *The Dying Negro, a Poetical Epistle* (London: W. Flexney, 1773).

DIBDIN, CHARLES, *A Complete History of the English Stage* (London, 1797–1800).

DODD, WILLIAM, *Poems, by Dr Dodd* (London: Dryden Leach, 1767).

[DODSLEY, JAMES (ed.)], *A Collection of Poems in Six Volumes. By Several Hands* (London: J. Dodsley, 1766).

[DOWNES, JOHN], *Roscius Anglicanus, or an Historical Review of the Stage* (London: H. Playford, 1708).

—— *Roscius Anglicanus . . . With Additions, by the late Mr. Thomas Davies* (London: Printed for the Editor, 1789).

DRYDEN, JOHN, *Alexander's Feast: or, the Power of Musick. An Ode. Wrote in Honour of St. Cecilia, Written by Mr. Dryden. And an additional New Act, call'd The Choice of Hercules. Both Set to Musick by Mr. Handel* (London: J. and R. Tonson and S. Draper, 1751).

——*The Letters of John Dryden,* ed. C. E. Ward (Durham, NC: Duke University Press, 1942).

—— *The Prologues and Epilogues of John Dryden: A Critical Edition,* ed. William Bradford Gardner (New York: Columbia University Press, 1951).

—— *The Works of John Dryden,* 20 vols. (Berkeley and Los Angeles: University of California Press, 1967–89).

—— *Poems and Fables,* ed. James Kinsley (Oxford: Oxford University Press, 1970).

[DRYDEN, JOHN (ed.)], *Miscellany Poems . . . By the most Eminent Hands* (London: Jacob Tonson, 1684).

—— *Miscellany Poems: The First Part . . . By the Most Eminent Hands. Publish'd by Mr Dryden. The Third Edition* (London: Jacob Tonson, 1702).

DRYDEN, JOHN, JUN., *The Husband His own Cuckold. A Comedy: As it is Acted at the Theater in Little Lincolns-Inn-Fields, By His Majesty's Servants* (London: J. Tonson, 1696).

Drydeniana XIV. On the Death of Dryden (New York and London: Garland Publishing Inc., 1975).

DUNCOMBE, JOHN, *The Feminiad* (London, 1754).

DUNLOP, JOHN, *The History of Fiction: Being a Critical Account of the most Celebrated Prose Works of Fiction, from the Earliest Greek Romances to the Novels of the Present Age,* 3 vols. (2nd edn., Edinburgh: James Ballantyne and Co., 1816).

D'URFEY, THOMAS, *Bussy d'Ambois, or the Husband's Revenge. A Tragedy. As it is Acted at the Theatre Royal. Newly Revised by Mr. D'Urfey* (London: R. Bentley. Jo. Hindmarsh, and Abel Roper, 1691).

—— *The Intrigues at Versailles: or, a Jilt in all Humours. A Comedy* (London: F. Saunders, P. Buck, R. Parker, 1697).

EGERTON, SARAH FYGE, *Poems on Several Occasions, together with a Pastoral. By Mrs. S.F.* (London: J. Nutt (1703?))

The English Review; or, an Abstract of English and Foreign Literature, vol. 15 (London: J. Murray. 1790).

EPHELIA [pseud.], *Female Poems on Several Occasions* (London: William Downing for James Courtney, 1679).

ETHEREGE, GEORGE, *The Man of Mode*, ed. W. B. Carnochan (London: Edward Arnold, 1967).

—— *She Would If She Could*, ed. Charlene M. Taylor (London: Edward Arnold, 1973).

—— *The Plays of Sir George Etherege*, ed. Michael Cordner (Cambridge: Cambridge University Press, 1982).

Familiar Letters of Love, Gallantry, and Several Occasions, By the Wits of the last and present Age . . . Together with Mr T. Brown's Remains, 2 vols. (London: Sam Briscoe, 1718).

FARQUHAR, GEORGE, *The Constant Couple; or a Trip to the Jubilee. A Comedy. Acted at the Theatre-Royal in Drury-Lane By His Majesty's Servants* (London: Ralph Smith and Bennet Banbury, 1700).

—— *The Beaux' Stratagem*, ed. Charles N. Fifer (London: Edward Arnold, 1977).

—— *The Recruiting Officer*, ed. John Ross (London: A & C Black Ltd., 1991).

—— *The Recruiting Officer and Other Plays*, ed. William Myers (Oxford: Oxford University Press, 1995).

A Farther Essay relating to the Female-Sex (London: A. Roper and E. Wilkinson, 1696).

Female Tatler, 69 (Monday 12 December–Wednesday 14 December 1709).

Female Tatler, 82 (Wednesday 11 January–Friday 13 January 1710).

[FERRIAR, JOHN], *The Prince of Angola, a Tragedy, altered from the play of Oroonoko. And adapted to the circumstances of the present times* (Manchester: J. Harrap, 1788).

FIELDING, HENRY, *Joseph Andrews and Shamela* (London: Oxford University Press, 1970).

—— *The History of Tom Jones, a Foundling*, ed. Martin C. Battestin and Fred Bowers (Oxford, 1974).

—— *The Journal of a Voyage to Lisbon*, ed. Tom Keymer (Harmondsworth: Penguin, 1996).

FINCH, ANNE, *see* WINCHILSEA

GARRICK, DAVID, *Isabella: or, the Fatal Marriage. A Play. Alter'd from Southern* (London: J. and R. Tonson, 1757).

—— *Cymon. A Dramatic Romance. As it is performed at the Theatre-Royal, in Drury-Lane.* (London: Printed for the Proprietor, 1766).

Gazetteer and New Daily Advertiser, 22 March–3 June 1777.

A General Dictionary, Historical and Critical, vol. iii (London: James Bettenham for G. Strahan, *et al.*, 1735).

[GENEST, JOHN], *Some Account of the English Stage, from the Restoration in 1660 to 1830*, 10 vols. (Bath: H. E. Carrington, 1832).

GENTLEMAN, FRANCIS, *Oroonoko: or the Royal Slave. A Tragedy. Altered from Southerne, by Francis Gentleman* (Glasgow: Robert and Andrew Foulis, 1760).

Gentleman's Magazine and Historical Chronicle, 8 (1738), 9 (1739).

[GILDON, CHARLES (ed.)], *Miscellany Poems upon Several Occasions: Consisting of Original Poems. By the late Duke of Buckingham, Mr. Cowly, Mr. Milton, Mr. Prior, Mrs. Behn, Mr. Tho. Brown, &c. And the Translations from Horace, Persius, Petronius Arbiter, &c. With an Essay upon Satyr, By the Famous M. Dacier* (London: Peter Buck, 1692).

GILDON, CHARLES (ed.) *Chorus Poetarum: or, Poems on Several Occasions. By the Duke of Buckingham, the late Lord Rochester, Sir John Denham, Sir Geo. Etherege, Andrew Marvel, Esq; The famous Spencer, Madam Behn, And several other Eminent Poets of this Age. Never before Printed* (London: Benjamin Bragg, 1694).

—— *The Post-Boy Robb'd of his Mail* (2nd edn., London: B. Mills for John Sprint, 1706).

—— *The Complete Art of Poetry*, 2 vols. (London: Charles Rivington, 1718).

[GOULD, ROBERT], *A Satyrical Epistle to the Female Author of a Poem, call'd Silvia's Revenge* (London: R. Bentley, 1691).

GOULD, ROBERT, *The Poetess: A Satyr. Being a reply to the Female-Author of a Poem call'd, Silvia's Revenge* (London: Printed, and sold by the Booksellers of London and Westminster, 1707).

[GRANVILLE, GEORGE], *The History of Adolphus, Prince of Russia; and the Princess of Happiness. By a person of Quality. With a Collection of Songs and Love-verses. By Several Hands* (London: R.T., 1691).

GRANVILLE, GEORGE, *The Genuine Works in Verse and Prose, of the Right Honourable George Granville, Lord Lansdowne* (London: J. Tonson and L. Gilliver, 1732).

—— *The Genuine Works in Verse and Prose, of the Right Honourable George Granville, Lord Lansdowne*, 3 vols. (London: J. and R. Tonson, and L. Gilliver and J. Clarke, 1736).

GREER, G., HASTINGS, S., MEDOFF, J., and SANSONE, M. (eds.), *Kissing the Rod: An Anthology of Seventeenth-Century Women's Verse* (London: Virago, 1988).

GRIFFITH, ELIZABETH, *A Collection of Novels, Selected and Revised by Mrs Griffith*, 3 vols. (London: G. Kearsley, 1777).

The Grove; or, a Collection of Original Poems, Translations, &c (London: W. Mears, 1721).

The Grove: or, the Rival Muses. A Poem. By the Author of a Pastoral Elegy on the Death of Mr Creech (London: John Deeve, 1701).

[HAWKESWORTH, DR.], *Oroonoko, A Tragedy . . . By Thomas Southern. With Alterations* (London: C. Bathurst, 1759).

HAYWARD, THOMAS, *The British Muse, or, a Collection of Thoughts Moral, Natural, and Sublime, of our English Poets: Who flourished in the Sixteenth and Seventeenth Centuries*, 3 vols. (London: F.Cogan and J. Nourse, 1738).

HAYWOOD, ELIZA, *Secret Histories, Novels and Poems* (2nd edn., London: Dan Browne and S. Chapman, 1725).

—— *The History of Miss Betsy Thoughtless*, 4 vols. (London: T. Gardner, 1751).

—— *The Invisible Spy. By Explorabilis*, 2 vols. (2nd edn., London: T. Gardner, 1759).

[HEARNE, MARY], *The Lover's Week: or, the Six Days Adventures of Philander and Amaryllis* (2nd edn., London: E. Curll and R. Francklin, 1718).

An Heroic Epistle, from Kitty Cut-A-Dash to Oroonoko (Dublin, 1778).

The History of the Athenian Society (London, 1693).

HITCHCOCK, ROBERT, *Historical View of the Irish Stage,* vol. i (Dublin: R. Marchbank, 1788); vol. ii (Dublin: William Folds, 1794).

HOOLE, JOHN, *Cleonice, Princess of Bithynia: A Tragedy. As it is performed at the Theatre Royal in Covent-Garden* (London: T. Evans, 1775).

HUNT, LEIGH, *Men, Women, and Books,* 2 vols. (London: Smith, Elder and Co., 1847).

INCHBALD, ELIZABETH (ed.), *The British Theatre,* 25 vols. (London: Longman, Hurst, Rees and Orme, 1808).

JACOB, GILES, *The Poetical Register: or, the Lives and Characters of the English Poets* (London: A. Bettesworth, 1723).

KEMBLE, JOHN PHILIP, *Love in Many Masks: As Altered by J. P. Kemble, from Mrs Behn's Rover, and first acted at the Theatre Royal in Drury Lane, March 8th, 1790* (London: T. and J. Egerton, 1790).

KILLIGREW, THOMAS, *Thomaso, or, The Wanderer: A Comedy. The Scene Madrid. Written in Madrid by Thomas Killigrew. In Two Parts* (London, 1663).

KING, WILLIAM, *The Art of Love: In Imitation of Ovid De Arte Amandi* (London: Bernard Lintot, 1709).

KNOX, VICESSIMUS, *Essays Moral and Literary,* 2 vols.(London: Charles Dilly, 1779).

Ladies Dictionary (London: John Dunton, 1694).

Ladies Journal (Dublin: W. Wilmot, 1727).

Ladies Magazine, By Jasper Goodwill, of Oxford, Esq., vols. i–iii (London: G. Griffith, 1749–52).

Lady's Poetical Magazine, or Beauties of British Poetry, 4 vols. (London: Harrison and Co., 1781–2).

LANGBAINE, GERARD, *Momus Triumphans: or, the Plagiaries of the English Stage* (London: N.C. for Sam Holford, 1688).

—— *An Account of the English Dramatick Poets* (Oxford: L.L. for George West, and Henry Clements, 1691).

—— [and GILDON, CHARLES], *The Lives and Characters of the English Dramatic Poets . . . First Begun by Mr Langbain, improv'd and continued down to this Time, by a Careful Hand* (London: Tho. Leigh and William Turner, 1699).

[LA PLACE, PIERRE-ANTOINE DE], *Oronoko, traduit de l'anglois de Mme Behn,* 2　parts in 1 vol. (Amsterdam: aux dépens de la Compagnie, 1745).

LA PLACE, PIERRE-ANTOINE DE, *Les Aventures curieuses et intéressantes d'Oronoko, prince afriquain . . . traduit de l'anglois de Mme Behn,* 2 parties en 1 vol. (La Haye: F. H. Scheurleer, 1755–6).

—— *Oronoko imité de l'anglois, nouvelle edition, revuë & corrigée* (Paris: Sebastien Jorry, 1756).

—— *Oronoko, imité de l'anglois, nouvelle édition revuë et corrigée par M. de la Place* (Londres; et se trouve à Paris: Vente, 1769).

—— *Oronoko, imité de l'anglois, nouvelle édition revuë et corrigée par M. de la Place*, 2 parts in 1 vol. (Versailles: S. Dasier, 1779).

—— *Oronoko, ou le prince nègre, imitation de l'anglois*, in *Collection de romans et contes imités de l'anglois*, vol. i (Paris, 1788).

A Letter from the Dead Thomas Brown, to the Living Heraclitus: With Heraclitus Ridens, his Answer (London, 1704).

LLOYD, ROBERT, *The Capricious Lovers; A Comic Opera. As it is performed at the Theatre Royal in Drury-Lane. The Music composed by Mr. Rush* (London: R. Withy and W. Griffin, 1764).

LOCKE, JOHN, *Two Treatises of Government*, ed. Peter Laslett (Cambridge: Cambridge University Press, 1967).

LOCKHART, J. G., *Memoirs of the Life of Sir Walter Scott, Bart.* (Edinburgh: Robert Cadell, 1842).

London Chronicle: or, Universal Evening Post, 22–4 February–12–15 March 1757.

London Daily Post and General Advertiser, 9 and 10 March, 1741.

The London Review of English and Foreign Literature. By W. Kenrick, LLD. and others, vol. vi (London: Printed for the Author, and sold by T. Evans, 1778).

LORD, GEORGE DE F., *et al.* (eds.), *Poems on Affairs of State: Augustan Satirical Verse, 1660–1714*, 7 vols. (New Haven and London: Yale University Press, 1963–70).

[MACKENZIE, ANNA MARIA], *Slavery: Or, The Times*, 2 vols. (London: G. G. J. and J. Robinson, 1792).

Man Superior to Woman; or, a Vindication of Man's Natural Right of Sovereign Authority over the Woman . . . By a Gentleman (London: T. Cooper, 1739).

MANLEY, DELARIVIER, *Letters Written by Mrs. Manley. To which is Added a Letter, from a supposed Nun in Portugal, to a Gentleman in France, in Imitation of the Nun's Five Letters in Print, by Colonel Pack* (London: R.B., 1696).

—— *The Lost Lover; or, the Jealous Husband: A Comedy. As it is Acted at the Theatre Royal by His Majesty's Servants* (London: R. Bentley, F. Saunders, J. Knapton, and R. Wellington, 1696).

—— *The Royal Mischief. A Tragedy. As it is Acted by His Majesties Servants* (London: R. Bentley, F. Saunders, and J. Knapton, 1696).

—— *The New Atalantis*, ed. R. Ballaster (London: Penguin, 1992).

MAXWELL, JOHN, *The Royal Captive. A Tragedy* (York: Printed by Thomas Gent, for the Use of the Author, 1745).

[MENDEZ, MOSES], *The Chaplet. A Musical Entertainment. As it is perform'd by His Majesty's Company of Comedians, at the Theatre Royal in Drury-Lane. The Music Compos'd by Dr. Boyce* (London, 1761).

Modern Novels: In XII Volumes, vol. i (London: R. Bentley, 1692).

Monthly Review, 89 vols. (London, 1749–94).

MORE, HANNAH, *Slavery, a Poem* (London: T. Cadell, 1788).

—— *Poems by Hannah More* (London: T. Cadell, 1816).

Morning Chronicle and London Advertiser, Friday 10 April 1778.

The Muses Mercury: or the Monthly Miscellany (London: J.H. for Andrew Bell, 1707).

The Nine Muses. Or, Poems Written by Nine Several Ladies Upon the Death of the Late Famous John Dryden, Esq. (London: Richard Basset, 1700).

Nouveau Dictionnaire Historique et Critique, 4 vols. (Amsterdam: Z. Chatelain *et al.*, La Haye, Pierre de Hondt, 1750).

[OLDYS, ALEXANDER], *The Fair Extravagant, or, The Humorous Bride. An English Novel* (London: Charles Blount, 1682).

OLDYS, ALEXANDER, *The Female Gallant or, The Wife's the Cuckold. A Novel* (London: Samuel Briscoe, 1692).

—— *An Ode, By Way of Elegy, on The Universally Lamented Death of the Incomparable M.* Dryden (London, 1700; rpr. in *Drydeniana XIV. On the Death of Dryden* (New York and London: Garland Publishing, Inc., 1975).

Oronooko: ein Trauerspiel. In *Deutsche Schaubühne* (Augsburg, 1789).

Oroonoko. A Tragedy. Altered from the Original Play of that Name, Written by the late Thomas Southern, Esq. (London: A. and C. Corbett, 1760).

OTWAY, THOMAS, *The Souldiers Fortune: A Comedy. Acted by their Royal Highnesses Servants at the Duke's Theatre* (London: R. Bentley and M. Magnes, 1681).

—— *The Prologue to the City Heiress, Or, Sir Timothy Treat All* (London: J. Tonson, 1682).

OULTON, W. C., *The History of the Theatres of London: containing an Annual Register*, 2 vols. (London: Martin and Bain, 1796).

PHILLIPS, EDWARDS, *Theatrum Poetarum, or a Compleat Collection of the Poets, Especially the most Eminent, of all Ages* (London: Charles Smith, 1675).

PILKINGTON, LETITIA, *Memoirs of celebrated Female Characters* (London: Albion Press, 1804).

PIX, MARY, *Ibrahim, the Thirteenth Emperor of the Turks: A Tragedy. As it is Acted by His Majesties Servants* (London: John Harding, and Richard Wilkin, 1696).

—— *The Spanish Wives. A Farce, As it was Acted by His Majesty's Servants, at the Theatre in Dorset-Garden* (London: R. Wellington, 1696).

—— *The Innocent Mistress. A Comedy. As it was Acted, by His Majesty's Servants at the Theatre in Little-Lincolns-Inn-Fields* (London: J. Orme for R. Basset, 1696).

—— *Queen Catharine, or, the Ruines of Love. A Tragedy. As it is Acted at the New Theatre in Little-Lincoln's-Inn-Fields, By His Majesty's Servants* (London: William Turner and Richard Basset, 1698).

—— *The Deceiver Deceived: A Comedy, As 'tis now Acted by His Majesty's Servants, At the Theatre in Little-Lincoln's-Inn-Fields* (London: R. Basset, 1698).

—— *The False Friend, Or, the Fate of Disobedience. A Tragedy. As it is Acted at the New Theatre in Little Lincolns-Inn-Fields* (London: Richard Basset, 1699).

—— *The Beau Defeated: Or, the Lucky Younger Brother. A Comedy. As it is now Acted By His Majesty's Servants at the New Theatre in Lincoln's-Inn-Fields* (London: W. Turner and R. Basset, 1700).

—— *The Czar of Muscovy. A Tragedy. As it is Acted at the Theatre in Little Lincolns-Inn-Fields By His Majesty's Servants* (London: B. Lintott, 1701).

—— *The Double Distress. A Tragedy. As it is Acted at the Theatre-Royal in Little Lincolns-Inn-Fields. By His Majesty's Servants* (London: R. Wellington and Bernard Lintott, 1701).

—— *The Different Widows: or, Intrigue All-A-Mode* [*sic*]. *A Comedy. As it is Acted at the New Theatre in Little Lincolns-Inn-Fields. By her Majesty's Servants* (London: Henry Playford and Bernard Lintott, 1703).

—— *The Inhumane Cardinal: or, Innocence Betray'd*, ed. Constance Clark (Delmar, N.Y.: Scholars' Facsimiles and Reprints, 1984).

Poems by Eminent Ladies, 2 vols. (London: R. Baldwin, 1755).

Poems by Eminent Ladies, 2 vols. (Dublin: D. Chamberlaine for Sarah Cotter, 1757).

Poems by the Most Eminent Ladies of Great-Britain and Ireland (London: T. Becket and Co. and T. Evans, 1773).

Poems by the most Eminent Ladies of Great Britain and Ireland. Re-published from the Collection of G. Colman and B. Thornton, Esqrs. With Considerable Alterations, Additions, and Improvements, 2 vols. (London: W. Stafford (c.1785?))

Poems on Affairs of State (London, 1696).

Poems on Affairs of State (London, 1697).

Poems on Affairs of State, ii. *From the Reign of K. James the first, To this present Year 1703* (London, 1703).

A Poetical Dictionary; or, the Beauties of the English Poets, Alphabetically Displayed, 4 vols. (London: J. Newbery, 1761).

POPE, ALEXANDER, *Pastoral Poetry and An Essay on Criticism*, ed. E. Audra and Aubrey Williams [The Twickenham Pope, vol. i] (London: Methuen and Co.; New Haven: Yale University Press, 1961).

—— *The Poems of Alexander Pope*, ed. John Butt (London: Methuen, 1963).

—— *The Prose Works of Alexander Pope*, ed. Rosemary Cowler (Oxford: Basil Blackwell, 1986).

PRATT, SAMUEL JACKSON, *Miscellanies* (London, 1785).

PRIOR, MATTHEW, *Dialogues of the Dead and Other Works in Prose and Verse*, ed. A. R. Waller (Cambridge: Cambridge University Press, 1907).

RADCLIFFE, ALEXANDER, *The Ramble* (London, 1682; inc. with sep. title-page and pagination in *The Works of Capt. Alex. Radcliffe* (3rd edn., London: Richard Wellington, 1696).

REEVE, CLARA, *The Progress of Romance*, 2 vols. (Colchester: W. Keymer, 1785).

RICHARDSON, SAMUEL, *Selected Letters of Samuel Richardson*, ed. J. Carroll (Oxford: Clarendon Press, 1964).

—— *Pamela: or, Virtue Rewarded*, ed. T. C. Duncan Eaves and Ben D. Kimpel (Boston: Houghton Mifflin, 1971).

—— *Clarissa: or the History of a Young Lady*, ed. Angus Ross (London: Penguin, 1985).

ROCHESTER, JOHN WILMOT, EARL OF, *The Poems of John Wilmot Earl of Rochester*, ed. Keith Walker (Oxford: Basil Blackwell, 1984).

[Rowe, Elizabeth Singer], *Poems on Several Occasions. Written by Philomela* (London: John Dunton, 1696).

—— *Philomela: Or, Poems by Mrs. Elizabeth Singer [Now Rowe]* (2nd edn., London: E. Curll *et al.*, 1737).

Rowe, Nicholas, *The Fair Penitent. A Tragedy. As it is Acted at the New Theatre in Little Lincolns-Inn-Fields. By Her Majesty's Servants* (London: Jacob Tonson, 1703).

Scarron, Paul, *The Whole Comical Works of Mon. Scarron. Translated by Mr. Tho. Brown, Mr Savage, and Others,* 3rd edn., revised and corrected (London: J. Nicholson, J. and B. Sprint, R. Parker, and Benj. Tooke, 1712).

Scott, Sir Walter, *Lives of the Novelists* (London: J. M. Dent, 1820).

—— *The Miscellaneous Prose Works of Sir Walter Scott, Bart.*, ii. *Life of Swift* (Edinburgh: Adam and Charles Black, 1853).

—— *The Letters of Sir Walter Scott*, ed. H. J. C. Grierson, vol. x (London: Constable and Co., 1936).

A Select Collection Of the Original Love Letters of Several Eminent Persons, of Distinguish'd Rank and Station, Now Living . . . To which are subjoin'd, Poems by Eminent Ladies (London: Printed for the proprietors, 1755).

Serious and Comical Essays (London: J. King, 1710).

Sophia [pseud.], *Woman's Superior Excellence over Man* (London: John Hawkins, 1740).

Southerne, Thomas, *The Fatal Marriage: or, the Innocent Adultery* (London: Jacob Tonson, 1694).

—— *Oroonoko: A Tragedy* (London: H. Playford, B. Tooke and S. Buckley, 1696).

—— *Oroonoko. A Tragedy . . . As Performed at the Theatres-Royal, Drury-Lane and Covent-Garden. Regulated from the Prompt-Books By Permission of the Managers* (London: John Bell, 1791).

—— *Oroonoko: A Tragedy . . . With Remarks by Mrs Inchbald*, in E. Inchbald (ed.), *The British Theatre*, vol. vii (London: Longman, Hurst, Rees, and Orme, 1808).

—— *Oroonoko*, ed. Maximillian E. Novak and David Stuart Rodes (London: Edward Arnold, 1977).

—— *The Works of Thomas Southerne*, ed. Robert Jordan and Harold Love, 2 vols. (Oxford: Clarendon Press, 1988).

[Steele, Richard], *The Lover. By Marmaduke Myrtle, Gent.* no. 23, Saturday 17 April 1714.

Steele, Richard, *The Plays of Richard Steele*, ed. Shirley Strum Kenny (Oxford: Clarendon Press, 1971).

A Supplement to the Athenian Oracle . . . To which is prefix'd The History of the Athenian Society, And an Essay upon Learning. By a member of the Athenian Society (London: Andrew Bell, 1710).

Swift, Jonathan, *A Tale of a Tub With Other Early Works, 1696–1707*, ed. Herbert Davies (Oxford: Basil Blackwell, 1939).

—— *The Poems of Jonathan Swift*, ed. Harold Williams (2nd edn., Oxford: Clarendon Press, 1958).

[THOMAS, ELIZABETH], *Miscellany Poems on Several Subjects* (London: Tho. Combes, 1722).

THORN-DRURY, G. (ed.), *A Little Ark Containing Sundry Pieces of Seventeenth-Century Verse* (London: P. J. and A. Dobell, 1921).

The Town and Country Magazine; or Universal Repository of Knowledge, Instruction and Entertainment, 22 (London: A. Hamilton Jnr, 1790).

[TROTTER, CATHARINE, later Cockburn], *Agnes de Castro, A Tragedy. As it is Acted at the Theatre Royal, By His Majesty's Servants. Written by a Young Lady* (London: H. Rhodes, R. Parker, S. Briscoe, 1696).

TROTTER, CATHARINE, *Fatal Friendship. A Tragedy. As it is Acted at the New-Theatre in Little-Lincolns-Inn-Fields* (London: Francis Saunders, 1698).

—— *Love at a Loss, or, Most Votes Carry It. A Comedy. As it is now Acted at the Theatre Royal in Drury-Lane, By His Majesty's Servants* (London: William Turner, 1701).

—— *The Unhappy Penitent: A Tragedy. As it is Acted, At the Theatre Royal in Drury Lane, by His Majesty's Servants* (London: William Turner and John Nutt, 1701).

—— *The Revolution of Sweden. A Tragedy. As it is Acted at the Queens Theatre in the Hay-Market* (London: James Knapton and George Starah, 1706).

—— *The Works of Mrs. Catherine Cockburn*, ed. Thomas Birch, 2 vols. (London: J. and P. Knapton, 1751).

[TRYON, THOMAS], *Friendly Advice to the Gentlemen-Planters of the East and West Indies. By* Philotheos Physiologus (n.p: printed by Andrew Sowle, 1684).

V——, M. (trans.), *Lebens und Liebes-Geschichte des Königlichen Sclaven Oroonoko in West-Indien* (Hamburg: Thomas von Wierings, 1709).

VANBRUGH, SIR JOHN, *The Relapse*, ed. Curt A Zimansky (London: Edward Arnold, 1970).

—— *The Provok'd Wife*, ed. James L. Smith (New Mermaids edn.; London: Ernest Benn Ltd., 1974).

—— and CIBBER, COLLEY, *The Provok'd Husband*, ed. Peter Dixon (London: Edward Arnold, 1975).

VICTOR, BENJAMIN, *The History of the Theatres of London and Dublin, from the Year 1730 to the present Time*, 2 vols. (London: T. Davies *et al.*, 1761).

—— *The History of the Theatres of London, from the Year 1760 to the present Time* (London: T. Becket, 1771).

WHALEY, JOHN, *A Collection of Poems* (London: John Willis and Joseph Boddington, 1732).

—— *A Collection of Original Poems and Translations* (London: Printed for the Author, and Sold by R. Manby, and H. S. Cox, 1745).

WHINCOP, THOMAS, *Scanderbeg: or, Love and Liberty. A Tragedy. To which are added A List of all the Dramatic Authors, with some Account of their Lives; and of all the Dramatic Pieces ever published in the English Language, to the Year 1747* (London: W. Reeve, 1747).

WHYTE, SAMUEL, *A Collection of Poems on Various Subjects* (Dublin: Robert Marchbank, 1792).

WILKES, THOMAS, *A General View of the Stage* (London: J. Coote, 1759).

WILKES, WETENHALL, *An Essay on the Pleasures and Advantages of Female Literature* (London: T. Cooper and R. Caswell, 1741).

WILLIAMS, IOAN (ed.), *Novel and Romance: A Documentary Record* (London: Routledge, 1970).

[WILLIAMS, JOHN], *Poems: By Anthony Pasquin* (2nd edn., London: J. Strahan, 1789).

WINCHILSEA, ANNE FINCH, COUNTESS OF, *The Poems of Anne Countess of Winchilsea*, ed. Myra Reynolds (Chicago: University of Chicago Press, 1903).

WORDSWORTH, DOROTHY and WILLIAM, *The Letters of William and Dorothy Wordsworth: The Later Years*, ed. Ernest de Selincourt, vol. i (Oxford: Clarendon, 1939).

WYCHERLEY, WILLIAM, *Miscellany Poems: As Satyrs, Epistles, Love-Verse, Songs, Sonnets, &c.* (London: C. Brome, J. Taylor, and B. Tooke, 1704).

—— *The Plain Dealer*, ed. Leo Hughes (London: Edward Arnold Ltd., 1967).

—— *The Plays of William Wycherley*, ed. Arthur Friedman (Oxford: Clarendon Press, 1979).

—— *The Country Wife*, ed. James Ogden (London: A & C Black Ltd., 1991).

YOUNG, EDWARD, *The Complete Works, Poetry and Prose, of the Rev. Edward Young, LL.D.*, 2 vols. (London: William Tegg and Co., 1854).

The Young Students Library . . . To Which is Added, A New Essay Upon All Sorts of Learning . . . By the Athenian Society (London: John Dunton, 1692).

SECONDARY SOURCES

ABBOTT, JOHN LAWRENCE, *John Hawkesworth: Eighteenth-Century Man of Letters* (Madison and London: University of Wisconsin Press, 1982).

ALLEMAN, G. S., *Matrimonial Law and the Materials of Restoration Comedy* (Wallingford, Pa., 1942).

ALLISTON, APRIL, *Virtue's Faults: Correspondences in Eighteenth-Century British and French Women's Fiction* (Stanford, Calif.: Stanford University Press, 1996).

ANDERSON, PAUL BUNYAN, 'Splendor Out of Scandal: The Lucinda-Artesia Papers in *The Female Tatler*', *Philological Quarterly*, 15 (1936), 286–300.

—— 'Innocence and Artifice: or, Mrs. Centlivre and *The Female Tatler*', *Philological Quarterly*, 16 (1937), 358–75.

ANDRADE, SUSAN Z., 'White Skin, Black Masks: Colonialism and the Sexual Politics of *Oroonoko*', *Cultural Critique*, 27 (1994), 189–214.

ATHEY, STEPHANIE, and ALARCÓN, DANIEL COOPER, '*Oroonoko*'s Gendered Economies of Honor/Horror: Reframing Colonial Discourse Studies in the Americas', *American Literature*, 65/3 (1993), 415–43.

BACKSCHEIDER, PAULA, *Daniel Defoe: His Life* (Baltimore and London: Johns Hopkins University Press, 1989).

—— *Spectacular Politics: Theatrical Power and Mass Culture in Early Modern England* (Baltimore and London: Johns Hopkins University Press, 1993).

—— 'The Shadow of an Author: Eliza Haywood', *Eighteenth-Century Fiction*, 11/1 (1998), 79–102.

BAKHTIN, M. M., *The Dialogic Imagination*, ed. Michael Holquist, trans. Caryl Emerson and Michael Holquist (Austin, Tex., and London: University of Texas Press, 1981).

BALLASTER, ROS, *Seductive Forms: Women's Amatory Fiction from 1684 to 1740* (Oxford: Clarendon Press, 1992).

BARASH, CAROL, *English Women's Poetry, 1649–1714: Politics, Community, and Linguistic Authority* (Oxford: Clarendon Press, 1996).

BARKER, K., 'The Revival of Theatre outside London (c.1700–1788) with Special Reference to the West Country', *Transactions of the Eighth International Congress on the Enlightenment, Studies on Voltaire and the Eighteenth Century*, 305 (1992), 1366–8.

BARRY, JONATHAN, 'Literacy and Literature in Popular Culture: Reading and Writing in Historical Perspective', in T. Harris (ed.), *Popular Culture in England, c.1500–1850* (Basingstoke: Macmillan, 1995), 69–94.

BARTHELEMY, ANTHONY GERARD, *Black Face, Maligned Race: The Representation of Blacks in English Drama from Shakespeare to Southerne* (Baton Rouge, La., and London: Louisiana State University Press, 1987).

BATE, W. JACKSON, *The Burden of the Past and the English Poet* (London: Chatto and Windus, 1971).

BATTERSBY, CHRISTINE, *Gender and Genius: Towards a Feminist Aesthetics* (London: The Women's Press, 1989).

BENEDICT, BARBARA M., *Making the Modern Reader: Cultural Mediation in Early Modern Literary Anthologies* (Princeton: Princeton University Press, 1996).

BERNBAUM, ERNEST, 'Mrs. Behn's Biography a Fiction', *PMLA* 28 (1913), 532–53.

BLACKBURN, ROBIN, *The Making of New World Slavery: From the Baroque to the Modern 1492–1800* (London and New York: Verso, 1997).

BLOOM, HAROLD, *A Map of Misreading* (New York: Oxford University Press, 1975).

—— *The Anxiety of Influence: A Theory of Poetry* (2nd edn., New York and Oxford: Oxford University Press, 1997).

BLOUCH, CHRISTINE, 'Eliza Haywood and the Romance of Obscurity', *SEL* 31 (1991), 535–52.

BOSWELL, E., *The Restoration Court Stage 1660–1702* (London: George Allen and Unwin, 1960).

BOUCÉ, PAUL-GABRIEL, 'Imagination, Pregant Women, and Monsters, in Eighteenth-Century England and France', in G. S. Rousseau and Roy Porter (eds.), *Sexual Underworlds of the Enlightenment* (Chapel Hill, NC: University of North Carolina Press, 1988), 86–100.

BOURDIEU, PIERRE, *The Field of Cultural Production: Essays on Art and Literature*, ed. Randall Jackson (Cambridge: Polity Press, 1993).

BOWYER, J. B., *The Celebrated Mrs Centlivre* (Durham, NC: Duke University Press., 1952).

BOYCE, BENJAMIN, *Tom Brown of Facetious Memory: Grub Street in the Age of Dryden* (Cambridge, Mass.: Harvard University Press, 1939).

BRADY, JENNIFER, 'Dryden and the Negotiations of Literary Succession and Precession', in E. Miner and J. Brady (eds.), *Literary Transmission and Authority: Dryden and Other Writers* (Cambridge: Cambridge University Press, 1993), 27–54.

—— 'Progenitors and Other Sons in Ben Jonson's *Discoveries*', in James Hirsh (ed.), *New Perspectives on Ben Jonson* (London: Associated University Presses, 1997), 16–34.

BREWER, JOHN, and PORTER, ROY (eds.), *Consumption and the World of Goods* (London and New York: Routledge, 1993).

BROADBENT, J. D., *Annals of the Liverpool Stage* (Liverpool, Edward Howell, 1908).

BROCKBANK, EDWARD M., *John Ferriar: Public Health Work, Tristram Shandy, Other Essays and Verses* (London: William Heinemann, 1950).

BROWN, HOMER O., *Institutions of the English Novel: From Defoe to Scott* (Philadelphia: University of Pennsylvania Press, 1997).

BROWN, LAURA, *Ends of Empire: Women and Ideology in Early Eighteenth-Century English Literature* (Ithaca, NY, and London: Cornell University Press, 1993).

BRUCE, D., *Topics of Restoration Comedy* (London: Victor Gollancz, 1974).

BURLING, W. J., '"Their Empire Disjoyn'd": Serious Plays by Women on the London Stage, 1660–1737', in Schofield and Macheski (eds.), *Curtain Calls*, 311–24.

—— *A Checklist of New Plays and Entertainments on the London Stage, 1700–1737* (London and Toronto: Associated University Presses, 1993).

CAMERON, JOANNA M. 'Centlivre, not Shirley: Correcting an Error in Joseph Wood Krutch's *Comedy and Conscience After the Restoration*'. *Notes and Queries*, NS 43/3 (1996), 292–6.

CAMERON, W. J., 'George Granville and the "Remaines" of Aphra Behn', *Notes and Queries*, 204 (1959), 88–92.

—— *New Light on Aphra Behn* (Auckland: University of Auckland Press, 1961).

CAMPBELL, ELAINE, 'Aphra Behn's Surinam Interlude', *Kunapipi* , 7/3 (1985), 25–35.

CARLSON, SUSAN, *Women and Comedy: Rewriting the British Theatrical Tradition* (Ann Arbor: University of Michigan Press, 1991).

—— 'Cannibalizing and Carnivalizing: Reviving Aphra Behn's *The Rover*', *Theatre Journal*, 47 (1994), 517–39.

—— 'Aphra Behn's *The Emperor of the Moon*: Staging Seventeenth-Century Farce for Twentieth-Century Tastes', *Essays in Theatre*, 14/2 (1996), 117–30.

CHERNAIK, WARREN, *Sexual Freedom in Restoration Literature* (Cambridge: Cambridge University Press, 1995).

CHIBKA, ROBERT L., ' "Oh! Do Not Fear a Woman's Invention": Truth, False-hood and Fiction in Aphra Behn's *Oroonoko*', *Texas Studies in Language and Literature*, 30/4 (1988), 510–37.

CLARK, WILLIAM SMITH, *The Early Irish Stage: The Beginnings to 1720* (Oxford: Clarendon Press, 1955).

—— *The Irish Stage in the County Towns 1720 to 1800* (Oxford: Clarendon Press, 1965).

COHEN, D., 'Nicholas Rowe, Aphra Behn, and the Farcical Muse', *Papers on Language and Literature*, 15/1(1979), 383–95.

CONOLLY, L. W., *The Censorship of English Drama 1737–1824* (San Marino, Calif.: The Huntington Library, 1976).

COPELAND, NANCY, 'Re-Producing *The Rover*: John Barton's *Rover* at the Swan', *Essays in Theatre*, 9 (1990), 45–60.

CORDNER, M., 'Marriage Comedy after the 1688 Revolution: Southerne to Vanbrugh', *Modern Language Review*, 86 (1990), 273–89.

CORMAN, B., 'Women Novelists in Histories of the Eighteenth-Century English Novel', *Transactions of the Eighth International Congress on the Enlight-enment, Studies on Voltaire and the Eighteenth Century*, 305 (1992), 1368–71.

CRAIG, D. H. (ed.), *Ben Jonson: The Critical Heritage 1599–1798* (London: Rout-ledge, 1990).

CROMPTON, VIRGINIA, ' "Forced to write for bread and not ashamed to owne it": Aphra Behn, Court Poetry and Professional Writing in the 1680s', Ph.D. thesis, University of East Anglia, Norwich, 1994.

CULLER, A. DWIGHT, 'Edward Bysshe and the Poet's Handbook', *PMLA* 63 (1948), 858–85.

DANCHIN, PIERRE, *The Prologues and Epilogues of the Eighteenth Century*, 4 vols. (Nancy: Presses Universitaires de Nancy, 1990–3).

DAVIS, DAVID BRION, *The Problem of Slavery in Western Culture* (New York and Oxford: Oxford University Press, 1988).

DAY, ROBERT ADAMS, 'Aphra Behn's First Biography', *Studies in Bibliography*, 24 (1969), 227–40.

DEJEAN, JOAN, *Fictions of Sappho 1546–1937* (Chicago and London: University of Chicago Press, 1989).

—— *Tender Geographies: Women and the Origins of the Novel in France* (New York: Columbia University Press, 1991).

DE LUNA, D. N., 'Mr *Higden*: Not a Dryden poem . . . but a Dryden Forgery', *Times Literary Supplement*, 4807 (19 May 1995), 13.

DERITTER, JONES, 'The Gypsy, *The Rover*, and the Wanderer: Aphra Behn's Revision of Thomas Killigrew', *Restoration*, 10/2, (1986), 82–92.

DHUICQ, BERNARD, 'Aphra Behn's Reflections on Morality, or, Seneca Unmasqued', *Notes and Queries*, NS 41 (1994), 175–6.

DIAMOND, ELIN, '*Gestus* and Signature in Aphra Behn's *The Rover*', in J. Todd (ed.), *Aphra Behn: Contemporary Critical Essays* (Basingstoke: Macmillan, 1999), 32–56.

DITCHFIELD, G. M., 'Manchester College and Anti-Slavery', in Barbara Smith (ed.), *Truth, Liberty, Religion*, 185–224.

DOBSON, MICHAEL, *The Making of the National Poet: Shakespeare, Adaptation, and Authorship, 1660–1769* (Oxford: Clarendon Press, 1992).

DODDS, J. W., *Thomas Southerne: Dramatist*, Yale Studies in English, 81 (New Haven: Yale University Press; London: Oxford University Press, 1933).

DONKIN, ELLEN, *Getting into the Act: Women Playwrights in London, 1776–1829* (London and New York: Routledge, 1995).

DOODY, MARGARET ANNE, *A Natural Passion: A Study of the Novels of Samuel Richardson* (Oxford: Clarendon Press, 1974).

DORAN, J., *Their Majesties Servants, or Annals of the English Stage, from Thomas Betterton to Edmund Kean* (2nd edn., London: W. H. Allen and Co., 1865).

DOWNIE, J. A., 'The Making of the English Novel', *Eighteenth-Century Fiction*, 9/3 (1997), 249–66.

DUFFY, MAUREEN, *The Passionate Shepherdess: Aphra Behn 1640–89* (London: Jonathan Cape, 1977).

EAST, JOYCE E., 'The Dramatic Works of Hannah Cowley', Ph.D. thesis, University of Kansas, (1979).

ELTIS, DAVID and JAMES WALVIN (eds.), *The Abolition of the Atlantic Slave Trade: Origins and Effects in Europe, Africa, and the Americas* (Madison: University of Wisconsin Press, 1981).

ERICKSON, ROBERT A., 'Mrs A. Behn and the Myth of Oroonoko-Imoinda', *Eighteenth-Century Fiction*, 5/3 (1993), 201–16.

EZELL, MARGARET, *Writing Women's Literary History* (Baltimore: Johns Hopkins University Press, 1993).

FALCO, RAPHAEL, *Conceived Presences: Literary Genealogy in Renaissance England* (Amherst, Mass.: University of Massachusetts Press, 1994).

FERGUSON, MARGARET, 'Transmuting Othello: Aphra Behn's *Oroonoko*', in Marianne Novy (ed.), *Cross-Cultural Performances: Differences in Women's Re-Visions of Shakespeare* (Urbana, Ill., and Chicago: University of Illinois Press, 1993), 15–49.

—— 'Juggling the Categories of Race, Class and Gender: Aphra Behn's *Oroonoko*', in Hendricks and Parker (ed.), *Women, 'Race' and Writing*, 209–24.

FERGUSON, MOIRA, *Subject to Others: English Women Writers and Colonial Slavery, 1670–1834* (New York and London: Routledge, 1992).

—— *Eighteenth-Century Women Poets: Nation, Class and Gender* (Albany, NY: State University of New York Press, 1995).

FERRIS, INA, *The Achievement of Literary Authority: Gender, History and the Waverley Novels* (Ithaca, NY, and London: Cornell University Press, 1991).

FITZSIMMONS, LINDA and MCDONALD, ARTHUR W., *The Yorkshire Stage 1766–1803: A Calendar of Plays* (Metuchen, NJ, and London: Scarecrow Press Inc., 1989).

FLETCHER, ANTHONY, *Gender, Sex and Subordination in England 1500–1800* (New Haven and London: Yale University Press, 1995).

FLYNN, E. A., and SCHWEICKART, P. P., *Gender and Reading: Essays on Readers, Texts and Contexts* (Baltimore and London: Johns Hopkins University Press, 1986).

FOGARTY, ANNE, 'Looks that Kill: Violence and Representation in Aphra Behn's *Oroonoko*', in Carl Plasa and Betty Ring (eds.), *The Discourse of Slavery*, 1–17.

FOXTON, R., 'Delariviere Manley and "Astrea's Vacant Throne"', *Notes and Queries*, NS 33 (1986), 41–2.

FRANCUS, MARILYN, 'The Monstrous Mother: Reproductive Anxiety in Swift and Pope', *ELH* 16 (1994), 829–852.

GALLAGHER, CATHERINE, 'Who was that Masked Woman? The Prostitute and the Playwright in the Comedies of Aphra Behn', in Heidi Hutner (ed.), *Rereading Aphra Behn: History, Theory and Criticism* (Charlottesville, Va., and London: University Press of Virginia, 1993), 65–85.

—— *Nobody's Story: The Vanishing Acts of Women Writers in the Marketplace, 1670–1820* (Oxford: Clarendon Press, 1994).

GARDINER, JUDITH KEGAN, 'The First English Novel: Aphra Behn's *Love Letters*, The Canon, and Women's Tastes', *Tulsa Studies in Women's Literature*, 8/2 (1989), 201–22.

GENEST, JOHN, *Some Account of the English Stage, from the Restoration in 1660 to 1830*, 10 vols. (Bath: H. E. Carrington, 1832).

GEWIRTZ, ARTHUR, *Restoration Adaptations of 17th Century Comedies* (Washington: University Press of America, 1982).

GOREAU, ANGELINE, *Reconstructing Aphra: A Social Biography of Aphra Behn* (Oxford: Oxford University Press, 1980).

GRAY, C. H., *Theatrical Criticism in London to 1795* (New York: Benjamin Blom, 1931).

GREENE, J., 'The Repertory of the Dublin Theatres, 1720–1745', *Eighteenth-Century Ireland*, 2 (1987), 133–48.

—— and CLARK, G. L. H., *The Dublin Stage, 1720–45: A Calendar of Plays, Entertainments and Afterpieces* (Bethlehem: Lehigh University Press; London and Toronto: Associated University Presses, 1993).

GREER, G., 'Honest Sam. Briscoe', in Robin Myers and Michael Harris, eds, *A Genius for Letters: Booksellers and Bookselling from the 16th to the 20th Century* (Winchester: St. Paul's Bibliographies; Delaware: Oak Knoll Press, 1995), 33–47.

—— *Slip-Shod Sibyls: Recognition, Rejection and the Woman Poet* (London: Viking, 1995).

GRIFFIN, DUSTIN, 'The Beginnings of Modern Authorship: Milton and Dryden', *Milton Quarterly*, 24/1 (1990), 1–7.

—— *Regaining Paradise: Milton and the Eighteenth Century* (Cambridge: Cambridge University Press, 1986).

GUFFEY, GEORGE, 'Aphra Behn's *Oroonoko*: Occasion and Accomplishment', in *Two English Novelists: Aphra Behn and Anthony Trollope: Papers Read at a Clark Library Seminar, May 11, 1974* (Los Angeles: Clark Library, 1975), 3–41.

GUILLORY, JOHN, *Poetic Authority: Spenser, Milton and Literary History* (New York: Columbia University Press, 1993).

—— *Cultural Capital: The Problem of Literary Canon Formation* (Chicago and London: University of Chicago Press, 1994).

GWILLIAM, TASSIE, *Samuel Richardson's Fictions of Gender* (Stanford, Calif.: Stanford University Press, 1993).

HAM, ROSWELL GRAY, *Otway and Lee: Biography from a Baroque Age* (New Haven: Yale University Press, 1931).

HAMMOND, BREAN S., *Professional Imaginative Writing in England, 1670–1740: 'Hackney for Bread'* (Oxford: Clarendon Press, 1997).

—— 'Mid-Century English Quixotism and the Defence of the Novel', *Eighteenth-Century Fiction* 10/3 (1998), 247–68.

HAMMOND, PAUL, *John Dryden: A Literary Life* (Basingstoke: Macmillan, 1991).

HARGREAVES, H. A., 'New Evidence of the Realism of Mrs. Behn's *Oroonoko*', *Bulletin of the New York Public Library*, 74 (1970), 437–44.

HARRIS, T. (ed.), *Popular Culture in England, c.1500–1850* (Basingstoke: Macmillan, 1995).

HARWOOD, JOHN T., *Critics, Values, and Restoration Comedy* (Carbondale and Edwardsville, Ill.: Southern Illinois University Press, 1982).

HELGERSON, R., *Self-Crowned Laureates: Spenser, Jonson, Milton and the Literary System* (Berkeley: University of California Press, 1983).

HENDRICKS, MARGO, and PARKER, PATRICIA (eds.), *Women, 'Race' and Writing in the Early Modern Period* (London and New York: Routledge, 1994).

HIGHFILL, PHILIP H., BURNIM, KALMAN, and LANGHANS, EDWARD (eds.), *A Biographical Dictionary of Actors, Actresses, Musicians, Dancers, Managers and Other Stage Personnel in London, 1660–1800*, 17 vols. (Carbondale and Edwardsville, Ill.: Southern Illinois University Press, 1973–87).

HIRSH, JAMES (ed.), *New Perspectives on Ben Jonson* (London: Associated University Presses, 1997).

HOBBY, ELAINE, *Virtue of Necessity: English Women's Writing, 1640–89* (London: Virago, 1988).

HOEGBERG, DAVID E., 'Caesar's Toils: Allusion and Rebellion in *Oroonoko*', *Eighteenth-Century Fiction*, 7/3 (1995), 239–58.

HOLLAND, PETER, *The Ornament of Action: Text and Performance in Restoration Comedy* (Cambridge: Cambridge University Press, 1979).

HOPKINS, P. A., 'Aphra Behn and John Hoyle: A Contemporary Mention, and Sir Charles Sedley's Poem on his Death', *Notes and Queries*, 41 (1994), 176–85.

HOROWITZ, MARYANNE CLINE, 'The "Science" of Embryology Before the Discovery of the Ovum', in Marilyn J. Boxer and Jean H. Quataert (eds.),

Connecting Spheres: Women in the Western World, 1500 to the Present (New York and Oxford: Oxford University Press, 1987), 86–94.

HOTSON, LESLIE, *The Commonwealth and Restoration Stage* (Cambridge, Mass.: Harvard University Press, 1928).

HOWARD, GEORGE ELLIOTT, *A History of Matrimonial Institutions: Chiefly in England and the United States*, 2 vols. (Chicago: University of Chicago Press, 1904).

HOWARD, JEAN E., *The Stage and Social Struggle in Early Modern England* (London: Routledge, 1994).

HOWE, ELIZABETH, *The First English Actresses* (Cambridge: Cambridge University Press, 1992).

HUET, MARIE-HÉLÈNE, *Monstrous Imagination* (Cambridge, Mass.: Harvard University Press, 1993).

HUGHES, DEREK, *English Drama 1660–1700* (Oxford: Clarendon Press, 1996).

HUGHES, LEO, *A Century of English Farce* (Princeton: Princeton University Press, 1956).

—— *The Drama's Patrons: A Study of the Eighteenth-Century London Audience* (Austin, Tex., and London: University of Texas Press, 1971).

HULME, PETER, *Colonial Encounters: Europe and the Native Caribbean, 1492–1797* (London and New York: Methuen, 1987).

HUME, ROBERT D., *The Development of English Drama in the Late Seventeenth Century* (Oxford: Clarendon Press, 1976).

—— 'The Multifarious Forms of Eighteenth-Century Comedy', in G. W. Stone (ed.), *The Stage and the Page: London's "Whole Show" in the Eighteenth-Century Theatre* (Berkeley and London: University of California Press, 1981), 3–32.

—— *The Rakish Stage: Studies in English Drama, 1660–1800* (Carbondale and Edwardsville, Ill.: Southern Illinois University Press, 1983).

—— *Henry Fielding and the London Theatre 1728–1737* (Oxford: Clarendon Press, 1988).

—— 'Before the Bard: "Shakespeare" in Early Eighteenth-Century London', *ELH* 64/1 (1997), 41–75.

HUTNER, HEIDI (ed.), *Rereading Aphra Behn: History, Theory and Criticism* (Charlottesville, Va., and London: University Press of Virginia, 1993).

INGRASSIA, CATHERINE, *Authorship, Commerce, and Gender in Early Eighteenth-Century England: A Culture of Paper Credit* (Cambridge: Cambridge University Press, 1998).

JAUSS, HANS ROBERT, *Toward an Aesthetic of Reception*, trans. Timothy Bahti (Brighton: Harvester, 1982).

JONES, J., 'New Light on the Background and Early Life of Aphra Behn', *Notes and Queries*, NS 37/3 (1990), 288–93.

JORDAN, ROBERT, 'Mrs. Behn and *Sir Anthony Love*', *Restoration and Eighteenth-Century Theatre Research*, 12/1 (1973), 58–9.

JORDANOVA, LUDMILLA, *Sexual Visions: Images of Gender in Science and Medicine between the Eighteenth and Twentieth Centuries* (Hemel Hempstead: Harvester Wheatsheaf, 1989).

KAUL, SUVIR, 'Reading Literary Symptoms: Colonial Pathologies and the *Oroonoko* Fictions of Behn, Southerne and Hawkesworth', *Eighteenth-Century Life*, 18/3 (1994), 80–96.

KEENER, F. M., and LORSCH, S. E. (eds.), *Eighteenth-Century Women and the Arts* (Westport, Conn.: Greenwood Press Inc., 1988).

KENNY, S. S., 'Theatrical Warfare, 1695–1710', *Theatre Notebook*, 27/4 (1973), 130–45.

—— 'Perennial Favorites: Congreve, Vanbrugh, Cibber, Farquhar, and Steele', *Modern Philology*, 73 (1976), S4–S11.

KEWES, PAULINA, 'Gerard Langbaine's "View of *Plagiaries*": The Rhetoric of Dramatic Appropriation in the Restoration', *Review of English Studies*, NS 48 (1997), 1–18.

—— 'Between the "Triumvirate of Wit" and the Bard: The English Dramatic Canon, 1660–1720', in Cedric C. Brown and Arthur F. Marotti (eds,) *Texts and Cultural Change in Early Modern England* (London: Macmillan, 1997), 200–24.

—— *Authorship and Appropriation: Writing for the Stage in England, 1660–1710* (Oxford: Clarendon Press, 1998).

KING, KATHRYN, with Jeslyn Medoff, 'Jane Barker and Her Life (1652–1732): The Documentary Record', *Eighteenth-Century Life*, 21/3 (1997), 16–38.

KRAMER, DAVID B., 'Onely Victory in Him: The Imperial Dryden', in E. Miner and J. Brady, *Literary Transmission and Authority: Dryden and Other Writers* (Cambridge: Cambridge University Press, 1993), 55–78.

KREISSMAN, BERNARD, *Pamela-Shamela* (Lincoln, Nebr.: University of Nebraska Press, 1960).

LAMB, MARY ELLEN, *Gender and Authorship in the Sidney Circle* (Madison: University of Wisconsin Press, 1990).

LANDRY, DONNA, *The Muses of Resistance: Laboring-Class Women's Poetry in Britain, 1739–96* (Cambridge: Cambridge University Press, 1990).

LANGHANS, EDWARD A., 'Three Early Eighteenth Century Promptbooks', *Theatre Notebook*, 20 (1966), 142–50.

—— *Restoration Promptbooks* (Carbondale and Edwardsville, Ill.: Southern Illinois University Press, 1981).

—— *Eighteenth Century British and Irish Promptbooks: A Descriptive Bibliography* (New York and London: Greenwood Press, 1987).

LETELLIER, ROBERT IGNATIUS, *The English Novel, 1660–1700: An Annotated Bibliography* (Westport, Conn., and London: Greenwood Press, 1997).

LEWCOCK, M. D., 'Computer Analysis of Restoration Staging, 1: 1661–72', *Theatre Notebook*, 47/1 (1993), 20–8.

LINK, FREDERICK M., *Aphra Behn*, Twayne's English Authors Series, 63 (New York: Twayne Publishers, Inc., 1966).

LOCK, F. P., 'Astraea's "Vacant Throne": The Successors of Aphra Behn', in

Paul Fritz and Richard Morton (eds.), *Woman in the 18th Century and Other Essays* (Toronto and Sarasota: Hakkert and Co., 1976), 25–36.

—— *Susanna Centlivre* (Boston: Twayne Publishers, 1979).

LOFTIS, J., *Steele at Drury Lane* (Berkeley and Los Angeles: University of California Press, 1952).

—— *The Spanish Plays of Neoclassical England* (New Haven and London: Yale University Press, 1973).

The London Stage 1660–1800, Part 1, ed. William Van Lennep; Part 2, ed. Emmet L. Avery; Part 3, ed. Arthur H. Scouten; Part 4, ed. G. W. Stone; Part 5, ed. C. B. Hogan (Carbondale, Ill.: Southern Illinois University Press, 1960–68).

LYNCH, JAMES J., *Box Pit and Gallery: Stage and Society in Johnson's London* (New York: Russell and Russell, 1971).

MCBURNEY, W. H. (ed.), *Four Before Richardson: Selected English Novels, 1720–1727* (Lincoln, Nebr.: University of Nebraska Press, 1963).

MACDONALD, JOYCE GREEN, 'Race, Women, and the Sentimental in Thomas Southerne's *Oroonoko*', *Criticism*, 40, no. 4 (1998), 555–70.

—— 'The Disappearing African Woman: Imoinda in *Oroonoko* after Behn', *ELH* 66 (1999), 71–86.

MCDOWELL, PAULA, 'Consuming Women: The Life of the "Literary Lady" as Popular Culture in Eighteenth-Century England', *Genre*, 26 (1993), 219–52.

MACHEREY, PIERRE, *A Theory of Literary Production*, trans. Geoffrey Wall (London: Routledge and Kegan Paul, 1979).

MCKENDRICK, N., BREWER, J., and PLUMB, J. H., *The Birth of a Consumer Society: The Commercialization of Eighteenth-Century England* (London: Europa, 1982).

MACMILLAN, D., *Catalogue of the Larpent Plays in the Huntington Library* (San Marino, Calif., 1939).

MCWHIRR, ANNE, 'Elizabeth Thomas and the Two Corinnas: Giving the Woman Writer a Bad Name', *ELH* 62/1 (1995), 105–20.

MANN, DAVID D., and MANN, SUSAN GARLAND, *Women Playwrights in England, Ireland, and Scotland 1660–1823* (Bloomington and Indianapolis: Indiana University Press, 1996).

MASSON, GEORGINA, *Queen Christina* (London: Secker and Warburg, 1968).

MAYO, ROBERT D., *The English Novel in the Magazines 1740–1815* (Evanston, Ill.: Northwestern University Press, 1962).

MEDOFF, JESLYN, 'New Light on Sarah Fyge (Field, Egerton)', *Tulsa Studies in Women's Literature*, 1/2 (1982), 170–1.

—— 'The Daughters of Behn and the Problem of Reputation', in Isobel Grundy and Susan Wiseman (eds.), *Women, Writing, History 1640–1740* (London: Batsford, 1992), 33–54.

MENDELSON, SARA HELLER, *The Mental World of Stuart Women: Three Studies* (Brighton: Harvester, 1987).

MIDGLEY, CLARE, *Women against Slavery: The British Campaigns, 1780–1870* (London and New York: Routledge, 1992).

MILHOUS, JUDITH, 'The Duke's Company's Profits, 1675–1677' *Theatre Notebook*, 32 (1978), 76–88.

—— *Thomas Betterton and the Management of Lincoln's Inn Fields 1695–1708* (Carbondale and Edwardsville, Ill.: Southern Illinois University Press, 1979).

—— 'The Multimedia Spectacular on the Restoration Stage', in S. S. Kenny (ed.), *British Theatre and the Other Arts, 1660–1800* (Washington: Folger Shakespeare Library; London and Toronto: Associated University Presses, 1984).

—— and HUME, R. D., *Vice Chamberlain Coke's Theatrical Papers 1706–1715* (Carbondale and Edwardsville, Ill.: Southern Illinois University Press, 1982).

—— —— *Producible Interpretation: Eight English Plays 1675–1707* (Carbondale and Edwardsville, Ill.: Southern Illinois University Press, 1985).

—— —— *A Register of English Theatrical Documents 1660–1737* (Carbondale and Edwardsville, Ill.: Southern Illinois University Press, 1991).

—— —— *The London Stage 1660–1800. Part 2: 1700–1729. A New Version . . . Draft of the Calendar for Volume I. 1700–1711. Facsicle 1: 1700–1707. Facsicle 2: 1707–1711* (Bound Draft, 'To be published by Southern Illinois University Press', 1996).

—— —— 'Thomas Doggett at Cambridge in 1701', *Theatre Notebook*, 51/3 (1997), 147–65.

MILLER, NANCY K., *Subject to Change: Reading Feminist Writing* (New York: Columbia University Press, 1988).

MINER, EARL, *The Cavalier Mode from Jonson to Cotton* (Princeton: Princeton University Press, 1971).

—— and BRADY, JENNIFER, *Literary Transmission and Authority: Dryden and Other Writers* (Cambridge: Cambridge University Press, 1993).

MISH, C. C. (ed.), *Restoration Prose Fiction, 1666–1700: An Anthology of Representative Pieces* (Lincoln, Nebr.: University of Nebraska Press, 1970).

MORNET, DANIEL, 'Les Enseignements des bibliothèques privées (1750–1780)', *Revue d'histoire littéraire de la France*, 17 (1910), 449–96.

MULLER, FRANS, 'Flying Dragons and Dancing Chairs at Dorset Gardens: Staging *Dioclesian*', *Theatre Notebook*, 47/2 (1993), 80–95.

MUNNS, JESSICA, 'Barton and Behn's *The Rover*: or, the Text Transpos'd', *Restoration and Eighteenth-Century Theatre Research*, 2nd ser. 3/2 (1988), 11–22.

MYERS, ROBIN, and HARRIS, MICHAEL (eds.), *A Genius for Letters: Booksellers and Bookselling from the 16th to the 20th Century* (Winchester: St Paul's Bibliographies, 1995).

NAGLER, A. M., *A Source Book in Theatrical History* (New York: Dover Publications, 1959).

NICOLL, A., *The Garrick Stage: Theatres and Audience in the Eighteenth Century* (Manchester: Manchester University Press, 1980).

NOVY, MARIANNE (ed.), *Cross-Cultural Performances: Differences in Women's Re-Visions of Shakespeare* (Urbana, Ill. and Chicago: University of Illinois Press, 1993).

NUSSBAUM, FELICITY, *Torrid Zones: Maternity, Sexuality and Empire in Eighteenth-Century English Narratives* (Baltimore and London: Johns Hopkins University Press, 1995).

ODELL, GEORGE C. D., *Annals of the New York Stage* (New York: Columbia University Press, 1927).

O'DONNELL, MARY ANN, *Aphra Behn: An Annotated Bibliography of Primary and Secondary Sources* (New York and London: Garland, 1986).

—— 'A Verse Miscellany of Aphra Behn: Bodleian Library MS Firth c. 16', in P. Beal and J. Griffiths (eds.), *English Manuscript Studies, 1100–1700*, vol. ii (Oxford: Blackwell, 1990).

OKIN, SUSAN MOLLER, *Women in Western Political Thought* (Princeton: Princeton University Press, 1979).

OLDFIELD, J. R., 'The "Ties of soft Humanity": Slavery and Race in British Drama, 1760–1800', *Huntington Library Quarterly*, 56 (1993) 1–14.

OLSEN, TILLIE, *Silences* (London: Virago, 1980).

OWENS, W. R., and GOODMAN, LIZBETH (eds.), *Shakespeare, Aphra Behn and the Canon* (London: Routledge with the Open University, 1996).

PACHECO, ANITA, 'Royalism and Honor in Aphra Behn's *Oroonoko*', *SEL* 34 (1994), 491–506.

—— 'Rape and the Female Subject in Aphra Behn's *The Rover*', *ELH* 65 (1998), 323–45.

PARKER, PATRICIA, *Literary Fat Ladies: Rhetoric, Gender, Property* (London and New York: Methuen, 1987).

PATTERSON, ORLANDO, *Slavery and Social Death: A Comparative Study* (Cambridge, Mass.: Harvard University Press, 1982).

PAYNE, DEBORAH C., '"And Poets Shall by Patron-Princes Live": Aphra Behn and Patronage', in Schofield and Macheski (eds.), *Curtain Calls*, 105–19.

PEARSE, NANCY COTTON, 'Mary Pix, Restoration Playwright', *Restoration and Eighteenth-Century Theatre Research*, 15/1 (1976), 12–23.

PEARSON, JACQUELINE, *The Prostituted Muse: Images of Women and Women Dramatists 1642–1737* (London: Harvester, 1988).

—— 'Gender and Narrative in the Fiction of Aphra Behn', *RES* 165 (1991), 40–56, and 166 (1991), 179–90.

—— 'The History of *The History of the Nun*', in H. Hutner (ed.), *Rereading Aphra Behn, History, Theory and Criticism* (Charlottesville, Va., and London: University Press of Virginia, 1993), 234–53.

PEARSON, JOHN, *Two Centuries of Testimony in Favour of Mrs. Aphra Behn* (London: John Pearson, 1872).

PEDICORD, HARRY WILLIAM, *The Theatrical Public in the Time of Garrick* (New York: King's Crown Press, 1954).

PLASA, CARL, and RING, BETTY J. (eds.), *The Discourse of Slavery: Aphra Behn to Toni Morrison* (London and New York: Routledge, 1994).

PLATT, HARRISON G. Jr., 'Astrea and Celadon: An Untouched Portrait of Aphra Behn', *PMLA* 49, (1934), 544–99.

PLOMER, HENRY R., *A Dictionary of the Printers and Booksellers who were at Work in England, Scotland and Ireland from 1668 to 1725* (The Bibliographical Society, 1968).

POINTON, MARCIA, *Strategies for Showing: Women, Possession and Representation in English Visual Culture 1665–1800* (Oxford: Oxford University Press, 1997).

POTTER, L., 'Transforming a Super-Rake', *Times Literary Supplement* (25 July 1986), 817.

POWELL, J., *Restoration Theatre Production* (London: Routledge and Kegan Paul, 1984).

PRESCOTT, SARAH, 'Penelope Aubin and *The Doctrine of Morality:* A Reassessment of the Pious Woman Novelist', *Women's Writing*, 1/1 (1994), 99–112.

—— 'British Women Writers of the 1720s: Feminist Literary History and the Early Eighteenth-century Novel', Ph.D. thesis, Exeter University, 1997.

PRICE, CECIL, *The English Theatre in Wales in the Eighteenth and Early Nineteenth Centuries* (Cardiff: University of Wales Press, 1948).

RAVEN, JAMES, *British Fiction, 1750–1770: A Chronological Check-List of Prose Fiction Printed in Britain and Ireland* (Newark, Del.: University of Delaware Press; London: Associated University Presses, 1987).

RIBEIRO, A., and BASKER, JAMES G. (eds.), *Tradition in Transition: Women Writers, Marginal Texts, and the Eighteenth-Century Canon* (Oxford: Clarendon Press, 1996).

RICH, JULIA A., 'Heroic Tragedy in Southerne's *Oroonoko* (1695): An Approach to a Split-Plot Tragicomedy', *Philological Quarterly*, 62 (1983), 187–200.

RICHETTI, JOHN, 'Voice and Gender in Eighteenth-Century Fiction', *Studies in the Novel*, 19 (1987), 263–72.

—— *The Columbia History of the British Novel* (New York: Columbia University Press, 1994).

RIGGS, DAVID, *Ben Jonson: A Life* (Cambridge, Mass., and London: Harvard University Press, 1989).

RIVERS, ISABEL, *Books and their Readers in Eighteenth-Century England* (Leicester: Leicester University Press, 1982).

ROGERS, PAT, '"Towering Beyond her Sex": Stature and Sublimity in the Achievement of Sarah Siddons', in M. A. Schofield and C. Macheski, *Curtain Calls: British and American Women and the Theater, 1660–1800* (Athens, Oh.: Ohio University Press, 1991), 48–66.

ROSENFELD, SYBIL, *Strolling Players and Drama in the Provinces, 1660–1765* (Cambridge: Cambridge University Press, 1939).

—— *The Theatre of the London Fairs in the Eighteenth Century* (Cambridge: Cambridge University Press, 1960).

—— *The Georgian Theatre of Richmond, Yorkshire, and its Circuit: Beverley, Harrogate, Kendal, Northallerton, Ulverston and Whitby* (London: Society for Theatre Research with William Sessions Ltd., 1984).

ROSENTHAL, LAURA J., 'Owning Oroonoko: Behn, Southerne, and the Contingencies of Property', *Renaissance Drama*, NS 23 (1992), 25–58.

—— *Playwrights and Plagiarists in Early Modern England* (Ithaca, NY, and London: Cornell University Press, 1996).

ROSS, TREVOR, 'The Emergence of "Literature": Making and Reading the English Canon in the Eighteenth Century', *ELH* 63/2 (1996), 397–422.

—— *The Making of the English Literary Canon: From the Middle Ages to the Late Eighteenth Century* (Montreal and Kingston: McGill-Queen's University Press, 1998).

RUNGE, LAURA, *Gender and Language in British Literary Criticism, 1660–1790* (Cambridge: Cambridge University Press, 1997).

SALVAGGIO, R., 'Verses on the Death of Mr Dryden', *Journal of Popular Culture*, 21/1 (1987), 75–91.

SCHIEBINGER, LONDA, *The Mind Has No Sex? Women in the Origins of Modern Science* (Cambridge, Mass., and London: Harvard University Press, 1989).

SCHNEIDER, BEN R., 'The Coquette-Prude as an Actress's Line in Restoration Comedy During the Time of Mrs Oldfield', *Theatre Notebook*, 22 (1967), 143–56.

SCHOFIELD, M. A., and MACHESKI, C. (eds.), *Curtain Calls: British and American Women and the Theater, 1660–1800* (Athens, Oh.: Ohio University Press, 1991).

SCHOR, NAOMI, *Reading in Detail: Aesthetics and the Feminine* (New York and London: Methuen, 1987).

SCOUTEN, ARTHUR H., and HUME, ROBERT D., '"Restoration Comedy" and its Audiences, 1660–1776', in R. D. Hume (ed.), *The Rakish Stage*, 46–81.

SEBBAR-PIGNON, LEÏLA, 'Le Mythe du bon nègre ou l'idéologie coloniale dans la production romanesque du XVIIIe siècle', *Les Temps modernes*, 29 (1974), 2349–75 and 2588–613.

SEEBER, EDWARD D., '*Oroonoko* in France in the XVIIIth Century', *PMLA* 51 (1936), 953–9.

SHAWCROSS, JOHN T., *John Milton and Influence: Presence in Literature, History and Culture* (Pittsburgh: Duquesne University Press, 1991).

—— (ed.), *John Milton: The Critical Heritage*, 2 vols. (London and New York: Routledge, 1995).

SHEFFEY, RUTHE T., 'The Literary Reputation of Aphra Behn', Diss., University of Pennsylvania, 1959.

SHELDON, ESTHER K., *Thomas Sheridan of Smock-Alley . . . including a Smock-Alley Calendar for the Years of his Management* (Princeton: Princeton University Press, 1967).

SHOWALTER, ENGLISH, *The Evolution of the French Novel 1641–1782* (Princeton: Princeton University Press, 1972).

SMITH, BARBARA (ed.), *Truth, Liberty, Religion: Essays Celebrating Two Hundred Years of Manchester College* (Oxford: Manchester College, 1986).

SMITH, BARBARA HERRNSTEIN, *Contingencies of Value: Alternative Perspectives for Critical Theory* (Cambridge, Mass., and London: Harvard University Press, 1988).

SMITH, HILDA L., *Reason's Disciples: Seventeenth-Century English Feminists* (Urbana, Ill., Chicago, London: University of Illinois Press, 1982).

—— and CARDINALE, SUSAN, *Women and the Literature of the Eighteenth Century: An Annotated Bibliography based on Wing's Short Title Catalogue* (Westport, Conn.: Greenwood Press, 1990).

SMITH, JOHN HARRISON, *The Gay Couple in Restoration Comedy* (Cambridge, Mass.: Harvard University Press, 1948).

SPEAIGHT, GEORGE, *The History of the English Puppet Theatre* (London, 1955).

SPEARING, ELIZABETH, 'Aphra Behn: The Politics of Translation', in J. Todd (ed.), *Aphra Behn Studies* (Cambridge: Cambridge University Press, 1996).

SPENCER, JANE, 'Creating the Woman Writer: The Autobiographical Works of Jane Barker', *Tulsa Studies in Women's Literature*, 2/2 (1983), 165–82.

—— *The Rise of the Woman Novelist: From Aphra Behn to Jane Austen* (Oxford: Basil Blackwell, 1986).

—— 'Not Being a Historian: Women Telling Tales in Restoration and Eighteenth-Century England', in Roy Eriksen (ed.), *Contexts of Pre-Novel Narrative: The European Tradition* (Berlin: Mouton de Gruyter, 1994), 319–40.

—— 'Adapting Aphra Behn: Hannah Cowley's *A School for Greybeards* and *The Lucky Chance*', *Women's Writing*, 2/3 (1995), 221–34.

—— '*The Rover* and the Eighteenth Century', in Janet Todd (ed.), *Aphra Behn Studies* (Cambridge: Cambridge University Press, 1996), 84–106.

—— 'Women Writers and the Eighteenth-Century Novel', in John Richetti (ed.), *The Cambridge Companion to the Eighteenth-Century Novel* (Cambridge: Cambridge University Press, 1996), 212–35.

SPENDER, DALE, *Mothers of the Novel: 100 Good Women Writers before Jane Austen* (London: Pandora Press, 1986).

STACKELBERG, JÜRGEN VON, '*Oroonoko* et l'abolition d'esclavage: le rôle du traducteur', trans. Geneviève Roche, *Revue de littérature comparée*, 63/2 (1989), 237–48.

STANTON, JUDITH P., 'Statistical Profile of Women Writing in English from 1660 to 1800', in Frederick M. Keener and Susan E. Lorsch (eds.), *Eighteenth-Century Women and the Arts* (Westport, Conn.: Greenwood Press, 1985), 247–52.

—— '"This New-Found Path Attempting": Women Dramatists in England, 1660–1800', in M. A. Schofield and C. Macheski (eds.), *Curtain Calls: British and American Women and the Theater, 1660–1800* (Athens, Oh.: Ohio University Press, 1991), 322–54.

—— 'The Production of Fiction by Women in England, 1660–1800: A

Statistical Overview', paper given at Eighth International Congress on the Enlightenment, Bristol, 1991.

STAVES, SUSAN, *Players' Scepters: Fictions of Authority in the Restoration* (Lincoln, Nebr.: University of Nebraska Press, 1979).

STONE, MARJORIE, 'Sisters in Art: Christina Rossetti and Elizabeth Barrett Browning', *Victorian Studies*, 32 (1994), 339–64.

—— *Elizabeth Barrett Browning* (London: Macmillan, 1995).

SUAREZ, M. F., SJ, 'Trafficking in the Muse: Dodsley's *Collection of Poems* and the Question of Canon', in A. Ribeiro and J. Basker (eds.), *Tradition in Transition* (Oxford: Clarendon Press, 1996), 297–313.

SUMMERS, JOSEPH H., *The Heirs of Donne and Jonson* (London: Chatto and Windus, 1970).

SUMMERS, MONTAGUE L., 'The Source of Southerne's "The Fatal Marriage"', *Modern Language Review*, 11/2 (1916), 149–55.

SUTHERLAND, JAMES R., 'The Progress of Error: Mrs. Centlivre and the Biographers', *RES* 18 (1942), 167–82.

SUTTON, JOHN L. Jr., 'The Source of Mrs Manley's Preface to *Queen Zarah*', *Modern Philology*, 82/2 (1984), 167–72.

SYPHER, WYLIE, *Guinea's Captive Kings: British Anti-Slavery Literature in the XVIIIth Century* (1942; rpr. New York: Octagon Books, 1969).

TAVARD, GEORGE H., *Woman in Christian Tradition* (Notre Dame and London: University of Notre Dame Press, 1973).

THOMAS, DAVID, *Theatre in Europe: A Documentary History. Restoration and Georgian England, 1660–1788* (Cambridge: Cambridge University Press, 1989).

THOMAS, HUGH, *The Slave Trade: The History of the Atlantic Slave Trade: 1440–1870* (London: Picador, 1997).

TOBIN, BETH FOWKES (ed.), *History, Gender and Eighteenth-Century Literature* (Athens, Ga., and London: University of Georgia Press, 1994).

TODD, JANET, *Gender, Art and Death* (Cambridge: Polity Press, 1993).

—— '"Pursue that way of fooling, and be damn'd": Editing Aphra Behn', *Studies in the Novel*, 27/3 (1995), 304–19.

—— *The Secret Life of Aphra Behn* (London: André Deutsch, 1996).

—— (ed.), *Aphra Behn Studies* (Cambridge: Cambridge University Press, 1996).

—— *The Critical Fortunes of Aphra Behn* (Columbia: Camden House, 1998).

—— (ed.), *Aphra Behn: Contemporary Critical Essays* (Basingstoke: Macmillan, 1999).

TURLEY, DAVID, *The Culture of English Antislavery, 1780–1860* (London and New York: Routledge, 1991).

TURNER, CHERYL, *Living by the Pen: Women Writers in the Eighteenth Century* (London: Routledge, 1992).

VERMILLION, MARY, 'Buried Heroism: Critiques of Female Authorship in Southerne's Adaptation of Behn's *Oroonoko*', *Restoration*, 16 (1992), 28–37.

VIETH, DAVID M., *Attribution in Restoration Poetry: A Study of Rochester's* Poems *of 1680* (New Haven and London: Yale University Press, 1963).

VON MALTZHAN, NICHOLAS, 'The First Reception of *Paradise Lost* (1667)', *Review of English Studies*, 188 (1996), 479–99.

WALL, WENDY, *The Imprint of Gender: Authorship and Publication in the English Renaissance* (Ithaca, NY, and London: Cornell University Press, 1993).

WALSH, MARCUS, *Shakespeare, Milton, and Eighteenth-Century Literary Editing: The Beginnings of Interpretative Scholarship* (Cambridge: Cambridge University Press, 1997).

WALVIN, JAMES, *England, Slaves and Freedom, 1776–1838* (Basingstoke: Macmillan, 1986).

WARD, CHARLES E., *The Life of John Dryden* (Chapel Hill, NC: University of North Carolina Press, 1961).

WARNER, WILLIAM B., 'The Elevation of the Novel in England: Hegemony and Literary History', *ELH* 59 (1992), 577–96.

—— *Licensing Entertainment: The Elevation of Novel Reading in Britain, 1684–1750* (Berkeley: University of California Press, 1998).

WEBSTER, CHARLES, and BARRY, JONATHAN, 'The Manchester Medical Revolution', in Barbara Smith (ed.), *Truth, Liberty, Religion*, 165–84.

WEINBROT, HOWARD D., *Britannia's Issue: The Rise of British Literature from Dryden to Ossian* (Cambridge: Cambridge University Press, 1993).

WILES, R. M., *Serial Publication in England Before 1750* (Cambridge: Cambridge University Press, 1957).

WILLIAMS, CAROLYN D., *Pope, Homer and Manliness: Some Aspects of Eighteenth-Century Classical Learning* (London and New York: Routledge, 1994).

WILLIAMSON, MARILYN, *Raising Their Voices: British Women Writers 1650–1750* (Detroit: Wayne State University Press, 1990).

WILSON, JOHN HAROLD, *A Preface to Restoration Drama* (Cambridge, Mass.: Harvard University Press, 1968).

WINN, JAMES ANDERSON, *John Dryden and His World* (New Haven and London: Yale University Press, 1987).

WOODCOCK, GEORGE, *The Incomparable Aphra* (London: T. V. Boardman and Co., 1948).

WOODMANSEE, MARTHA, 'The Genius and the Copyright: Economic and Legal Conditions of the Emergence of the "Author"', *Eighteenth-Century Studies*, 17 (1983–4), 425–48.

—— *The Author, Art, and the Market: Rereading the History of Aesthetics* (New York: Columbia University Press, 1994).

WOOLF, VIRGINIA, *A Room of One's Own* (London: Vintage, 1996).

ZWICKER, S. N., *Lines of Authority: Politics and English Literary Culture, 1649–1689* (Ithaca, NY, and London: Cornell University Press, 1993).

Index